1996

Zara Steiner's contribution to the history of modern British foreign policy has shown successfully the connexion between the attitudes of those who have been responsible for British diplomacy and the policies they produced. Thus, in honouring Dr Steiner, the contributors to this volume explore a number of case studies involving personality and foreign policy: examining the attitudes of those who made or influenced British diplomatic strategies; how these attitudes were shaped by and, occasionally, shaped events; and how British foreign policy in a few instances was fashioned as a result.

The contributors have concentrated their efforts on the years 1890–1950, the period of Dr Steiner's interest. This is an important juncture in both international and British history, when Britain's position as the only world power was undermined by the nature of the first and second world wars, and when British diplomats and others had to make adjustments to changed domestic and external conditions in war and peace. The volume therefore adds to the explanations about how and why transition in Britain's status as a Great Power occurred in the way it did.

Diplomacy and world power

Zara Steiner

Diplomacy and world power

STUDIES IN BRITISH FOREIGN POLICY, 1890–1950

EDITED BY

MICHAEL DOCKRILL

AND BRIAN McKERCHER

CAMBRIDGE
UNIVERSITY PRESS

Published by the Press Syndicate of the University of Cambridge
The Pitt Building, Trumpington Street, Cambridge CB2 1RP
40 West 20th Street, New York, NY 10011-4211, USA
10 Stamford Road, Oakleigh, Melbourne 3166, Australia

First published 1996

Printed in Great Britain at the University Press, Cambridge

A catalogue record for this book is available from the British Library

Library of Congress cataloguing in publication data

Diplomacy and world power: studies in British foreign policy,
1890–1950/edited by Michael Dockrill and Brian McKercher.
    p. cm.
  Includes bibliographical references and index.
  ISBN 0 521 46243 6
  1. Great Britain – Foreign relations – 20th century. 2. Great
Britain – Foreign relations – 1837–1901. 3. World politics – 20th
century. I. Dockrill, M. L. (Michael L.) II. McKercher, B. J. C.,
1950–.
DA566.7.D57 1996
327.41 – dc20 95–8659 CIP
ISBN 0 521 46243 6 hardback

Contents

Contributors

VALERIE CROMWELL, former Reader in History at the University of Sussex, is Director of the *History of Parliament*, associated with the Institute of Historical Research, University of London. She is the author of articles on British foreign policy and diplomacy in the nineteenth and early twentieth centuries, and on British parliamentary and administrative history. Two articles, on 'The Foreign Office before 1914' and 'The Foreign Office between the wars' were written jointly with Zara Steiner.

MICHAEL DOCKRILL is Reader in War Studies at King's College, London. He has written books and articles on various aspects of British foreign policy in the twentieth century including *The Mirage of Power: British Foreign Policy 1902-1923* (Batsford, 1981), *British Defence since 1945* (Blackwell, 1988), and *The Cold War, 1945-1963* (Macmillan, 1988). He is general editor of the Macmillan/ King's College series *Studies in Military and Strategic History*. Two articles, 'The Foreign Office reforms, 1919-1921' and 'The Foreign Office at the Paris Peace Conference' were written jointly with Zara Steiner.

ERIK GOLDSTEIN is Reader in International History at the University of Birmingham. He has written a number of books and articles on British foreign policy during the First World War and the post-war period, including *Winning the Peace: British Diplomatic Strategy. Peace Planning and the Paris Peace Conference 1916-1920* (Clarendon Press: Oxford, 1991) and he is joint editor of *Diplomacy and Statecraft*. He is also author of *Wars and Peace Treaties, 1816-1991* (Routledge, 1992) and co-editor of *The End of the Cold War* (Cass, 1990) and of *The Washington Conference 1921-1922* (Cass, 1994).

RICHARD LANGHORNE is the Director of Wilton Park, Foreign and Commonwealth Office and Hon. Professor of International Relations, University of Kent at Canterbury. He was the Director of the Centre of International Studies at the University of Cambridge from 1987 to 1993, and was Fellow of St John's College, Cambridge, from 1975 to 1993. He has written books and articles on international history in the late nineteenth and early twentieth centuries including *The Practice of Diplomacy* (with K.A. Hamilton) (1994) and *The Collapse of the Concert of Europe 1890–1914* (London: Macmillan, 1982), *The Twentieth Century Mind* (Oxford 1972) and contributions to *The Cambridge History of British Foreign Policy under Sir Edward Grey* (edited by F.H. Hinsley) (Cambridge, 1977).

BRIAN MCKERCHER is Associate Professor of International History at the Royal Military College of Canada, Kingston, Ontario. He has written widely on Anglo-American relations during the twentieth century, and his books include *The Second Baldwin Government and the United States, 1924–1929* (Cambridge: Cambridge University Press, 1984), *Esme Howard* (Cambridge University Press, 1989) and he is currently writing a book on *Transition: Britain's Loss of Global Pre-eminence to the United States, 1930–1945* (forthcoming from Cambridge University Press). He has also edited a number of books on British foreign policy, intelligence and arms limitation and written articles and chapters in books on twentieth-century diplomacy and foreign policy.

KEITH NEILSON is Professor of History at the Royal Military College of Canada, Kingston, Ontario. He is the author of *Strategy and Supply: Anglo-Russian Relations 1914–1917* (London: Allen and Unwin, 1984), and has co-edited *The Cold War and Defense* (New York: Praeger, 1990), *Men, Machines and War* (Waterloo: Wilfred Laurier Press, 1988) and *Go Spy the Land: Military Intelligence in History* (New York: Praeger, 1992). He has also written articles on Anglo-Russian and Anglo-Soviet relations during the twentieth century.

DAVID REYNOLDS is a Fellow of Christ's College, Cambridge University. His publications include *The Creation of the Anglo-American Alliance, 1937–1941: A Study in Competitive Co-operation* (1981), which was awarded the Bernath Prize in 1982; *An Ocean Apart: The Relationship Between Britain and America in the Twentieth Century* (1988 – co-author); *Britannia Overruled: British Policy and World Power in the Twentieth Century* (1991); and *Rich Relations: The American Occupation of Britain, 1942–1945* (1995).

KEITH ROBBINS was formerly Professor of Modern History at the University of Glasgow and is currently Vice-Chancellor of University College, University of Wales, Lampeter. He has written widely on British foreign and domestic affairs during the nineteenth century. His publications include *Munich 1938* (1968), *Sir Edward Grey* (1971), *Churchill* (1992) and *The Eclipse of a Great Power: Modern Britain 1870–1992* (1994). He is the General Editor of the Longman series *Profiles in Power*.

GEOFFREY WARNER took early retirement from the Open University in 1989 after teaching at the Universities of Reading, Hull and Leicester. He is currently College Lecturer in Modern History at Brasenose College, Oxford, and is also a Visiting Fellow in the Department of Politics and International Studies at the University of Birmingham. His articles and essays on the history of British foreign policy and the Cold War have appeared in *International Affairs, Diplomacy and Statecraft, Diplomatic History* and the *Vierteljahreshefte fur Zeitgeschichte*, as well as in various symposia. He has written the chapter on Ernest Bevin in Gordon Craig and Francis Lowenheim (eds.) *The Diplomats 1939–1979* (Princeton University Press, 1994), and has prepared a selection from the diaries and papers of the late Sir Kenneth Younger for publication.

DONALD CAMERON WATT was formerly Stevenson Professor of International History at the London School of Economics. His numerous publications include *Personalities and Policies, Too Serious a Business, Succeeding John Bull* and *How War Came: The Immediate Origins of the Second World War 1938–1939*. He has recently completed the official history of the central organisation of defence in the United Kingdom, 1954–1964, for the Cabinet Office Historical Branch.

Preface

In the last forty years or so, 'diplomatic history' has died; from its ashes has arisen 'international history'. In Britain's case, during the 1950s, the study of British diplomatic history had fallen into the doldrums. Many of the monographs produced in this field during that decade tended to be rather turgid accounts of the minutiae of diplomacy and were, more often than not, based on published volumes of despatches released by European foreign ministries. These works contained little in the way of explanation of how foreign policies were actually formulated by governments, except for what could be gleaned from these publications and a limited number of archives. Thus, 'the realities behind diplomacy' tended to be ignored, and strategic, economic and social factors as they affected foreign policy-making were hardly mentioned. Zara Steiner was one of a new generation of historians at the time who began to investigate the process of foreign policy formulation, especially its administrative and institutional aspects – Cabinet and Cabinet ministers, Cabinet committees, the Committee of Imperial Defence after 1902, the Foreign Office, other Departments of State and their officials. Born in the United States, educated there and in Great Britain, and practising her craft as an historian in Great Britain, Zara brought to the emerging field of 'international history' a transnational view of Great Power politics. Freed by her background from a parochial view of foreign policy-making that had long distinguished 'international history' – the study of a Power's foreign policy was subsumed within its national history so much that its historians ignored the wider world in their evaluations – she helped to pioneer a broader, more comprehensive approach to the subject that demanded multi-archival research, comparative analyses of national diplomatic strategies, and whilst not ignoring 'national histories', successfully showed how and why it is crucial to look at the impact of any Power's diplomacy from *both* a national and an international perspective.

Her intellectual odyssey can be seen in the high points of her career. Zara was educated at Swarthmore College, St Anne's College and Harvard University, where she completed her Ph.D. In 1958 she published *The US State Department and the Foreign Service* and in 1961 *The Present Problems of the US Foreign Service*. In 1965 she became a Fellow of New College, Cambridge where she was to remain until the present. Having settled in the United Kingdom, she turned her attention from the State Department to a study of the British Foreign Office and of British foreign policy in the twentieth century. Initially she was interested in the evolution of the British Foreign Office during the 1900s. This did not involve merely 'what one clerk said to another', since the staff at the Foreign Office had secured a more prominent role in the determination of foreign policy since Lord Salisbury's day, when the work of the clerks was mostly of a routine and tedious nature. The practice of allowing individual officials to minute and write comments and recommendations on incoming despatches and telegrams and to draft outgoing correspondence gave them a crucial role in the policy-making process. On important subjects, their views were read, if not necessarily accepted, by the permanent under-secretary and the foreign secretary. Zara's monograph, *The Foreign Office and Foreign Policy, 1898–1914*, published in 1969, examined 'the actual work and underlying stance of these men who began as clerks, exerting an influence within a narrow, often traditional bureaucratic radius, and who, by the time the First World War began, had won a permanent place in the conception of British foreign affairs'.

In fact she was too modest: her book is a thorough examination of the Foreign Office input into decision-making and the interaction between the Foreign Office, the Cabinet and other Departments of State in the crises-ridden years before Britain went to war with Germany. In other words Zara has gone a long way towards explaining how and why Britain chose to adopt the particular foreign policy stance she did before 1914: generally pro-French and pro-Russian and certainly highly suspicious of German aims and ambitions. Her descriptions of the personalities and concepts of Sir Edward Grey, Sir Charles Hardinge, Sir Arthur Nicolson, Sir Eyre Crowe, Sir William Tyrrell and other officials who were influential in the pre-1914 Foreign Office are penetrating and revealing while the book is lively, readable and interesting – a world away from some of the work published by diplomatic historians in the previous decade.

She has also published a large number of articles which extended her work into the First World War and the post-war era. These have included an examination of the war-time Foreign Office, the effects of the Foreign Office reforms of 1918 and 1919 and of the work of the Foreign Office delegation to the Paris Peace Conference. In 1977 she published *Britain and the Origins of the First World War*, a clear and concise analysis of Britain's role before 1914, which remains the standard text on this subject. In 1982 she edited an ambitious project, *The Times Survey of the Foreign Ministries of the World*, which contained articles by specialists, herself included, from across the globe and is the standard reference book on the subject. She is currently completing *The Reconstruction of Europe, 1919–1941* in the *Oxford History of Modern Europe* series. This will also be a major contribution to our understanding of the interaction of the European powers in the inter-war period.

Zara is an inspiring and enthusiastic teacher to generations of undergraduates at Cambridge. She has also supervised postgraduates from the United Kingdom and from overseas reading for the Cambridge Ph.D. She has therefore encouraged many students who subsequently became university teachers themselves. All the contributors to this volume have known Zara for many years and many have worked with her as colleagues and friends. Many, including the editors, have been much influenced by Zara's approach to the study of, and understanding of, diplomacy and diplomatic history. And importantly, her work has never ignored the human dimension in foreign policy-making: indeed, taken as a whole, her published studies show the important connection between personality and policy. Overall this volume is intended to reflect Zara's deep interest in diplomatic history and all the contributions deal with aspects of British foreign policy and diplomacy.

The chapters have been arranged in chronological order, with the first three concerned with the more general aspects of diplomacy and arbitration. Valerie Cromwell's 'A World Apart?' examines diplomatic practice and behaviour during the nineteenth and twentieth centuries and reflects on the continuity and distinctiveness which has been the hall mark of the British Foreign Service down to the present day, despite numerous attempts to reform the system, of which the most recent was the abortive Central Policy Review Staff recommendations of 1977. As the author suggests, the late twentieth century diplomatic service still sees itself as a *corps d'élite* distinct from the home civil service, reflecting its belief that 'personality counts for more in diplomacy than in any other public service' (p. 7). As late as 1949 the service felt it necessary to issue advice on etiquette to new entrants, which, when leaked to the press, greatly embarrassed the Labour foreign secretary, Ernest Bevin.

Keith Robbins' 'Experiencing the Foreign' looks at the extent of the exposure of British politicians to foreigners and foreign countries before 1939 and how this affected their attitudes to foreign affairs. Some, like Edward Grey and Asquith, had little experience of foreign countries – indeed Grey abhorred overseas travel. Others, like Curzon and Ramsay MacDonald, had had more to do with the British Empire and the

Dominions than Europe, while Lloyd George spent a good deal of his time as prime minister travelling to the Continent for conferences with European, usually French, politicians. Robbins does not think that personal knowledge – or lack thereof – of foreign countries had much effect on British foreign policy before 1914, while after 1914 the record is unclear: Lloyd George's personal diplomacy after all did not meet with much success, at least after 1919.

Richard Langhorne's chapter examines the increasing resort to arbitration by states after 1870, and concludes that this tendency indirectly reflected the profound and unsettling change in the international system after the Franco-Prussian War and, at the same time, the greater administrative role of governments. To many contemporaries arbitration was regarded as a possible future alternative to war but this was hardly a likely outcome given that all arbitration treaties excluded the national honour, dignity and vital interests of the powers involved from their remit. Useful in the resolution of relatively minor disputes, it is doubtful whether it will ever be acceptable where serious issues involving political circumstances arise.

The fourth contributor, Keith Neilson, deals with the influence of ambassadors on British foreign policy between 1904 and 1914, and chooses as his examples the Washington Embassy and the St Petersburg Embassy. The record is patchy. After 1904 particularly, ambassadors to the capitals of the great powers were selected because they were thought to be sympathetic to the current trend in British foreign policy, which was designed to encourage American Anglophile sympathies where they existed, and to ensure after 1907 that Russia remained loyal to the Entente. In this connection the successive ambassadors to Russia in the period – Hardinge, Nicolson and Buchanan – were successful, despite the fact that they sometimes found it difficult to disguise in their reports their repugnance for many aspects of the czarist autocracy. On the other hand, in the United States, only Lord Bryce can be regarded as a success in dealing with the administration and with Congress: Durand did not get on with Teddy Roosevelt nor Spring-Rice with Woodrow Wilson. However, they usually had able deputies who could establish a rapport with Americans.

Brian McKercher's chapter plots the fall, rise and fall of Foreign Office influence on foreign policy between 1919 and 1939. After Lloyd George's unfortunate experiments with personal diplomacy before 1922, when the influence of the Foreign Office was at its nadir, it was able to reassert its control over foreign policy, particularly after 1925. McKercher asserts that the 'Edwardian' tradition in the Office, which had little patience for collective security, disarmament and the League of Nations, and concentrated on the balance of power and national interest, remained paramount down to about 1937. Crowe, Tyrrell and Vansittart were, successively, exemplars of this tradition, which may have saved Britain from many of the disasters which afflicted her foreign policy after Neville Chamberlain, who had a totally different philosophy, extended prime ministerial control over foreign affairs after 1937. McKercher concludes, from his study of this subject, that recent works which have asserted the primacy of the Treasury over foreign policy-making in the period have little validity.

Erik Goldstein's chapter also concentrates on the resurgence of Foreign Office influence in the 1920s, examining the particular case of the Locarno Pact in 1925. Here, with the crucial support of Eyre Crowe shortly before his death, Austen Chamberlain was able to establish his ascendancy over foreign policy against the formidable combination of Curzon, Balfour, Amery, Churchill and Birkenhead. Chamberlain's threat to resign if he did not get his way and Baldwin's eventual backing enabled him to secure an agreement which offered France at least a limited guarantee in the West for the first time since the abortive Anglo-American guarantee of 1919.

Donald Cameron Watt's article on Chamberlain's ambassadors, whom he identifies as Sir Nevile Henderson in Berlin, Lord Perth in Rome, Sir Robert Craigie in Tokyo and Sir Eric Phipps in Paris, surveys a much wider field than the title suggests. It encompasses Neville Chamberlain's relations with the Foreign Office and diplomatic service after he became prime minister in 1937 and examines how he exploited his contacts with these three ambassadors to short circuit the official channels to further his own goals. Watt is scathing, not only about the way in which Chamberlain acted in a constitutionally dubious manner in dealing with these ambassadors, but also for the grave ethical and moral misjudgements Chamberlain made in the course of pursuing his policies.

Michael Dockrill's chapter surveys Anglo-French relations during the 'phoney war,' chiefly from the point of view of the Foreign Office. Traditional Foreign Office Francophilia reasserted itself in 1939 and, at least in the case of civilian relations, the Office was able to iron out differences between the two countries and to make a substantial contribution towards the smooth operation of the Entente before May 1940, to the extent that the two countries were beginning to move towards a much closer association before Germany invaded the Low Countries. Such an outcome would have been unthinkable before 1939.

David Reynolds, in a timely contribution, takes issue with recent historiography which suggests that Winston Churchill sacrificed the power and independence of the United Kingdom by continuing with the war against Nazi Germany after the fall of France, since the end result was that Britain became a satellite of the United States. In other words this outcome could have been avoided by a negotiated peace with Germany in 1940 or 1941. In fact the notion of a compromise peace with Hitler was unthinkable given British experiences of his untrustworthiness before 1940 and the half-suspected ambitions for future global power which he harboured. Any lingering doubt about the possibility of a lasting accommodation with Hitler should have been removed by Germany's assault on her former ally, the Soviet Union, in 1941. Despite the criticisms of Roosevelt by British historians, the president was forced into a formidable struggle with Congress to secure Lend Lease for Britain in 1941, while Britain had no strategy for defeating the Axis on her own: she had never fought on the European continent without the support of powerful allies. How anybody with even the slightest knowledge of Nazi atrocities during the Second World War could advocate that Britain should have sought a compromise peace with such a monster state defies comprehension.

Finally, Geoffrey Warner examines Anglo-Soviet relations from 1941 to 1948, from alliance to outright hostility. The brief period of cooperation between the two countries, which was scarcely cordial or trusting, was in many ways an aberration: their relations between 1917 and 1941 had been characterised by suspicion and hostility and once Germany had been defeated they were bound to resume this 'natural' pattern, given the extent of their differences over the ordering of the post-war world. He concludes that, contrary to the assertions of recent historians, Britain did not deliberately provoke tensions between the two countries – she was quite prepared to accept a sphere of influence for Russia in Eastern Europe but not beyond it, that is, into the region of British interests.

This assessment of Britain as a world power has been written to honour our friend and colleague. Needless to say, it also gives practical form to something that she has impressed on most of us over the years in her gentle but firm way: if you have all the answers, you have not asked all the questions. Collectively, therefore, we have explored a series of unanswered questions in a way that not only shows our debt to her, but also reflects the scope of her important contributions to the field of modern British foreign policy in particular, and of international history, in general. Zara Steiner has been to the fore amongst a select number of scholars who have distinguished themselves since the mid-1950s as 'international historians', a group including Jean-Baptiste Duroselle, Pierre Renouvin, Ernest May and Donald Cameron Watt. She has asked critical questions about how and why British foreign policy in the first half of the twentieth century evolved as it did. She has offered new ways of looking at how foreign policy – and not just British foreign policy – has been made, and how the vagaries of time, circumstance and human agency have affected the issues of war and peace since the 1890s. She has impressed on colleagues and students the need to go beyond a national perspective to understand more fully those issues, and to put them in the context of 'the realities of diplomacy', especially strategic, economic and social factors. She has by her work, advice and critical judgement helped point the way for others to follow. As this collection shows, we owe her an immense debt of gratitude; as it also shows, other 'international historians' who labour in this field of academe owe her the same debt.

Michael Dockrill and Brian McKercher

Acknowledgements

Unpublished Crown copyright material in the Public Record Office and in the India Office Records is reproduced by permission of the Director of the Public Record Office. Material from the Newspaper Library, Colindale, is reproduced by permission of the British Library Newspaper Library. The Master, Fellows and Scholars of Churchill College, Cambridge, have given us permission to quote from the papers of Lord Hankey, Sir Eric Phipps and Sir J.W. Headlam-Morley in the Churchill Archives Centre, Cambridge. Quotations from the papers of Lord Vansittart at Churchill College are reproduced with the permission of Sir Colville Barclay. The Syndics of the Cambridge University Library have granted us permission to quote from the papers of Lord Baldwin of Bewdley, Lord Hardinge of Penshurst, Lord Templewood and Lord Crewe. The Trustees of the Liddell Hart Centre for Military Archives, King's College, London, have given us permission to examine and reproduce extracts from the papers of Sir Basil Liddell Hart, and from the papers of Field Marshal Lord Alexander. Extracts from the papers of Lord Bertie, Lord Balfour and Lord Robert Cecil at the British Library are reproduced by permission of the British Library and of Professor A.K.S. Lambton. Extracts quoted from a Memorandum by Lord Halifax in May 1940 (Hickleton Papers) in the Borthwick Institute of Historical Research, the University of York, are reproduced with the permission of Lord Halifax and of the director of the Borthwick Institute. Extracts from the Selborne Papers at the Bodleian Library are reproduced with the permission of the present Earl of Selborne. Extracts from the private papers of David Lloyd George, which are in the custody of the House of Lords Record Office, are reproduced by permission of the Clerk of the Records. Extracts from Lord Howard of Penrith's papers at the Cumbria Record Office are reproduced by permission of the present Lord Howard of Penrith. Quotations from the papers of Philip Kerr, Marquis of Lothian, at the National Library of Scotland, are reproduced with the permission of the Keeper of the Records of Scotland. Extracts from Hugh Dalton's papers are reproduced with the permission of the Librarian, the British Library of Economic and Political Science. Extracts from the Austen and Neville Chamberlain papers at the University Library, Birmingham, are reproduced with the permission of the University of Birmingham. Extracts from the papers of Lord Morley are reproduced with the permission of the India Office Library and Records. The holder of the copyright for the Beaumont papers, held at the Department of Documents at the Imperial War Museum, could not be traced. We apologise if we have unwittingly infringed any other copyrights.

CHAPTER 1

'A world apart': gentlemen amateurs to professional generalists

In celebrating the achievements of Zara Steiner, this chapter seeks to thread through a number of aspects of the British diplomatic world since 1815, a world on which together we have shared and share ideas and projects. Its focus is on some of the ways in which, despite external pressures for change, the Foreign Office and diplomatic service retained and protected well into the twentieth century many styles and patterns of behaviour established during the previous century.

After the Foreign Office and diplomatic service were amalgamated in 1919, it was soon clear that the ostensibly merged service had assumed most of the traditions and practices of the latter. Successive governments since 1945 have continued, sometimes somewhat reluctantly, to tolerate and accept the justification for such traditions and practices, even after the harsh review in 1977 by Kenneth Berrill's Central Policy Review Staff investigation. This acceptance, and the consequent associated financing, have ensured the survival within the diplomatic service of a sense of distinctiveness within the civil service. That sense of distinctiveness has in its turn helped to perpetuate those traditions and practices. Sir David Kelly even went so far as to assert that, when he joined the diplomatic service, 'it was regarded as part of the King's Household and not really part of the Civil Service at all'.[1] The series of investigations, which began in 1962 with the Plowden inquiry, have all with different emphasis focused and continue to focus on the benefits and disadvantages of the distancing of the service from the home civil service. To a certain extent, the late twentieth-century British

---

[1] Sir David Kelly, *The Ruling Few* (London, 1952), p. 367.

1

diplomatic service still sees itself as 'an institution apart ... a corps d'élite'.[2]

That *esprit de corps*, that genuine sense of 'specialness', that distancing of the diplomatic service from the rest of the British civil service, derived not only from its particular political functions but also from the peculiar nature of the Embassy and legation abroad as it had become established by 1815. It was the enduring concept of the mission abroad as a family, and a particular type of family at that, which was to characterise the service till long after 1919. Lady Paget remembered how much business had been transacted after dinner at the Embassy in Vienna as late as the early 1890s and how she had helped to decipher telegrams.[3] Once recruited and successfully set on the salaried career ladder, for the ambitious young diplomat the choice of bride was obviously important. The persistence of the family embassy and the continuing importance of social hospitality in the diplomat's representational role ensured and still ensure a particularly high profile for the diplomatic wife. In the years before 1914, experience of an aristocratic or even a royal social *milieu* was to prove invaluable for a young woman faced with managing a diplomatic household in one of the major European capitals. Such women as Lady Elizabeth Yorke, wife of Sir Charles Stuart, and Lady Henrietta Cavendish, wife of Lord Granville, both ambassadors at Paris, could face the early nineteenth-century diplomatic world with equanimity. In 1885 Sir Edward Malet reported with some smugness on his wife, Lady Ermyntrude Sackville Russell, to the foreign secretary, a later Lord Granville, soon after their arrival in Berlin, 'I am glad to say that Ermyn seems to take to her public duties as if she were to the manner born.'[4] Marriage to the daughter of a senior diplomat could prove particularly advantageous as in the case of Cecil Spring-Rice who was fortunate enough as first secretary at Berlin to marry Florence Lascelles, only daughter of Sir Frank Lascelles, his ambassador: after the death of her mother she had run the Embassy for him most successfully. Horace Rumbold, son of a diplomat, proposed to and was accepted by Ethel Fane, daughter of a diplomat, on promotion to first secretary in 1904. As long as the Embassy remained a home as well as an office the family concept survived and continued long after to be admired. Sir David Kelly commented on the 1920s image of 'a small family corporation' and on the lack of demarcation between private and official life.[5] An obituary tribute to Lady Sherfield commented on the atmosphere in the 1950s at

[2] Sir Julian Bullard, quoted in Simon Jenkins and Anne Sloman, *With Respect, Ambassador: an inquiry into the Foreign Office* (London, 1985), p. 24. In 1994 the Foreign and Commonwealth Office felt confident enough to permit the filming by the BBC of a television series 'True Brits' within the office and in embassies overseas, which underlined the distancing.

[3] Walpurga, Lady Paget, *Embassies of Other Days*, 2 vols. (London, 1923), II, p. 555.

[4] Public Record Office, Granville Papers, PRO 30/29/172. 18 Apr. 1885.

[5] Kelly, *Ruling Few*, pp. 75, 134.

the Embassy at Washington when her husband was ambassador there, 'Under them, the Embassy was a true diplomatic family.'[6] It was only with the gradual separation of the Embassy's offices from the official diplomatic residence that the family ethos began to weaken. Its influences remain.

Not only did the staff work in offices at the residence. The junior staff were unpaid and often lived there. There can be no doubt that the persistence of unpaid staff living and working in missions abroad aided the survival of the family concept. In the eighteenth century it had been quite common for young men, sons of friends or relatives of a minister, to arrange informally to spend time in the diplomatic household helping in the work, considering such experience helpful to a future political career. Attempting to increase efficiency in 1825, Canning instructed that all such people could only be attached to a mission with the written consent of the secretary of state. In 1856, in the hope of ensuring at least a basic competent educational standard for recruits, examinations for unpaid attachés were instituted. They were designed to test handwriting, English and French dictation, French and one other language, geography, *précis* and modern history. The introduction of even these basic examinations inevitably weakened the personal links between ambassadors and their attachés, but various moves, led by Clarendon, were made to reduce their impact on young men who, it was argued, were going to give as much as five years unpaid service to the state. Any real control of such unpaid staff was bound to remain difficult as long as it had to be assumed that some recruits were not aiming at a diplomatic career. Nineteenth-century public concern for the abolition of personal and political patronage in public appointments consequently had a somewhat muted effect on the diplomatic service. At the same time increasing pressure of all types of diplomatic work after 1815 was leading to substantial operational difficulties since such unpaid staff could drift in and out of the service and could not always be expected to be reliable. As a result, to cope with the gradually increasing administrative and clerical load, a few paid attachés were appointed to serve below the secretary of embassy but above the unpaid attachés. Their number grew steadily. By 1825 there were seven paid attachés serving abroad by comparison with thirty-five unpaid: in 1853 that ratio had become 29:28. After persistent criticism from within the service, the rank and title of paid attaché were replaced in 1862 by those of second and third secretaries. These established appointments were however still only to be made after a young man had satisfactorily completed his probationary period as unpaid attaché, six months of which was to be spent in the Foreign Office. Not only was the first period of work in the diplomatic service to remain unpaid till 1919, but a £400-a-year income

6 *The Times*, 1 June 1985.

requirement also continued. A pattern of close and informal relationships pervaded the atmosphere of work.

Britain's major European Embassies and legations, in the same way as those of the other great powers, including even France after 1871, continued to be characterised by an aristocratic life-style suitable for the reception of social equals at the peak of local politics and society. It was consequently deemed desirable that unpaid and also paid junior diplomatic staff should be recruited from an appropriate social and educational background such as to enable them to melt into the background, not to put a foot wrong and to be welcome at the ambassador's formal and family dining tables. It was essential, as Sir David Kelly insisted, that, if they were to do their job, 'they had to be accepted as "Court-worthy," people of the same class who observed the same standards'.[7] Although the standards of the qualifying examination were to be raised gradually till they approached those of university final degree examinations, the continuing need by candidates for nomination on first application ensured that young men from families unknown to the foreign secretary or to his private secretary only rarely applied for the diplomatic service. Recruitment of junior staff throughout the nineteenth century remained largely the preserve of the sons of either the landed or professional classes. These young men came more and more however from the major public schools. The introduction in 1870 of open competitition for the administrative class of the home civil service was strongly and successfully resisted by the foreign secretary for the Foreign Office and diplomatic service. The argument rested on the different nature and requirements of diplomatic work. Eton came to dominate the entry despite the examination changes of 1904 and 1907: 67 per cent of the 1900–14 entrants were Etonians.[8] What had changed by 1914 was that they had now, in addition, also attended a university, usually Oxford or Cambridge. Sir David Kelly describes his May 1914 interview by the selection board:[9]

I did not come from one of the very small group of schools from which practically the whole Foreign Office and Diplomatic Service were at the time recruited, and had no family connections with it . . . I presented myself at the Foreign Office in an ordinary suit, and saw to my horror that the other ten or twelve candidates (for that was all there were) were all in tail coats! When my name was called, as I went to the board room I heard an awed whisper of, 'Good Lord, he got a First!' . . . Entering the Board Room I found some half dozen elderly diplomatists under the chairmanship of, I understood, Sir A. Nicolson . . . I was asked why I wanted to go in for the Diplomatic Service and could think of nothing better to reply than

[7] Kelly, *Ruling Few*, p. 117.
[8] For a full account of the social and educational background of entrants to the diplomatic service up to 1914, see R.A. Jones, *The British Diplomatic Service, 1815–1914* (Ontario, 1983), chapters 2 and 8.
[9] Kelly, *Ruling Few*, pp. 76–7.

that I liked foreign travel. I was asked one other question, about Balkan affairs, and was then politely bidden good-day and walked out feeling that my inadequate dress had damned me at sight ... However, within a few days I received notice of my nomination ...

Sir John Barnes was sure that 'It is of course true that the old diplomatic service was drawn from a pretty narrow circle and that this state of affairs to some extent persisted between the wars. There were some shining exceptions, such as William Strang, Robert Howe (son of an engine driver, I believe) and Knox Heber; but perhaps they prove the rule.'[10] Between the wars Eton's grip on diplomatic recruitment weakened. In 1929, of ten appointments, four were from Eton: the rest, however, came from the major public schools. All, bar one who went to no university, came from either Oxford or Cambridge.[11]

There had been pressure since the 1861 select committee on the diplomatic service for the interchange of staff between the Foreign Office and the diplomatic service, but this continued to be successfully rebutted on the grounds that the work of the two staffs was totally different and that the junior staff abroad were unpaid and consequently cheap. Following the MacDonnell Commission's publication of highly critical evidence with its 1914 report, the Foreign Office finally accepted in 1916 the principle of amalgamation. Although the £400 entrance private income requirement was abolished and a joint Foreign Office and diplomatic service seniority list was agreed in 1919, the old division between home staff in the Foreign Office and those appointed for the diplomatic service survived *de facto* until 1943.[12] Pay in the service remained inadequate for those with limited means. During the greater part of his career (1919–51), Sir David Kelly found that his official pay covered only about three-quarters of his total expected expenses and still less if he was posted to the Foreign Office.[13] The continued recruitment of those who could afford such a career consequently ensured the survival of the bulk of diplomatic service traditions. The limitation on the joint seniority list and the persisting difference in pay and expenses aided that survival despite recurrent Treasury pressure for conformity. Thus, when David Scott began his campaign in January 1938 to merge the consular with the diplomatic service and the Foreign Office, the full amalgamation of those two, agreed in 1919, had still not been effected. The interview by the special Board of Selection continued to be used to weed out the unsuitable. The practice of interviewing candidates before the written examinations had been revived in 1921. Sir John

[10] Sir John Barnes to the author, private letter, 6 Mar. 1984.
[11] PRO, FO 366/882. Table of examination results, 1925–9.
[12] Valerie Cromwell and Zara Steiner, 'Reform and retrenchment: the Foreign Office between the Wars', in Roger Bullen, ed., *The Foreign Office, 1782–1982* (Frederick, MA, 1984).
[13] Kelly, *Ruling Few*, p. 134.

Barnes who entered the Office in 1946 had found his interview 'a pernicious piece of snobbery and ought to have been abolished long before it was. Mine consisted of Rab Butler looking at me as if I was a beetle at the wrong end of a microscope, although I came to love him dearly later.'[14]

The social and educational background of recruits in the interwar period inevitably encouraged expectations of official and social life in the diplomatic service based on assumptions of an upper class life-style, even for junior staff. Sir Berkeley Gage was probably one of the liveliest examples.[15] Despite his Eton and Trinity College, Cambridge education, he only managed to pass the entry examination in 1928 at the third attempt and was first appointed to the Rome Embassy because, he understood, the ambassador wanted a man who hunted on his staff. A young man of considerable means, he arrived with his 300 guinea horse and proved a great success. After spells in China, in London early in the second world war he co-founded the Thursday Dining Club which met at the Carlton Club, and which he considered his greatest achievement. His Cosy Club in Bangkok and Pink Elephant Club in Lima continued the tradition and his official residences were inevitably known as 'The Berkeley Arms'. Descendant of General Thomas Gage of Bunker Hill fame, he arrived in Chicago in 1950 with a golden retriever, cocker spaniel, brand new Bentley and Dutch valet. The Chicago press was delighted, which was to prove no bad thing in view of the then strong anti-British feeling in the city, which Gage was eventually to soothe. He published privately in 1989 his memoirs, *A Marvellous Party*. It was clear that, even for the many less colourful recruits, the rising academic standards for diplomatic entrants had barely affected the expected and assumed life-style. Diplomatic memoirs of the interwar years together with the records of the Foreign Office chief clerk's department chronicle the continuity. Extensive correspondence on unhappiness with housing provision is a significant indicator. On arriving in Buenos Aires in September 1933 from his Embassy in Chile, Sir Henry Chilton opened a lengthy and increasingly desperate negotiation with London about the state of his official residence. He became so angry that he cabled the Foreign Office to persuade the Prince of Wales to support a new house or a new building: he pleaded that it was a pity to waste money on so rotten a house by building servants' rooms in the roof. He also cabled the Office of Works on 4 September 1933, 'My excellent English servants quite naturally refuse to be housed in dingy mildewed cellars. I shall either therefore have to place them in spare rooms upstairs and be unable to put up guests or lodge them outside, an additional expenditure which I trust would be borne by His Majesty's government.'[16] The transfer of the costs of all Embassies and legations

[14] Sir John Barnes to the author, private letter, 6 Mar. 1984.
[15] *The Times* obituary, 8 Mar. 1994.
[16] PRO, FO 366/913.

abroad from the diplomatic vote to that of the Office of Works in that year inevitably made such special pleading more difficult. Diplomatic allowances were another constant source of friction. Nevertheless, even after 1945, much of the life-style remained. In 1949, Sir David Kelly set off to Moscow as new ambassador with his wife, his wife's Swiss secretary, a Belgian chef, an English butler and their Saluki dog.[17]

Such a glamorous career has to be seen against a background of ever sharper snapping at the foreign secretary's heels by the Treasury, who were determined to bring the Foreign Office and diplomatic service into line with the home civil service in terms of recruitment, promotion, pensions and retirement age. Between the wars that pressure was intensified by the determination of the permanent under-secretary at the Treasury and head of the home civil service, Sir Warren Fisher, to limit the role of the Office as his relationship seriously deteriorated with Sir Robert Vansittart, its permanent under-secretary, in the area of policy-making. By the mid-1930s the Office had agreed to match the same level of accountability as the home departments and, by 1938, Vansittart's successor, Sir Alexander Cadogan, had very reluctantly conceded the argument in consenting to become accounting officer. At the same time dispute rumbled on until 1939 between the Treasury, the Foreign Office and the Civil Service Commission as to appropriate examinations for entry. In 1936, in collaboration with the universities of Oxford, Cambridge and Bristol, the Treasury and Civil Service Commission had devised a new syllabus for admission to the administrative class of the home civil service without consulting the Foreign Office and expected it to conform to the scheme. Criticism was expressed of the Office's insistence on obligatory papers and also a higher mark in the viva examination. This encountered strong resistance: as Lord Cranborne put it, 'Personality counts for far more in diplomacy than in any other public service. It is no question of enabling socially favoured candidates to obtain jobs. It is the question of securing suitable candidates for the very special work they have to do.'[18] One of the main arguments for the new scheme was the importance of enabling candidates to take the civil service examinations immediately after their degree examinations in June and, if successful, to start work in October, thereby assisting candidates without private means to compete. Wrongfooted by the Treasury, the Foreign Office still continued to argue for a higher qualifying mark than that for the home civil service in the viva examination and for obligatory papers in French, German, Modern History and Economics, despite constant repetition of the point that such requirements weighted the scales even more in favour of those with means. In 1937, Anthony Eden, the foreign secretary, offered to reconsider the matter if, after four or five

[17] Kelly, *Ruling Few*, p. 369.
[18] PRO, FO 366/975/X1455: correspondence Jan.–Mar. 1936.

years' experience, the fears of the vice-chancellors' committee were proved justified. The claim of special career needs was repeated. Nervousness as to the likelihood of a debate on the issue in the House of Commons in 1938, however, encouraged the drafting of proposals closer to those for the home civil service but nothing had been resolved by the outbreak of war.

The persistence of earlier patterns of behaviour, the leisurely pace and casual approach to work by clerks within the Foreign Office in London is well known. Sir Edward Hertslet's nostalgic memories of the life of young Office clerks in the 1850s with their 'nursery', an attic equipped with diversions for idle hours, their piano, 'foils, single-sticks, boxing gloves, and other sources of amusement'[19] were given to contrast them with the difference in approaches to work in 1900. That late nineteenth-century change can now, however, be seen to have been only relative. In commenting to Zara Steiner and myself on our paper on the interwar Foreign Office, Sir John Barnes suggested a much later date for significant change:[20]

One thing you do not mention is that the whole pace of Foreign Office activity changed utterly with the advent of the Spanish Civil War in 1935 or whenever. Until then, it had been a leisurely life, and they raced their dogs along those lovely, long, wide corridors. But after Franco they had to take life rather more seriously and were worked off their feet. Or so Donald Maclean once told me, but you may think him a prejudiced witness.

Such a change was to become visible in the working practices of Embassies overseas after 1945 at the same time as the Foreign Office, diplomatic and consular services were merged following the 1943 White Paper. A fundamentally different role was envisaged for the diplomatic service: 'economics and finance have become inextricably interwoven with politics; an understanding of social problems and labour movements is indispensable in forming a properly balanced judgement of world events'.[21] Nevertheless, despite pressure for a change of emphasis, many of the existing patterns of behaviour and traditional attitudes continued.

Very soon after the war and the merger of the three services, with new entrance examinations for the unified service becoming only special variants of those for the home civil service, it became clear that the new, more open methods of recruitment were resulting in the arrival at British embassies abroad of young people and ex-servicemen, who, though often educated to a high standard, came from a much less privileged social background than their pre-1939 predecessors. On the considerable assumption that established traditions and practices would continue, it

[19] Sir Edward Hertslet, *Recollections of the Old Foreign Office* (London, 1901), p. 23.
[20] Sir John Barnes to the author, private letter 6 Mar. 1984.
[21] Parliamentary Papers, 1943: HC Cmd. 6420.

was obvious to some that, if these new recruits were to be assimilated into the life-style customary in the diplomatic service, they were going to need more than the traditional acquisition of drafting skills and diplomatic expertise. They were now going to need some sort of social acculturation. It was to prove more than a little embarrassing to the Foreign Office that the means chosen for that was to attract colourful publicity. Marcus Cheke now enters the story. Cheke had had an unusual career. Having been a Liberal parliamentary candidate in 1929, he entered the diplomatic service as an honorary attaché at Lisbon (1931–4), in Brussels (1934–7), then was press attaché (1938–42) and later appointed on special attachment with rank of first secretary (1942–5) in Lisbon before becoming vice-marshal of the Diplomatic Corps in 1946. In January 1949 Cheke produced a hand-book for members of the foreign service on their first posting abroad.[22] It appeared a useful and constructive idea and was circulated with a covering letter to posts abroad.

What the Foreign Office was not to need was the publicity the handbook received once it was 'leaked' to the press. On 23 February 1949, two national newspapers carried lively stories from their Washington correspondents. 'You, too, can be the life of the Embassy: 8 easy lessons' was the headline for Ralph Izzard's racy report in the *Daily Mail* on what had given the American capital's society 'its biggest chuckle of the season', 'this modern "The Chesterfield Letters"'. The editor even footnoted that reference for the help of readers. Some choice handbook entries were selected, including Cheke's indication that the book might be of particular use to those in the same situation as Hilaire Belloc's Lord Lucky, who

> ... rose in less than half an hour
> To riches, dignity and power.

It also reported the comment of a Washington society hostess, on reading Cheke's advice on funerals, that 'A line must be drawn somewhere. I won't have any diplomat, British or otherwise, making political connections at my funeral. I am making a will to that effect.' The *Daily Express* published on its front page, together with a jaunty photograph of Cheke and his wife, a short piece from R.M. MacColl, headlined 'Diplomats told how to handle bores: Mr Cheke's secret leaks out'. This also included selections from Cheke's extensive advice and carried a remark from 'an Embassy official tonight: "It is unfortunate this has got out. Those references to boring guests – oh dear."' MacColl recounted the furore in Washington and how the British Embassy was desperately trying to uncover the source of the 'leak'. This was indeed true and the *Evening News* later the same day headlined its story 'BEVIN CALLS FOR "BOOK" PROBE: HOW DID ETIQUETTE

---

[22] Marcus Cheke, *Guidance on foreign usages and ceremony, and other matters, for a Member of His Majesty's Foreign Service on his first appointment to a Post Abroad*, Jan. 1949, 81 pp.

Mr and Mrs Marcus Cheke, *Daily Express*, 24 February 1949

NOTES LEAK OUT?' and reported that the Foreign Office had ordered an immediate inquiry into how a copy of a confidential booklet had come into unauthorised hands in Washington. Sir Orme Sargent, permanent under-secretary, was reported as having 'warned all recipients that the booklet was not to be published, if for no other reason than that it sometimes poked fun at foreign mentality, which might not always be understood'. A few choice items from the handbook were again summarised. Cheke himself was reported as having 'admitted that there "had been a leak", but he would not say how or when'. Whitehall fears were also reported that some passages from the booklet might be seized on by Russia and other unfriendly nations as anti-British propaganda.

At the Foreign Office, Bevin, as was his wont, had come in early and read the day's newspapers. He was deeply concerned that the tone of the reports would cause immense harm for what had long since become, for an experienced trade unionist, his loyal service.[23] He was obviously irritated that such an embarrassing text had been circulated without his knowledge. The next day, 24 February, Frank Roberts, coming to the end of his time as principal private secretary to the foreign secretary and equally disturbed that he had not been warned of the decision to circulate the handbook, prepared a careful minute for the secretary of state,[24]

You wanted to see for yourself Mr Cheke's booklet on Guidance to Members of the Foreign Service on Appointment to a Post Abroad. A copy is attached, together with the covering circular, which clearly stated why such guidance was being given, i.e. because there had been an exceptionally large new entry into the Service after the war, and many Heads of Missions were now too hard-pressed to give individual guidance as they used to do when I joined the Service in 1930. The circular also makes it very clear that Mr Cheke's book is only intended to deal with certain minor aspects of diplomatic life, and that there is no suggestion that social behaviour is the be all and end all of a Foreign Service officer's career. The main purpose is to warn members of the Foreign Service that conditions in foreign countries vary between countries and, above all, are not necessarily the same as conditions in the United Kingdom.

I should perhaps add that Mr Cheke produced this book on his own initiative as a result of many warnings and complaints he had had from Heads of Missions abroad. As similar complaints have reached Sir O. Sargent and Mr Caccia, it was felt that Mr Cheke's book, suitably revised and provided the whole affair was kept in its proper proportion, would fill a gap.

When the original draft was circulated for comments, many suggestions were made and subsequently incorporated by Mr Cheke to meet possible criticism that his book was too largely concerned with social occasions in small capitals. For example you will find in Chapter 8 and again in Chapter 10 a good deal of advice

---

[23] Private conversation with Sir Frank Roberts, 18 July 1994. Roberts makes two points: 1. that some sort of guidance was indeed then necessary; 2. that Cheke's experience had been limited to small and somewhat old-fashioned capitals.

[24] PRO FO 366/2831. F.K. Roberts to secretary of state, 24 Feb. 1949.

on handling such important categories of people as journalists, visitors from the United Kingdom, etc.

Special attention was paid at that stage, while the book was in draft, to the question of possible criticism in the House of Commons if there were any leak and as a result garbled publicity. I myself said that it was most important that this aspect of the question should not be overlooked, and consequently Mr Mayhew [Parliamentary Under Secretary] was fully consulted, and, I understand, took the line that he was quite prepared to deal with any Parliamentary criticism, and that he thought the book served a useful purpose and should be circulated confidentially, even at the risk of leakage and misleading publicity.

I am sorry that you were not yourself informed of what was on foot. When the first draft came my way in May no decision had been taken as to whether the book should be circulated or not, and, while I drew attention to certain snags and made various suggestions, I did not think I need trouble you until the question had been discussed with Mr Mayhew and some definite recommendation was being made. I was not, however, aware of the final decision to circulate the amended document, and could not, therefore bring it to your attention.

It is, of course, too soon to give you a full account of general reactions, but they are certainly not uniformly critical. You may like to know that the News Chronicle have rung up to say that they consider the idea to be an excellent one, and to offer their help in combatting any adverse publicity. At an American diplomatic dinner which I attended last night, although there was a good deal of good-humoured fun, the Americans took the line that such a book should be most useful, and that they ought to have one themselves. There is, I gather, already a State Department booklet on similar lines, but according to members of the American Embassy here, they could do with further guidance.

Sargent had telegraphed the Embassy in Washington on 23 February requesting information on the leak and, in the early hours of the morning of 25 February, received a full reply from Sir Oliver Franks, the ambassador, reporting on the Embassy's efforts to trace the source of it.[25] All six copies of the handbook received with the circular letter in Washington had been accounted for together with those sent by the Personnel Department to new entrants. MacColl had insisted his sole source was the two *Washington Post* articles by their social columnist, Mrs Thayer, on 22 and 23 February. On 23 February, the minister had had the opportunity to question Mrs Thayer, who had volunteered spontaneously the information that she had received the book by post from England. She had refuted the suggestion that it had come from some British government office. She explained that she had in fact received the book three weeks before and had not indeed then bothered to look at it: on reading it recently, she had however realised what good 'copy' it was. In conclusion, Franks then reported an agitated phone call on the morning of 24 February from Mrs Thayer, who had been very upset by the commotion caused and indicated that she had had no idea of the attention her articles would attract or any

[25] PRO FO 366/2831. Telegram 1085 sent 24 Feb. 1949.

wish to make trouble with the British. She had said that she had now returned the book by air mail to its sender in England, though was still careful not to say who this was, and implied generally that she would not write any more articles about the handbook. Sargent cannot have been pleased to see later that morning that the *News Chronicle* had headed its column of Vicky's cartoons of his own illustrated version of a manual with the note that the Foreign Office had been convulsed by the worst leak in its history. The cartoons would hardly seem to have been much help in 'combatting any adverse publicity'.[26]

So, what was in the handbook?[27] Its foreword by Orme Sargent explained that it aimed to give guidance to a new recruit (Grade 8 or 9) on first posting abroad, finding himself 'thrown into a society with which he is wholly unfamiliar' and, while not intended to deal with work and duties generally, was limited to how he was 'to establish and conduct those social relationships which it is his duty to cultivate in such a post'. It also pointed out that it did not cover the question of social contacts and behaviour at consular posts 'where the circumstances and requirements are somewhat different'. After an introduction justifying the textbook, Marcus Cheke then presents ten chapters taking Mr John Bull, a married man with two years' experience working in the Foreign Office in London, through 'the many pitfalls which surround his footsteps both in the drawing-room of his own Ambassadress and in the houses of foreign acquaintances' after his arrival as a second or third secretary on the staff of Sir Henry Sealingwax, His Majesty's ambassador to Mauretania.

What to do on being nominated to a post abroad inevitably comes first. Cheke underlines that there are two types of Embassy and two sorts of ambassadors. An Embassy to a major power 'in a large and civilised capital' might mean that the ambassador and Lady Sealingwax would be somewhat remote personages to all but the most senior staff members and the staff itself would be loosely knit with many alternative social distractions. At a smaller capital, especially at a great distance, 'the whole Embassy staff forms a sort of family, of which His Majesty's Ambassador is *pater familias*'. Much detailed advice is given on what Mrs John Bull should do, on their dress and on their choice of housing. Bull is warned that, despite the earlier caution to avoid familiarity, 'Nowadays his Foreign Service colleagues will begin to call him by his Christian name at once, and after a day or two, during which Mr Bull may prefer to avoid giving them any name at all, he may return this vulgar compliment.'[28] Cheke then moves

---

[26] Sir Frank Roberts confirms in conversation (18 July 1994) that the source of the leak was not traced. Marcus Cheke remained vice-marshal of the Diplomatic Corps until 1957, after which he was appointed minister to the Holy See till his death in 1960. In 1957 he was also appointed extra gentleman usher to the queen and KCVO.

[27] It is known that the handbook was being issued to new recruits in the 1960s.

[28] Cheke, *Guidance*, p. 9.

Diplomacy Without Tears

CONTACTS

Be careful whom you cut. He may be the next Prime Minister.

RECEPTIONS

Don't form a queue at official functions. Undisciplined foreigners do not understand.

CARD GAMES

Always remember that your partners are foreigners and make allowances.

ANIMAL LOVE

If a foreign politician doesn't like your dog he is not necessarily a cad.

The Foreign Office has been convulsed by the worst leak in its history.

A secret guide to young diplomats on how to behave abroad has been bootlegged—or hi-jacked in Washington.

To console the Foreign Office Vicky offers his own illustrated Manual to Good Manners in High Places.

CONVERSATION

Don't discuss the weather. Remember that foreigners have other topics of conversation.

SENSE OF HUMOUR

When diplomatic talks become strained give him a copy of "Punch."

Vicky's 'Handbook', *News Chronicle*, 25 February 1949

on to the first social and formal moves to be faced on arrival and reminds Bull of the difference between British and foreign styles of invitation. He emphasises the reasons why British Embassy invitations must take first priority. Having underlined the advice that 'at Embassy parties Mr and Mrs Bull must consider themselves to be on duty', it is explained that one of their chief duties will be to be affable to bores as 'nothing ruins the appearance of a party as surely as dreary individuals standing in gloomy and solitary silence'.[29] It is also vital for them both to watch the situation of Lady Sealingwax and to provide her with appropriate assistance. Bull is warned always to sit on the ambassador's left in a car and to walk on his left.

The niceties of engraved visiting cards and their use, the complex formalities of introductions within and outside the diplomatic circle and the importance of correct *placement* at table are carefully spelt out. Having in his introduction pointed out that an extra allowance was paid for hospitality abroad, Cheke warns that if Bull finds the forms of ceremony 'so intolerable that he is inclined to refuse to conform to them, he would be wise to ask himself – however confident he may feel of his efficiency at his desk – whether the Foreign Service is, after all, really in his line'.[30] For Bull's future career, the importance of the social world of the diplomatic corps and of the personal links forged in it is emphasised. Small but telling points are made. Bull is advised to learn how to play bridge. As a junior, he must not leave Embassy or foreign dinners before important guests go: 'it is generally necessary for him to stay to the bitter end of even the most tedious dinners, and he will find it much more agreeable to play a hand of cards than have to sit up half the night making conversation to some boring, important old lady'.[31] He must also find out about the local custom on tipping servants.

Having worked through such matters of a formal nature, Cheke becomes more discursive about the value to an ambassador of having at least one staff member who is out and about in society regularly because of the need for a regular supply of 'the sort of intelligence that only personal contacts can give to correct the information coming in to him from official quarters and from the press'.[32] The value of contacts with the commercial and financial worlds, the press, politicians, the academic world, 'drawing-room society', the 'Smart Set' and labour leaders is discussed. Cheke cites in his favour the success between the wars of Alfred Horstmann, German minister in Lisbon, who dissipated anti-German feeling and made a hundred influential contacts which were to be richly exploited by his successor during the Spanish Civil War. In some countries

[29] Ibid., p. 13.
[30] Ibid., p. 24.
[31] Ibid., pp. 45–6.
[32] Ibid., p. 47.

where it is rare to be invited to private houses, cafés, theatre foyers and clubs offer the best opportunities for keeping up contacts. Public funerals in some countries prove unrivalled as occasions for cultivating acquaint-anceships. 'How many an interesting political connection was first conceived by a certain foreign Head of Mission in a convulsive handshake in a funeral cortège and cemented by giving his man a lift home in his car from the cemetery!'[33]

Bull must work hard to identify the distinguishing traits of the Mauretanian national character. Mauretania is identified as a Latin society in Cheke's discussion of foreign mentality. Latins, he explains from his experience, are more complex than the Anglo-Saxons, 'more suspicious-minded', always seeking evidence of sentimental attachments and sinister motives; they are generally touchy and full of vivacity. Bull is warned not to joke about politics or to pay too obvious attention to a young married lady there. A short appendix offers short hints provided by Cheke's colleagues of guidance for recruits to North America, 'never behave as if their name was Mr and Mrs Cholmondeley Haugh-Haugh', Russia and behind the Iron Curtain, beware of microphones and telephone tapping, the Far East, 'Truth, he would argue, is after all relative', the Middle East, 'Bull must learn to practise patience' and Scandinavia, 'give your host his full titles on every occasion, however informal'. At the same time Bull is cautioned on his relationship with the British community at his overseas posting and is advised to follow the practice established there. Cheke is clearly critical of those British diplomats who view such communities with distaste. He also warns Bull to remember that failure to show appropriate attention to British visitors to Mauretania, often members of official delegations, 'may do more harm to the individual Ambassador and to the Foreign Service as a whole on their return home than almost any other sin of omission or commission in diplomatic life'.

Cheke's constant theme is 'that all people outside the British Isles lay a much greater emphasis on ceremony in their official and social relations than Englishmen do'. The total absence of ceremony in America he considers must be regarded as a kind of ceremony. There are signs that he was well aware that he was issuing a counsel of perfection: 'It is the Englishman's (and the American's) ignorance or contempt of ceremony and his refusal to adapt himself to the social etiquette of the foreign country where he is residing which explains how seldom an English Third Secretary succeeds in acquiring a position in foreign society comparable to that enjoyed by his European colleagues.'[34] There can be no doubt that there was not only much good sense buried in the guidebook but also there was a need for something like it. What was ill judged was its tone

[33] Ibid., p. 56.
[34] Ibid., p. 58.

and the substantial probability that such a widely circulated text would become public. It was issued to all new recruits and to all overseas missions.

The publicity was particularly unfortunate since it came as the Foreign Office and diplomatic service were undergoing an unprecedented period of change. It was perhaps significant that just as Cheke was producing his guidebook, the Office was approaching the Treasury on the subject of simplifying the existing diplomatic uniform in view of the importance of standardising the various uniforms 'in order to promote the idea of unity of the Services which were amalgamated by the 1943 Act'.[35] The amalgamation and complete integration of the Foreign Office, the diplomatic service, the commercial diplomatic service, the consular service and the overseas information services from the Ministry of Information into a single unified foreign service meant that senior positions in the Foreign Office and abroad were open to all staff who could be called on for any type of work. Little sense of the effects of these immense changes is to be found in Cheke's guidebook.

The successive post-war investigations into the foreign service have revealed how much of the world described by Cheke has survived despite structural administrative and functional change. Looking back nostalgically in 1973, Humphrey Trevelyan pointed sadly to the changes he had seen since joining the service in 1947:[36]

In the old days the ambassador was purely political. In his heyday he took with him to his post his wife, perhaps his mistress, his butler, his son or his nephew as an attaché and a few footmen and secretaries to round it off. In later times he allowed some inferior life to form part of his entourage, having to do with commercial or consular affairs; but he disdained such menial occupations himself and gladly admitted to a total ignorance of anything to do with the country in which he lived other than the political and amorous intrigues of the court or presidency. Nowadays, whatever his personal predilections, he will recognise that he must give serious attention to matters other than politics. He must regard himself as an economist, a commercial traveller, an advertising agent for his country; he wields the weapon of culture for political ends; he promotes scientific and technical exchanges and administers development aid. He cannot wholly detach himself from the technicalities and personal inconveniences which accompany the battle for intelligence. He must concern himself with the relations not only of governments, but also of politicians, scientists, musicians, dancers, actors, authors, footballers, trade unionists and even women and youth, these two new technical professions in the modern world. But he continues to have a basic political job to negotiate with the other government and to keep his own government informed about anything in the country to which he is accredited which affects his country's interests.

[35] PRO FO 366/2814 A.J. Gardener to J.D.K. Beighton, Treasury, 5 Jan. 1949.
[36] Humphrey [Lord] Trevelyan, *Diplomatic Channels* (London, 1973), p. 15.

There was however a persisting reluctance to recognise the need for new skills and roles and a continuing defence of traditional practices, although the range of entrants widened out of all recognition, becoming more representative of the society the service is supposed to represent.

The report of the 1977 Central Policy Review Staff on Britain's overseas representation fundamentally reviewed the distribution of the relevant functions between the home civil service departments and the foreign service in the light of Britain's declining international position.[37] Alongside their structural recommendations, they made clear recommendations for change in the diplomatic life-style. They found the current level of spending on entertainment of £5.6 million, which included some of the associated extra housing costs, unjustified. Underlining the link between the over-generous provision of housing and assumptions about the effectiveness of social entertaining 'for purposes of general cultivation', they acknowledged that the Foreign and Commonwealth Office had, with its own review, moved a little down the road of linking the size of allowances more closely to the entertainment needs of the individual's job but wished it to go much further. They recommended the replacement of individual allowances by a mission fund, funding it by halving the entertainment allowance. They wished the FCO to reduce its entertainment budget by 50 per cent and to encourage a reduction in entertainment at home, less entertainment involving spouses and 'more entertainment of the business lunch type'. They pointed out that these big reductions would still leave the average counsellor able to entertain approximately 400 people a year. They had identified a particular social problem beginning to face the foreign service, that of spouses with jobs. They made various recommendations for the reduction of standards of diplomatic accommodation, having reviewed housing for other countries and also for equivalent Ministry of Defence staff overseas.

Very little changed as a result of the 1977 report. By the time Simon Jenkins and Anne Sloman prepared a series of broadcasts in 1984 on the Foreign Office, they found much of the traditional life-style had survived.[38] They found the British diplomat 'lives, works and entertains in surroundings which bespeak a grander age than ours, a world of protocols and butlers, memoranda and Daimlers'. They also made many of the points advanced by the CPRS and hoped for a merger of the foreign with the home civil service. That has not happened. The world apart has been protected.

---

[37] *Review of Overseas Representation: Report by the Central Policy Review Staff* (London, 1977).
[38] Jenkins and Sloman, *With Respect, Ambassador*, based on five BBC broadcasts.

CHAPTER 2

'Experiencing the foreign': British foreign policy makers and the delights of travel

It is fitting that a paper to honour a historian of British foreign policy should focus on the role of diplomats and politicians as 'go betweens' whose task it is to understand the 'foreign' but who must not, in the process, 'go native'. It is all the more pertinent when that historian has herself approached British foreign policy as an 'outsider', though happily she has largely 'gone native'! This chapter does not attempt a comprehensive study of the 'mental maps' of the British foreign-policy-making elite, but rather explores the ways in which 'the foreign' was experienced. It asks how far such perceptions, in particular or in general, had any direct or even tangible consequences for the formulation or execution of foreign policy. Perceptions of 'the foreign', in turn, presuppose certain assumptions about the nature of 'Britishness'.

Lord Salisbury surveyed foreigners from the olympian English redoubt of Hatfield House. As prime minister and foreign secretary, he dominated British policy-making for some fifteen years in the late century when Britain's global role was both impressive and burdensome. Foreigners, of some sort, could not be avoided in an imperial outreach which encompassed the world. Yet in the course of his long life his contact with them was relatively limited, though we may also note that he was extraordinarily shy and his contact with 'the English' themselves was not excessive – he succeeded his father in the House of Lords in 1868. Foreigners were not conspicuous in the Eton and Oxford of his youth. In 1851–3, just before he entered the House of Commons, he was exposed not to Europeans or Asians but sent to convalesce from a nervous breakdown, to the 'British' in South Africa, New Zealand and Australia. The fact that the intrepid pioneers he encountered were not 'foreigners' did not stop them being rather boring – from his youthful perspective. He had not been brought up amongst gold-diggers.

We read that although predictably well grounded in Latin and Greek, he was 'proficient in the German language and very widely read in its history and literature. He was fully acquainted with the French language, history and literature and, to a lesser extent, with those of Italy.'[1] In the years between 1859 and 1864 he wrote a series of reviews, usually monthly, of books in German, in which he considered approximately 500 books dealing with historical, political, philosophical and theological topics.[2] Other pieces show a wide interest in events in France, Italy and elsewhere – though it is Germany which is the predominant foreign interest. An aristocratic MP who reviews Schleiermacher and Karl Marx cannot be accused of blinkered insularity. We can with justice speak of Salisbury possessing 'an European mind', though besides comment on British domestic matters he also writes on the United States and New Zealand, to give but two examples. Such an attribution does not, of course, preclude a robust preference for English ways. He sternly criticises contemporary attempts in London to 'ape' the French and he hints at an underlying incompatibility of temperament between the two peoples.[3]

In his celebrated essay on 'Foreign Policy' of 1864 Salisbury suggested that while Englishmen were perhaps never very popular on the Continent and the 'angular peculiarities that mark our national character' had long been the subject of continental amusement, things had now reached a pretty pass. English character was now summed up as 'a portentous mixture of bounce and baseness'.[4] It was evidently possible to deal in 'national characters' and in the late 1850s he took the view that 'it is to Germany alone that we can look for an alliance of a people – the only alliance that will avail us now ...'[5] It is apparent, however, that Salisbury's interpretations of foreign developments did not derive from personal contact with foreigners in their native habitats. Limited family holidays, as son and parent, were preferably taken in the security of neutral Switzerland. In any case, where the 'alliance of a people' was concerned, he had grave reservations. He took the sensible view that statesmen could not consult the wishes of the peoples since the peoples had no enduring and settled interests to be consulted.[6]

Such a view was no hindrance to becoming Secretary of State for India

---

[1] M. Pinto-Duschinsky, *The Political Thought of Lord Salisbury* (London, 1967), p. 25; J.A.S. Grenville, *Lord Salisbury and Foreign Policy; The Close of the Nineteenth Century* (London, 1970), p. 6, perhaps surprisingly, underplays the importance of Salisbury's knowledge of German.

[2] Pinto-Duschinsky, *Political Thought of Lord Salisbury*, p. 42.

[3] 'Hospitality to Foreigners', 31 May 1862.

[4] *Essays by the late Marquess of Salisbury K.G.* (London, 1905), pp. 152–3.

[5] Pinto-Duschinsky, *Political Thought of Lord Salisbury*, p. 130.

[6] Ibid., pp. 120–1.

which he did briefly in 1866–7 and then again in 1874–8. To Salisbury's great dismay, Disraeli had 'shot Niagara' in 1867, but he certainly saw no reason to suppose that command from above should cease in India. In any case, what chiefly excited Salisbury were the problems posed by India's external relations rather than its own future internal development. About the latter, he had a shrewd sense of 'the nakedness of the sword on which we really rely'.[7] He expressed scepticism about the notion that Indians could be made other than alien by means of an education in English, describing this view as 'a deadly legacy from Metcalfe and Macaulay'. Such people would constitute an opposition in quiet times and become rebels in times of trouble.[8] As prime minister and foreign secretary at the time of Queen Victoria's Jubilee in 1887 he observed the curious assemblage of foreigners with puzzled amusement – black queens, Indian feudatories, Persian, Siamese and Japanese princes. They were indubitably foreign though the Black Queen of Hawaii looked exactly like Lady Rosebery stained walnut.[9] Simple observation as much as racial arrogance suggested to him that when 'you bring the English in contact with inferior races, they will rule, whatever the ostensible ground for their presence'. The level of administrative, technical and scientific skill they possessed made this predominance, in the non-European world, inevitable.[10] It was an axiom which he confirmed twenty years later, in his 1898 Primrose League speech when he roughly divided the nations of the world into the living and the dying, arguing that 'the living nations will gradually encroach on the territory of the dying and the seeds and causes of conflict among nations will speedily appear . . . These things may introduce causes of fatal difference between the great nations whose mighty armies stand opposite threatening each other.'[11] At the same time, however, he deplored mani- festations of arrogance on the part of his fellow countrymen in India, though admitting that he was a voice in the wilderness in this matter.[12]

It was in November 1876 that Salisbury made his international debut when he was sent by Disraeli as British delegate to the conference assembling at Constantinople. He travelled on a route that took him to Paris, Berlin, Vienna and Rome. He was absent for approximately a month. It is his contacts with 'the leading statesmen' of the Continent that has led Palmer to comment that he thus acquired 'a personal knowledge of

[7] Anil Seal, *The Emergence of Indian Nationalism: Competition and Collaboration in the Later Nineteenth Century* (Cambridge, 1968), p. 193.
[8] Ibid., pp. 133–4.
[9] Cited in Grenville, *Lord Salisbury and Foreign Policy*, p. 9.
[10] Cited and discussed by D.R. Gillard, 'Salisbury', in Keith M. Wilson, ed., *British Foreign Secretaries and Foreign Policy: From Crimean War to First World War* (London, 1987), p. 132.
[11] Cited in James Joll, ed., *Britain and Europe: Pitt to Churchill 1793–1940* (Oxford, 1967), pp. 192–4.
[12] Grenville, *Lord Salisbury and Foreign Policy*, p. 20.

the workings of Europe's chancelleries such as no British Cabinet Minister had possessed for half a century'.[13] Transferring to the Foreign Office in the spring of 1878, he was soon travelling abroad again when he accompanied Disraeli to the Congress of Berlin which opened in June 1878.[14]

These foreign visitations between 1876 and 1878 sealed with personal experience the book knowledge on which his previous images of different societies and countries had been based. They form an essential background to his handling of foreign policy during the subsequent period of his prime. He was not seduced, however, into taking the view that one kind of foreigner was to be preferred to another. Foreign policy required a constant willingness to be flexible. He was not taken with the notion that there were underlying affinities between peoples which dictated alignments. Nothing would be gained by further rounds of visits to the capitals and chancelleries of Europe to update his personal impressions of the foreign. There was no enthusiasm for a visit to the troublesome new power, the United States. His nephew (and private secretary at the Berlin Congress), A.J. Balfour, had apparently concluded, after his visit there in 1875, that no pleasure he experienced on the other side of the ocean compensated for the misery of crossing it. It was also galling that the seats in American Pullman cars were so low that he could not rest his head against them and read a book. He was forced to look at the scenery.[15] No doubt he passed on this information to his uncle.

In short, Salisbury seems to have concluded that in his prime he had enough experience, knowledge and wisdom to be able to interpret, as he saw fit, the excellent reports which flowed in from those exiles in foreign lands: Her Majesty's ambassadors and ministers. While the map of the world was being painted red, all he was prepared to do was occasionally to take the packet boat from Newhaven and holiday at his villa near Dieppe. Such residence, however, in no way predisposed him to be sympathetic to the aspirations of Captain Marchand.

Lansdowne's background and experience also indicated an aristocratic and imperial 'Britishness'. Educated at Eton and Balliol, his opposition to Gladstonian Home Rule – he held substantial estates in Ireland – indicated hostility towards local nationalism and led him to the Conservatives. Between 1883 and 1894 he embodied aristocratic Britishness in distant places, as governor-general of Canada and viceroy of India, successively.[16] Europe was very far away. By 1900, however, when Lansdowne became

[13] A.W. Palmer, 'Lord Salisbury', in H. van Thal, ed., *The Prime Ministers*, II (London, 1975), p. 135.
[14] Robert Blake, *Disraeli* (London, 1966), pp. 645–54.
[15] Blanche F.E. Dugdale, *Arthur James Balfour*, I (London, 1939), p. 31.
[16] Lord Newton's *Lord Lansdowne* (London, 1929) remains the only published biography but see also P.J.V. Rolo, 'Lansdowne', in Wilson, ed., *British Foreign Secretaries*.

foreign secretary (after serving as war secretary since 1895), he was much more aware of the intensifying inter-state rivalries in Europe, rivalries made more acute by national animosities. The substantial agreements signed during his period of office – the Hay–Pauncefote treaty, the Anglo-Japanese treaty and the Anglo-French agreement – have been widely discussed by historians. In France, it was perhaps time to adjust an unfavourable stereotype of 'John Bull'.[17] In Britain, it was time to initiate societies and contacts which would ensure that the entente became cordiale. A few years ahead lay the celebrated Franco-British exhibition which attracted an attendance of millions. It seems fairly clear that Lansdowne himself, however, wished to keep open the prospect of a future arrangement with Germany and distrusted the clamant voices in the press and elsewhere who saw the Entente as a public indication that the government was 'anti-German' and 'pro-French'.

At another level, French and German were the languages in which aspirants to the Diplomatic Service had to show considerable proficiency (in addition to Latin) – optional papers were also available in Italian, Spanish, Portuguese and Russian. They were also expected to have a not insubstantial private income, a limitation which did not apply to Foreign Office clerks. It was usually necessary not only to attend a London crammer but also to spend time in France or Germany. Sometimes, months with a *curé de campagne* in France or a pastor in Germany passed pleasantly enough without having any lasting 'pro-French' or 'pro-German' consequence. At the turn of the century, however, both aspirants and established diplomats found themselves in situations where Britain was unpopular. The cause was the Boer War. Young men from Eton, like Robert Vansittart, were astonished at the animosity they encountered. His German contemporaries gloated at every British defeat and, on his own account, 'There was no escape from gibes in the house, press, theatre, street.'[18] On a subsequent visit he narrowly avoided a duel which stemmed from an incident during a game of tennis. Here, it is sometimes said, were the sources of a profound suspicion of all things German which Sir Robert Vansittart was to manifest as permanent under-secretary thirty years later. The 'Black Record', in other words, was first discovered on a tennis court. Yet Vansittart's contemporaneous experiences in France were scarcely any more encouraging. Indeed, 'anglophobia' could be encountered right across the continent. 'All classes seemed to grudge and belittle our successes and to rejoice over our reverses' was Charles Hardinge's recollection of the mood in St Petersburg where he was ambassador.[19] The experience of 'anti-British' sentiment in continental Europe by

---

[17] R. Marx, 'Stéréotype et décision; le paradoxe du rapprochement franco-britannique de 1903–1904', *Recherches Anglaises et Nord-Américaines*, 25 (1992), 21–34.
[18] Lord Vansittart, *The Mist Procession* (London, 1958), p. 29.
[19] Lord Hardinge of Penshurst, *Old Diplomacy* (London, 1947), p. 74.

no means led to a simple and pervasive 'anti-German' attitude in diplomatic circles.

Lansdowne's successor, Sir Edward Grey, cannot be supposed to have allowed his policy to be guided by his personal experience of Europe. It has frequently been noted that in August 1914, when he had been foreign secretary for eight years and eight months, he had been abroad only once – to France three months earlier.[20] Nor was this reluctance novel. His experience of 'the foreign' was limited to India (1887) and the West Indies (1897).[21] He retained memories and prejudices from his earlier experience as parliamentary under-secretary at the Foreign Office under Rosebery and Kimberley but had not first-hand knowledge of the mood or mind of Germany. He knew not Paris, Berlin, St Petersburg or Rome. He was believed to have a modest understanding of French, but the cast of his mind and the content of his reading were emphatically English. It followed that his conception of policy was in no sense determined by his personal experience of those countries with which he had chiefly to deal. He had prejudices concerning foreign lands, but did not care to expose them to reality. Winchester and Balliol had not turned him into a European. Well-bred and addicted to country pursuits – though of an unusually harmless character – he seemed to his European counterparts an enigmatic English gentleman.

Grey's indifference to travel was unusual amongst his Liberal Cabinet colleagues in its determined insularity. Socially and educationally they were more of a 'mixed bag' than their Conservative predecessors. Sir Henry Campbell-Bannerman was more unambiguously a Scot than the previous prime minister, A.J. Balfour. We learn that his father, a Glasgow merchant, 'believed in foreign languages' and sent his sons early on a grand tour of Europe. The proper object of education was to get knowledge of the world rather than knowledge of books. Foreign travel indeed became something of a passion and, after his marriage in 1860, he and his wife normally spent six weeks each year on the European mainland, recording their impressions of people and places in great detail. His biographer suggests that he was 'storing up that curious and intimate knowledge of foreign countries which made him in after days one of the most European of British public men'.[22] By the twentieth century, when his wife was ill, he had come to settle for regular and substantial attendance at Marienbad. It was only with great difficulty (and with no discernible sense of urgency on his part) that his Liberal colleagues had persuaded him that the imminent outbreak of the Boer War required his

---

[20] Keith Robbins, *Sir Edward Grey: A Biography of Lord Grey of Fallodon* (London, 1971).

[21] See 'Sir Edward Grey and the British Empire' reprinted in Keith Robbins, *Politicians, Diplomacy and War in Modern British History* (London, 1994), pp. 165–75.

[22] J.A. Spender, *The Life of Sir Henry Campbell-Bannerman* (London, 1923), I, pp. 9, 230.

presence in London in October 1899. He had been in residence in Bohemia since early August.

His fellow Scot, Lord Elgin, whom he made colonial secretary, seemed by ancestry and experience fully equipped with the requisite imperial/foreign experience. His father, described as 'perhaps the most successful of Britain's pro-consuls', had been shipwrecked in both western and eastern hemispheres, had faced a Montreal mob at the risk of his life, had come under fire in China and was buried in the Himalayas – he died as viceroy of India. Indeed, the scale of his service on the peripheries of the British Empire was such that to be abroad was to be at home.[23] The son, the new colonial secretary, had been born in Montreal (though educated at Eton and Balliol) and had himself been lately a somewhat reluctant viceroy. His family home, Broomhall by Dunfermline, was full of echoes of its foreign activities which, with the particular exception of certain Marbles, were largely non-European. Two thousand visitors who gathered to celebrate Queen Victoria's golden jubilee in 1887 at Broomhall seem not to have been surprised to have been shown a crutch which had belonged to the Empress of China.[24]

Asquith, prime minister after 1908, had no such items in his family cupboard nor, as he made his way upwards through the law and politics, did he engage in foreign travel or seek out foreigners. He was a Liberal imperialist, but did not know the empire at first hand. Of course, he had to visit Scotland frequently. When he arrived in Downing Street he preferred cruising, even in the company of Churchill, to visiting European cities, and was therefore prepared to venture to the Dalmatian coast or to Cannes.[25] The primary purpose of these excursions was not to deepen perceptions of the main currents of European politics. However, the invention of reasonably reliable motor cars did tempt the more adventurous – that is to say, Lloyd George and Churchill – to traverse terrain not often frequented by British government ministers in the past.[26] Lloyd George reckoned that two punctures a day represented reasonably good going on foreign jaunts. Both men also penetrated into Germany on personal study tours to investigate social insurance and military matters at first hand. Lloyd George, however, took particular pleasure in the fact that, for one reason or another, he was taken to have a particular affinity with France.[27] Certainly it suited him to let it be known that as a Welshman, he did not identify with Saxons, and perhaps not even with Anglo-Saxons. There was no disguising, however, that R.B. Haldane had not only

[23] Sydney Checkland, *The Elgins 1766–1917: A Tale of Aristocrats, Proconsuls and their wives* (Aberdeen, 1988), p. 200.
[24] Checkland, *The Elgins*, p. 209.
[25] R. Jenkins, *Asquith* (London, pbk, 1967), pp. 124–5n, 290.
[26] Keith Robbins, *Churchill* (London, 1992), pp. 44–5.
[27] J. Grigg, *Lloyd George: The People's Champion, 1902–1911* (London, 1978), pp. 162–3, 306.

157,387

studied in Germany, he had a strong liking for German philosophy. Here was an elevated engagement with Kultur not often found in a British Cabinet.[28] It was accepted that his Scottishness explained this peculiarity. Herbert Samuel, another philosopher, liked cycling through France, Belgium, Switzerland and Italy.[29] James Bryce was known simply to have an insatiable appetite for travelling to any country you cared to mention, particularly if mountains were thrown in, and this enthusiasm, coupled with his celebrated work on *The American Commonwealth*, seemed an excellent reason for sending him to the United States as ambassador after an initial short period as Irish Secretary.[30] Lord Ripon had been fired with enthusiasm for *associations ouvrières* in Paris – but that was in 1848.[31]

Taken in the round, therefore, with the conspicuous exception of the foreign secretary, Liberal ministers possessed a degree of foreign experience which included but also extended beyond the British Empire. That knowledge conformed to no set pattern but, in aggregate, it was not insignificant. Even so, it is difficult to believe that the miscellaneous accumulated perceptions of the outside world possessed by the pre-1914 Liberal governments correlated to any discernible extent with the course of British foreign policy during these years. No Liberal minister had penetrated as far as Russia, the Anglo-Russian Convention notwithstanding. A Russian foreign minister, had, however, been encountered at Balmoral in 1912.

It remained the case, therefore, that leading members of the Foreign Office continued to believe that they had the edge over their political masters because, by one means or another, they knew about foreign countries almost from the 'inside'. Concerning Grey's first permanent under-secretary, Hardinge, Zara Steiner remarks that initially his 'main areas of concern were Germany, Russia and Turkey, all key places of diplomatic activity' – and all places (amongst others) where Hardinge had himself spent time at various stages in his career. Nicolson, Hardinge's successor, came to his post in 1910 directly from four years in the Embassy in St Petersburg. His experience elsewhere was more restricted, in part because of an excessive incarceration in Tangier as British minister for nearly a decade until 1904. Mrs Steiner characterises Nicolson as 'strongly Russophile', a judgement which seems basically sound, but why was he 'Russophile'?[32] Are we to assume, in his case, that it was because he was ambassador in Russia that he was sympathetic to Russia? It is clear that we cannot infer any general rule. Sir Edward Goschen, successively ambassador in Vienna (1905–8) and Berlin (1908–14), certainly cannot be

---

[28] R.B. Haldane, *An Autobiography* (London, 1929), pp. 12–21.

[29] Herbert Samuel, *Memoirs* (London, 1945) p. 30.

[30] Viscount Bryce, *Memories of Travel* (London, 1923); E. Ions, *James Bryce and American Democracy* (London, 1968); Hugh Tulloch, *James Bryce's* American Commonwealth (Woodbridge, 1988).

[31] A. Denholm, *Lord Ripon 1827–1909: A Political Biography* (London, 1982), p. 4.

[32] Z.S. Steiner, *The Foreign Office and Foreign Policy 1898–1914* (Cambridge, 1969), p. 97.

thought to be 'Germanophile' as a result of his postings despite the fact that he was of German descent and had inherited a Schloss in Carinthia – his only real home. Goschen could not resist the view, on relatively rare visits, that England was a jolly place. He remarked in December 1901 à propos his brother's biography of their grandfather, a Leipzig publisher, that he would rather that the book had not appeared 'for – tho' I oughtn't to – I hate the Germans and dislike being descended from one'.[33] His command of German does not seem to have been fluent. Even so, it does appear that Goschen's feelings towards Germans mellowed during his Berlin years – and his two sisters married two German brothers. It is indeed arguable that this mellowing led, in the final months of his mission, to too generous an interpretation of the intentions of the German government and of Bethmann Hollweg, a fellow music lover, in particular.[34]

It may be, indeed, that it was a mistake to have an ambassador in Berlin, at what turned out to be so crucial a juncture, whose interpretation of Germany was bound up with his own ancestry. Such personal complications, of course, were not confined to Goschen. They applied, perhaps above all, to Eyre Crowe, born in Leipzig, where his father was British consul-general, to a German mother. It was not until 1882 that he first visited England as a seventeen-year-old, with a very imperfect knowledge of English. He married his widowed German cousin in 1903. His uncle, Henning von Holzendorff, was to become Chief of the German Naval Staff in the first world war. It was a background (and manner allegedly derived from it) which led some of his contemporaries to wonder whether Crowe was really English – a suspicion which would have been strengthened had it been generally known that he read Marx's Das Kapital in German. Yet his well-known memorandum of 1907 demonstrated no generosity in interpreting German foreign policy. It could indeed be argued that his German background and connections made him particularly acute in his assessments. It could equally be argued that his personal desire to emphasise his Englishness made him unduly disinclined to give German policy the benefit of any doubt that existed. On the other hand, Crowe was anxious to reassure his German mother that he had 'no personal hatred of Germany' and that he was 'not one of the prejudiced anti-German herd'.[35]

Once the first world war had begun, it was entirely predictable that that herd would be in the ascendancy. As Haldane, amongst others, was to

---

[33] C.H.D. Howard, ed., *The Diary of Edward Goschen 1900–1914* (London, 1980), p. 69.

[34] Ibid., pp. 35–53.

[35] Sibyl Crowe and Edward Corp, *Our Ablest Public Servant: Sir Eyre Crowe c. 1864–1925* (Braunton, 1993), p. 72. In correspondence, Dr Corp acknowledges that n 35 (pp. 191–2) which claims that a statement made in my biography of Grey is 'quite untrue' is itself quite untrue.

find, to have had a special link with Germany could prove fatal to a political career. Indeed, nuanced (or balanced) perceptions, based on previous experience, of any country with which Britain was at war could not be entertained. The exigencies of warfare required only blacks and whites. The war also contributed to the undermining of the more or less explicit sense of 'spheres of activity' between politicians and the Foreign Office which we have sketched in the years before 1914. I have noted elsewhere the foreign secretary's sense of his own impotence in time of war.[36] Decision-making in wartime came to demand new structures and channels. These tendencies accelerated after Lloyd George became prime minister and the work of the 'Garden Suburb' is well known.[37] The prominence of the prime minister himself needs little emphasis. His wartime visits to France further fuelled an already well-developed sense of the importance of personal diplomacy. The thirty-five-year old Philip Kerr became his 'additional private secretary' in January 1917 and was to remain in that position until March 1921, giving advice on imperial, Irish and general foreign policy issues. It is notable that he came to the post from service in South Africa and travels in widely separated parts of the British Empire in connection with the Round Table movement. St Moritz and Biarritz apart, the European Continent had seen little of him since he sailed for South Africa after leaving Oxford, with the exception of a visit to Paris, Munich, Nuremberg and Berlin in October 1911 to collect material for a long article on 'Britain, France and Germany'.[38] What filled his mind, rather, was the unity of the British Empire and the benefits of federalism. What was to be the relationship between the white race and subject peoples? He thought about these things in Cairo and Cape Town, in Delhi and Vancouver.

The travels of the four members of the War Cabinet who served under the prime minister – with the exception of the Labour politician, Arthur Henderson, whose travels lay ahead of him – showed a comparable imperial/global rather than European emphasis. Few major British politicians had made more strenuous efforts to prepare themselves for high office than Lord Curzon by intense foreign travel. Prior to becoming foreign under-secretary (1895–8), he had spent a good deal of the preceding six years in extensive travel which he largely financed by journalism and three major volumes on Russia, Persia and the Far East. He also travelled extensively in North America. His reputation as an expert with first hand knowledge of the Middle East and Asia made him seem an obvious choice as viceroy of India, (1898–1905) though his tenancy of that post ended in disappointment and bitterness. His conviction of the provi-

---

[36] F.H. Hinsley, ed., *British Foreign Policy under Sir Edward Grey* (Cambridge, 1977), pp. 532–3.
[37] J. Turner, *Lloyd George's Secretariat* (Cambridge, 1980).
[38] J.R.M. Butler, *Lord Lothian, 1882–1940* (London, 1960), p. 48.

dential character of British imperial rule did not, however, desert him and his Asian travels and residence continued to dominate his thoughts. Beside Curzon sat Lord Milner who was indeed born in Germany and partly brought up there, but a man for whom the British Empire was central to his life and thought. His appointment to the Egyptian finance ministry (1889–92) led him to write *England and Egypt* (1892), a vigorous defence of imperial mission. It was as high commissioner for South Africa (1897–1905) that he came into controversial prominence. Later, he travelled widely in the Empire and in such works as *The Nation and the Empire* he argued against the centrifugal tendencies which he detected. Bonar Law, leader of the Conservative Party, the final member of the quartet, had served in Asquith's Coalition as colonial secretary, but he took no delight in the prospect of foreign travel, or indeed of anything else for that matter, though he had honeymooned in Paris. Even so, given that he was born and brought up in rural New Brunswick, Canada, before moving to Glasgow, such preconceptions as he brought to foreign policy were imperial.

The contrast between the well-travelled Curzon and Milner, on the one hand, and Henderson, on the other, could scarcely have been greater. Henderson's travels had been limited to two or three trips to Germany before 1914 on trade union and Labour Party business.[39] In the summer of 1917, however, he seemed a suitable person to send on an official mission to Russia to try to keep the Provisional Government in the war. Even the most detailed scrutiny of Curzon's writing on Russia would not have greatly assisted him in this task. This particular piece of foreign travel did not convert him to the Bolshevik cause, but it did turn him into an enthusiastic advocate of British Labour's participation in the proposed international socialist conference at Stockholm, which would include representatives from all belligerent countries. Lloyd George saw no need for further foreign travel of this kind and forced Henderson's resignation.[40] The very fact that Henderson had gone to Russia in the first place was, however, an important straw in the wind. Politicians were finding it more and more difficult to resist the notion that they should present themselves in person to deal with difficulties on site.

The Paris Peace conference demonstrated this conviction magnificently. For the first time, even a president of the United States would feel obliged to engage in foreign travel to negotiate a peace, although, as we know, a 'summit conference' developed almost by accident.[41] No lengthy analysis of the work of the Council of Four and the complex issues that had to be

---

[39] Chris Wrigley, *Arthur Henderson* (Cardiff, 1990), p. 74.
[40] J.M. Winter, 'Arthur Henderson, the Russian Revolution and the Reconstruction of the Labour Party', *Historical Journal*, 15 (1972), 753–73.
[41] K. Eubank, *The Summit Conferences 1919–1960* (Norman, 1966), pp. 9–31.

resolved is possible here.[42] Most commentators, however, have stressed that, for better or worse, the outcome did indeed depend on the principals. 'Three men made the peace,' writes Elcock 'and their beliefs, ambitions and desires, and the interaction of their personalities, made the Treaty what it was.'[43] It is well known that Lloyd George preferred Hankey over Hardinge – who was consoled with the deceptive title 'Organizing Ambassador'.[44] Anybody with any knowledge of foreign politics or of European affairs, Hardinge later told him, would have realised that the peace treaties contained clauses which were 'opposed to every principle of national life and existence'.[45] Such a lament was only to be expected from such a quarter. Yet the obloquy into which 'secret diplomacy' had fallen meant that the store of wisdom, so treasured by the Foreign Office, could not be drawn upon. It was Lloyd George who now stood forth in Paris as the representative of the people. Clemenceau was on home ground but by 1919 Lloyd George seems to have felt under no disadvantage by the fact that he had to travel. It was undoubtedly a greater distance, literally and metaphorically, that President Wilson had to journey. The magnetic manoeuvring of Lloyd George, whether seen as Machiavellian or merely Welsh, carried the day.[46] The prime minister was rewarded on his apparently triumphant return to London from his protacted foreign adventures by the treat of travelling in the royal carriage. There was a delightful irony in the fact that Viscount Grey of Fallodon was prevailed upon to experiment with the travel bug by making a mission to Washington – in what turned out to be an abortive attempt to persuade the US Senate to ratify.[47] If even Grey began to travel, it was clear that most post-war politicians could be expected to succumb to the habit.

Certainly, Lloyd George himself could not resist it in his remaining years of power. He was present at the San Remo conference in April 1920 where reparations and Near Eastern issues were high on the agenda. He conferred with Millerand at Boulogne in mid-June. The following month he sparred with the German delegates at Spa. And so it continued, either in the form of bilateral meetings or short multilateral conferences. The apotheosis of this personal 'diplomacy by conference' was the Genoa conference of April 1922. Lloyd George did not lack enemies who criticised

[42] M.L. Dockrill and J.D. Goold, *Peace without Promise: Britain and the Peace Conferences 1919–23* (London, 1981).

[43] H. Elcock, *Portrait of a Decision: The Council of Four and the Treaty of Versailles* (London, 1972), p. 322.

[44] M.L. Dockrill and Zara Steiner, 'The Foreign Office at the Paris Peace Conference', *International History Review*, 2 (1980), 54–86.

[45] B.C. Busch, *Hardinge of Penshurst: A Study in the Old Diplomacy* (Hamden, 1980), p. 290.

[46] A. Lentin, *Guilt at Versailles: Lloyd George and the Pre-History of Appeasement* (London, 1985), pp. 105–23.

[47] Keith Robbins, *Sir Edward Grey: A Biography of Lord Grey of Fallodon* (London, 1971), pp. 351–3.

his constant travels. They pointed out that these heads of government meetings in fact achieved very little in their attempt to reconcile French demands for security with German demands for modification of the peace settlement. Were his journeys really necessary? Lloyd George believed that the international system was so uncertain that only the prime minister could act, in person and abroad. Besides, he liked being abroad, though he did succeed in getting the organist at Lucerne cathedral to play Welsh hymn tunes so that he would not feel completely cut off.[48] It was a situation transparently not pleasing to Lord Curzon, foreign secretary since 1919. It seemed to him that just at the point when he had reached the office for which, above all, his own travels had best prepared him in the past, the scope for his own initiative had been sharply curtailed. However, the problem went deeper than that. His irritation was also an expression of the fact that, with the exception of the Middle East, his own expertise now seemed so tangential to the pressing issues of post-war Europe. To have been to the source of the Oxus did not throw much light on the problem of Upper Silesia.

However, in the end, it was to prove the Near East that both Lloyd George and Kerr were to find unmanageable and which led to their downfall – ironically, it seemed during the Chanak crisis that they were more concerned to safeguard imperial prestige than was Curzon. During the two short-lived Conservative governments that followed, under Bonar Law and Baldwin respectively, Curzon was able to gain something of the prestige which he thought was his due, though he smarted under his failure to become prime minister. He had to deal with the Ruhr crisis and was only able to display some aspects of his personal expertise in the negotiations which led to the Treaty of Lausanne of July 1923.

The advent of a minority Labour government in 1924 caused some consternation in the Foreign Office. In fact, although new to office, Ramsay MacDonald's interest in foreign policy was substantial. His criticism of British policy in 1914 was well known. He had also been a substantial traveller. In 1897 he had visited New York and Chicago. After becoming an MP in 1906 he carried out an extensive tour of Canada, Australia and New Zealand, followed, in 1909, by a visit to India. His itinerary, in short, corresponded closely to that of Round Table enthusiasts – though the conclusions he drew in such books as *Labour and the Empire* (1907) differed from theirs. He had attended the 1904 Congress of the Second International in Amsterdam and took a lively interest in subsequent congresses in other European cities, but he could not yet be said to know Europe at first hand. After the war he visited Germany again for the first time in July 1920 and was shocked by conditions in Berlin. A few weeks later, he visited the Menshevik Republic of Georgia where he was somewhat

[48] K.O. Morgan, ed., *Lloyd George Family Letters 1885–1936* (Cardiff/London, 1973), p. 192.

perturbed by the wild gallop of virile horsemen who proceeded ahead of his car.[49] The reality of his foreign interest found expression in the fact that he became his own foreign secretary – a step not even Lloyd George could have taken. In the event, however, the government did not last long and its performance permitted few longer-term conclusions about how a Labour government, perhaps with an overall majority, would conduct foreign policy.[50]

The Baldwin/Austen Chamberlain partnership that followed until 1929 presented interesting contrasts both with Lloyd George and Labour. Baldwin went to extravagant lengths, despite his own ancestry, to seem quintessentially English. His pipe, the baggy clothes, the rustic image, the fondness for pigs all combined to make him the very embodiment of the English spirit.[51] Yet Baldwin was not insular. In 1890 he visited his firm's associates in North America, travelling through Quebec, Montreal, New York, Philadelphia, Washington, Richmond, Chicago and New Orleans. The implications of the introduction of the McKinley Tariff were not lost on him. More generally, we read that for twenty years the Baldwins were in the habit of taking a month's winter sports in Switzerland and a month or more touring the Continent. During their first visit to Paris in 1894, Baldwin expressed the wish to find a simple place to live *en pension* so that he could work earnestly at French. By 1914, his knowledge of Western Europe was substantial, ranging from the cathedrals of France to the lakes of Italy on the one hand, and the cities of Berlin, Dresden and Munich on the other. His German was passable and he could read Russian without difficulty.[52] These were facts which Baldwin did not care to advertise. They certainly did not lead him, when he unexpectedly emerged to fill high office, to follow Lloyd George into 'Diplomacy by Conference'. Here, indeed, was another way in which to mark out his regime from that of his unpredictable predecessor. It may be that his experience, as chancellor, of being sent to Washington in January 1923 to conduct debt negotiations, put him off the attractions of personal diplomacy. 'Is it not possible', Bonar Law wrote, 'that you are too much under the influence of Washington which is not even the New York atmosphere? What would you have thought of such proposals before you left?'[53] Nor should we forget how uncomfortable travel could be. The weather on the outward journey was atrocious and the trip was only made even tolerable by a piano recital from Wilhelm Backhaus who happened to be a fellow traveller.[54]

[49] D. Marquand, *Ramsay MacDonald* (London, 1977), pp. 206–10.
[50] Keith Robbins, 'Labour Foreign Policy and International Socialism: MacDonald and the League of Nations', reprinted in Robbins, *Politicians, Diplomacy and War*, pp. 239–72.
[51] David Cannadine, 'Politics, Propaganda and Art: The Case of Two "Worcestershire Lads" ', *Midland History* (1977), 106–7.
[52] K. Middlemas and J. Barnes, *Baldwin: A Biography* (London, 1969), pp. 22–3, 32–3.
[53] Ibid., p. 142.
[54] Ibid., pp. 136–44.

As prime minister, Baldwin had domestic problems enough to occupy him and, in any case, in Austen Chamberlain, had a foreign secretary whose background, experience and attributes seemed to fit him admirably for the position. Baldwin was to be content largely to survey Europe from the delights of Aix-les-Bains – which he discovered for the first time in September 1921 and visited annually thereafter. Only in his first government, however, in September 1923, did he travel to Paris for a *tête-à-tête* in the British Embassy over lunch with Poincaré. At the close of their session Poincaré assured Baldwin of the value he placed on personal conversations, in the first instance, as opposed to conferences. The fact that he did not repeat them with foreign leaders suggests that Baldwin was less sure.[55]

Joseph Chamberlain had concluded that travel would be a necessary element in Austen's development so as to prepare him for political greatness. Balance required that Cambridge should be supplemented by study both in Paris and Berlin in the mid-1880s – Austen had the necessary languages.[56] There was also time to visit Constantinople, Athens and Bulgaria. He paid another extended visit to the Near East in the autumn of 1901. Such knowledge on the ground did not enable him, fifteen years later, to avoid 'Mesopotamian miseries' and his resignation as secretary of state for India. He met the lady who was to be his wife in Algiers in 1906 where he was seeking a cure following the Liberal election victory. In subsequent years it was Switzerland or the Italian lakes to which he often retired to recuperate. He could not have anticipated, however, that in October 1925 he would be at Locarno, cruising on the lake in the launch *Orange Blossom* with the French and German foreign ministers.[57] The value of personal diplomacy and foreign travel was apparently restored. In time, of course, the 'Locarno spirit' came to seem somewhat elusive and perhaps illusory.[58] Chamberlain himself was not averse to being thought a 'good European', though Britain's general position in relation to European issues had to be 'semi-detached'.[59] It may be a reasonable inference that it was the fact that his travel was largely European and not, despite the fact that his father had been colonial secretary, imperial which led him to elevate the importance of European issues and a British role in attempting to shape their outcome.

In any case, in the person of the chancellor of the Exchequer, Churchill, and the colonial secretary, Amery, the Cabinet had two formidable travellers who were not reticent. Amery was born in the North-Western provinces

[55] Ibid.
[56] Sir Austen Chamberlain, *Down the Years* (London, 1935), pp. 18–47.
[57] David Dutton, *Austen Chamberlain: Gentleman in Politics* (Bolton, 1985), p. 231.
[58] Anne Orde, *Great Britain and International Security, 1920–1926* (London, 1978), pp. 184–212.
[59] Sir Austen Chamberlain, *Peace in Our Time: Addresses on Europe and the Empire* (London, 1928).

of India where Churchill had served as a soldier. The South African War featured prominently in both of their young lives. Amery covered the Balkans as a young correspondent. Churchill had been to Cuba. Churchill had been to the United States – where Amery's father had gone to live. Amery's mother was Hungarian, Churchill's mother was American. Both knew what it was like to fight in Europe. It is not surprising that the perspectives they derived from travel and reflection gave Chamberlain some difficulty.

Nor is it surprising that the 'traditional' aspects of the Locarno agreements gave him, on the other hand, difficulty from his colleague Lord Robert Cecil, whose enthusiasm for the League of Nations knew no bounds. Lord Robert's travels complemented the range of travel experience round the Cabinet table. A barrister, he undertook a big arbitration in Singapore in 1905, the year before he entered parliament. He travelled there across Canada and sailed from Vancouver to Yokohama. He just happened to travel in the train to Tokyo with Prince Ito, who was fresh from the signature of the Treaty of Portsmouth. The British ambassador, having a great regard for Cecil's late father, Lord Salisbury, arranged for him to meet the Mikado. Cecil found it 'an uninteresting interview' and contented himself with noting that the Mikado's clothes fitted even worse than his own – a major achievement since Cecil was awkwardly shaped. The Japanese were all charming but not very interesting. The journey continued to Shanghai and Hong Kong before finally Cecil reached Singapore.[60] These experiences, however, had little immediate bearing on the European problems which chiefly concerned the League of Nations and Cecil in the early 1920s.

When Ramsay MacDonald headed the second Labour government in 1929 he felt obliged this time to appoint Arthur Henderson as his foreign secretary, though their personal relations were not good and the prime minister did not share unreservedly his colleague's enthusiasm for the League of Nations. Henderson's post-war travelling had increased. He and MacDonald had presented the views of the Berne Socialist conference to the Big Four at the Paris Peace Conference. He went to the United States in May 1919 for conversations with Sam Gompers which were not very productive. There were other Socialist gatherings in Amsterdam and Switzerland. During the life of the first Labour government he had paid several visits to Geneva in support of the Protocol. However, despite (or perhaps because of) Henderson's increased knowledge of the world, there was no doubt that MacDonald wished to have more than the last word.

The last years of the Baldwin government had witnessed a deterioration in Anglo-American relations on navy levels and other issues. Baldwin apparently said to Neville Chamberlain that he had got to loathe the Amer-

[60] Viscount Cecil of Chelwood, *A Great Experiment* (London, 1941), p. 28.

icans so much that he hated meeting them.[61] It fell to MacDonald to
attempt a solution and President Hoover somewhat reluctantly agreed that
the British prime minister should invite himself to Washington as part of
this process. Claud Cockburn maliciously but deliciously put it about that
MacDonald's chief preoccupation on the voyage across was whether he
should wear a top hat or a cloth cap. As the first prime minister in office
to visit the United States, Macdonald (hatless) received a ticker-tape welcome in Broadway, New York in October 1929, was photographed (hat in
hand) with Hoover outside the White House and addressed the US Senate.
The private discussion with Hoover, however, was distinctly tough. Indeed,
although the London Naval Conference did subsequently take matters
forward, it has been argued that 'the only success MacDonald had in the
United States was in obtaining popular acclaim at his public appearances'.[62] While Hugh Dalton wrote in his diary that the prime minister's
visit had 'made for himself an eternal niche in the temple of history',
other old Foreign Office hands expressed scepticism about the benefits of
foreign travel.[63]

In fact, by visiting Canada in August 1927, during which time he delivered twenty-eight speeches in nineteen days, Baldwin secured an earlier
niche for himself as the first prime minister in office to visit North America – and also to visit a British Dominion. Baldwin accompanied the Prince
of Wales who happened to have a ranch in Alberta. Mackenzie King, the
Canadian prime minister, was surprised by how much the British delegation (with the exception of the Prince of Wales) hated the Americans.
Indeed, one of Baldwin's purposes on such an extended tour in all nine
provinces was to shore up the British link and prevent the 'loss' of Canada
to its southern neighbour. Neville Chamberlain wrote to the prime minister to say that the visit had done more than anything else could have done
to make separation improbable. Baldwin's sacrifice of his summer holiday
had rendered great service to Britain and the Empire.[64]

In the pre-war decade, the tendencies identified since 1919 were confirmed and strengthened. Baldwin found the attractions of Aix-les-Bains
as great as ever but he was distinctly selective in the official visits he was
prepared to undertake. In 1932 he again travelled to Canada to negotiate
what became the Ottawa Agreements on Commonwealth trade. At the
end of 1933, when Hitler was filling the air with talk of non-aggression
pacts, intermediaries made suggestions that Baldwin himself should visit

---

[61] D. Cameron Watt, *Succeeding John Bull: America in Britain's Place 1900–1975*
   (Cambridge, 1984), pp. 59–61.
[62] D. Carlton, *MacDonald versus Henderson: The Foreign Policy of the Second Labour
   Government* (London, 1970), pp. 114–18.
[63] H. Dalton, *Call Back Yesterday* (London, 1953), p. 246.
[64] D. Dilks, *Three Visitors to Canada: Baldwin, Chamberlain and Churchill* (London, 1985?),
   pp. 13–18.

Germany and see for himself this Führer who had a spark of genius. In the event, he decided against the journey.[65] In the summer of 1936, the possibility of a meeting between Hitler and Baldwin was more energetically pursued, with both Ribbentrop and Tom Jones involved. But should Hitler visit Britain or Baldwin visit Germany – should they perhaps meet on a ship off Dover? Momentarily, at least, Baldwin appears to have been tempted but in the end he did not motor back from Aix through the Black Forest. It was left to Lloyd George to pay his celebrated personal visit in September. 'Your Welsh friend', wrote Baldwin to Tom Jones, who supplied him with a note of Lloyd George's talks, 'is, as I have always said, a most remarkable little man.'[66] One factor behind Baldwin's reluctance to engage in official travel in his last premiership was the fact that it was a tiring business. MacDonald, in the last years of his premiership had come to the same conclusion, although, in April 1935, he allowed himself to lead the British delegation at the Stresa conference. We gather that the strain of even three days of high-level diplomacy was too much for him. He rambled in discussion and his interpreter was compelled to invent a coherent speech. The delights of travel were clearly exhausted.[67]

A reason advanced by Baldwin for not travelling to meet Hitler was that travelling was best left to Foreign Office ministers. By the 1930s, that was indeed something which had come to be assumed to be implicit in the job. It was a duty to which they did not respond with uniform relish. Their reactions, in turn, depended in some measure on the travel in which they had engaged before taking office. Among their number, only Lord Reading had sailed at the age of sixteen as a ship's boy on the run between Cardiff and Rio de Janeiro – a seven-week trip. He had earlier been sent to Hanover by his father for six months to learn German. As solicitor-general, from the summer of 1910 onwards each year until 1914, he and his wife joined the fashionable company at Marienbad. At the end of the war, Reading became a frequently absentee ambassador to the United States. His residence in India, as viceroy (1921–6) proved a more demanding and enduring experience. When, somewhat unexpectedly, he became foreign secretary in 1931 at the age of seventy-one – the third though not the last twentieth-century foreign secretary to have been viceroy – it could not be said that he lacked experience of the world. In the event, however, he only had the opportunity to fit in one visit in September to the League of Nations Assembly in Geneva. The Cabinet wanted him to explain 'the aims and intensive activities of the National Government, and say a strong word about the maintenance of the £ sterling'.[68]

---

[65] Middlemas and Barnes, *Baldwin*, pp. 748–50.
[66] Ibid., pp. 955–8. A comprehensive account of British travellers to National Socialist Germany is provided in Angela Schwarz, *Die Reise ins Dritte Reich* (Göttingen, 1993).
[67] Marquand, *MacDonald*, pp. 772–3.
[68] D. Judd, *Lord Reading* (London, 1982), pp. 14, 16–20, 256.

Simon, his successor in November 1931, was to find himself frequently in Geneva until in turn he made way for Hoare in 1935. The foreign secretary could, apparently, have addressed the delegates in French, Spanish, Portuguese and Italian, but in fact he spoke English. He could also read German and had some knowledge of Russian and Hindustani.[69] Such unusual linguistic fluency, however, should not lead to the conclusion that Simon was an endemic traveller with an intimate knowledge of Europe. On the contrary, there is no record of European travel before he was sent on a mission to Paris during the first world war, and likewise no record of travel in the immediate post-war years. His Hindustani had presumably been acquired in India where he headed the Statutory Commission (1927–30) into Indian government. It was India and not Europe which had dominated the new foreign secretary's recent thoughts. That was perhaps not inappropriate, insofar as the Far East had to be uppermost in his mind. Early in 1932, however, the Disarmament Conference finally met in Geneva under the presidency of Henderson. Simon shuttled reluctantly to and fro: 'Geneva is an appalling drag', he wrote to Runciman in March, 'and something will have to be done about it . . . presence at Geneva means absence from London and I feel that during the next few months London is the more important'.[70] He described Geneva to Baldwin as a dreadful place, 'well worthy of Calvin'.

A solution of a kind was to hand in the person of Anthony Eden. Eden's interest in foreign policy appeared to make him an ideal person to assist Reading and Simon. He was a rising star of the new generation. Required to learn French and German in childhood, he had also been despatched to Nice and Dresden to improve his spoken language. After war service, it was not French and German which he studied at Oxford but Persian and Arabic – with unexpected distinction. It is not surprising that it was to the Middle East that Eden travelled for six weeks in the mid-1920s after he had become an MP. It was agreed that Eden would stay in Geneva and exercise a watching brief for the foreign secretary – whom he did not like.[71] However, while Eden did indeed mind the shop in Geneva, this responsibility not only contributed to his first-hand knowledge of European politicians but assisted the rise of his own political stock. In February 1934 he was sent on an exploratory mission to Paris – 'there is the rot of corruption in the whole parliamentary system' – Berlin and Rome. In Berlin, he had several meetings with Hitler whom he rather liked. It was difficult not to giggle at the sight of people saluting the Führer, but there was a suspicion that Hitler possessed a sense of humour. Eden was attracted by Hitler's current proposals, was convinced that Germany was

[69] David Dutton, *Simon: A Political Biography of Sir John Simon* (London, 1992), p. 92.
[70] David Dutton 'Simon and Eden at the Foreign Office, 1931–1935', *Review of International Studies*, 20: 1 (January 1994), 35–52.
[71] Robert Rhodes James, *Anthony Eden* (London, 1987), pp. 19, 60–1, 84–5, 123.

not rearming *au grand galop* and wrote to the prime minister that the chancellor would not go back on his word.[72]

The lord privy seal's visit to Berlin (and that to see Mussolini which followed) epitomised, to critics, all the dangers implicit in travelling diplomacy. Did Eden's long train journey across Germany, his childhood memories of Dresden and his less than perfect command of German make him a sensible interpreter of German intentions at this critical juncture? He was indeed to find that his report was to be criticised in Cabinet – and by the stay-at-home foreign secretary. Eden also saw the hand of Vansittart, the permanent under-secretary, behind an article in *The Observer* which questioned his competence to negotiate.

Whatever might be the legitimacy of such observations, travel seemed inescapable, but it remained fraught with problems. Difficulties returned at the beginning of 1935 when another official visit to Berlin was in prospect. Neville Chamberlain noted that Simon 'was jealous of Eden and does not like his going alone to any foreign country'. Hitler's reaction to the British Defence White Paper in March placed the visit in jeopardy but it had already been decided that Simon and Eden would together go to Berlin and then Eden would go on to Moscow, Warsaw and Prague without the foreign secretary. Naturally, in the conversations with Hitler, Simon took the lead. Even though there was reasonable, though inconclusive, discussion of current issues, Simon looked at the Führer's hands – 'the hands of a musician' – and kept thinking of his part in the Roehm assassinations.[73] Leading figures in the Foreign Office fluctuated between thinking that politicians gained 'a sense of realities' from such visits and alarm about their consequences – in this case, the possible jeopardising of a future Stresa 'Front'. In the event, Simon returned from Berlin a puzzled rather than a triumphant or disillusioned man.[74]

Eden, together with Cranborne, continued eastwards, reaching parts not previously visited by a twentieth-century government minister. It seemed a long train journey to Moscow. Eden's impressions of Stalin were favourable. He knew him to be a man without mercy, but he respected the quality of his mind and felt a sympathy for him. No one could have been less doctrinaire. Eden himself, though no Bolshevik, did not look upon the Soviet system with appalled hostility, though he would have been unwise to conclude that the Soviet people enjoyed the scale of entertainment lavished on the visitors by their hosts. It was only as the train departed for Warsaw that Eden remembered that he had kept London completely in the dark. His expectation that Whitehall would not be pleased was to prove justified. From Prague, Eden took a flight which apparently hurled him about with a seismic violence and he had to land in Cologne. Exhausted,

---

[72] Ibid., pp. 134–5.
[73] Viscount Simon, *Retrospect* (London, 1952), p. 202.
[74] Dutton, *Simon*, pp. 200–1.

he had to make the rest of the journey by train and boat and a heart attack was (wrongly) suspected. It was Eden's illness which led to the prime minister going to Stresa. Eden was angry that his condition prevented him from adequately explaining to his colleagues what he believed the lessons of his visits had been.[75] The experience was a reminder, however, that there were personal disadvantages to set against whatever advantages foreign travel might bring.

It was ironic that Simon's successor as foreign secretary, Hoare, not only spoke Russian and knew (pre-revolutionary) Russia more than just from a railway carriage, but also was a passionate enthusiast for flight. The Italian he had learnt after Oxford, and the Russian he learnt later, both proved invaluable for his wartime intelligence activities in Russia and Italy. Hoare was not simply a transient traveller in Europe. As secretary of state for air during much of the 1920s, he not only safeguarded the RAF but must also be regarded as the politician most responsible for the development of civil aviation. He was an enthusiast for the key routes to India and South Africa by Imperial Airways. In 1926/7, with his wife – who thus became the first woman to fly to India – he inaugurated the new Indian route, a round trip of 12,000 miles. Even though, by later standards, the statistics of civil flights through the 1920s seem modest, contemporaries found them phenomenal. A new era in travelling was clearly dawning.[76] There was a certain appropriateness, therefore, in the fact that Hoare served as secretary of state for India, though throughout his term (1931–5) he did not again hurtle through the sky to the east. In this capacity he piloted through the contentious Government of India Act (1935) against the rhetoric of an earlier Indian traveller – Winston Churchill.

This background suggested that Hoare might make an admirable foreign secretary – with Eden still the second minister but brought into the Cabinet as minister for League Affairs. Ironically, however, it was travel which was to be Hoare's undoing. The discussions which he held at the Quai d'Orsay with Laval in December 1935, from which emerged the Hoare–Laval 'Pact' aimed at settling the Abyssinian crisis, proved unacceptable to his Cabinet colleagues. What was even worse was that he could not be present to defend them in person, having broken his nose in two places on a Swiss ice rink. His resignation followed. Having grumbled for some time about the inadequacies of his superiors, Eden at last achieved his ambition.

But, in February 1938, exhausted by the imperiousness of his superior, the prime minister, Neville Chamberlain, Eden resigned. The immediate causes need not detain us, but the clash partly stemmed from his sense

[75] Rhodes James, *Eden*, pp. 144–5.
[76] J.A. Cross, *Sir Samuel Hoare: A Political Biography* (London, 1977), pp. 9, 38–58, 100–2.

that his travels over the previous four years had given him a sense of European realities which the prime minister lacked. It was not the case, however, that Neville lacked interest in travel as such. Indeed, as a young man, in assorted family company he had travelled in France and, in 1889, he journeyed with his father to Egypt – an experience which his new stepmother thought opened his eyes to the world.[77] It is well known that he had a closer acquaintance with the Bahamas than most British politicians. There were visits to Spain, Switzerland, Italy and the Low Countries. His honeymoon took him to French North Africa. In 1912 he holidayed with his family at Karlsbad in Bohemia. After the war, when he emerged onto the national stage, he undertook a substantial five-week tour of Canada in 1922. As his father's son, he took pride in expressing his belief in the genius of the British race for government and colonisation. A decade later, with Baldwin, he was again in Canada, but in rather more difficult circumstances. The Ottawa agreements proved taxing to negotiate, putting to the hard economic test, as they did, the rhetoric of Commonwealth unity. It could not be said, therefore, that the new prime minister was only a landlocked Birmingham politician, even though in the 1930s, when in government, his travels in Europe could not match Eden's.

Halifax, Eden's replacement, had conformed in his early travels to the imperial mode. In 1904, having finished his probationary year at All Souls, he set out on a Grand Tour, though one that was imperial rather than European in its focus. Travelling first to South Africa, he then proceeded to India (where he stayed with Lord Curzon) before visiting Ceylon, Australia and New Zealand, returning to South Africa and thence to Canada.[78] He had short holidays in France but his imperial knowledge was incomparably greater. In 1910, however, when as a fledgling MP he was asked to speak in a debate on Egypt he replied that he knew nothing about it. Prevailed upon to speak, nevertheless, and perhaps recollecting that he had visited Port Said, he confidently stated that the Egyptians were a black people.[79] After the war, he served as colonial under-secretary under Winston Churchill, and became minister of agriculture. In 1926 he went out to India as viceroy. On his return, after the War Office, he became lord privy seal in 1935 under Baldwin and lord president of the Council on Baldwin's resignation. In this last office he visited Germany in November 1937, ostensibly to shoot foxes in East Prussia. Included in the visit, however, was a meeting with Hitler – the third British minister in office to call. The records of the conversation are well known. What emerges from them is that, on his first visit, Halifax did not seem entirely at home in the nuances of German politics and policies. He was experienced enough as a negotiator, but not with a sincere German Führer. Halifax did recog-

[77] D. Dilks, *Neville Chamberlain, Vol. 1 1869–1929* (Cambridge, 1984), pp. 36–7.
[78] Lord Birkenhead, *Halifax: The Life of Lord Halifax* (London, 1965), pp. 68–76.
[79] Ibid., pp. 95–6.

nise, however, that they had a different set of values and were speaking a different language (literally and metaphorically).[80]

Nearly a year later, however, it was not Halifax (as foreign secretary) who set out to visit Hitler but the prime minister himself. Neville Chamberlain's celebrated trips to Germany during the Czechoslovak crisis can be considered as the most politically charged and dramatic piece of foreign travel which any British prime minister had attempted. We have already noted that Chamberlain had not been an enthusiast for official foreign travel and did not undertake it between 1932 and 1937. Hoare's misfortunes provided a salutary lesson.[81] That reticence made his travels by air in September 1938 even more striking. In the immediate aftermath of the Munich conference, when it was widely believed that war had been averted, the advantages of personal diplomacy were emphasized by commentators. Only a face to face encounter between the men who mattered could get anywhere. Correspondingly, when the optimism of Munich disappeared and war came, the tide again turned against travelling prime ministers. Fresh emphasis was placed on the merits of tried and tested diplomatic method, though it was not easy to believe that the advice received from the British Embassy in Berlin proved the point beyond all argument.[82]

Whatever his criticisms of the Munich agreement, when he became prime minister, Winston Churchill – himself an early flyer – showed no tendency to moderate his zest for travel, often in circumstances of considerable personal discomfort and strain. It was to prove impossible, indeed, to persuade statesmen that they should remain grounded. For better or worse, as the speed and comfort of air travel inexorably improved, the delights of foreign travel proved irresistible in the post-1945 world. Diplomats could not reverse the situation and could only accommodate themselves to behaviour which would have shocked their predecessors in the days of 'Old Diplomacy'.

The patterns of travel which have been touched on in this chapter do not readily admit of any general conclusions. Travel both did and did not 'broaden the mind' of the British political elite which engaged in it. Prejudices were sometimes modified but as often confirmed. Sometimes foreigners scarcely made an appearance in foreign countries – for distinguished Britons liked the company of their own kind when abroad. The travellers rarely lingered long enough to enter into the spirit of the country being visited. It is noteworthy that few travellers established lasting relationships with their counterparts in the countries they visited. Yet, the itineraries followed and the impressions formed by British visitors in the

---

[80] Andrew Roberts, *The Holy Fox: A Biography of Lord Halifax* (London, 1991), pp. 66–75.
[81] I am grateful to Professor David Dilks for confirmation of these points.
[82] Keith Robbins, *Munich 1938* (London, 1968).

period under review are not without significance, even if it is impossible to establish clear policy outcomes. 'It is one thing to go touring about two continents', Beatrice Webb noted, 'and another thing going as a delegate to important international assemblies.'[83] She was contrasting the activities of such men as MacDonald and Henderson with those of Conservative ministers, but, although her observation is not without some validity, it was a comparison which was ceasing to be an accurate description by the time of the second world war. Looked at over the half century sketched in this chapter, we may indeed be driven to conclude that a little travel is a dangerous thing – but we must also conclude that its delights have proved irresistible.

[83] Cited in Wrigley, *Henderson*, p. 165.

RICHARD LANGHORNE

CHAPTER 3

Arbitration: the first phase, 1870–1914

Arbitration has been identified in various primitive forms in several international systems, and in the modern system its emergence predated the later nineteenth century.[1] There were 70 arbitrations between 1794 and 1850. But between 1851 and 1875, there were 100 and in the following twenty-five years almost exactly twice that number[2] and no less than 149 in the following fourteen years. The number of arbitration treaties also rose sharply: 90 were concluded between 1880 and 1900 and 100 were in force by 1914.[3] Thus, there is no doubt when the device took off as a feature of international practice; nor was its arrival lost on contemporary observers. 'We have got rid of private wars between small magnate and large magnate in this country; we have got rid of the duel between man and man, and we are slowly, as far as we can, substituting arbitration for struggles in international disputes.'[4] The source of this rather noticeably qualified observation was the great Lord Salisbury. The reasons for Salisbury's observation can be seen relatively easily: the reason for the qualification will be discussed later.

The development of arbitration during the nineteenth and early twentieth centuries falls into three main sections: the period before the *Alabama*

[1] See, e.g., M. Wight, *Systems of States* (Leicester, 1977), pp. 50–3.
[2] See table 3.1. The tables have been compiled from three sources each of which provides its evidence for different purposes. Only by making a (highly tedious) combination of what they contain can a full picture be arrived at and even then it is hard to be certain that every case has been included or correctly described. However, the general trends are quite clear. Stuyt is the basic text, assisted by Ralston, who gives 44 treaties not mentioned by Stuyt, and by Manning, who gives 157 that neither Stuyt nor Ralston quote: A.M. Stuyt, *Survey of International Arbitrations, 1794–1938* (Leiden, 1939); J.H. Ralston, *International Arbitration from Athens to Locarno* (Oxford, 1929); W.O. Manning, *Commentaries on the Law of Nations* (London, 1975).
[3] F.S. Northedge, *The League of Nations* (Leicester, 1986), p. 15.
[4] Lord Salisbury in the *Review of Reviews* (March 1898).

claim (1871), the period between 1871 and the first Hague Conference (1899) and finally that between 1899 and the establishment of the League of Nations. The characteristic technique for arbitrations in the first period involved the setting up of mixed commissions, formed of varying numbers of commissioners from each party to the dispute, who were often required to add to their number by agreement or by drawing lots. Failure to agree might be resolved by reference to a disinterested head of state, or some other umpire (see table 8, p. 55). Simpson and Fox summed up the effect of this approach as follows:

> Later experience was to confirm that the success of a mixed commission often depended on the ability of the commissioners appointed by the parties to give agreed decisions on the questions submitted to them without recourse to the umpire or arbitrator. This in turn meant that the mixed commission worked best where the subject-matter of the dispute allowed or encouraged the commissioners to act to some extent as negotiators rather than judges, to temper justice with diplomacy, to give a measure of satisfaction to both sides, for example, in a territorial dispute.[5]

A particular difficulty that could emerge from referring a failure to agree to a head of state was shown in the *Bulama Island* case of 1870, where an Anglo-Portuguese dispute over a west African island was referred to the president of the United States, who ruled in favour of the Portuguese. This was not so much because of the merits of the case but because the US had a consistent policy of not recognising the validity of a cession of territory by natives who did not have permanent possession of it. The president's adviser merely commented that the parties must have known of this American doctrine before choosing the arbitrator.[6] The *Alabama* case, however, produced a change, not just by increasing confidence in the effectiveness of arbitration, but through the procedure employed. The issues were too significant to be dealt with by a mixed commission and reference to a head of state represented too great a risk and this led to the establishment of a different type of tribunal. In this case, the tribunal consisted of one member appointed by each side and others appointed by the king of Italy, the president of the Swiss Confederation and the emperor of Brazil. The result was a kind of collegiate international court, and it set a pattern which gradually superseded its predecessor, though both operated side by side during the later nineteenth century, the latter particularly in questions of frontier delimitation, as for example between Britain and the South African Republic in 1884. The newer process, however, was used in three major arbitrations in the 1890s: the Newfoundland lobster fisheries dispute between Britain and France (1891), the Behring Sea seal fishery dispute between the USA and Britain (1892) and the British

---

[5] J.L. Simpson and Hazel Fox, *International Arbitration. Law and Practice* (London, 1959).
[6] Ibid., p. 7.

Guiana and Venezuela boundary dispute, first between Britain and Venezuela and subsequently on the intervention of the United States, between
Venezuela, Britain and the USA (1897).

In 1899 and 1907, the Hague Conferences, whose original purpose had
been to calm the developing and expensive contemporary armaments race,
contributed to the development of arbitration by setting up the Permanent
Court of Arbitration in 1899, and making some modifications in 1907.
There were some severe limitations in this development which meant that
the Permanent Court is neither permanent nor a court in any strict sense.
It was and is a panel of names from which arbitrators can be selected to
form a tribunal in the event of disputants wishing to use the procedure
made available under the Convention for the Pacific Settlement of International Disputes. The persons nominated to the panel by signatory
governments must not exceed four each and must be 'of known com-
petency in questions of international law, of the highest moral reputation
and disposed to accept the duties of arbitrator'. There was an administrative bureau which was genuinely permanent and at the disposal of tribunals, and there was, perhaps most importantly, a full description of the
procedure to be adopted by tribunals, unless the parties themselves have
agreed to vary them. These rules, together with the minor modifications
of 1907, remain the basis upon which international arbitrations are conducted. As can be seen from table 8, rapid use was made of the Permanent
Court after 1899; but the generally insignificant disputes dealt with confirmed the limited ambitions of the powers who signed the Convention.
All that could be agreed upon after the discussions of both 1899 and 1907
was the following:

In questions of a legal nature, and especially in the interpretation or application
of International Conventions, arbitration is recognised by the Signatory Powers as
the most effective, and at the same time the most equitable, means of settling
disputes which diplomacy has failed to settle. [The following was added in 1907]:
'Consequently, it would be desirable that, in disputes regarding the above-
mentioned questions, the Contracting Powers should, if the case arise, have
recourse to arbitration, in so far as circumstances permit'.[7]

This limitation and the hesitations that lay behind it were the source
of the obvious qualification in Lord Salisbury's statement referred to earlier. It was also put bluntly by the American delegate to the Hague Peace
Conference in the following year: 'Not a single power was willing to bring
itself to submit to arbitration all questions, except in minor matter – as
for example postal or monetary difficulties and the like.'[8] When the Hague
Conference was reconvened in 1907, there was a greater willingness to
discuss making arbitration compulsory in certain circumstances, and

[7] Ibid., p. 14.
[8] Quoted in F.H. Hinsley, *Power and the Pursuit of Peace* (Cambridge, 1963), p. 269.

making the court genuinely permanent. But there was enough opposition, particularly strong on the part of the German government which wished to protect its freedom of action to the last extremity, to prevent any such development. Thus arbitration remained, fundamentally as it had always been, deeply constrained by the fact that it depended on the consent of the parties at every level and at every stage and ultimately to the carrying out of any award made. When powers began to try to make bilateral generalised arbitration treaties, they expressed the reality of the situation very clearly. The first of these was made in 1903 between Britain and France and its formula of listing the types of disputes covered and inserting a disclaimer in respect of any dispute which affected the 'vital interests, the independence or the honour of the two contracting States and do not concern the interests of third parties' became typical.[9] This style was used in ten other such treaties made by Britain before 1905, and was used in the Anglo-American Arbitration Convention of 1908, together with the additional restriction that it could only be brought into operation after an exchange of Notes between the two governments on each occasion of its potential use. In 1910, President Taft suggested making a more comprehensive arbitration treaty with Britain, a proposition which the British foreign secretary, if not the British Foreign Office, took up enthusiastically. The resulting treaty of 1911, and a similar one negotiated with France, were rejected in the US Senate, not so much on grounds of Anglophobia as on objections to the limitation of the sovereignty of the Senate which the proposed joint commission was particularly held to imply. A hint of more immediate concerns was apparent in the objections of Theodore Roosevelt, who agreed that disputes with Britain were never likely to be unsuitable for arbitration but feared the possible precedent that might be set for treaties with powers whose intentions might not be so benign.[10]

It thus seems reasonable to ask, in the light of such doubts, why the pace of arbitration increased so sharply at the time. One answer to this question emerges clearly from the figures set out in tables 5 and 6 (pp. 54–5). If the first line of table 6 is added to the Latin America total in table 5, it can be seen that 274 arbitrations (a large number) originated in Latin America. American influence in favour of arbitration in the continent partly accounted for this: the Americans were both litigious in cast of mind and believed themselves to act in an individual and particularly fair minded way in foreign affairs. The high proportion of boundary claims was also significant – forty-nine out of ninety-four – a type of claim which proved singularly amenable to the process of arbitration. It should also be noted that the instability and poverty of most Latin American states were

[9] Simpson and Fox, *International Arbitration*, p. 16, n.54
[10] B. Perkins, *The Great Rapprochement* (London, 1969), p. 254.

powerful motivations towards finding alternatives to possibly unsuccessful warfare. It is clear, moreover, that performance rates were significantly poorer outside arbitrations arranged by the US and Great Britain. Latin American states may have been prone to resort to arbitration, they were less willing to accept the results: see table 7 (p. 55). It is also plain from table 3 (p. 52) that Latin America scored heavily in the other main area where arbitration was prevalent, with thirty-six examples of private claims cases.

Other motives for the development of arbitration cannot, however, be so easily gleaned from the tables. The contemporary international environment was probably the most important factor. By the later 1870s the European powers were beginning to suffer the first effects of the contradiction between their need to cooperate at technical levels and the intensity of their demand for sovereign independence of action. The development of the much more complex systems of administration which the industrial revolution had brought to the most advanced states had coincided with and reinforced the complete acceptance of the nation itself as an essential component of a legitimate state. The 'national state' was never so powerful an idea or fact as it was in the last quarter of the nineteenth century, and while on the one hand it completed the ruin of Turkey and brought irreversible decline to Austria-Hungary, it also brought a heightened sense of national dignity to those who had been able to profit from its effects. This sense was to bring greater tension to international relations just at the moment when long-term adjustments were changing the bases of the international system, both globally and regionally. The rise of Germany in Europe, and the emergence of the crisis over China in the Far East, created tensions that greatly weakened the European states system and emphasised the need to find alternative means of guaranteeing security. Three main responses became visible: an arms race, expressed in various styles, but so compelling as to cause governments to lose control over defence expenditure; the making of alliances, which neatly embodied the dilemma they were in, as they wished to control their affairs independently, but were nonetheless forced to embrace the greater security offered by highly limited alliances, often actually intended to act as a restraint on their partner. The third response took the form of a much increased consciousness of the possible uses of international law. Because it was the alliances and their military and naval combinations which seemed after 1914 to have caused rather than prevented the war, it is easiest to go to the form in which the League of Nations was created to see how deeply the legal approach had bitten. At the time, the discussion in journals, at conferences of lawyers and peace associations of varying kinds, the calling of the two Hague Conferences (1899 and 1907), the extended argument over the law of the sea embodied in the Declaration of London, all created an atmosphere which greatly raised the profile of legal routes to the resolution of disputes and made them publicly popular: amongst the most discussed was certainly arbitration.

There were two principal origins of this effect: the first arose out of the resurgence of warfare in the mid-nineteenth century, and particularly out of the American Civil War. Even before, the 1856 Peace of Paris, which brought the Crimean War to an end, had urged 'States, between which any serious misunderstanding may arise, should, before appealing to Arms, have recourse as far as circumstances might allow, to the Good Offices of a friendly Power.' Northedge correctly noted that this novel provision came at the end of the first serious war between great powers whose horrors had been widely reported to the public by the press.[11]

There was a tendency for proposals to codify the whole of international law to emerge as a precondition for creating a general treaty which at its best would prevent warfare and even at its least effective greatly mitigate its effects.[12] The foundation in 1873 of the Institute of International Law followed the individual efforts of the 1860s and while there was no political will to pick up the ball on the part of governments, the lawyers made substantial progress, particularly over diplomatic law,[13] over the laws of war, where actual treaties emerged, leading to the existing Geneva Conventions, and in 1875 over arbitration. For this the Institute published draft rules for arbitral tribunals which were interesting both because they came, though not immediately, to be widely accepted and because they reflected the changes in practice which had been fuelled by the *Alabama* case.

There was already a body of arbitration experience derived largely from Anglo-American relations beginning with the Jay Treaty of 1794 and proceeding successfully through thirty-two arbitrations up till 1850, with only two serious failures.[14] The prevalence of boundary questions in Anglo-US relations, as well as the very conservative general interests of the British Empire help to explain this. Despite this experience, however, it was the *Alabama* case which really sharpened interest in the possibilities of arbitration. The point was not the nature of the dispute, but the fact that it was submitted to arbitration, and that the decision, widely regarded as hard on Britain, was accepted by the British government, and the amount of the award paid up. It seemed as if this particular legal route to a resol-

---

[11] Northedge, *League of Nations*, p. 16, n.15

[12] For example, J.K. Bluntschli, Die Organisation des Europäischen Staatsvereins in *Gesammelte Kleine Schriften*, Berlin, 1879, I, chapter 12, 1868.

[13] See R. Langhorne, 'Regulating Diplomatic Relations: From the Beginnings to the Vienna Convention (1961)', *Review of International Studies*, 18 (1992), 3–17.

[14] Under the Jay Treaty (1794) commissioners set up under article 6 could not agree a decision upon debts owing to British creditors by persons who had become US citizens. The second concerned the Lakes Huron and Superior boundary, where arbitration failed in December, 1827.

ution was acceptable to a great power, and that the prospects for its further elaboration now looked bright.

The second factor played, despite what has sometimes been thought, an indirect rather than any direct part. Nation states found it distasteful to make political and military alliances with one another because of the inroads into their freedom of action which they implied. In the field of administrative cooperation, however, the later nineteenth century witnessed a flood of what was in effect international legislation on a very wide range of activities. The very growth in the scope of government which on the one hand had had the effect of confirming the national individuality of states, compelled them at levels lower than the high political to enter broadly based agreements on topics ranging from the prevention of cattle disease to the movement of international rail freight. Most such agreements contained provisions for dealing with any disputes by legal rather than diplomatic means; and there was a marked tendency for states to accept without much question the decisions thus arrived at. This development was important both in itself and for its effect in increasing the legal atmosphere in which significant areas of international relations were being conducted. But very few such provisions entailed arbitration (see tables 3, 4 and 5) though one important arbitration did initiate an administrative consequence of its own. The Tribunal of 1892 which decided the *Behring Sea Seal Fishing* dispute between the United Kingdom and the United States drew up a set of regulations for the seal fisheries.[15] The reasonable number of arbitrations on treaty interpretation contain some that fall into the 'administrative' category, but it is noticeable that boundary and private claims considerably exceed them in number. Perhaps surprisingly in view of what has been thought before,[16] the growth of arbitration, if not the resort to legal processes, did not flow directly from the needs of states newly regulating international administrative needs among themselves.

If it is clear what the main sources of the legal background were, it is also apparent that they were far from being an adequate explanation of the phenomenon. The example of Anglo-American arbitration is particularly apt – it was the oldest, frequently the most effective, almost a tradition; yet there is little doubt that the basis of British willingness to employ the procedure was diplomatic rather than legal. American attitudes likewise suggest that it was the tendency of decisions to favour them which sustained their interest as much as any moral standpoint, however much the latter might speak to a perceived American tradition. For much of the nineteenth century, British governments were concerned not to allow Anglo-American hostility to add to their other anxieties, and this became particularly true at the turn of the century. They were conscious of the latent, latterly patent,

[15] Simpson and Fox, *International Arbitration*, p. 7.
[16] Hinsley, *Power*, p. 261.

power of the US, and in naval affairs decided that security could only be achieved by political means, since any attempt to include the US in the usual calculations of relative naval strength would demand construction on a scale beyond Britain's capacity. But these political means were always at risk from the possibility of disputes arising about the Canadian boundary, let alone other matters of commerce or maritime law which tended to dominate the direct disputes between the US and the British Empire. In this context, there was no doubt that Britain generally sacrificed the interests of Canada on the altar of appeasement in Washington, the most obvious example being the Alaska boundary settlement of 1903. As Kenneth Bourne put it: 'the appeasement of the United States at the end of the nineteenth century was the natural, if belated, conclusion of a policy which Great Britain had long since adopted in the interests of her security'.[17] To do this with the minimum of embarrassment was most easily achieved by means of arbitration: it took a long time, it was supposedly impartial and technical, but, above all, it was at one remove from the government itself, thus making the process more acceptable to public opinion in Britain itself, if not always in Canada. In the case of the Alaska Boundary Award of 1903, although the British very pointedly nominated three 'men of honour' to the commission while the Americans used three notoriously *parti pris* politicians, they nevertheless put considerable private pressure on the leading Briton, Lord Alverstone, to side with the Americans.

There was another aspect to this factor. As the age of the yellow press dawned and flourished, at the same time as all governments became more than ever concerned to maintain public support, they were capable both of trying to manipulate the press and frightened of unfavourable publicity on nationalist issues emerging in it. To lose a sensitive issue in foreign relations for an indefinite period of time while the process of arbitration ensued and then to present the result as a success if the award was favourable and morally unavoidable if it was not, had an obvious domestic political dividend. The time factor was plainly important. It took time for tribunals to be established – or after 1899, for the Hague procedure to get under way, should that be the chosen route – time for commissioners and umpires to accept appointment, time for them to assemble, time for evidence to be gathered, presented and cross-examined, time for summing up, for reflection before an award was given and time for governments to respond. In many Latin American arbitration treaties, the value of time was specifically recognised by including a 'cooling off' period in their provisions – an idea that was to have a distinguished future after 1919. Another essentially political motive emerges from the tables. It is clear from the nature of the issues generally arbitrated that the device had a role in removing less important matters of

---

[17] K. Bourne, *Britain and the Balance of Power in North America* (London, 1967), p. 382. For further discussion of this point see P.M. Kennedy, *The Rise and Fall of British Naval Mastery* (London, 1976), pp. 205–13.

dispute from the field while more serious questions were negotiated. It was convenient not to have a public row about a case of illegal arrest while trying to negotiate an alliance.

The increasing number of arbitrations, and the good effect which they appeared to have on Anglo-American relations, led the German government to reverse the true positions of cause and effect, and to try to improve their position with the US by getting in ahead of the British with a general arbitration treaty in the early twentieth century. They were unsuccessful, and might have been wiser to think about Theodore Roosevelt's domestic manoeuvres, and about their own tactics off Manila Bay in 1898, after which the Americans believed themselves to have been saved from German hostility by the British navy.

The intrinsic fallibility of the arbitration process seen as an isolated, legal, phenomenon, may also be judged from the difficulties that arose when General Arbitration treaties came under discussion. From the Hague Conference of 1899 onwards, it became clear that states were only prepared to agree to treaties which contained crippling reservations, or were general only in the sense that they contained a list of pre-agreed issues that were arbitrable. This was a characteristic of Latin American treaties which began to appear earlier than others. When the question of General Arbitration treaties arose among the greater powers in the early twentieth century, they contained reservations which were both vague and restricting – matters to do with national honour, dignity and vital interests were excluded; and, even then, the treaties were often not ratified, particularly by the US – most notably during the weary months of negotiations between the Administration and Congress concerning the celebrated, but failed, Anglo-American treaty of 1911.

Are there any lessons to be learnt? It is obvious that there was a connection, albeit an indirect one, between the fact that the international system was undergoing profound and uncomfortable change at the end of the nineteenth century and the increasing tendency to turn to arbitration as a mechanism of the international political system. It was clearly also partly a function of the changed and greater administrative responsibilities of governments. Profound change both in the international system and in the role of states also characterises the present, and there has certainly been an increase in the number of relatively small disputes, some about boundaries, between relatively small states. A corresponding increase in resort to arbitration might be expected. But, if it occurs, most probably through the machinery of the United Nations, it will without doubt be accompanied by the more purely political motivations which characterised its first extensive phase, and is unlikely to be allowed to invade the areas of really serious loss and gain. Legal routes to resolution of disputes tend not to work well when what is really at issue is the desire of states to improve or defend their political circumstances.

Table 1. *Arbitration treaties 1794–1914*

1794–1914	All	GB	US
1794–1800	7	3	4
1801–1825	26	11	7
1826–1850	37	8	7
1851–1875	100	28	29
1876–1900	199	46	38
1901–1914	149	23	34
Total	518	119	119

Table 2. *Issues by period*

	1794–1800	1801–1825	1826–1850	1851–1875	1876–1900	1901–1914	Total
Boundary questions	2	4	2	17	43	2	89
Debt recovery	2	0	0	0	0	0	2
Maritime seizure	2	0	2	8	8	5	25
Territorial questions	0	3	2	4	10	7	26
Private claims	0	1	9	12	23	37	82
Mutual claims	0	2	2	9	12	0	25
Claims after insurrection or civil war	0	0	1	4	9	4	18
Fisheries	0	0	1	1	1	1	4
Claims made due to act of war	0	0	4	2	11	1	18
Illegal arrest	0	0	0	3	7	1	11
General	0	4	8	19	35	37	103
Total	6	14	31	79	159	114	403

Table 3. *Main US arbitrations by issue*

Main US arbitrations	GB	S. America	Europe	Asia	Africa	Misc.	Total
Boundary questions	7	3	0	0	0	0	10
Debt recovery	1	3	0	0	0	0	4
Maritime seizure	1	4	5	0	0	0	10
Territorial questions	1	0	0	0	0	0	1
Private claims	1	25	1	2	0	0	29
Mutual claims	1	10	2	1	0	0	14
Claims following insurrection or civil war	2	3	2	1	0	1	9
Illegal arrest	0	3	0	1	1	0	5
Fisheries	0	3	0	1	1	0	3
General	0	12	12	0	0	0	24
Total	14	66	22	6	2	1	109

Table 4. *Main GB arbitrations by issue*

Main GB Arbitrations	US	S. America	Europe	Asia	Africa	Misc.	Total
Boundary questions	7	2	7	0	2	2	20
Debt recovery	1	0	0	0	0	0	1
Maritime seizure	1	2	3	0	0	0	6
Territorial questions	1	3	8	0	0	0	12
Private claims	1	0	1	0	0	0	2
Mutual claims	1	8	7	1	1	1	19
Claims made following insurrection or civil war	2	2	1	0	0	2	7
Illegal arrest	0	2	2	0	0	0	4
Fisheries	3	0	1	0	0	0	4
General	0	0	0	0	0	0	0
Total	17	19	30	1	3	5	75

Table 5. *Arbitrations by issue, excluding US and GB*

	Europe	South America	Asia	Af	Europe America	Europe Asia	Europe Africa	America Asia	America Africa	Asia Africa	Total
Boundary questions	8	44	6	2	3	1	0	0	0	0	64
Debt recovery	1	0	0	0	0	0	0	0	0	0	1
Maritime seizure	4	1	0	0	1	0	0	1	0	0	7
Territorial questions	9	1	0	0	3	0	0	0	0	0	13
Private claims	6	11	1	0	15	0	0	0	0	0	33
Mutual claims	0	4	0	1	1	0	0	0	0	0	6
Claims: following insurrection or civil war	0	1	0	0	3	0	0	0	0	0	4
Illegal arrest	1	0	0	0	0	0	0	0	0	0	1
Fisheries	0	0	0	0	0	0	0	0	0	0	0
Claims: Act of War	1	7	0	1	7	0	0	0	0	0	16
Treaty Interpretation	2	12	0	0	1	0	0	0	0	0	15
Sub-total	32	81	7	4	34	1	0	1	0	0	160
General		91									91
Total	32	172	7	4	34	1	0	1	0	0	251

Table 6. *Arbitration by region*

Arbs by region	GB	US
S. & C. America	28	74
US/GB	29	29
Europe	41	11
Asia	5	5
Africa	5	1
Others	12	5
Total	120	125

Table 7. *Acceptance and performance rates (including dismissal of claim), 1794–1914*

Between	Total nos.	Performances
US and others, except GB	62	24
GB and others, except US	83	40
US and GB	25	18
Other countries	167	36

Table 8. *Main umpires by period*

	1794/ 1800	1801/ 1825	1826/ 1850	1851/ 1875	1876/ 1900	1901/ 1914	Total
Swiss Federation					5	1	6
The Pope					2	1	3
US president				1	7	3	11
US judge						1	1
US citizen	2			6	9	6	23
British sovereign			1		1	1	3
British judge			1			1	2
British citizen	1		1	11	14	1	28
Russian sovereign	1	1	1	1	1		5
Spanish sovereign					7	2	9
Spanish citizen				1	6	1	8
Italian citizen				4	3	1	8
Belgian citizen				3		1	4
US Domestic Tribunal		1			1	1	3
Permanent Court						18	18
Canadian judge					1	3	4
Mixed nationalities		2		1	6		9
Friendly nation: South America				13	8	2	23
Central American government				2	10		12
French president				2	3	2	7
Nationality of Umpire unknown	1	2		18	16	26	63
Umpire not chosen	2	14	18	18	46	34	132
Total	7	20	22	81	146	106	382

CHAPTER 4

'Only a d. . .d marionette'?
The influence of ambassadors
on British foreign policy,
1904–1914

In 1904, Sir Francis Bertie, the British ambassador at Rome, complained about his lack of influence. Recalling fondly his days at the Foreign Office, Bertie lamented: 'In Downing Street one can at least pull the wires whereas an Ambassador is only a d. . . .d marionette.'[1] Bertie's view is generally accepted by historians, who argue that the role of diplomats declined in the late nineteenth and early twentieth centuries.[2] At one level, there is little doubt that such a view is correct; after the invention of the telegraph, British diplomats did not make policy in the fashion supposedly done by Stratford Canning at Constantinople before the Crimean War.[3]

To note that ambassadors did not make policy is one thing; to then assert that they counted no more than as marionettes is another. To do so is both to oversimplify the role of ambassadors and to underestimate the influence that they were able to exert on policy by other than direct means. British ambassadors affected British foreign policy in a number of ways. First, ambassadors and their staffs provided the Foreign Office with the bulk of information about the countries to which they were accredited. This was important, both in the wider sense that ambassadors were responsible for keeping the Foreign Office well informed about such matters as their host country's economic and military strength, and in

---

[1] As cited in Chirol to Hardinge, 10 Aug. 1904, Hardinge Papers (Cambridge University Library, Cambridge) 7.

[2] Wholeheartedly by R.A. Jones, *The British Diplomatic Service 1815–1914* (Waterloo, ON, 1983), pp. 116–38; and in a more nuanced fashion by Zara Steiner in *The Foreign Office and Foreign Policy 1898–1914* (Cambridge, 1969), pp. 173–85 and 'Elitism and Foreign Policy: The Foreign Office before the Great War', in B.J.C. McKercher and D.J. Moss, eds., *Shadow and Substance in British Foreign Policy 1895–1939* (Edmonton, 1984), pp. 19–55. Both Steiner's and Jones' books approvingly cite Bertie's remark.

[3] Even Canning's independence is now in doubt; recent research suggests that his actions at Constantinople more reflected British policy than made it; see D.M. Goldfrank, *The Origins of the Crimean War* (London, 1994), pp. 276–9.

the narrower sense that the ambassadors were expected to provide their superiors in Whitehall with an accurate assessment of the personalities and political influence of those in positions of power. By doing so, ambassadors helped to create the 'mental map' that served to determine British policy.[4] Second, ambassadors were the embodiment of Britain abroad. The prestige of an individual ambassador not only reflected Britain's own prestige, but also helped to augment or diminish that prestige. Further, an ambassador who, for whatever reason, was able to establish an exceptional position in a foreign country was likely able to carry out British policy more effectively than someone who was unable to do so. This influenced what policies the Foreign Office initiated, since, for example, it would be folly to attempt delicate negotiations with an unsatisfactory ambassador in place.

Third, British foreign policy generally consisted of achieving what was possible, and was rather flexible in its execution. In an era before shuttle diplomacy, this normally meant that two parallel sets of negotiations were carried on simultaneously, one in London between the foreign secretary and a foreign ambassador, the other in the opposing capital between the foreign secretary's opposite number and the British ambassador. Progress in negotiations was incremental, with each small achievement paving the way to the next. The path to the goal was rarely a straight one. This meant that the ambassador and the foreign secretary acted as partners, with each needing to keep the other closely informed. And, since the British ambassador was negotiating directly with the person responsible for policy, in some ways the ambassador's observations were more important than were the foreign secretary's. In this circumstance, ambassadors could both determine the way in which British policy was implemented and suggest modifications to that policy.

Some evidence for these assertions can be found by considering the choice of British ambassadors to the United States and Russia in the last decade before the first world war and the way in which these ambassadors shaped the 'mental maps' of the two countries. The selection of these two countries is arbitrary, but not done without reason. The United States and Russia serve as complementary case studies: America was democratic and linked by culture and history to Britain; tsarist Russia was autocratic and linked to Britain only by the fact that it posed the greatest long-term threat to the British Empire. Britain and the United States had a large and burgeoning trade; Britain and Russia did not. British and American interests were opposed only marginally; British and Russian

---

[4] The concept is from A. Henrickson, 'The Geographical "Mental Maps" of American Foreign Policy Makers', *International Political Science Review*, 1:4 (1980), 495–530 and explored in Steiner, 'Elitism and Foreign Policy', 44–51, and Keith Neilson, *Britain and the Last Tsar. British Policy and Russia 1894–1917* (Oxford University Press, 1995), chapters 1 and 2.

interests clashed world-wide. On the other hand, both Russia and the United States were exotic countries for most Britons, despite (or perhaps because of) the commonality of language in the case of the latter. In addition, both were continental-sized states, whose domestic affairs were not easily appreciated from abroad. Thus, the Foreign Office was dependent on its representatives in Washington and St Petersburg for information to a greater extent than was the case with respect to the Western European Powers.

I

What sort of country did British diplomatists find the United States in the years before 1914? How did the British ambassadors – Sir Mortimer Durand (1903–7), James Bryce (1907–13) and Sir Cecil Spring-Rice (1913–18) – and their staffs perceive America? The answer to this is complex, and what follows is necessarily somewhat of an overview, but the outlines are clear. In essence, the United States was a land of contradictions and novelty, where the sublime and the ridiculous seemed often to meld into one – in short, the United States was the California of its time.

While, as the British Embassy's annual report for 1907 noted, 'no country changes so quickly as does the United States', certain things seemed constant.[5] One was, in the words of Durand, 'the prevalence in the United States of violent crime'.[6] The particular focus of this for British diplomats was the treatment of blacks, but to this was added the exploits of night riders and other vigilante groups, leading Durand to the conclusion that 'all over the United States life seems to be held cheap, and criminals are encouraged by the slowness of the courts'. Such conditions led, as was observed in 1908, to the 'continued insecurity of life and property in many parts of the country'.[7]

These observations are worth examining closely. There were a variety of reactions to the frequent lynching of blacks. First, there was no scepticism about the conventional explanation about the cause – black assaults on white women – for the lynchings. But, second, what was not accepted was either that the lynchings should be permitted or that the attacks were triggered by a lusting after miscegenation. Durand's remarks are instructive:

There is much to be said for the southern view that assaults on white people justify swift and summary punishment; but the people are becoming too much accustomed to taking the law into their own hands and to lynching men for all

---

[5] Bryce to Grey, desp. 152, 30 Apr 1908, in D. Cameron Watt and K. Bourne, eds., *British Documents on Foreign Affairs*, pt. I, ser. C, vol. 12, doc. 177. (Hereafter in the style, *BDFA I*, C12, 177.)

[6] Durand to Grey, desp. 16, 25 Jan. 1906, ibid., 10.

[7] Bryce to Grey, desp. 152, 30 Apr. 1908, ibid., 177.

sorts of crimes. Sooner or later this must be stopped, and the sooner the better. The lawlessness which now prevails in many of the oldest States of the Union is surprising, and discreditable to the nation.[8]

Esme Howard, counsellor at the Embassy from 1906 to 1908, advanced the idea that the assaults by blacks were in reality political acts rather than *crimes passionneles* – he saw them as the revenge of a people illegally deprived of their political rights.[9]

Another striking feature was the open corruption – 'the most conspicuous blot upon the political life of the United States' – of American cities.[10] Municipal corruption, Bryce wrote in 1907, is 'notoriously bad, in degrees varying from the murky turpitude of Philadelphia and Pittsburgh to the comparatively mild form of jobbery and corruption which exists in Boston and Cleveland'.[11] Other cities did not escape censure. San Francisco, for example, was alleged to approach Philadelphia in the depths of its corruption. But, as Bryce also noted, 'the American seems to be making fresh efforts to shake off the tyranny of the "boss" and the so-called "machine" in politics'.[12] For this reason, the Embassy reported carefully on the various experiments in municipal government that abounded in the United States before 1914.

A negative feature of the United States in British eyes was its newspapers. The annual report for 1906 characterised them simply as 'immeasurably inferior to the English press. The best American newspapers, compared with ours, are vulgar and sensational, wanting in all reticence and dignity, and the rest are thoroughly unscrupulous and bad.'[13] A year later, opinion had not changed. The Embassy reported on the 'unbridled licence, the mendacity, the recklessness, and nauseous vulgarity of a large section of the press'.[14] But this did not mean that newspapers could be ignored. In a long evaluation of the American press, one of the junior members of the Embassy pointed out their significance:

The press is very powerful in the United States, more so perhaps than in England ... the papers seldom try to lead, but by feeling carefully the pulse of the masses form that intimate connection which is so demoralising for the writers and gives the impression that the whole press is popular.[15]

Americans, he continued, were 'insatiable readers', but ignorant, and as their opinions were thought to be those found in the newspapers, 'immense deference' was paid to them by American politicians. Obviously,

---

[8] Durand to Grey, desp. 49 confidential, 2 Apr. 1906, ibid., 18.
[9] Howard to Grey, desp. 262, 17 Aug. 1908, *BDFA I*, C13, 69.
[10] Bryce to Grey, desp. 78A, 1 Apr. 1909, ibid., 110.
[11] Bryce to Grey, desp. 255, 28 Nov. 1907, ibid., 163.
[12] Bryce to Grey, desp. 124, 29 May 1907, ibid., 128.
[13] Bryce to Grey, desp. 238 confidential, 28 Dec. 1906, *BDFA I*, C12, 101.
[14] Bryce to Grey, desp. 152, 30 Apr. 1908, ibid., 177.
[15] Grant Watson's report in Bryce to Grey, desp. 120, 3 Apr. 1908, *BDFA I*, C13, 59.

the Embassy would have to pay careful attention to the handling of the American press if British policies were to succeed.

Nor was great store set by other American institutions. At the end of his term in Washington, Bryce wrote of his puzzlement over 'the co-existence in this country of so much that is good in the people with so much that is bad in their Government'.[16] While, as we shall see, Bryce thought well of many prominent men in the American government, this feeling did not extend to Congress, and particularly to the Senate. Writing to Lord Grey, the governor general of Canada, in late 1907, Bryce was sharp in his condemnation: 'The Senate is practically inexhaustible. It is a coarse body, a more selfish & grasping body, & unfortunately a more powerful body for the purpose of obstruction, than it ever was before.'[17] While the Senate's power was 'abominable' and 'pernicious to the US itself', Bryce realised that it 'was a fact; we may lament, but we cannot ignore it'. The understanding of this fact must therefore underlie all relations with America.

Such a root-and-branch condemnation of the United States was carried over into the realm of foreign affairs. 'Americans are self-centred', lamented a British ambassador, adding on another occasion that, 'The first thing that strikes an Englishman in America is the indifference shown by Americans to the affairs of foreign countries.'[18] This did not mean, though, that that was necessarily a negligible quantity in world affairs. While Americans 'confidently assert their claim to be the greatest of all [Powers]', many among the British elite realised that this boast, if premature, had a ring of future truth. The first lord of the Admiralty, writing in 1902, noted that the United States was potentially a major threat to British naval supremacy: 'Of course', he wrote, 'if the United States chooses, it could build and maintain a bigger Navy than ourselves, because they have the longer purse; but I do not think that is at present a probable policy on their part.'[19] Valentine Chirol, the well-travelled foreign editor of *The Times*, expressed the feelings of many upon his return from the United States in 1904: 'As usual I have returned from America rather depressed by the greatness & vitality of that huge & young nation with which it seems hopeless for us to compete in the long run on anything like equal terms.'[20] But the key phrases here were 'could' and 'in the long run'. For, in 1914 the United States was only a potential power. The idea, moreover, of an Anglo-American conflict was anathema to many. F.H. Villi-

---

[16] Bryce to Grey, desp. 124, 16 May, *BDFA I*, C15, 49.
[17] Bryce to Grey, 28 Dec. 1907, Bryce Papers, FO (Foreign Office Archives, Public Record Office, Kew) 800/331.
[18] Durand to Grey, desp. 16, 1 Jan. 1906, *BDFA I*, C12, 10; Durand to Grey, desp. 238 confidential, Annual Report for 1906, 28 Dec. 1906, ibid., 101.
[19] Selborne to Sir Charles Dilke, 21 Mar. 1902, Selborne Papers (Bodleian Library, Oxford) 33.
[20] Chirol to Hardinge, 25 Dec. 1904, Hardinge Papers 7.

ers, a prominent clerk in the Foreign Office, speaking in the aftermath of the Venezuelan crisis, put it clearly: 'The American scare is I hope dying away. I never believed that there was any serious danger, or that, for such a cause, the atrocious folly & crime of a war between us & the US was possible.'[21]

The above litany of despair and dislike needs to be treated carefully. The three men who were British ambassadors to the United States in this period were all pro-American, and the negative remarks cited above need to be counter-balanced by their more positive assessments. For example, while San Francisco was corrupt in the fashion of American cities, after the earthquake there 'the attitude of the American people, as usual in such emergencies is one of confidence and courage'.[22] If Americans tended to be seen as less refined than their British counterparts, they had 'that sort of easy, breezy friendliness of manner' that many Britons found attractive.[23] The standard of living of working people was much higher than in Britain, and the growth of industry and wealth phenomenal. Though American government was corrupt and often incompetent, 'the standard of public virtue is rising'.[24] Bryce, with his long experience of the United States, put things in perspective in 1909:

But something is also due to a real improvement in the tone of American public men. There is less rudeness, less arrogance, less of a brutal self-assertion, and wider outlook upon the world than there was among the prominent men of the last generation. When one sees instances of inordinate national vanity and assertion now, one marks them as exceptional. Thirty years ago they would have been the rule.[25]

However, British views of individual American statesmen were often divided.

This was particularly true in the case of Theodore Roosevelt. 'The divine Teddy', as he was frequently called, was as great a conundrum to his British contemporaries as he has been to historians subsequently. Chirol, an astute observer of the high-and-mighty, made clear after his first meeting with Roosevelt, the difficulty of fathoming the president:

His is certainly a very striking personality, but he takes a lot of knowing, & I cannot profess to have read him. That he is forceful & impulsive everybody knows & he talks very freely & with every appearance of frankness, but I doubt whether the reality quite corresponds to the appearance.[26]

Lansdowne, the British foreign secretary at the time, was only too aware

---

[21] Villiers to Lascelles, 26 Dec. 1895, Lascelles Papers FO 800/15.
[22] Durand to Grey, desp. 75, 20 Apr. 1906, *BDFA I*, C12, 27.
[23] Bryce to Grey, desp. 152, 30 Apr. 1908, *BDFA I*, C13, 177.
[24] Bryce to Grey, desp. 49A, Annual Report for 1909, 4 Mar. 1910, ibid., 134.
[25] Bryce to Grey, desp. 96, 26 Apr. 1909, ibid., 77.
[26] Chirol to Hardinge, 25 Dec. 1904, Hardinge Papers 7.

of the conflicting aspects of Roosevelt. Writing to Durand, the foreign secretary referred to the president as a 'strange being', but confessed that he found Roosevelt 'an attractive personality'.[27] Tellingly, he compared the president to that other enigmatic and erratic contemporary, Kaiser Wilhelm II, a view that was shared by others. Prince Louis of Battenberg, the British director of Naval Intelligence and a man who knew the kaiser well, also found the two leaders 'men of similarity of character and temperament'.[28]

If many found Roosevelt attractive, the British were also aware of another side to him. Durand observed that the president often assumed an 'intolerably didactic, not to say dictatorial' tone to Congress, and that 'his confidence in his own views and his vehement energy have, at various times during his career, led him into a rather high-handed course of action'.[29] And Hardinge, the permanent under-secretary (PUS) at the Foreign Office from 1906 to 1910, could not 'get over the falseness' that Roosevelt had displayed towards Durand when the former had assured the outgoing ambassador that he left Washington with the president's full support.[30] Roosevelt was clearly an elemental and mercurial force. Perhaps Lansdowne put it best, when he concluded his letter to Durand, cited above, with the observation that 'I should be sorry to have to deal with him [Roosevelt] if he happened to be in the wrong mood.'

Views of Roosevelt's secretary of state, Elihu Root, were more consistent. In Root, while he had flaws, the British had found someone they liked and with whom they could work. Durand's summary of the man also speaks volumes about Englishmen's views of Americans generally:

He is, I think, friendly to England, and honest in so far as a keen American politician can be. He has great ability, and a quiet but keen sense of humour. He works very hard – too hard – and is a practised and powerful speaker. His fault is that, though a man of broad and statesmanlike views in most respects, he enters on all negotiations after the manner of a lawyer, anxious to score technical advantages and to make the most of his brief. With much good-will and good feeling he is yet capable, for the sake of his country, of being aggressive and grasping. In short, he is an American, with the leading characteristics of an American, the tendency towards the fault of the Dutch, of giving too little and asking too much.[31]

While Durand was censorious of Root's faults, Bryce was less so. Remembering what he termed the 'brusquerie [and] brutality' of Richard Olney, President Cleveland's secretary of state, Bryce was more than willing to

---

[27] Lansdowne to Durand, 4 Feb. 1905, Lansdowne Papers FO 800/144.
[28] Battenberg to Edward VII, extract, 5 Nov. 1905, Lansdowne Papers FO 800/116.
[29] Durand to Grey, desp. 9, 11 Jan. 1906, *BDFA I*, C12, 3.
[30] Hardinge to Howard, 1 Feb. 1907, Howard Papers (Cumbria County Record Office, Carlisle) DHW 2/11.
[31] Durand to Grey, desp. 238 confidential, Annual Report for 1906, 28 Dec. 1906, *BDFA I*, C12, 101.

overlook any small flaws in Root.[32] 'No one regrets his departure', Bryce wrote as Root left office, 'from the State Department more than I do.'[33] And, the ambassador ventured that Root's impending election to the Senate would 'not only improve the quality of that body, which much needs such improvement, but is of good augury for our relations with the United States'.

As president, William Howard Taft was a disappointment to the British. When he was Roosevelt's secretary of war, Taft had been considered by Durand as a 'really honest' man, with marked 'ability and energy'.[34] This favourable assessment may have been partly due to a certain temperamental affinity between the straightforward giant and the reserved British ambassador, for the latter noted approvingly that Taft was 'the only prominent American politician that I know who can make a well reasoned temperate political speech, without bombast, and without abusing his opponents'.[35] Be that as it may, by the time that his tenure as president had expired, the British were certain that Taft's time in office had not met with success. Bryce thought this due partly to those very qualities that Durand had lauded. 'A little touch of distrustfulness or even of cynicism', the ambassador wrote in April 1911, 'might make him a shrewder judge of men.'[36]

If Taft were regarded as a genial mediocrity, the same might be said of Philander Knox, his secretary of state. From the first, Bryce's opinion of him was mixed. The ambassador found him a man of

shrewd keen intellect of the business lawyer, quick to see where he can gain an advantage, desirous of making his personality felt . . . inclined to be autocratic, rapid in his decisions, and not easy to move from one which he has made, neither indulgent in his judgements, nor sufficiently considerate of the feelings of weaker nations.[37]

Offsetting this, in Bryce's view, was the fact that Knox was 'an upright man, not swayed by unworthy motives, nor masking schemes or intrigues behind his overt acts'. But, by the end of Knox's time in office, Bryce's initial hopes that the secretary might rise to the occasion were disappointed. 'I have never known so singular a case of the failure of a high official to realise the importance of his post.'[38]

The final tandem under consideration was that of President Woodrow Wilson and his secretary of state, William Jennings Bryan.[39] During the

[32] Bryce to Grey, desp. 49A, Annual Report for 1909, 4 Mar. 1910, *BDFA I*, C13, 134.
[33] Bryce to Grey, desp. 36, 6 Feb. 1909, ibid., 105.
[34] Durand to Grey, desp. 238 confidential, Annual Report for 1906, *BDFA I*, C12, 101.
[35] Ibid.
[36] Bryce to Grey desp. 97A, 5 Apr. 1911, *BDFA I*, C14, 44.
[37] Bryce to Grey, desp. 49A, 4 Mar. 1910, *BDFA I*, C13, 134.
[38] Bryce to Grey, desp. 134, 16 May 1912, *BDFA I*, C15, 49.
[39] For British views of Wilson before the war, see G.R. Conyne, *Woodrow Wilson. British Perspectives, 1912–21* (London, 1992), pp. 7–43.

election campaign of 1912, Bryce had remarked that Wilson was 'the standard-bearer' in the Democratic Party 'of radicalism and ultra-democracy'.[40] Wilson represented the new and untried – a true reflection of the American tendency to throw up the novel. He was not long found congenial in the field of foreign policy. In the first encounter between his administration and Britain, Wilson quickly gained the enmity of Sir Arthur Nicolson, Hardinge's successor as PUS. 'The whole policy of President Wilson towards Mexico', Nicolson wrote to his predecessor, 'has been a most inane and futile one. It is worthy of a pedantic university professor, who has no knowledge of the world or practical politics.'[41]

If Wilson was 'a pedantic university professor', Bryan was regarded as even less capable. During the 1908 presidential race, he had been dismissed rather cavalierly by the embassy as

an honest, well-meaning man, with a fine voice, a wonderful flow of words, considerable rhetorical skill in dressing up commonplaces, but little knowledge and no thinking power. He is really rather a Young Man's Christian Association lay preacher rather than a statesman in the European or even in the American sense of the word.[42]

This description had changed little in 1913, when Bryce described the personnel of the new Wilson administration: 'it may be difficult for him [Bryan]', Bryce added condescendingly, 'at his age to accustom himself to a totally different point of view and discipline himself to reticence and caution'.[43]

These were the men with whom the British had to deal. While opinions of their abilities varied, it is clear that Roosevelt and Root were considered by far the strongest pairing. Taft and Knox were considered mediocre, while Wilson and Bryan were thought, respectively, unprepared and incompetent. And it is important to remember that generally Americans were not considered up to the mark socially. When a member of the British Embassy in Washington wrote to Hardinge in 1909 suggesting that the Foreign Office should try and ease the way for Americans visiting London to join clubs, Hardinge's reply was discouraging and disparaging: 'one can realise that members of select clubs would not care to have them invaded by a noisy class of Americans, spitting and drinking cocktails'.[44]

This was not quite the British image of Russia; however, the views of the British ambassadors to St Petersburg – Sir Charles Hardinge (1904–6), Sir Arthur Nicolson (1906–10) and Sir George Buchanan (1910–18) – were not particularly more laudatory concerning the tsarist state.

[40] Bryce to Grey, desp. 120, 26 Apr. 1912, *BDFA I*, C15, 2.
[41] Nicolson to Hardinge, 25 Feb. 1914, Nicolson Papers FO 800/372. For British views of Wilson's Mexican policy generally, see Conyne, *Woodrow Wilson*, pp. 16–41.
[42] Bryce to Grey, desp. 152, 30 Apr. 1908, *BDFA I*, C12, 177.
[43] Bryce to Grey, desp. 84, 31 Mar. 1913, *BDFA I*, C15, 75.
[44] Hardinge to Mitchell Innes, 'Counsellor, Washington', 25 Mar. 1909, Hardinge Papers 17.

For most Englishmen, Russia was an exotic and alien land, the home of despotic government, a land with few civil liberties and a threat to the British Empire.[45] In fact, with a few modifications, most of the reproaches – antisemitism, the Gulag, the prevalence of spies and so on – made concerning the Soviet Union were made just as strongly about tsarist Russia before the first world war.[46]

A noticeable sore point for the British was Russian law, especially its arbitrary nature and the use of police agents. Hardinge had particular reason to be angered about this, for during his tenure as ambassador the Russian government attempted to compromise the security of the Embassy and steal the British cyphers.[47] For Hardinge, these actions were outside the pale of proper behaviour: 'they cannot even be regarded as mediaeval but as simply barbarious and unworthy of any Government with any pretensions to be treated as that of a civilized country'.[48] This 'disgraceful state of affairs' continued for more than two years, with Hardinge and the rest of the Embassy staff moving carefully to counter the Russian endeavours.[49] Nicolson also found espionage a difficult business. The intertwining of police agents and revolutionaries left him scratching his head as to the truth of such matters. 'It is impossible to judge', he wrote to Hardinge about one such case, 'what is true, or what is untrue in the tangled mass of "revelations" which are daily published. Spies & informers are always a shady lot.'

Spies were not the only problem that Hardinge encountered in his brushes with the Russian justice system. British newspaper correspondents often ran afoul of the Russian government, who suspected them of being overly sympathetic to Russian revolutionaries and felt that their reportage was overly critical of the tsarist regime. In December 1904, J.S. Marshall, the correspondent of the *Daily Express*, was summarily ejected from Russia on the suspicion that he was providing secret information to the British naval attaché, a belief that Hardinge rejected.[50] Instead, the ambassador believed that Marshall was expelled in retaliation for

[45] Neilson, *Last Tsar*, chapters 2 and 3.
[46] Keith Neilson, 'Tsars and Commissars: W. Somerset Maugham, *Ashenden* and Images of Russia in British Adventure Fiction, 1890–1930' *Canadian Journal of History*, 28:3 (1992), 475–500; E. Feldman, 'British Diplomats and British Diplomacy and the 1905 Pogroms in Russia', *Slavonic and East European Review*, 65:4 (1987), 579–608; Feldman, 'Reports from British Diplomats in Russia on the Participation of Jews in Revolutionary Activity in Northwest Russia and the Kingdom of Poland, 1905–6', *Studies in Contemporary Jewry*, 3 (1987), 181–203.
[47] Christopher Andrew and Keith Neilson, 'Tsarist Codebreakers and British Codes', *Intelligence and National Security*, 1:1 (1986), 6–12.
[48] Hardinge to Spring Rice, 28 Mar. 1906, Hardinge Papers 8.
[49] Hardinge diary entry, 21 Oct. 1904, Hardinge Papers 5; an interesting memoir account of these activities is in Nevile Henderson, *Water Under the Bridges* (London, 1945), pp. 29–33.
[50] Hardinge to Bertie, 21 Dec. 1904, Bertie Papers, FO 800/176; Hardinge to Knollys, 22 Dec. 1904, and Hardinge to Sanderson, 22 Dec., both Hardinge 6.

Hardinge's efforts to thwart the secret police in their quest to penetrate the Embassy. Hardinge generalised from the Marshall case: 'What makes this place quite odious is the perpetual intrusion everywhere of the secret police.'[51] In 1911, Buchanan had a similar difficulty with the Russians when Harold Williams, the Russian correspondent for the *Morning Post* (owned by Buchanan's sister-in-law, Lady Bathurst) was accused of espionage.[52] Buchanan believed none of the charges; instead, he felt that Williams was merely a pawn in a larger game being played by the Russian secret service, whose object was to manufacture evidence in a separate case.[53] In any case, neither Hardinge nor Buchanan had any reason to believe in Russian justice.

Nor did they have any confidence in the honesty of the Russian government. When Hardinge had served earlier in St Petersburg, as first secretary of the embassy, he had been responsible for keeping track of Russian budgets. This experience led him to note that 'a Russian budget is very easy to "fake" as there is practically no control'.[54] Equally, Hardinge found Russian officials lacking in veracity and likely to go back on their word: 'Verbal statements', he wrote to the Foreign Office, 'or conversations with Russians Ministers are like water on a duck's back, & when inconvenient are forgotten, but anything in writing, however unofficial its form, is remembered.'[55] Business dealings in Russia were often fraudulent, and the embassy was well aware of the need to bribe officials in order to ensure contracts.[56] Hardinge, in fact, went to far as to describe corruption as 'the Russian system', a belief shared by Buchanan.[57]

In foreign affairs, the Russians were generally considered extremely difficult and untrustworthy. In Hardinge's view, the Russians understood only force and strength in international relations. As he noted after a successful challenge to Russian actions in China, the British success was 'entirely due to the firmness with which the question has been treated at home. I am *quite* sure that that is the proper way to treat the Russians.'[58] Further, the Russians could not be trusted; on the eve of the Russo-Japanese War, Hardinge opined that, 'The responsibility [for the crisis]

---

[51] Hardinge to Bertie, 21 Dec 1904, Bertie Papers FO 800/176.

[52] See the account of this incident by Williams' wife: A. Tyrkova-Williams, *Cheerful Giver: the Life of Harold Williams* (London, 1935), pp. 123–24.

[53] Buchanan to Grey, tel. 53, 13 Feb. 1912, and minutes FO 371/1467/6442.

[54] Hardinge to Sanderson, 24 Nov. 1900, Hardinge Papers 3; and see Hardinge to Lansdowne (foreign secretary), desp. 40, 16 Jan. 1905, FO 65/1698.

[55] Hardinge to Sanderson (PUS), 9 Oct. 1901, Hardinge Papers 3; see also, Hardinge to Lansdowne, 24 Nov. 1904, Lansdowne Papers FO 800/141.

[56] Keith Neilson, 'Russian Foreign Purchasing in the Great War: A Test Case', *Slavonic and East European Review*, 60 (1982), 572–90; O'Beirne (British chargé d'affaires, St Petersburg) to Grey, desp. 308, 16 Oct. 1913, FO 371/1747/47540.

[57] Hardinge to Howard (British minister, Stockholm), 28 Apr. 1917, Howard Papers, DHW 4/Official/9; Buchanan to Grey, tel. 1205, 22 Aug. 1915, FO 371/2454/117261.

[58] Hardinge to Bertie, 15 Nov. 1900, Bertie Papers (British Library, London) Add MSS 63014.

seems to me to rest entirely with the Russians who have shown their usual bad faith throughout.'[59] However, Hardinge's opinions were not entirely shared, particularly by Nicolson. Nicolson served in Russia when Anglo-Russian relations were on a better footing than they had been during Hardinge's time in St Petersburg. Partly because of this, and partly because of a more trusting nature, Nicolson had more confidence in Russian diplomacy and Russian officials than did his predecessor.[60] Like Nicolson, Buchanan got along well with the Russians, but Sir George shared Hardinge's exasperation with Russian methods, feeling that it 'requires an enormous amount of patience in dealing with Russians'.[61]

The nature of the Russian government was of particular interest to the British. For Hardinge, there was no doubt that Russia was misgoverned and badly in need of reform. Writing to Sir Thomas Sanderson, the PUS at the Foreign Office, the ambassador noted that 'all thinking persons seem now to be agreed . . . that the Autocracy on its present basis cannot continue. Reforms & large reforms must be introduced. As it is, the Autocracy has many able & honest servants, a large number of courtiers but no partisans.'[62] Nicolson, who came to Russia in the midst of the revolutionary turmoil of 1906, agreed with Hardinge, but was realistic in his appraisal of how fast reform could be undertaken in a country where liberal institutions had few or shallow roots. 'As we find it necessary to govern India by an autocracy', he noted in his diary, 'so it is necessary to govern Russians.'[63] And, in a remark that revealed the cultural superiority – not to mention a certain degree of hypocrisy – that most Englishmen felt towards the tsarist state, Nicolson added that 'in India it is an enlightened & benevolent autocracy & hitherto this cannot be said in respect to this country'. Buchanan, whose war-time experience with Russia left him frustrated by the administrative incompetence of the tsarist government, believed that, 'unless drastic measures are taken to reform the administration', revolution was likely.[64]

In a country where the government was intensely personal, the significance of individuals loomed large. At the centre of the government stood the enigmatic figure of Nicholas II. Of the three British ambassadors, perhaps Hardinge had the best opportunity to know the emperor personally, for the ambassador's close personal ties to Edward VII gave him a special *entrée* to court circles. Hardinge liked Nicholas II, but found him exasperating. During the Russo-Japanese War, the ambassador was shocked by what he termed the 'mystic fatalism which is deeply imbued'

[59] Hardinge to Bertie, 8 Feb. 1904, Bertie Papers FO 800/176.
[60] Morley to Minto, 2 Nov. 1906, Morley Papers (India Office Library, London) Eur D 573/1.
[61] Buchanan to Howard, 20 Oct. 1916, Howard Papers DHW 5/5.
[62] Hardinge to Sanderson, 1 Feb. 1905, Hardinge Papers 7.
[63] Nicolson diary entry, 27 July 1906, Nicolson Papers PRO (Private MSS Collection, Public Record Office, Kew) 30/81/13.
[64] Buchanan to Grey, tel. 1205, 22 Aug. 1915, FO 371/2454/117261.

in Nicholas.[65] Further, he felt that Nicholas did not 'realise the extreme gravity of both the external and internal situations', and thus 'sees nobody and spends his time playing with the baby [the heir apparent]'.[66] Nicolson, who had few opportunities to see the emperor, as the latter spent most of his time carefully guarded from potential assassins, shared some of Hardinge's concerns.[67] While Nicolson found Nicholas 'strongly liberal in all his views and leanings', he noted that the ruler 'has intensely domestic tastes, and is devoted to the joys of home and family' to the detriment of his public duties.[68] During the first world war, Buchanan often spoke with Nicholas, but was always cognisant of the need to avoid the appearance of interference in Russian domestic politics, any semblance of which Nicholas resented.[69] This policy was adhered to generally, but there was immense frustration with Nicholas's approach to government: 'The contrast between what he might do & what he is doing', Sir Edward Grey, the British foreign secretary, noted in 1916, 'is intolerable!'[70] Nonetheless, while Buchanan also was critical of Nicholas's choice of political advisers, the ambassador was certain that Nicholas was a reliable ally.[71]

Such an evaluation did not apply to all of Nicholas's advisers and ministers. The British Embassy kept a careful watch on the personnel of the Russian government, since their views would affect Russia's policy towards Britain. Perhaps the most important man to hold office during this time was Sergei Witte, who acted variously as Nicholas II's minister of finance and chief minister. Witte, who had been a favourite when he advocated a pacific foreign policy favourable to Britain, drew mixed reviews from the British ambassadors. 'Once he is in power', Hardinge wrote of Witte in 1905, 'he is all right, but he fishes for his own advantage in troubled waters, and he is likely to continue to stir up the mud until his position is assured.'[72] This was particularly the case when Witte was removed from office in 1906. From the margins of power, Witte advocated a pro-German Russian foreign policy, which Nicolson and Hardinge both felt dangerous to British interests.[73] However, as Witte possessed an overbearing personality that the emperor found offensive, most were convinced that Nicholas II would not restore Witte to favour.[74]

[65] Hardinge to Sanderson, 15 Feb. 1905, Hardinge Papers 6.
[66] Hardinge to Bertie, 14 Feb. 1905, Bertie Papers FO 800/176.
[67] Nicolson to Hardinge, 22 Feb. 1908, Hardinge Papers 12.
[68] Reported in Morley to Minto, 17 June 1908, Morley Papers Eur D 573/3.
[69] Keith Neilson, 'Wishful Thinking: The Foreign Office and Russia 1907–1917', in McKercher and Moss, eds., Shadow and Substance, pp. 162–3.
[70] Grey to Crewe (acting foreign secretary), 24 July 1916, Crewe Papers (Cambridge University Library, Cambridge) C/17.
[71] Buchanan to Grey, desp. 19, 28 Jan. 1916, FO 371/2745/25836; Buchanan to Nicolson, 4 Feb. 1916, FO 371/2743/22897.
[72] Hardinge to Lansdowne, 4 Jan. 1905, Lansdowne Papers FO 800/141.
[73] Nicolson to Grey, desp. 95, 15 Feb. 1907, and Hardinge's minute, FO 371/321/6333.
[74] Hardinge to Lansdowne, desp. 42, 17 Jan. 1905, FO 65/1698; Buchanan to Grey, desp. 102, 2 Apr. 1912, and minutes, FO 371/1468/14640; Nicolson to Buchanan, 18 May 1914, Nicolson Papers FO 800/374.

Another significant figure was Peter Stolypin, the chairman of the council of ministers from 1906 until his assassination in 1911. Stolypin was Nicolson's favourite minister. The ambassador was impressed by the strong measures taken by the Russian in order to quell the domestic disturbances in the wake of the revolution of 1905. Early in Stolypin's time as chairman, Nicolson reported him as 'wonderfully calm & determined'.[75] Nicolson's admiration for Stolypin grew with time, and was widely shared at the Foreign Office.[76] While Buchanan had only a brief experience of Stolypin, he, too, found him admirable: 'the more I see of Stolypin', Sir George wrote in May 1911, 'the more I like him'.[77] Upon Stolypin's death, Nicolson wrote with real sorrow and noted that he would be 'difficult to replace'.[78]

Naturally, the British were particularly interested in Nicholas II's foreign ministers. Aleksandr Izvolskii (minister 1906 to 1910) and Sergei Sazonov (minister 1910 to 1916) were the two most prominent in the decade before the first world war. Izvolskii was felt initially to be a man of 'much intelligence and a very hard worker' if somewhat vain and susceptible to 'flattery'.[79] This opinion, which stemmed from a British diplomat who had known Izvolskii well earlier in the Russian's career, soon became the accepted one.[80] Even Nicolson, who initially had found Izvolskii 'timorous & afraid of responsibility' and 'disinclined to submit to any drudgery', changed his mind, and came to accept the earlier evaluation of Izvolskii.[81] Most important for the British, Izvolskii came to be regarded as a staunch advocate of a Russian foreign policy friendly to Great Britain. Hardinge was of this opinion when Izvolskii came to office, and, during the negotiations for the Anglo-Russian Convention of 1907, Nicolson came to share this view.[82] Indeed, when Izvolskii seemed likely to be removed from office as a result of the Bosnian crisis of 1908–9, both Hardinge and Nicolson made efforts to shore up his position by praising his abilities.[83] While Nicolson was aware that Izvolskii did not always tell 'the *whole* truth', Izvolskii was generally well regarded in British circles.[84]

So, too, was Sazonov. Just before he came to office, Sazonov was not

---

[75] Nicolson diary entry, 6 Sept. 1906, Nicolson Papers PRO 30/81/13.

[76] Nicolson to Grey, desp. 383, 27 Aug. 1908, and minutes, FO 371/519/30064; Nicolson to Hardinge, 11 Mar. 1909, Nicolson Papers FO 800/337; Nicolson to Grey, tel. 234, 30 Apr. 1909, and minutes, FO 371/729/1636; Nicolson to Grey, desp. 327, 25 May 1909, and minutes, FO 371/731/21127.

[77] Buchanan to Nicolson, 4 May 1911, Nicolson Papers FO 800/348.

[78] Nicolson to Grey, memo, 18 Sept. 1911, Grey Papers FO 800/93.

[79] Johnstone (British minister, Copenhagen) to Grey, very confidential desp., 56, 9 May 1906, FO 371/125/17344.

[80] Spring Rice to Grey, 10 May 1906, Grey Papers FO 800/72.

[81] Nicolson to Grey, 5 July, 12 Sept., 21 Nov. 1906, all Nicolson Papers FO 800/337.

[82] Hardinge's undated minute on Johnstone to Grey, tel. 6, 7 May 1906, FO 371/121/15601; Nicolson to Grey, 26 Sept. 1906, Nicolson Papers FO 800/337.

[83] Hardinge to Nicolson, private tel., 8 Apr. 1909, FO 371/729/13412.

[84] Goschen (British ambassador, Berlin) diary entry, 9 July 1910, in C.H.D. Howard, ed., *The Diary of Edward Goschen 1900–1914* (London, 1980), p. 208, original emphasis.

felt likely to be 'equal to the occasion', an opinion that was reinforced when the new minister travelled to Potsdam late in 1910 and, in British eyes, appeared to have been 'lamentably weak in his dealings with the Germans'.[85] However, for the British, Sazonov improved with time. After his brief flirtation with Germany, Sazonov began to steer a firmly pro-British course. By early 1914, when there were rumours of Sazonov's dismissal, he had become a favourite:

We all know his defects, and I must say he has lost few opportunities in displaying them, but at the same time he is a thoroughly sincere adherent to our understanding and is acquainted in a certain measure with the English character and opinions. Here is moreover, a thoroughly straightforward man and anxious to remain on the very best footing with us.[86]

Indeed, during the war, Sazonov's continued tenure in office was regarded by the British as an indicator of the tsarist regime's continued adherence to the Entente. His dismissal in 1916 was felt to adumbrate a more reactionary policy by the Russian government, with possible serious consequences for Anglo-Russian relations and for the existence of the autocracy itself.[87]

II

Quite evidently, ambassadors and their embassies helped to draw the 'mental maps' of the United States and Russia that served to guide British foreign policy with respect to those two states. And, equally clearly, each country and its leaders were felt to have specific characteristics and natures. These, in turn, meant that, if British policy were to be determined and implemented effectively, the individuals serving in the embassies had to be selected with care.

Durand's supersession in Washington illustrates this perfectly. Despite Sir Mortimer's personal warmth towards America, he failed to get on with Roosevelt.[88] From 1904 through 1907, a series of stop-gap measures were employed by the Foreign Office, in the hope of creating a conduit between Britain and America independent of Durand. The first step in this endeavour was Chirol's visit to America in 1904. Armed with a letter of introduction from Spring Rice (an old friend of Roosevelt), Chirol went to Washington with Lansdowne's blessing to sound out Roosevelt on the latter's attitude to the Russo-Japanese War and on Durand's effectiveness as

---

[85] Hardinge to Nicolson, 27 Sept. 1909, Nicolson Papers FO 800/342; Buchanan to Grey, 26 Jan. 1911, Grey Papers FO 800/74.

[86] Nicolson to Hardinge, 25 Feb. 1914, Nicolson Papers FO 800/372.

[87] The minutes on Buchanan to Grey, private and secret tel., 20 July 1916, FO 371/2750/ 144394; Grey to Crewe, 22 July 1916, Crewe Papers C/17.

[88] Bradford Perkins, *The Great Rapprochement. England and the United States, 1895–1914* (New York, 1968), pp. 227–8.

ambassador.[89] While Chirol was unable to resolve the differences in the British and American positions in the Far East, he was able to impress 'very strongly' on Lansdowne the need for a change in the personnel at the embassy, 'in view of Durand's limitations'.[90] The best solution, Chirol argued, was to appoint a new counsellor at the Embassy, especially one 'very well posted in the Far Eastern question'. The same conclusion was reached by Spring Rice, who, with the approval of the Foreign Office, followed Chirol across the Atlantic to spend his holidays with Roosevelt.

Upon his return to London, Spring Rice reported to Lansdowne about the state of British representation in Washington.[91] While Spring Rice realised that: 'owing to the differences of age & character Sir M. Durand was at a disadvantage in dealing with the President', 'Springy' felt that this could be overcome – given that Roosevelt appeared to like Durand personally – by means of a change in the personnel at the Embassy. Spring Rice's suggested candidates made it evident just how the perceptions could influence postings.

As counsellor, Spring Rice suggested that Lansdowne should send Hugh O'Beirne, already 'well known in Washington' from his time there in the 1890s. At a lower level, Spring Rice added, 'a man like [Ronald] Lindsay would be popular & respected'. Why did Spring Rice suggest these two individuals and what did the reasons that he had for doing so say about Washington? From the very beginning of his career, O'Beirne had been marked as a high flyer. When he left his first post, O'Beirne did so with the accolades of his ambassador following him.[92] Subsequent employment had confirmed this assessment, and when it was proposed, as Spring Rice suggested, that O'Beirne be sent to Washington from Paris, the British ambassador there immediately protested against his loss.[93] Bertie's objections were overridden in London: 'I am pretty well convinced', Grey's private secretary replied, 'that it [sending O'Beirne] is the best thing that we can do to put things right in Washington.'[94]

In the event, this did not occur. But two things emerge clearly from the fact that someone with O'Beirne's abilities, particularly his facility to get along with people (O'Beirne is 'very useful socially' a Foreign Office official noted) was suggested for Washington.[95] First, Washington was now significant enough that someone thought likely to rise to the top of the diplomatic service should be sent there. Second, it was clear that the American capital required a certain type of personality. In this respect, it

---

[89] Chirol to Hardinge, 15 Nov. 1904, Chirol to Hardinge, 17 Jan. 1905, both Hardinge Papers 7.
[90] Chirol to Hardinge, 9 Jan. 1905, Hardinge Papers 7.
[91] Spring Rice's memo, Feb. 1905, Lansdowne Papers FO 800/116.
[92] Lascelles to Sanderson, 22 May 1895, Lascelles Papers FO 800/17.
[93] Bertie to Drummond, 22 Feb. 1905, Bertie Papers FO 800/183.
[94] Mallet to Bertie, 23 Feb. 1905, Bertie Papers FO 800/183.
[95] Mallet to Nicolson, 21 June 1906, Nicolson Papers FO 800/338.

is significant that Spring Rice's other suggestion, that Ronald Lindsay be moved to Washington, *was* acted upon. For Lindsay, 'the tall blue eyed extremely handsome Ronald Lindsay', as a colleague described him, was of the type certain to be successful in Washington.[96] With his good looks, affable personality and love of polo, Lindsay was ideal for Washington, and, indeed, would crown his career with his own appointment as ambassador in 1930. If Spring Rice himself was still too young and too junior to be made ambassador to Washington in 1905 – the course preferred by Roosevelt[97] – it was evident that suitable substitutes would be despatched in his place.

This should be borne in mind when considering Durand's replacement. By late 1906, Roosevelt's disdain for Durand had reached a point where it was manifest that the ambassador would have to be removed. Spring Rice, newly installed as minister to Teheran, was still unavailable and still too junior. The question became: who should be sent? In his memoirs, Hardinge recollected that he had suddenly seized upon Bryce in a flash of inspiration.[98] The reality was more complex. First, the policy of substitutes had not ended with the employment of Lindsay. Lord Edward Gleichen, a cousin of Edward VII and a wounded war veteran, was sent to Washington as military attaché in 1906 in the hope that he and the president would prove compatible.[99] When Gleichen failed to come up to the mark, Hardinge found another, more successful, candidate.

This was Esme Howard. Howard, a contemporary and friend of Spring Rice, had pursued a somewhat unusual career.[100] After entering the diplomatic service, Howard served for only five years and resigned at the age of twenty-eight. For the next dozen years, he pursued various careers – he ran unsuccessfully for parliament, he worked among the urban poor in London, he prospected for gold in South Africa and fought there in the Boer War, and he travelled up the Amazon and in various other remote areas. In 1903, he resumed his diplomatic career, and, between 1903 and 1906, made a name for himself by his careful handling of the Cretan imbroglio and the irascible personality of Prince George. Here was a man well-suited for Washington and Teddy Roosevelt. Howard had the requisite qualities of the outdoorsman and man of action that the president demanded and a proven ability to get along with unpredictable people. With Howard as counsellor of embassy and Lindsay as secretary, Hardinge had overcome the weakness in personnel at Washington.

---

[96] Sir Henry Beaumont, *Diplomatic Butterfly*, typescript memoir (microfilm copy, Imperial War Museum, London).

[97] Knollys to Bertie, 28 Nov. 1903, Bertie Papers FO 800/163.

[98] Hardinge of Penshurst, *Old Diplomacy* (London, 1947), pp. 131–2. Conyne, *Woodrow Wilson*, pp. 7–8, argues that it was Grey who thought of Bryce. Both are simplistic.

[99] Perkins, *Great Rapprochement*, p. 228.

[100] See B.J.C. McKercher, *Esme Howard. A Diplomatic Biography* (Cambridge, 1989), pp. 1–70.

The search for Durand's replacement underlined the difficulty that finding a suitable person for Washington entailed. Edward VII, prone to meddle in diplomatic postings, had no doubts as to the proper successor. The king wrote to the prime minister, Sir Henry Campbell-Bannerman, in November 1906 that Hardinge himself should go to Washington.[101] In a couple of years, the king suggested, Hardinge 'might then be succeeded by Sir Cecil Spring Rice'. This galvanised Hardinge. He had taken the post of PUS in order to shape general policy, and was not to be deflected from this course by going to America. He immediately set his good friend and the king's private secretary, Lord Knollys, to persuade Edward that such a move was out of the question, and, pursued by Knollys' rejoinder that if he wished to avoid Washington, 'pray put forward some eligible man for the post as soon as you are able', began to search hard for the requisite person.[102]

Given that, as Hardinge later informed Bryce, 'we have not got a soul in the FO who has ever been to Washington except myself & it is nearly 20 years since I left' (and how significant this remark was with its implication for the relative insignificance of the United States as a post before 1900), it was not surprising that the net had to be cast wide.[103] As one wit at the Foreign Office wrote to Spring Rice: 'The Washington stakes are still very undecided & every day brings a new starter most of whom I consider rankers.'[104] Among those considered, in addition to Hardinge, were Lord Rosebery, a former prime minister, who declined the post and Gerard Lowther, the incumbent British minister to Morocco, who did not wish to accept for personal reasons.[105] Unable to find either a suitable luminary outside the diplomatic service or an established diplomat within it, it seems plausible to think that Hardinge seized upon Bryce as the candidate of last resort.

Certainly, Bryce's candidacy was not looked upon with favour in some corners. Chirol, writing in the mistaken belief that Bryce had been considered but rejected, was caustic: 'Bryce's candidature was at one moment seriously considered. He is the one conspicuous failure in the Cabinet – obviously a high qualification for one of the most difficult of the diplomatic posts. Fancy him in the grip of the forceful Teddy!'[106] Chirol went on to outline what qualities a successful candidate should possess: he should be 'quite able to go riding & shooting & "humbug" with the Presidential Nimrod'. Recalling his earlier visit to Washington, Chirol pointed out that he had attempted to emphasise these points to Durand two years before,

---

[101] Edward VII to Campbell-Bannerman, 20 Nov. 1906, Hardinge Papers 9.
[102] Knollys to Hardinge, 24 Nov. 1906, ibid.
[103] Hardinge to Bryce, 26 Dec. 1906, Bryce Papers (Bodleian Library, Oxford) USA 27.
[104] Tyrrell to Spring Rice, 28 Nov. 1906, Spring Rice Papers FO 800/241.
[105] Lowther to Nicolson, 12 Jan. 1907, and Villiers to Nicolson, 30 Jan. 1907, both Nicolson Papers FO 800/339.
[106] Chirol to Nicolson, 27 Nov. 1906, Nicolson Papers FO 800/338.

and had told the ambassador that 'the "discretion" & "reserve" which are the qualities that you deem most important in British Ambassador in Washington may come to be mistaken for aloofness & indifference, if not for actual outrageousness'. Durand had been obdurate. 'But nothing', concluded Chirol in 1906, 'I suppose, could permanently have unfrozen him.'

Despite Chirol's forebodings, which were shared by some in the diplomatic service, Bryce's appointment had much to recommend it.[107] First, Bryce was a well-known academic authority on the United States. Second, he had travelled widely in that country, had the kind of wide-ranging mind that Roosevelt found congenial and, despite his advancing years, was an avid outdoorsman. Further, Bryce was the first chairman of the Anglo-American League, founded in 1898 to promote friendship between the two countries. And, if Bryce had been a failure, as Chirol alleged, in the Cabinet as Irish secretary, his well-known support for Home Rule would serve to mollify the highly irrational and vocal Irish-American element. With his Embassy buttressed by keen, capable young men like Howard and Lindsay, Bryce seemed well situated to repair any damage done to Anglo-American relations by Durand.

This proved to be the case. Leaving much of the nuts and bolts of diplomacy to the younger men, particularly Howard, Bryce moved with consummate grace and tact to restore the vital personal element in Washington.[108] Within a few months of Bryce's arrival, Howard could write admiringly that:

The Bryces are making a very good impression indeed, so far as I can judge. He is cultivating the politicians vigorously, & she does not snub the millionaires as I feared she might, but treats everyone with the same friendly spirit, which is just the right thing. I am afraid, poor man, he has let himself in for a terrible job, as he has invitations to make speeches in every town of the States & in every college & university, let alone attending ceremonial dinners.[109]

Further, during his time in America, Bryce travelled to every state in the Union. This assiduous cultivation of the public in America, coupled with deft bargaining on outstanding diplomatic issues, meant that Bryce left the United States in 1913 with the strained atmosphere of the Durand era just a memory.

This brings us back to Spring Rice.[110] By 1913, he seemed set to inherit his patrimony. At fifty-three and having been minister at Teheran and Stockholm, he now possessed the age, experience and seniority the lack of which had disbarred him from being appointed to Washington ten years

---

[107] Lowther to Nicolson, 12 Jan. 1907, and Villiers to Nicolson, 30 Jan. 1907, both Nicolson Papers FO 800/339.
[108] McKercher, *Howard*, pp. 71–100.
[109] Howard to his brother, Stafford, 7 Mar. 1907, Howard Papers DHW 5/86.
[110] There is a recent biography: D.H. Burton, *Cecil Spring Rice. A Diplomat's Life* (London and Toronto, 1990).

before. But there were adumbrations that his time in Washington might not prove to be the unalloyed success that a first glance would suggest was likely. The first pertained to his personality. Spring Rice had always been well known for his caustic wit and inability to suffer fools gladly. Had his good friend Roosevelt been president, this trait would not have mattered; with the egregious Bryan and the hypersensitive and pedantic Wilson in office, problems were likely. Spring Rice himself knew that he might have difficulties succeeding the immensely popular Bryce, due to the quirks in his own personality. 'I shall get a good many bricks hurled at my head', he wrote of his appointment in 1913, 'especially when they realise that I am not a Bryce and do not intend to kiss Sunday school girls or lay foundation stones.'[111] Second, Spring Rice's judgement had not always impressed his seniors at the Foreign Office. In particular, during his time in Persia he had objected strenuously to the proposed Anglo-Russian Convention, and complete confidence was no longer freely given in London to his views.[112] Still, he seemed the obvious man for the job. As his former chief at the Foreign Office wrote of Spring Rice's appointment: 'I am afraid he will not have a very congenial Secretary of State to deal with, but he quite understands Americans, and has a strong sense of humour.'[113] Perhaps he did, but the combination of Spring Rice's personality and the changes in personnel in the American administration meant that he began as ambassador in 1913 with a far smaller chance of a successful tenure than he would have had a decade earlier. By 1918, he was ambassador in name only, isolated from Wilson's administration and completely bypassed in the essentials of Anglo-American relations.[114] The lessons of 1905 to 1913 had been ignored, and the result was chaos.

The selection of an ambassador for Russia was seen as a much more important matter than the choice of Whitehall's man in Washington. Russia was one of the European great powers and the possessor of a sprawling empire that impinged on Britain's own imperial possessions. If it were important that Anglo-American relations remain on an even keel, it was imperative that Anglo-Russian relations were not strained.

Whereas there was a shortage of suitable candidates for Washington, this was not the case for St Petersburg. As one of the plum appointments in the diplomatic service, it was avidly coveted by most senior diplomats and filling the post was more a matter of choosing the most suitable candidate. Hardinge's appointment was due to a combination of his own talents, Hardinge's royal connections and the lobbying efforts of Sir Frank Bertie,

---

[111] Spring Rice to Howard, 26 Mar. 1913, Howard Papers DHW 4/Personal/18.
[112] Morley to Minto, 28 Feb. 1907, Morley Papers Eur D 573/2; Hardinge to Nicolson, 8 Jan. 1907, Nicolson Papers FO 800/339.
[113] Sanderson to Hardinge, 25 Apr. 1913, Hardinge Papers 93.
[114] Burton, *Spring Rice*, pp. 153–203; Kathleen Burk, *Britain, America and the Sinews of War 1914–1918* (London, 1985).

the British ambassador to Rome and Hardinge's close friend.[115] But, Hardinge had wished for St Petersburg for reasons other than pure ambition; he was convinced of the need for better Anglo-Russian relations, a belief he shared with Lord Lansdowne. As Hardinge was one of the brightest stars in the diplomatic service, it was not surprising that the foreign secretary had been susceptible to the pleas to appoint 'Capability' Hardinge to Russia.

Hardinge's time as ambassador was brief, but tumultuous. After the Russo-Japanese War, he returned to the Foreign Office as PUS, determined to use this key position to ensure that his view of policy was followed. Russia was central to his vision, and thus he worked hard to ensure that his successor as ambassador to St Petersburg shared his views on foreign policy.[116] His choice was an old friend, Sir Arthur Nicolson. While Nicolson and Hardinge saw eye-to-eye on the correct line to take with Russia, and Nicolson had been a success as ambassador to Madrid, convincing Lansdowne that he was 'quite to be trusted anywhere', there was one factor that came close to blocking Nicolson's appointment.[117] This reflected the nature of Russia. In a country where much of diplomatic life swirled around public engagements and social gatherings, the fact that Nicolson and, especially, his wife did not possess social graces militated against him. It was only with some reluctance that Nicolson's proven abilities were thought to outweigh the fact that social *gaucheries* might reduce the effectiveness of his embassy.

Nicolson spent four years in Russia, during which time he helped bring an end to a century of Anglo-Russian enmity by negotiating the Anglo-Russian Convention. In 1910, when Hardinge was appointed viceroy of India, Nicolson succeeded his friend as PUS. For both Nicolson and Hardinge, finding a successor to the former as ambassador was a key task, since Russia remained at the centre of their common plan for maintaining Britain's own pre-eminence. With the Convention in place, what was required in St Petersburg was a man of tact and discretion who could deal comfortably with Nicholas II. The first choice fell upon Gerard Lowther, whom Grey wished to move from Constantinople, but the ambassador turned the appointment to Russia down.[118] This left the way open to the man whom Nicolson later described to Hardinge as 'your candidate and mine', Sir George Buchanan.[119] Buchanan's qualifications were solid, but

[115] Steiner, *Foreign Office*, pp. 73–4; B.C. Busch, *Hardinge of Penshurst: A Study in the Old Diplomacy* (Hamden, 1980), pp. 68–9.
[116] The following, except where otherwise noted, is based on Keith Neilson, ' "My Beloved Russians": Sir Arthur Nicolson and Russia, 1906–1916', *International History Review*, 9:4 (1987), 524–5.
[117] Lansdowne to Balfour (prime minister), 28 Sept. 1905, Balfour Papers (British Library, London) Add MSS 49729.
[118] Hardinge to O'Beirne, 5 July 1910, Hardinge Papers 21.
[119] Nicolson to Hardinge, 2 Mar. 1911, Nicolson Papers FO 800/347.

not exceptional. He had done well at all his posts, and had proved particularly adroit in handling the difficult and slippery character of King Ferdinand of Bulgaria. It was Buchanan's tact and level-headedness that made him attractive to Hardinge. 'I am glad to hear that Buchanan is doing well in St Petersburg', the viceroy wrote, 'I felt sure he would as he is a gentleman and quite sensible although not overburdened with brains.'[120] Indeed, Buchanan fulfilled Hardinge's and Nicolson's expectations. Nicolson admired the way in which Buchanan was able to 'use forcible language without causing the slightest irritation in Sazonoff's mind', and, during the war, both the PUS and Grey were confident that Buchanan could approach Nicholas II on the most delicate topics and cause as few difficulties as possible.[121]

III

What, in light of the above, are we to make of Bertie's oft-quoted remark concerning the influence of ambassadors? First, it is important to consider the circumstances. In August 1904, when Bertie made the remark, the British ambassador at Rome was temporarily in London, standing in as PUS for Sir Thomas Sanderson, who was ill.[122] The 'Bull', as Bertie was often termed due to his thrusting personality, had not enjoyed his time in Rome, where he felt isolated socially and unable to influence decisions. His five months as acting PUS must have reinforced his discontent. Thus, at least in part, his remark can be discounted as reflecting only his personal dissatisfaction and not the general situation. Second, Bertie's argument by analogy was misleading. Whereas marionettes are inert instruments, manipulated by the puppeteer, ambassadors were not passive playthings, manoeuvred by foreign secretaries. Instead, they were active participants in the *process* of formulating and carrying out foreign policy. While foreign policy was ultimately the responsibility of the foreign secretary and the Cabinet, what that policy was, the way it was determined and the fashion in which it was carried out was the province of a wider body of individuals, a foreign-policy-making elite, including the ambassadors.[123]

The care taken with ambassadorial appointments reflected this fact. As each country was perceived by the Foreign Office as having particular and

---

[120] Hardinge to Nicolson, 29 Mar. 1911, Nicolson Papers FO 800/348.

[121] Nicolson to Goschen, 18 May 1914, Nicolson Papers FO 800/374; Nicolson to Grey, note, 18 Oct. 1915, Grey Papers FO 800/75; Buchanan to Grey, 26 May 1917, and minutes, FO 371/3010/107040.

[122] Keith Hamilton, *Bertie of Thame. Edwardian Ambassador* (London, 1990), pp. 51–2, 60–3.

[123] The notion is from D.C. Watt, 'The Nature of the Foreign-Policy-Making Elite in Britain', in Watt, *Personalities and Policies. Studies in the Formulation of British Foreign Policy in the Twentieth Century* (London, 1965), pp. 11–15.

unique characteristics – and the ambassadors also helped to determine what these characteristics were thought to be – each country demanded an ambassador whose personality, talents and training were deemed congruent with the requirements of the post. An ambassador suitable for America might not be suitable for Russia. It was, indeed, a case of 'horses for courses'. That Bertie was not the correct choice for Rome demonstrates this point clearly, and it imparts a certain irony to the way in which his observation on the role of ambassadors has been interpreted. For, if ambassadors were marionettes, then they were more like Pinocchio – with ambitions and influences of their own – than Bertie would have allowed.

CHAPTER 5

Old diplomacy and new: the Foreign Office and foreign policy, 1919–1939

Before the war I was called obstinate, prejudiced, unbalanced; during and after it the epithets clung and grew. They may be true; if they are not they are an interesting record of the anger that one can rouse by hampering the desire for a compromise never possible with regimes whose nature rejects it. Vansittart, 1958[1]

It's the old complex – the old ideology . . . I haven't got such lack of faith in our diplomacy that I daren't open up with friend or foe. This was the grand fault of our policy 1933–1938 . . .

Cadogan, August 1943[2]

Between 1918 and 1939, the Foreign Office lacked the influence over British foreign policy that it had exercised before the outbreak of the Great War.[3] Part of the reason stemmed from other departments of state seeking to force their views on the Cabinet and its advisory bodies about what British interests were and how best to protect them. Another came from the fact that far more than before 1914 there existed a range of articulate individuals and powerful domestic organisations that, having their intellectual roots in wartime criticism of the 'old diplomacy' practised before 1914, were both interested in foreign policy and sought to influence its

---

[1] Lord Vansittart, The Mist Procession. The autobiography of Lord Vansittart (London, 1958), p. 550.

[2] Cadogan diary, 11 Aug. 1943, in D. Dilks, ed., The Diaries of Sir Alexander Cadogan 1938–1945 (London, 1971), p. 551.

[3] Here, Zara Steiner's work must be considered the last word. See her The Foreign Office and Foreign Policy, 1898–1914 (Cambridge, 1969); 'The Foreign Office under Sir Edward Grey', in F.H. Hinsley, ed., British Foreign Policy Under Sir Edward Grey (Cambridge, 1977), pp. 22–69; and 'Elitism and Foreign Policy: The Foreign Office Before the Great War', in B.J.C. McKercher and D.J. Moss, eds., Shadow and Substance in British Foreign Policy 1895–1939. Memorial Essays Honouring C.J. Lowe (Edmonton, 1984), pp. 19–55.

nature and content. Finally, there were the efforts of the two prime ministers at the beginning and end of the period, respectively, David Lloyd
George and Neville Chamberlain, to bring foreign policy under Downing
Street's control. Still, less Foreign Office influence did not necessarily
translate into a loss of authority for politically powerful foreign secretaries
and their 'professional' advisers. By 1925, three years after Lloyd George
fell from power, his revolution in having Downing Street control British
external relations had all but evaporated thanks to a counter-attack by
three of these foreign secretaries – Lord Curzon, James Ramsay MacDonald and Austen Chamberlain – and the Foreign Office permanent under-
secretary (PUS), Sir Eyre Crowe. Thereafter, until late 1937, the Foreign
Office dominated the foreign policy-making process. This situation was
helped by Crowe's successors, especially Sir Robert Vansittart, PUS from
January 1930 to December 1937. As the civil service head of the Foreign
Office and, in essence, the chief diplomatic adviser to the Cabinet, each
PUS proved to be a good bureaucratic infighter able to demonstrate to
his political masters the efficacy of 'old diplomacy' in protecting British
external interests. Thus, for a dozen years after 1925, the Foreign Office
served prime ministers who largely deferred to the advice of the 'professionals', blunted the encroachments of other ministries and neutralised
the admonitions of those private individuals and pressure groups working
to influence the shape and content of the government's diplomatic strategies. Only when Neville Chamberlain renewed prime ministerial control
over foreign policy – in large part by removing Vansittart from office – was
Foreign Office influence severely curtailed. This meant that in the last
years of peace before the outbreak of the second world war, amateurs
determined and implemented British foreign policy, amateurs who
thought that they had struck upon a new kind of diplomacy to safeguard
Britain and its Empire.

Until Vansittart's ouster, interwar foreign secretaries, their principal
advisers in London, and most senior members of the Diplomatic Service
comprised the leading element of a generation of men who had gained
control of British foreign policy in the decade and a half before 1914. An
insightful recent analysis has labelled this group the 'Edwardians', named
for King Edward VII, who succeeded to the throne in January 1901 and
shared its world view.[4] They replaced the 'Victorians', diplomatists like
the third Marquess of Salisbury, who had dominated British foreign policy
since Lord Palmerston's death in 1865. Given the late nineteenth century
supremacy of the Royal Navy and a relative political equilibrium on continental Europe – the centre of great power and, thus, world affairs – 'Victorians' as diverse as Salisbury, Benjamin Disraeli and William Gladstone

---

[4] K.E. Neilson, *Britain and the Last Tsar: British Policy and Russia, 1894–1917* (Oxford, 1995), pp. 48–50.

eschewed alliances with other powers that involved future British commitments to go to war. As Salisbury wrote as late as 1896:

in 1892, as now, we kept free from any engagements to go to war in any contingency whatever. That is the attitude prescribed to us on the one hand by our popular constitution, which will not acknowledge the obligations of an engagement made in former years – and on the other hand by our insular position which makes the burdensome conditions of an alliance unnecessary for our safety.[5]

But changing circumstances at the turn of the nineteenth century – widespread international antipathy towards Britain crystallised by the Boer War, Germany's determination to build a high seas fleet coupled with Berlin's hegemonic designs on the Continent, and increasingly dangerous imperial rivalries with France and Russia – suggested to a newer group of men that formal commitments were necessary for British security.[6] These men came to share the belief that Britain had to combine with those powers that shared its interests, at the price of offering pledges of future support, to maintain the balances of power in Europe and the wider world crucial to British interests. The result was the Anglo-Japanese alliance of 1902, the ententes with France (1904) and Russia (1907), and the advent of secret Anglo-French staff talks beginning in 1906.[7] This does not suggest that the 'Victorians' and their successors disagreed with the maxim that Britain had no eternal friends or enemies, only eternal interests. Nor does it indicate that they disagreed about the ends of policy: maintaining the balances of power in Europe and elsewhere to ensure peace and security. Rather, it is to say that the 'Victorians' and the 'Edwardians' disagreed on diplomatic means. However, when pressed to protect perceived British interests, neither the 'Victorians' nor the 'Edwardians' shied away from using or threatening force to underpin their foreign policy, something seen in both Disraeli's willingness to send the fleet to Constantinople in 1878 and the Liberal government's decision to go to war in 1914.

The 'Edwardians', therefore, had a profoundly different conception about how to protect Britain's position as a global power than did those who dominated foreign policy for the generation after 1865; and prior to the July crisis of 1914, although there might be differences in emphasis,

---

[5] Salisbury to Lascelles (British ambassador, Berlin), 10 Mar. 1896, in C.J. Lowe, *The Reluctant Imperialists. British Foreign Policy 1878–1902*, II, *The Documents* (London, 1967), pp. 110–11. Cf. K. Bourne, *The Foreign Policy of Victorian England, 1830–1902* (Oxford, 1970).

[6] Not all 'Edwardians' were younger men. Joseph Chamberlain, Salisbury's colonial secretary, was born in 1830, the same year as the prime minister. Even before the Boer War, reckoning that Britain needed allies, he advocated an Anglo-German alliance. See R. Jay, *Joseph Chamberlain. A Political Study* (Oxford, 1981), pp. 216–27, 253–6.

[7] Cf. C.J. Lowe and M.L. Dockrill, *The Mirage of Power*, vol. I, *British Foreign Policy 1902–14* (London, 1972); A.L. Friedberg, *The Weary Titan. Britain and the Experience of Relative Decline, 1895–1905* (Princeton, 1988); Neilson, *Last Tsar*; I.H. Nish, *The Diplomacy of Two Island Empires* (London, 1966).

these views were shared by those responsible for making and executing foreign policy: Lord Lansdowne, the foreign secretary from 1900 to 1905; Sir Edward Grey, his successor who held office until December 1916; a range of senior politicians from both major parties like Arthur Balfour, the Unionist prime minister from 1902 to 1905, and Herbert Asquith, the Liberal prime minister from 1908 to 1916; and career diplomats like Sir Charles Hardinge, twice PUS (1905–10, 1916–20), Sir Arthur Nicolson, who held that post in the interim, Crowe, then a rising star in the Foreign Office, and Sir William Tyrrell, Grey's private secretary. Along with Vansittart, who joined the Diplomatic Service in 1903, most of those who achieved positions of prominence in the interwar Foreign Office and Diplomatic Service began their careers in the fifteen years or so before 1914: these included Sir George Clerk (1898), successively ambassador at Prague, Constantinople and Paris from 1919 to 1937; Sir Cecil Hurst (1902), the legal adviser from 1918 to 1929; Sir Miles Lampson (1903), the ambassador at Peking from 1926 to 1933 and then, in Egypt, high commissioner to 1936 and ambassador until 1946; Sir Ronald Lindsay (1899), the ambassador at Berlin from 1926 to 1928, at Washington from 1930 to 1939, and PUS from 1928 to 1930; Sir Eric Phipps (1898), the ambassador at Berlin from 1933 to 1937 and Paris from 1937 to 1939; Sir Orme Sargent (1906), one of the chief Foreign Office German experts after 1919; and Sir Victor Wellesley (1899), the deputy under-secretary for ten years after 1925.

After serving apprenticeships doing menial departmental and chancellery tasks and, if showing promise, receiving increased responsibilities, these diplomats and their contemporaries approached diplomacy as the preserve of 'professionals'. Harold Nicolson, Sir Arthur Nicolson's son and a gifted diplomat in his own right, called this 'the Foreign Office mind'; more prosaically, Owen O'Malley, who entered the Foreign Office in 1911, talked of 'the brotherhood'.[8] Such attitudes derived from the relative homogeneity of the class and educational background of the 'professional' diplomats, the unstated assumption that they were members of the most socially exclusive and prestigious department of state in Whitehall, and the shared notion that only a particular individual – 'the type of man who is fit for this international career called diplomacy' – could succeed.[9] The continuity of beliefs amongst pre- and post-war 'Edwardians' can be seen in their memoirs.[10] Those of Hardinge and Vansittart, the

---

[8] Nicolson's comment, made in parliament in 1939, is quoted in Steiner, 'Elitism', p. 53; O. O'Malley, *The Phantom Caravan* (London, 1954), p. 157.

[9] Cf. R. Jones, 'The Social Structure of the British Diplomatic Service 1815–1914', *Histoire Sociale – Social History*, 14:27 (1981), 59–66; Steiner, 'Elitism'. The quotation is from the 'Fifth Report of the Royal Commission on the Civil Service' (1914), quoted in Steiner, *Foreign Office*, p. 19.

[10] Representative are L. Collier, *Flight from Conflict* (London, 1944); J.D. Gregory, *On the Edge of Diplomacy: Rambles and Reflections, 1902–1928* (London, 1929); N.M. Henderson,

permanent under-secretaries at the beginning and end of the 'Edwardian' period of the Foreign Office, are exemplary.[11] They laud professional expertise; they disparage what they perceive were the ill-conceived ideas of Lloyd George and Neville Chamberlain that endangered Britain's security because they ignored diplomatic realities like maintaining the balances of power;[12] they have little use for public opinion groups like the Union for Democratic Control (the UDC) and the League of Nations Union (the LNU) that, supposedly, were willing to subordinate British narrow interests to a wider international morality; and they argue that foreign policy is successful only if buttressed by the combined economic and armed strength of the state. Implicit in both memoirs is the notion that the will to pursue a hard line, including armed force against menacing powers, is a *sine qua non* for effective diplomacy; the 'professionals', of course, possessed such will. The ideal was to deter threatening powers but, if necessary, such powers had to know that Britain would fight rather than back down. Although elements of self-justification and dishing old enemies permeate these recollections, they testify to the style and attitudes – 'old diplomacy' in Hardinge's phrase – of the 'Edwardian' generation of 'professionals' that dominated the Foreign Office until at least 1937.

It is critical to understand that the idea of the balance of power suffused 'Edwardian' thinking about foreign policy, especially in the interwar period. The creation of the League of Nations at the Paris Peace Conference in 1919 begat a belief amongst contemporary critics of 'old diplomacy' that a new era of openness and cooperation had emerged whereby, within the international organisation, states would sublimate their narrow interests and forego dangerous alliances to foster the general international good.[13] The emergence of the League has also suggested to more recent scholars that 'collective security' underpinned British diplomatic strategies for most of the next twenty years – and, as a corollary, that the ultimate failure of collective security occurred largely because of British wavering over whether to commit their strength to support League endeavours such as international arms limitation and oppose transgressors

---

Water Under the Bridges (London, 1945); F.O. Lindley, *A Diplomat Off Duty* (London, 1928); L. Oliphant, *An Ambassador in Bonds*, 2nd edn (London, 1947); V.A.H. Wellesley, *Diplomacy in Fetters* (London, 1944). Then see Z. Steiner, 'The Diplomatic Life: Reflections on Selected British Diplomatic Memoirs Written Before and After the Great War', in G. Egerton, ed., *Political Memoir. Essays on the Politics of Memory* (London, 1994), pp. 167–87.

[11] Hardinge of Penshurst, *Old Diplomacy. The Reminiscences of Lord Hardinge of Penshurst* (London, 1947); Vansittart, *Mist Procession*.

[12] This was not retrospective criticism. See Hardinge's disdain for 'amateur diplomacy and illicit bargains' in Hardinge to Rennell Rodd (British ambassador, Rome), 26 May 1917, Hardinge MSS (University Library, Cambridge) 32.

[13] Cf. R. Cecil, *The Moral Basis of the League of Nations* (London, 1923); R. Dell, 'Peace, Disarmament and the League', *New Statesman*, 23 (2 Aug. 1924), 485–6; J.E. Grant, *The Problem of War and Its Solution* (London, 1922).

of peace.[14] Such criticism is misdirected because it fails to appreciate that, except for the first few years after the Great War, interwar British external policies were not based on the collective will of the League to maintain international peace and security. For the post-war 'Edwardians', collective security was an illusion. Admittedly, a number of politicians, including Anthony Eden, the foreign secretary from December 1935 to February 1938, became committed to the goals of the Covenant.[15] Even some Foreign Office officials, like Sir Alexander Cadogan, responsible for League affairs in the Foreign Office Western Department from 1924 to 1933 and Vansittart's successor as PUS, possessed a belief in the League's ability to maintain international peace and security. And given the large membership of organisations like the LNU, political leaders paid lip service to the ideals of the Covenant.[16] However, the 'Edwardians' prided themselves on seeing the world for what it was, not what it should be. For them, essential British interests had not changed because of the war, indeed, they were compounded thanks to the acquisition of mandated territories in the Middle East and Africa; after 1918, only the constellation of powers that threatened those immutable interests had altered.

Consequently, those who dominated the Foreign Office until 1937, both the permanent officials and the foreign secretaries – except Eden – saw the League only as another tool in the British diplomatic arsenal. If tying particular foreign policies to Geneva benefited Britain, for instance, supporting League-sponsored disarmament discussions after 1926 that might allow for arms cuts by all the powers, there was little opposition. But if diplomatic success meant concluding agreements outside the purview of the international organisation, as occurred with the conclusion of the Locarno Treaty in October 1925, a regional security arrangement in western Europe, then the dictates of *realpolitik* shaped British foreign policy. Like the 'Victorians' before them, the interwar 'Edwardians' did not see a balance existing only on continental Europe. Rather, they saw several balances in those areas of the globe judged vital to British and imperial security. Though they gave expression to these multiple balances in terms of questions needing answers – the 'Mediterranean question', the 'Chinese question', and so on – they approached the issue of national security as one of meeting specific threats in particular parts of the world. Grand

---

[14] Cf. P. Kyba, *Covenants without the Sword: Public Opinion and British Defence Policy, 1931–1935* (Waterloo, ON, 1983); B.A. Lee, *Britain and the Sino-Japanese War, 1937–1939. A Study in the Dilemmas of British Decline* (Stanford, 1973); P.J. Noel Baker, *The First World Disarmament Conference, 1932–1933, and Why It Failed* (London, 1979); D. Richardson, *The Evolution of British Disarmament Policy in the 1920s* (London, 1989).

[15] See FO memorandum (FP 36(5)), 'Reform of the League of Nations', 13 July 1936, CAB (Cabinet Archives, Public Record Office, Kew) 27/626. Cf. Earl of Avon, *Facing the Dictators* (London, 1963), pp. 317–18.

[16] S. Baldwin, 'War and Peace. The League of Nations', in Baldwin, *The Torch I Would Hand to You* (London, 1937), pp. 32–43.

strategy, thus, entailed pursuing foreign and defence policies that considered a series of interlocking questions on a global scale.

Within the post-1919 Foreign Office, therefore, the doctrine of the balance of power held sway; and in this regard, Crowe provided its intellectual basis. In 1907, he had penned a 'Memorandum on the present state of British relations with France and Germany' that later came to be seen as the classic exposition of the principles of the balance of power.[17] By defending Britain's 1904 entente with France as a means of containing German ambitions, and in stressing that British foreign policy was based on the strength of the Royal Navy, respected the independence of smaller powers, and promoted unrestricted commerce, Crowe's analysis laid out the axioms of the balance of power:

The only check on the abuse of political predominance derived from such a position has always consisted in the opposition of an equally formidable rival, or of a combination of several countries forming leagues of defence. The equilibrium established by such a grouping of forces is technically known as the balance of power, and it has become almost an historical truism to identify England's secular policy with the maintenance of this balance by throwing her weight now in this scale and now in that, but ever on the side opposed to the political dictatorship of the strongest single State or group at a given time.

Whilst the circle of those who read this paper in 1907 seems to have been limited – and its initial impact uncertain[18] – Crowe's juniors embraced it after 1920. Nurtured in the ethos of the pre-1914 Foreign Office and, after the war, being promoted to important diplomatic posts during Crowe's time as PUS, these men subsequently poured undiluted praise on Crowe because of their appreciation of his diplomatic skills and his wide strategic vision.[19] Vansittart, for one, called his memorandum 'one of the few diplomatic documents that achieved fame in a world of technicians'; he also pointed out that it 'advocated friendship with neighbours and banishment of fear by maintenance of strength'.[20] It has been argued, correctly, that the 'Crowe doctrine' became the litmus by which all policy discussed within the Foreign Office was measured until the early 1950s:[21] it was only briefly – and disastrously – superseded by the new approach to foreign

---

[17] Crowe, 'Memorandum on the Present State of British Relations with France and Germany', 1 Jan. 1907, in G.P. Gooch and H. Temperley, eds., *British Documents on the Origins of the War* (hereafter *BD*), III (London, 1928), pp. 397–420.

[18] Cf. Steiner, *Foreign Office*, p. 112, n1.

[19] For instance, I. Kirkpatrick, *The Inner Circle* (London, 1959), p. 12; H. Nicolson, *Peacemaking 1919* (London, 1933), p. 211; Lord Strang, *Home and Abroad* (London, 1956), pp. 271–3.

[20] Vansittart, *Mist Procession*, pp. 62–3; *Events and Shadows* (London, n.d.), p. vii. Cf. B.J.C. McKercher, 'The Last Old Diplomat: Sir Robert Vansittart and the Verities of British Foreign Policy, 1903–1930', *Diplomacy and Statecraft*, 6 (1995), 1–38.

[21] This is the thrust of J. Connell, *The 'Office': A Study of British Foreign Policy and Its Makers, 1919–1951* (London, 1958).

policy that marked the two peacetime years of Neville Chamberlain's brief tenure as premier; then because of the exigencies of fighting a second 'Great War', it fell into suspended animation until 1945.

Finally, stress must also be made on the fact that the 'Edwardians' were not consistently for or against particular powers; rather, they understood that international conditions were such that Britain had no permanent friends or enemies. For instance, in the decade before 1914 and in the 1930s, especially after Adolf Hitler became German chancellor in January 1933, Foreign Office officials held deep suspicions about German foreign policies. Such feelings arose because of the perception that German diplomacy had as its aim the weakening of other European powers in order to make Germany dominant on the Continent. But the charge that the interwar Foreign Office was so permeated with Germanophobia that such attitudes blinkered its advice fails to consider the world view of the 'Edwardian' professionals. Any power that threatened the European balance or those others integral to imperial and trade defence was treated with equal distrust. Before the war, Hardinge, Crowe and other advisers were just as wary when the Russians or the French threatened perceived interests.[22] The same attitude informed 'professional' advice after 1919 and, in this regard, Vansittart is probably the best example. He has long been characterised as the leading 'anti-German' in the interwar Foreign Office, the legacy of contemporary criticisms by his adversaries in the British government, like Neville Chamberlain and Eden, who sought to discredit him and win unrestrained control over foreign policy.[23] As Eden said in his memoirs:

[Vansittart] clearly saw the growing military power and political ambition of Nazi Germany as the principal danger. To meet this he was determined to keep the rest of Europe in line against Germany, and would pay almost any price to do so ... he expressed himself with such repetitive fervour that all except those who agreed with him were liable to discount his views as too extreme.[24]

Yet, it remains that, like other 'Edwardians', Vansittart had a more subtle view of external threat. In the 1920s, France and the United States were far stronger than Germany. Paris looked to keep Germany in a weakened

---

[22] For instance, Hardinge to Bertie (British ambassador, Paris), 28 Sept. 1904, Bertie MSS FO (Foreign Office archives, Public Record Office, Kew) 800/15; Hardinge to Nicolson, 22 Feb. 1907, Nicolson MSS FO 800/339; Crowe minute, 24 Jan. 1910, FO 371/825/2602/ 2602; Crowe memorandum, 14 Jan. 1912, BD, VII, 821–6.

[23] For contemporary criticism, see Harvey (Eden's private secretary) diary, 7 Mar. 1937, in J. Harvey, ed., The Diplomatic Diaries of Oliver Harvey, 1937–1940 (London, 1970), p. 22; Neville Chamberlain to Ida, his sister, 14 Nov. 1937, NC (Neville Chamberlain MSS, the University Library, Birmingham) 18/1/1028. Then cf. M. Gilbert and R. Gott, The Appeasers (London, 1963), pp. 23–4; H. Montgomery-Hyde, Neville Chamberlain (London, 1976), p. 109; R. Rhodes James, Anthony Eden (London, 1986), p. 116; N. Rose, Vansittart. Study of a Diplomat (London, 1977), pp. 35, 37.

[24] Avon, Facing the Dictators, pp. 242–3.

position so as to enhance its security, and, thereby, lead in continental affairs; Washington's consistent efforts to affect Anglo-American naval parity struck at the heart of imperial defence. In those years, Vansittart did not shirk from advocating the hardest line *vis-à-vis* either power, especially towards the latter when he headed the Foreign Office American Department from 1924 to 1928.[25] But as the passage of time brought changes to the international array of power, especially following Hitler's capture of the German chancellorship, his perception of what constituted the greater threat changed. As he told Phipps in September 1934, when charges of his anti-Germanism circulated in Berlin: 'I recollect with some entertainment that [Tyrrell] used to think me rather anti-French at one time. You are certainly right in saying I am pro-British.'[26] 'It is a question of our policy', he informed some of his senior advisers sixteen months later, 'the one that suits us best, not of any pro-this or anti-that, for the Northern Department that favours the loan [to Russia] is no more pro-Russian than the Central Department that favours credits is pro-German.'[27]

Foreign Office ability to influence interwar British diplomatic strategies derived from two factors: the determination of the two immediate post-war permanent under-secretaries, Hardinge and Crowe, to ensure that diplomats who thought as they did held key positions in the Foreign Office and Diplomatic Service; and the efforts of Curzon, MacDonald, and Austen Chamberlain to repel as much as possible outside interference in policy-making. As noted earlier, the zenith of Foreign Office authority over policy occurred in the fifteen years before 1914. Lansdowne and Grey each had strong political bases in the governing parties in parliament; each had the unqualified support of the prime ministers under whom they served; and each guarded their right to control policy by fending off other ministers. As a consequence, especially after administrative reforms in 1905 designed to handle better the increasing amounts of information that reached London by despatch bag and telegraph, Foreign Office advisers had great authority over British external relations. In Hardinge's case, thanks to a close friendship with Edward VII, his views also found a receptive audience in influential circles outside Whitehall that added to the political clout of the permanent officials in high policy-making circles. Naturally, Lansdowne, Grey and other politicians did not follow 'professional' advice unquestioningly. Grey's views reflected his own attitudes, plus the political

---

[25] For instance, Vansittart minute, 23 Mar. 1927, Vansittart to Howard (British ambassador, Washington), 4 Apr. 1927, both FO 371/12038/2249/128.

[26] Vansittart to Phipps, 29 Sept. 1934, PHPP (Phipps MSS, Churchill College, Cambridge) 2/17.

[27] Vansittart minute, 15 Jan. 1936, FO 371/20338/4794/20. I am indebted to Michael Roi for this reference.

reality of public opinion represented in the House of Commons.[28] Consequently, when Crowe pushed too hard for an early British commitment
to go to war against Germany during the 1914 July crisis, Grey admonished
him and blocked his certain promotion to succeed Nicolson as PUS.[29] But
this sort of incident constituted an intradepartmental dispute that did not
weaken Grey's political hand; the foreign secretary's success in August
1914 in convincing both the Cabinet and the House of Commons about
the need for Britain to go to war is almost legendary. By 1914, the Foreign
Office stood at the peak of its power within the British government.

This had changed by 1918. Much of the reason obtained from the
nature of wartime diplomacy. To speed decision-making, the Treasury,
the armed services, and other departments like the Ministry of Munitions
negotiated directly with their Allied counterparts to coordinate economic
and strategic policies.[30] Added to this, the Foreign Office became the
target of domestic critics, like the radical UDC, for its pre-war pursuit of
'old diplomacy'.[31] Battles like Ypres and the Somme seemed only to confirm the charge made by E.D. Morel, the UDC leader, in September 1914:
'Potentates, diplomatists, and militarists made this war.'[32] Most important,
after rising to the premiership in December 1916 at the head of a coalition
ministry, Lloyd George arrogated control of foreign policy for himself. He
distrusted professional diplomats, saw the Foreign Office and Diplomatic
Service as strongholds of aristocratic privilege, and wanted to revolutionise
foreign policy by directing British external relations from Downing
Street.[33] When Balfour succeeded Grey in December 1916, Lloyd George
denied him a seat in the new War Cabinet; by the end of the war, Foreign
Office ability to influence policy-making had been severely constrained.
Although prime ministerial control of wartime diplomacy irked 'pro-

---

[28] Cf. K. Robbins, *Sir Edward Grey. A Biography of Lord Grey of Fallodon* (London, 1971),
pp. 125–297; Robbins, 'The Foreign Secretary, the Cabinet, Parliament and the Parties',
in F.H. Hinsley, ed., *British Foreign Policy Under Sir Edward Grey* (Cambridge, 1977),
pp. 3–21.

[29] M.G. Eckstein and Z. Steiner, 'The Sarajevo Crisis', in Hinsley, *Grey*, pp. 397–410. For
a different interpretation, see S. Crowe and E.T. Corp, *Our Ablest Public Servant. Sir
Eyre Crowe, GCB, GCMG, KCB, KCMG, 1864–1925* (Braunton, Devon, 1993), pp. 255–
73. A thorough treatment of its subject, this study must be read with an eye to its tenden-
tious nature and its gratuitous dialectical slaps at anyone who ever criticised, even mildly,
Crowe.

[30] Cf. D. French, *British Strategy and War Aims, 1914–16* (Boston, 1986); K.E. Neilson,
Strategy and Supply. The Anglo-Russian Alliance, 1914–17 (London, 1985).

[31] Cf. C.A. Cline, *E.D. Morel 1973–1924. The Strategies of Protest* (Belfast, 1980); M. Swartz,
The Union of Democratic Control in British Politics During the First World War (Oxford,
1971).

[32] UDC Pamphlet No. 1 (anonymous, but Morel), *The Morrow of the War* (London, n.d.,
but Sept. 1914), p. 14.

[33] Cf. K.O. Morgan, 'Lloyd George's Premiership: A Study in "Prime Ministerial Government"', *Historical Journal*, 13 (1970), 130–57; R.M. Warman, 'The Erosion of Foreign
Office Influence in the Making of Foreign Policy, 1916–1918', *Historical Journal*, 15
(1972), 133–59.

fessionals' like Hardinge, the unpleasant fact was that, in wartime, diplomacy became secondary to coordinating more important issues of strategy and supply.[34]

Just before the armistice on the western front, Hardinge began the campaign to reassert Foreign Office authority over foreign policy when he lobbied Balfour to have only Foreign Office officials and leading members of the Diplomatic Service serve on the British Delegation to the Peace Conference.[35] Apart from wanting an 'ambassador' – himself – to run the Delegation secretariat, he contemplated having six senior 'professionals' – all 'Edwardians' who had achieved success during the war – serve as 'diplomatic advisers' responsible for policy touching the regions of Europe and the world where post-war adjustments had to be made: Crowe, who had coordinated the wartime blockade, would handle north-western Europe; Sir Esme Howard, the minister at Stockholm, north-eastern and eastern Europe; Sir Ralph Paget, the minister at Copenhagen, southern and south-eastern Europe; Sir Louis Mallet, the pre-war ambassador at Constantinople, the Middle East; Gerald Spicer, the senior clerk, Africa; and James Macleay, the counsellor at the Peking Embassy until 1916, the Far East. Lloyd George scotched these plans.[36] With his coalition returned to office following a general election in December 1918, he continued with his diplomatic revolution. The Cabinet secretary, Sir Maurice Hankey, beholden to Lloyd George, was put in charge of the administration of the Delegation.[37] On the Delegation itself, the 'professional' diplomats were reduced to a 'Political Section', outnumbered by numerous friends of the premier, serving officers, and a flood of officials from the Treasury, the Board of Trade and other ministries. Moreover, Lloyd George and the American, French and Italian leaders, respectively Woodrow Wilson, Georges Clemenceau and Vittorio Orlando, were determined to shape the peace treaties. Staffing sub-committees and commissions, lower level

---

[34] On Hardinge's discomfort, see Hardinge to Bertie (British ambassador, Paris), 18 May 1917, Hardinge MSS 32; Hardinge to Spring Rice (British ambassador, Washington), 4 Oct. 1917, ibid., 34. On Hardinge admitting the limitations of regular diplomacy in wartime, see Hardinge to Wingate, 28 Aug. 1918, ibid., 38.

[35] Hardinge to Balfour, 10 Oct. 1918, enclosing Hardinge memorandum, 'Peace Negotiations', 10 Oct. 1918, Lloyd George MSS (House of Lords Record Office, London) F/3/3/35; Hardinge to Howard (British minister, Stockholm), 8 Nov. 1918, enclosing Hardinge memorandum, 'Preparations for the Peace Conference', 8 Nov. 1918, Howard MSS (Cumbria County Record Office, Carlisle) DHW 9/29. Cf. E. Goldstein, *Winning the Peace. British Diplomatic Strategy, Peace Planning, and the Paris Peace Conference, 1916–1920* (Oxford, 1991), pp. 23–6.

[36] Nicolson, *Peacemaking*, p. 26. Cf. M.L. Dockrill and J.D. Goold, *Peace Without Promise. Britain and the Peace Conferences 1919–23* (London, 1981); Goldstein, *Winning the Peace*.

[37] '[Hankey] is an admirable Secretary, but with no diplomatic experience and no knowledge of Europe, and it is apparently regarded as a very grave slight to the Foreign Office and to Lord Hardinge ...'; Headlam-Morley (FO Historical Adviser) diary, 19 Jan. 1919, in A. Headlam-Morley, R. Bryant, and A. Cienciela, eds., *Sir James Headlam-Morley. A Memoir of the Paris Peace Conference 1919* (London, 1972), p. 8.

delegates were to give these decisions shape. Hence, high level decisions by-passed the experts, including Hardinge. And isolation from the centre of peace-making was not restricted only to the Foreign Office PUS; Balfour also found himself kept at a distance from the 'Big Three'.

Yet, despite their diminished role, several Foreign Office experts were able to influence the territorial and other settlements by virtue of their work on the sub-committees and commissions. Vansittart, for instance, having served before 1914 in Teheran and Cairo, worked on the Turkish settlement – the Treaty of Sèvres – which was not completed until August 1920. Indeed, when the Treaty of Versailles with Germany was signed on 28 June 1919 and the senior statesmen, including Hardinge, departed the Peace Conference, Vansittart and other experts remained in Paris. He worked closely with Lord Derby, the ambassador, and because Curzon, interested in the Middle East, succeeded Balfour in October 1919, as the new foreign secretary.[38] In Derby's estimation, Vansittart's contribution was 'admirable';[39] allied with Curzon's equally favourable view of his abilities, this led to Vansittart's promotion as Curzon's private secretary in December 1920. Similarly, Harold Nicolson over Balkan questions, Spicer on African issues, Hurst over legal matters, and others helped fashion the remaining four peace treaties.[40] Admittedly, on some major questions, Lloyd George refused to endorse 'professional' advice. The most spectacular example concerned Howard's support for defensible Polish frontiers necessary to maintain the Eastern European balance of power.[41]

Still, it remains that Foreign Office counsel was felt on a range of issues touching Britain's position in the post-war world. The most important came from Crowe. In the first phase of the Conference, he found himself immersed in a range of questions concerning the German settlement.

---

[38] Cf. Vansittart memorandum, 'British Desiderata in Regard to the Baghdad Railway', n.d. (but Feb. 1919), Vansittart, Forbes Adam, 'Memorandum on Turkish Settlement by Political Section of British Peace Delegation', 18 Dec. 1919, both *British Documents on Foreign Affairs*, pt. II, ser I, vol. 11 (hereafter in the style *BDFA*, II, 11I), 131–6, 236–44; Vansittart minute, 25 Aug. 1919, FO 608/152.

[39] Derby to Curzon, 11 May 1920, Curzon MSS (India Office Library, London) F/6/3.

[40] Cf. Nicolson minute, 9 May 1919, FO 608/54; Nicolson to Kerr (Lloyd George's private secretary), 27 May 1919, Lothian MSS (Scottish Record Office, Edinburgh) GD 40/17/ 216; Nicolson minute, 1 July 1919, FO 608/51; Spicer memorandum, 'Some of the principal points concerning Africa to be dealt with at the Peace Conference', 17 Jan. 1919, Spicer memorandum, 20 Jan. 1919, both FO 608/219; Spicer minute, 27 Jan. 1919, FO 608/217; Hurst memorandum for Balfour, 20 July 1919, FO 608/152; Hurst minute, 29 July 1919, FO 608/145; Hurst minute, 23 Aug. 1919, FO 608/141.

[41] See Howard diary, 1 July 1919, Howard MSS DHW 1/5. The myth that Howard's Catholicism, rather than his regard for the balance of power, informed his attitudes towards the Polish settlement is repeated mindlessly in Crowe and Corp, *Crowe*, p. 375, n.11. Cf. B.J.C. McKercher, *Esme Howard. A Diplomatic Biography* (Cambridge, 1989), pp. 197–233.

Juggling his prime minister's demands with those of the French, Italians and Americans, plus the sensitivities of smaller powers like Belgium, he looked to establish stability on the continent.[42] This meant seeking to arrange a post-war European balance between the French, now the strongest power on the continent, and Germany, whose defeat had whetted its neighbours' appetite for territory and revenge. Moreover, as Hardinge distanced himself from the day to day diplomacy of peace-making, Crowe gradually emerged as the dominant Foreign Office personality at Paris. His labours during the war, chiefly over the nettled question of blockade, had done much to restore his career damaged by the dispute with Grey in July 1914. Then, showing his diplomatic skills at Paris, he was charged by Lloyd George in the autumn of 1919 to serve as the British delegate on the 'Council of Five', the chief policy-making body of the Conference, when senior British statesmen were absent.[43] Crowe's subsequent contributions to the remaining peace negotiations won accolades from Curzon and others.[44]

Although Lloyd George was not always happy with Crowe's work – Crowe's attitudes did not always accord with those of the prime minister[45] – by mid-1920 Crowe's rehabilitation was complete. This turned out to be crucial to the reemergence of the Foreign Office at the centre of British foreign-policy-making as the new international order established by the Paris peace settlement came into effect. Tired, disillusioned by his marginalisation during the Peace Conference, and with a personal animus towards Curzon[46] – both men were former Indian viceroys – Hardinge accepted the offer of the Paris Embassy in August 1920. Despite Hardinge's campaign to have his protégé, Sir Ronald Graham, a career diplomat, succeed him as PUS, Crowe had the support of more powerful political patrons, including Curzon, Balfour, and Lord Robert Cecil, the assistant foreign secretary during the war who had doubled as minister of blockade.[47] Not surprisingly – except, perhaps, to Hardinge – Crowe became PUS in October 1920. In partnership with Curzon, he continued

---

[42] Cf. Crowe memorandum, 22 Jan. 1919, FO 608/2; Crowe minute, 29 Jan. 1919, FO 608/125; Crowe minute, 5 Mar. 1919, FO 608/46; Crowe minute, 7 May 1919, FO 608/137; Crowe minute, 19 Jun 1919, FO 608/151.

[43] Lloyd George to Crowe, 15 Sept. 1919, FO 608/162.

[44] For instance, Crowe despatch (1966) to Curzon, 16 Oct. 1919, FO 608/46; Crowe despatch (2133) to Curzon, 12 Nov. 1919, FO 608/50; Crowe to Kerr, 18 Nov. 1919, Lothian MSS GD 40/17/208. On support for Crowe's work, Curzon to Lloyd George, 9 Dec. 1919, enclosing Derby to Curzon, 8 Dec. 1919, Curzon MSS F/12/2/10.

[45] Kerr to Crowe, 14 Nov. 1919, and reply, 18 Nov. 1919, both Lothian MSS GD 40/17/208; Lloyd George to Curzon, 10 Dec. 191, Curzon MSS F/12/2/11.

[46] Hardinge to Graham, 10 Apr. 1920, Hardinge MSS 42.

[47] On promoting Graham, see Graham to Hardinge, 25 July 1916, Hardinge MSS 3; on criticism of Crowe, see Bertie note of a conversation, 16 Aug. 1916, Bertie MSS FO 800/163. On Crowe's selection, see Crowe and Corp, *Crowe*, pp. 397–9.

the campaign to reassert the control of the 'professionals' in the Foreign Office and Diplomatic Service so as to shape foreign policy.[48]

By mid-1920, three of the four most important embassies were held by the prime minister's friends and political cronies: Paris by Derby; Berlin by Lord D'Abernon, a financier; and Washington by Sir Auckland Geddes, a former president of the Board of Trade – Sir George Buchanan, a career diplomat, was in Rome. In addition, private secretaries in Downing Street, chiefly Philip Kerr, conducted interviews with foreign dignitaries and fashioned policies in the prime minister's name with little reference to the Foreign Office.[49] Curzon lent his support to his officials' drive to undermine Lloyd George's foreign policy revolution. By late 1920, he was annoyed both personally and politically with Lloyd George for having 'evolved a Foreign Policy of his own, & of which the Foreign Office were often unaware'.[50] In fact, Curzon considered resigning several times between 1919 and 1922. However, his political colleagues, chiefly, Balfour and Austen Chamberlain, the Unionist Party leader, asked him to stay in office to prevent one of Lloyd George's political confederates from succeeding him – Winston Churchill was named specifically; and, just as important, 'the Foreign Office implored me to stay on as the only antidote to Lloyd George's dictatorship'.[51] It cannot be denied that Lloyd George's diplomacy – conducted in a series of conferences at Cannes, Genoa and other continental resorts and, at crucial capitals, through the medium of hand-picked dilettantes – severely curtailed Foreign Office influence over British foreign policy.[52] However, this did not prevent Crowe and Curzon from laying the ground for the Foreign Office's recapture of the centre of policy-making once Lloyd George left office – which he did unexpectedly in October 1922 when he lost the confidence of the Unionist wing of the coalition.

In terms of reestablishing 'professional' authority over policy, Crowe and Curzon ensured that as second level embassies and legations fell vacant, they were filled by career diplomats who shared their views.[53] Thus,

---

[48] Helping was a delayed pre-war reform that came into force by 1921 and combined the Foreign Office and Diplomatic Service into a single body within the government. See Z. Steiner and M.L. Dockrill, 'The Foreign Office Reforms, 1919–1921', *Historical Journal*, 17 (1974), 131–56.

[49] Cf. Kerr, 'Notes. Of discussion with Mr Tardieu and Dr Mazes', 11–12 Mar. 1919, FO 608/142; Kerr to under-secretary, Foreign Office, 17 July 1919, Lothian MSS GD 40/17/74; Kerr to Hardinge, 28 Jan. 1920, ibid., GD 40/17/210; Drummond (secretary-general, League of Nations) to Kerr, 10 Dec. 1919, and reply, 24 Dec. 1919, both ibid., GD 40/17/56; Kerr to Grigg (Lloyd George's secretary), 9 Sept. 1921, ibid., GD 40/17/82.

[50] Curzon 'Memo on some aspects of my tenure of the Foreign Office', Nov. 1924, Curzon MSS F/1/7 (Box Z).

[51] Ibid.

[52] A. Sharp, 'The Foreign Office In Eclipse, 1919–1922', *History*, 61 (1976), 198–218.

[53] For general biographical information on these officials, see the relevant volumes of the *Dictionary of National Biography*, *Who's Who* and the *Foreign Office List*. Gregory, Lindley, Tilley, Vansittart and Wellesley left memoirs; Loraine, Rumbold and Vansittart are the subjects of biographies.

between October 1920 and October 1922, such men were transferred to Brazil (Sir John Tilley), China (Macleay), Denmark (the Earl of Granville), Greece, (Sir Francis Lindley), Iran (Sir Percy Loraine), the Netherlands (Sir Charles Marling) and Turkey (Sir Horace Rumbold). Just as crucial, the same desire was reflected in the appointment of leading Foreign Office officials: Lampson, head of the Central Department, responsible for German affairs; Vansittart, Curzon's private secretary; John Gregory, an assistant secretary; Gerald Villiers, head of the Western Department, which had responsibility for France and the League of Nations; and Wellesley, the head of the Far Eastern Department. Returning the three major embassies to 'the brotherhood', however, had mixed results. Although Hardinge's transfer to Paris was a signal achievement, despite pre-dating Crowe's appointment as PUS, and Graham succeeded Buchanan in November 1921, Berlin and Washington had to wait until after Lloyd George fell from power; and, in late 1922, back-sliding occurred when Hardinge retired and a Liberal politician, Lord Crewe, went to Paris. Still, when Geddes announced his intention to resign at the end of 1923, Curzon and Crowe agreed immediately to have Howard, the ambassador at Madrid since November 1919, succeed him. At that juncture, the 'Conservative' government led by Stanley Baldwin had just fought a general election and was now a minority in the House of Commons – the 'Conservatives' had dropped the name 'Unionist' after Lloyd George's overthrow a year earlier. With the Labour Party certain to form its own minority government once parliament reconvened in the New Year, Curzon and Crowe wanted to prevent another interloper from taking the Washington embassy.[54] Thus, Curzon told Howard: 'I thought you the best appointment & indeed the only *one in the service* [emphasis in original] that I could contemplate with sending, as I did not want to have Ramsay MacDonald send out a Labour man.' 'It is a critical moment for our much-suffering service', said Crowe more directly, 'and to recapture the embassies from outsiders is a thing which I have very much at heart.'

In essence, Curzon and Crowe played a bureaucratic waiting game until Lloyd George left office – placing the right men in positions of authority. After October 1922, the matter entered the political realm whereby Curzon, and after him, MacDonald and Austen Chamberlain, brought control of foreign policy back within the confines of the Foreign Office. This process was aided by two years of weak ministries that followed Lloyd George's overthrow. Austen Chamberlain, the Unionist leader in October 1922, had supported Lloyd George against the wishes of Unionist junior ministers and backbenchers. Resigning after failing to contain this rebellion, he and his followers went into the political wilderness; this action

54 Curzon to Howard, 15 Dec. 1923, Crowe to Howard, 9 Jan. 1924, both Howard MSS DHW 9/39.

weakened the 'Conservative' government that ruled until January 1924. Its Labour successor, MacDonald's minority government, held office for just nine months when, in the general election of October 1924, the Conservatives won a decisive majority and Baldwin healed the rift in his party by offering Austen Chamberlain the olive branch of the Foreign Office. Added to domestic political considerations was the fact that the prime ministers after October 1922 had markedly different attitudes towards the Foreign Office than did Lloyd George.[55] The two Conservative premiers, Andrew Bonar Law and Baldwin, both uninterested in international questions, allowed the Foreign Office greater latitude in policy-making. MacDonald, conversely, was consumed by foreign policy; but wanting to keep other ministers out of policy-making – the reason he served as his own foreign secretary – he came to rely on expert advice in fashioning his diplomatic initiatives.

Freed from Lloyd George's meddling, Curzon achieved a great diplomatic success through his part in concluding the Treaty of Lausanne, the new Turkish peace settlement, in July 1923. The Treaty of Sèvres had collapsed via the overthrow of the sultan and the advent of a new nationalist republican regime based in Ankara. Apart from domestic issues like his handling of the Irish question, Lloyd George's policies concerning Turkey had eroded Unionist support for his government in parliament. To keep Turkish nationalists in line, for example, he had supported Greek military intervention. But once Lloyd George departed, Curzon worked with Crowe to secure British gains originally achieved by Sèvres and establish a balance between British and French interests in the Middle East.[56] Even reconciling competing Anglo-French interests in Morocco seemed possible thanks to discussions at Paris beginning in mid-1923.[57] Nonetheless, Curzon was unable to resolve the interminable problem caused by a French determination to keep Germany weak – this through the abortive 'Draft Treaty of Mutual Assistance', a security arrangement tied to the League.[58] The European situation had assumed crisis proportions when in January 1923, after Germany defaulted on its reparations payments, the French and Belgians occupied Germany's industrial heartland, the Ruhr Valley. Still, Curzon could later observe:

I was held to be associated with [Lloyd George's] pro-Greek madness, which I

---

[55] Cf. K. Middlemas and J. Barnes, *Baldwin. A Biography* (London, 1969), pp. 342–6; Vansittart, *Mist Procession*, p. 347.

[56] B.C. Busch, *Mudros to Lausanne: Britain's Frontier in West Asia, 1918–1923* (Albany, NY, 1976); Crowe and Corp, *Crowe*, pp. 418–22.

[57] Curzon despatch to Crewe, 2 May 1923, with Crowe and Curzon minutes, both 5 May 1923, all FO 371/9458/3476/1; Curzon to St Aulaire (French ambassador, London), 24 May 1923, FO 371/9458/4029/1.

[58] A. Orde, *Great Britain and International Security, 1920–1926* (London, 1978), pp. 38–43.

had all along done my best to modify and [?conciliate], and was therefore regarded with natural suspicions by the Turks: and further I became identified by French public opinion with the man whom they disliked more than any one in the world.

I cannot recall however that during this time my administration of the Foreign Office was subject to any attack – nor was it ever challenged in either House of Parliament . . .[59]

MacDonald's brief time as foreign secretary led him to value Foreign Office expertise in constructing diplomatic strategies. Although finding a resolution to the Franco-German cold war also eluded him – his government proposed an unsuccessful initiative, the 'Geneva Protocol', to refine the 'Draft Treaty' – he sought to bring British foreign policy in line with socialist ideals.[60] An important element of this translated into establishing formal ties with Bolshevik Russia, including a trade agreement. During the October 1924 election campaign, however, with MacDonald out of London on a speaking tour, the Foreign Office acquired a letter supposedly written by Gregory Zinoviev, a Bolshevik leader, which called on the British Communist Party to foment revolution. Probably leaked to journalists by members of the intelligence services connected to the Conservative Party – a conspiracy in which the Foreign Office had no part – the 'Zinoviev letter' was published in the press in the last days of the campaign.[61] Whilst MacDonald had been consulted by the Foreign Office and the letter's authenticity remained uncertain, Gregory gave it legitimacy by sending a formal protest to the Russian government. An unfavourable public reaction helped the Conservatives win a majority, and some Labour Party officials subsequently considered means of controlling the Foreign Office whenever they next took office by filling the posts of the PUS and head of the News Department with Labour political appointees.[62] But MacDonald believed Crowe and the Foreign Office innocent of intrigue; although he thought them insensitive to socialist diplomatic aims, he surmised:

---

[59] See note 51, above. Thus, I disagree with the emphasis of the otherwise excellent Sharp, 'Eclipse'.

[60] On 'socialist' foreign policy, A. Henderson, *Labour and Foreign Affairs* (London, 1922); J.R. MacDonald, *The Foreign Policy of the Labour Party* (London, 1923). On the 'Protocol', see J.R. Ferris, *Men, Money, and Diplomacy: The Evolution of British Strategic Policy, 1919–26* (Ithaca, 1989), pp. 144–52; Orde, *International Security*, pp. 68–75.

[61] J.R. Ferris and U. Bar-Joseph, 'Getting Marlowe to Hold his Tongue: The Conservative Party, the Intelligence Services and the Zinoviev Letter', *Intelligence and National Security*, 8:4 (1993), 100–37. Cf. C.M. Andrew, 'The British Secret Service and Anglo-Soviet Relations in the 1920s: Part I, From Trade Negotiations to the Zinoviev Letter', *Historical Journal*, 20 (1977), 673–706; S. Crowe, 'The Zinoviev Letter', *Journal of Contemporary History*, 10 (1975), 407–32.

[62] Trades Union Congress and Labour Party Joint International Department, Sub-Committee on Foreign Services memoranda, 'The Foreign Office and Labour Governments', Feb. 1925, 'Proposals for a Public Programme', Mar. 1925, 'Foreign Office and Labour Governments. Public Programme', Apr. 1925, all MacDonald MSS PRO (Private Collections, Public Record Office, Kew) 30/69/5/132.

'A more prolonged tenure of office by us would have changed the spirit of the office and that is the thing that we have to work for.'[63] He therefore used his position as party leader to squelch any attempt to politicise the Foreign Office by appointing outsiders to leading positions.[64] This incident shows that MacDonald developed a high opinion of Foreign Office competence in 1924 – and the feeling was largely mutual;[65] when he formed his second government in June 1929, he had no desire to exhume Lloyd George's ideas about weakening 'professional' control of foreign policy.

Austen Chamberlain came to the Foreign Office in November 1924 intent on reviving his political fortunes that had suffered from standing by Lloyd George two years earlier. To this end, within five months of taking office, he forced the Cabinet to accept a Foreign Office strategy designed to end the continuing crisis on the continent. Supported by Crowe and Foreign Office experts like Harold Nicolson, he sought in his own words to be 'the honest broker' in continental affairs[66] – to arrogate for Britain the key role in maintaining the European balance. The 'Draft Treaty' and the 'Protocol' had each failed for a variety of reasons, the most important of which arose from their contemplating British participation in League-defined collective security anywhere on the globe.[67] Chamberlain, his advisers and other members of the Baldwin government agreed that British interests were limited to the Far East, the Mediterranean and western Europe. The Washington conference of 1921–2 had constructed a system of security in China and the western Pacific, no matter how fragile that system was.[68] With the situation in the Mediterranean bolstered by the Treaty of Lausanne, agreements with the Egyptians to preserve British control of the Suez Canal and the Moroccan negotiations, only the European question remained unsolved.

By December 1924, Chamberlain was considering an Anglo-French-

---

[63] MacDonald to Noel-Baker (Labour Party member), 25 May 1925, MacDonald MSS PRO 30/69/5/36.

[64] MacDonald to Henderson (Labour Party secretary), 30 Mar. 1925, ibid.

[65] Crowe and Corp, *Crowe*, pp. 447–8. Cf. Tyrrell to MacDonald, 12 Dec. 1928, MacDonald MSS PRO 30/69/5/39.

[66] Crowe to Chamberlain, 11 Mar. 1925, FO 371/10728/3569/459; Chamberlain to D'Abernon, 18 Mar. 1925, Chamberlain to Crewe, 2 Apr. 1925, both Chamberlain MSS FO 800/257; Nicolson memorandum, 'British Policy Considered in Relation to the European Situation', 20 Feb. 1925, FO 371/11064/2201/459.

[67] For instance, Crowe memorandum, 24 June 1923, FO 371/9419/5047/30; Crowe 'Memorandum on Cecil's Scheme of Guarantees, Treaties and Disarmament', 25 June 1923, CAB 16/56; Campbell (FO Western Department) memorandum, 'A Review of the Protocol for the Pacific Settlement of International Disputes', 20 Nov. 1924, *BDFA*, II, J1, 392–405.

[68] T.H. Buckley, *The United States and the Washington Conference, 1921–1922* (Knoxville, TN, 1970); M.G. Fry, *Illusions of Security. North Atlantic Diplomacy, 1918–22* (Toronto, 1972), pp. 154–86; S.W. Roskill, *Naval Policy Between the Wars*, I (London, 1968), pp. 300–1.

Belgian alliance in place of the 'Protocol'; he felt that such a mechanism would show a British commitment to go to war on the Continent to help France and Belgium, give France security and aid the evacuation of the Ruhr. By March 1925, this idea transformed into one that included Germany – sensing that the British were considering a separate deal with the French, Gustav Stresemann, the German foreign minister, mooted a treaty by which Germany would join with the former Allies in guaranteeing the inviolability of the Franco-German-Belgian border and sign arbitration agreements for the peaceful readjustment of Germany's eastern frontiers.[69] A corollary of this strategy involved bringing Germany into the League with one of the coveted permanent seats on the Council. Although Chamberlain, Crowe and Foreign Office advisers like Nicolson grasped the merit of Stresemann's proposed 'Rhineland pact'[70] – it would give Britain influence in the continental balance and limit its commitments only to the region judged vital to British security – the bulk of the Cabinet, especially Churchill, the chancellor of the exchequer, remained unenthused: 'It is by standing aloof', Churchill told Chamberlain, 'and not by offering ourselves that we shall ascertain the degree of importance which France really attaches to our troth.'[71] Disagreeing, Chamberlain and the Foreign Office impressed on Baldwin and other ministers the danger of remaining isolated from continental politics; whether British leaders liked it or not, Britain was tied to the Continent and could not avoid crises arising there.[72] When the Cabinet moved to reject the proposal, Chamberlain threatened resignation.[73] Not wanting another intra-party division, Baldwin immediately supported his foreign secretary; and Chamberlain then embarked on intricate diplomacy that, by October, transformed the 'Rhineland pact' into the Locarno treaty. In purely political terms, his success meant that he reestablished his political strength after the debacle of October 1922, which augured well for Foreign Office authority over foreign policy. In all of this, Crowe played a central role,[74] as much to force the Foreign Office vision of foreign policy on recalcitrant politicians as to revitalise 'the brotherhood'. Although he died in April 1925, his successors – and Chamberlain's – built on these accomplishments for the next dozen years.

The remaining years of the 1920s were the salad days of the interwar

---

[69] A. Kaiser, 'Lord D'Abernon und die Enstehung der Locarno-Verträge', *Vierteljahrshefte für Zeitgeschichte*, 34 (1986), 85–104.

[70] Nicolson memorandum, 'British Policy Considered in Relation to the European Situation', 20 Feb. 1925, FO 371/11064/2201/459/18.

[71] Churchill to Chamberlain, 23–25 Feb. 1925, with enclosure, Chamberlain MSS FO 800/257.

[72] Crowe to Chamberlain, 11 Mar. 1925, FO 371/10728/3569/459; Crowe to Chamberlain, 12 Mar. 1925, AC (Austen Chamberlain MSS, University Library, Birmingham) 52/240.

[73] Chamberlain to Crowe, 14 Mar. 1925, AC 52/241.

[74] See the posthumous appreciation of Crowe's talents in Chamberlain to Wellesley, 24 Apr. 1925, AC L.Add.84.

Foreign Office.[75] Through close personal ties with Stresemann and Aristide Briand, who commanded French foreign policy, Chamberlain used the Locarno treaty as the basis of Britain's European policy. His surmise in early 1925 that Britain could serve as the 'honest broker' in continental affairs proved true. He attended the quarterly League Councils, and there, and at the annual League Assembly each September, he was regularly sought out by the French, Germans, Italians and representatives of the lesser powers as a mediator. 'It is very difficult', he wrote to Baldwin in September 1927, 'to convey to anyone who is not here, and not only here but here in a position to know what goes on behind the scenes, how difficult and at the same time how influential is our position.'[76] There is truth in the retrospective charge that Chamberlain's freedom of action was constrained by Locarno[77] – he had always to consider the health of Franco-German relations in his calculations. But when compared with the period 1919–25 when the British lacked influence on the Continent and the European disequilibrium posed a danger to general security, the reconstruction of the balance and the ability to have a voice in how it evolved cannot be overstated. Importantly, unlike the 'Draft Treaty' and the 'Protocol', Locarno limited British commitments. Coupled with the Washington treaty system in the eastern reaches of the Empire and the lack of a Mediterranean flashpoint, immediate threats to British security had gone into abeyance.

During the second Baldwin government – it held office until June 1929 – the Foreign Office recovered from the calamity of Lloyd George's diplomatic revolution. Chamberlain's success by March 1925 in reducing outside ministerial influence to a minimum was mirrored by his achievement in preventing LNU advocates inside and outside the government from deflecting diplomatic strategy. After 1919, British League policy had usually been the preserve of a minister, other than the foreign secretary, with interest in League affairs. At the September 1924 Assembly, Gilbert Murray, a senior British delegate and LNU chairman, had threatened the Greeks with sanctions over a minor matter concerning the protection of minorities.[78] This occurred without reference to either MacDonald's Cabinet or the Foreign Office, with the result that when Chamberlain took office, his senior advisers implored him to control League policy. Chamberlain then won an intra-Cabinet dispute with Cecil, the chancellor of the Duchy of Lancaster and LNU leader, who assumed he would handle

[75] B.J.C. McKercher, 'Austen Chamberlain's Control of British Foreign Policy, 1924–1929', *International History Review*, 6 (1984), 570–91.
[76] Chamberlain to Baldwin, 16 Sept. 1927, Chamberlain MSS FO 800/261.
[77] J. Jacobson, 'The Conduct of Locarno Diplomacy', *Review of Politics*, 34 (1972), 67–81.
[78] See Selby minute, 1 Dec. 1924, Chamberlain MSS 800/256; FO Central Department memorandum, 6 Jan. 1925, with Lampson and Crowe minutes, both 6 Jan. 1925, both ibid., 800/257.

League policy.[79] During the subsequent life of Baldwin's second government, and beyond, Foreign Office men controlled official British relations with the League. This created friction between Chamberlain and the LNU Executive, which disliked the Foreign Office view that the League was not an end in itself but, rather, another device by which British diplomatic interests could be furthered.[80] Whilst Chamberlain supported League goals respecting the maintenance of international peace and security,[81] neither he nor his advisers were about to be brow-beaten into pursuing policy demanded by the LNU or its partisans in the Cabinet.

In addition, Tyrrell succeeded Crowe as PUS; responsible for promotions and transfers, he continued to place 'Edwardians' in important embassies and legations and in vacancies within the Foreign Office. Thus, in the Diplomatic Service, amongst other appointments, Clerk was sent to Constantinople (1926), Tilley to Tokyo (1926), Granville to The Hague (1926), Macleay to Prague (1927), Henry Chilton to the Vatican (1928) and Phipps to Vienna (1928). Within the Foreign Office, officials like Wellesley rose to become deputy under-secretary (1925), Sargent became a counsellor (1926), Lancelot Oliphant, an assistant under-secretary (1928), and Robert Craigie followed Vansittart as head of the American Department (1928). Tyrrell's ability to make the experts' position clear within the government was aided by a personal friendship with Baldwin – Tyrrell spent at least one weekend a month at Chequers, the prime minister's official country house – and the development of a close relationship with Chamberlain.[82] In addition, Chamberlain felt affection for the group of experts who had advised him during the negotiation of Locarno: Lampson, Hurst, Walford Selby, his private secretary, George Steward, the press officer at the Brussels Embassy, John Sterndale Bennett, a member of the Central Department, and Victor Cavendish-Bentinck, a second secretary at The Hague. He called them the 'Locarnoites' and, not surprisingly, they all received tangible rewards – Cavendish-Bentinck, for instance, was transferred to the Foreign Office whilst Lampson became a Companion of the Order of the Bath in the January 1926 Honours List before being posted to Peking in October.[83] Subsequently, 'Locarnoite' counsel found

---

[79] Cecil to Baldwin, 10 Nov. 1924, with enclosure, Cecil, 'Memorandum of Conversation with the Prime Minister on 10, 11 Nov. 1924', both Cecil (British Library, London) Add MSS 51080; Chamberlain to Salisbury (Cecil's brother), 2 Jan. 1925, Chamberlain MSS FO 800/257.

[80] Cf. Murray to Chamberlain, 6, 13 Jan. 1928, and replies, 11, 28 Jan. 1928, all Chamberlain FO 800/262.

[81] A. Chamberlain, The League (Glasgow, 1926).

[82] Cf. Middlemas and Barnes, Baldwin, p. 344; Tyrrell to Chamberlain, 1 June 1925, AC 24/7/27.

[83] The relevant entries in the Foreign Office List 1930 have information on these individuals' career patterns in the latter half of the 1920s.

especial sympathy with the foreign secretary.[84] Just as important, after Lindsay held the Berlin Embassy, a crucial Locarno post, for two success-ful years, he was chosen to succeed Tyrrell as PUS in July 1928.[85] Indeed, the summer of 1928 was an important point in the history of the interwar Foreign Office. At that time, there was a wholesale change of ambassa-dors – Tyrrell went to Paris, Rumbold to Berlin, Odo Russell to The Hague, Granville to Brussels, and Sir George Grahame, Granville's prede-cessor, to Madrid.[86] With the departure of Crewe, the Diplomatic Service was free of outsiders, a situation that lasted until 1939.

Perhaps the most significant appointment made by Tyrrell concerned Vansittart. Whilst Chamberlain wrestled with European problems and, in early 1927, the outbreak of anti-foreign violence in China that was largely suppressed by sending 10,000 marines to the Yangtse Valley, Vansittart played the leading role in obviating a major crisis in Anglo-American relations. In 1926, he defused an American legal challenge to British poli-cies of maritime belligerent rights pursued during the war.[87] The next year came the failure of the Coolidge naval conference, which had at its base an American attempt to emasculate those rights by forcing Britain to concede full naval equality to the United States. Vansittart's advice in the aftermath of the conference helped Chamberlain convince Baldwin that the Committee of Imperial Defence (the CID), the Cabinet's princi-pal advisory body on foreign and defence policy, should examine political means to parry the American assault of British naval preeminence.[88] Then, in February 1928, Tyrrell seconded him to Downing Street as a private secretary 'to get [Baldwin] interested in foreign affairs'.[89] The suggestion that the Treasury PUS and head of the civil service, Sir Norman Warren Fisher, engineered this transfer to weaken Foreign Office elitism in Whitehall might have validity.[90] But whatever the reasoning behind this action, a senior Foreign Office official now worked in the prime minister's office – it had never occurred before; it meant that Lloyd George's revol-ution was completely reversed as the Foreign Office view was now at the fore within 10 Downing Street.

[84] Cf. Lampson to Chamberlain, 26 Dec. 1926, Chamberlain FO 800/259; Chamberlain to Lampson, 11 Jan. 1927, ibid., FO 800/260; Chamberlain minutes, 19–20 Jan. 1928, FO 371/12789/592/1; Hurst minute, 7 May 1928, FO 371/12791/3022/1.

[85] For instance, Lindsay to Chamberlain, 21 Dec. 1928, AC 38/3/55.

[86] Chamberlain to Graham, 20 Feb. 1928, Chamberlain MSS FO 800/262 shows when these decisions were made.

[87] B.J.C. McKercher, 'A British View of American Foreign Policy: The Settlement of Block-ade Claims, 1924–1927', *International History Review*, 3 (1981), 358–84.

[88] For instance, Vansittart memorandum, 16 Nov. 1927, enclosing Craigie memorandum, 16 Nov. 1927, *DBFP IA*, IV, 440–5. Cf. B.J.C. McKercher, *The Second Baldwin Government and the United States, 1924–1929: attitudes and diplomacy* (Cambridge, 1984), pp. 77–103. On the Coolidge conference, see Roskill, *Naval Policy*, I, pp. 498–516.

[89] Vansittart, *Mist Procession*, p. 347.

[90] E. O'Halpin, *Head of the Civil Service. A Study of Sir Warren Fisher* (London, 1989), pp. 158–9.

Over the next two years, Vansittart showed both Baldwin and, after the 1929 general election, MacDonald that he was a sage adviser and skilled diplomat. This occurred over a renewed crisis in Anglo-American relations, caused by the naval question, that began in the late autumn of 1928 and lasted until MacDonald made a visit to Washington in October 1929. The inability of London and Washington to find a solution to their naval differences, clear in League-sponsored international disarmament discussions beginning in 1926, reached crisis proportions on 11 November 1928 after a speech by Calvin Coolidge, the American president. Angry at the failure of arms discussions, blaming the European powers for the lack of progress, and about to surrender office to a newly elected president, Herbert Hoover, Coolidge called for American naval supremacy over Britain by throwing his weight behind Congressional legislation to authorise the construction of fifteen new cruisers.[91] Vansittart subsequently took a leading role in resolving the crisis: consulting with Craigie and Howard, using American contacts like William Castle, a senior State Department official and a friend of Hoover, and supporting a prime ministerial visit to Washington to settle the crisis. Central to the expert advice of Craigie and Howard was the idea of reaching a political settlement – that is, avoiding technical questions that Admiralty and United States Navy Department staff officers had been using since 1926 to stymie agreement. In fact, Howard argued that paper parity would undercut the anglophobia of American Congressional navalists, thereby diminishing support for naval expansion. When MacDonald unexpectedly succeeded Baldwin in June 1929, Vansittart brought the Foreign Office case before the new premier, especially the notion that a settlement would protect future British belligerent rights.[92] Although the new Cabinet sought to put a 'socialist' imprimatur on arms limitation policy, MacDonald relied heavily on Vansittart and Craigie in settling Anglo-American differences. Moreover, Vansittart coordinated Downing Street's handling of the issue and, in September, went secretly to Washington to prepare for MacDonald's visit. Significantly, when MacDonald arrived in Washington in October, the only advisers he took with him were Vansittart and Craigie. Working with Howard, they helped make the MacDonald–Hoover conversations a success, paving the way for the formal settlement of Anglo-American differences at the London naval conference of January–April 1930.

Vansittart's achievements marked him as Lindsay's successor as PUS. Although Lindsay had worked well with Chamberlain, his patrician bearing

[91] Except where noted, this paragraph is based on B.J.C. McKercher, 'From Enmity to Cooperation: The Second Baldwin Government and the Improvement of Anglo-American Relations, November 1928–June 1929', *Albion*, 24(1992), 65–88.

[92] Craigie memoranda, 'Question of an Agreement with the United States in regard to Maritime Belligerent Rights', 'Question of the conclusion of an Anglo-American Arbitration Treaty, the Naval Disarmament Question', all 10 June 1929, all MacDonald MSS PRO 30/69/1/267.

and discomfort with 'socialist' politicians created personal differences with the new foreign secretary, Arthur Henderson, and the political under-secretary, Hugh Dalton.[93] Taking the opportunity of Howard's retirement, MacDonald decided to send Lindsay to Washington and replace him in the Foreign Office with Vansittart. Although Vansittart had critics within the Labour Party,[94] echoes of the 'Zinoviev letter', MacDonald wanted someone on the other side of Downing Street whom he could trust and rely upon to do the right thing. Moreover, MacDonald and Henderson were political rivals within the Labour Party – MacDonald had reluctantly appointed Henderson as foreign secretary.[95] Thus, MacDonald told Vansittart as he left for his new post: 'the F.O. needs the most efficient guidance it can get. The amateurs must be controlled. You may not have an easy time but you will have very important work.'[96] MacDonald's attitude, shared by Baldwin, is important in understanding Vansittart's subsequent authority over British foreign policy. Whereas before 1914, Hardinge had strength in Whitehall through his association with Edward VII, his post-war successors relied on connections with political leaders. Crowe, Tyrrell and Lindsay each used their relationships with their political masters to ensure the Foreign Office voice was heard amongst the din of other ministries and public groups like the LNU. Vansittart conformed to this pattern. And, significantly, when MacDonald's second government was replaced by a coalition, the 'National Government' of Conservatives, pro-MacDonald Labourites and anti-Lloyd George Liberals in August 1931, both MacDonald and Baldwin dominated the Cabinet. As long as they held office, Vansittart had sympathetic ears at the highest level of government. However, when they left in mid-1937 – Baldwin by retirement and MacDonald by death – Vansittart and the 'Edwardians' needed new patrons. Neville Chamberlain's advent to the premiership robbed them of support; indeed, it meant a prime minister who not only wanted to direct foreign policy but who had a different diplomatic philosophy.

Vansittart's leadership of the Foreign Office marked the high point of interwar 'Edwardianism'. His series of so-called 'Old Adam' memoranda circulated to the Cabinet – 'Old Adam' was the spectre of militarism abroad – were classic expositions of the 'Crowe doctrine'.[97] In these papers, along with submissions to specialist Cabinet and CID sub-

[93] Connell, The 'Office', pp. 99–100. Cf. Dalton to Lindsay, 15 Aug. 1929, Lindsay to Dalton (two letters), 16 Aug. 1929, all Dalton Papers (British Library of Economic and Political Science, London) II 1/1.
[94] N. Rose, Vansittart: Study of a Diplomat (London, 1977), p. 67.
[95] D. Carlton, MacDonald versus Henderson. The Foreign Policy of the Second Labour Government (London, 1970), pp. 15–17, 23–29.
[96] MacDonald to Vansittart, 26 Dec. 1929, VNST (Vansittart Papers, Churchill College, Cambridge) II 6/9.
[97] See Vansittart memoranda CID 991 B, CAB 4/19; CP 317(31), CAB 24/225; CP 4(32), CAB 24/227; CP 52(33), CAB 24/239; CP 212(33), CAB 24/243; CP 104(34), CAB 24/248; CP 42(36), CAB 24/260.

committees, he and his advisers advocated activist foreign policy strategies that had at their heart the maintenance of a global balance of power.[98] These arguments had especial significance in that between 1930 and 1936 the international order constructed after the Great War at Paris, Washington and Locarno, and in the settlement of war debts and reparations, vanished through economic dislocation created by the Great Depression, Japanese expansion in Manchuria, the rise of Hitler and his rearming of Germany, and the development of enmity between Britain and fascist Italy.[99] Britain had the diplomatic resources to maintain this balance, especially after the National Government revived the country's economic and financial strength after 1931 and, later, embarked on a programme of rearmament.[100] The central resource in this equation, however, was not a material one. As 'Edwardians' from Hardinge to Vansittart understood, what was needed was the political will to act decisively. During Vansittart's tenure as PUS, the Foreign Office dedicated itself to steeling the politicians with this will, to showing them that 'old diplomacy' – maintaining balances on continental Europe, in the Mediterranean and in the Far East – offered the best protection of British economic, strategic and imperial interests.

In all of this it is critical to realise that Vansittart, and not the foreign secretaries under whom he nominally worked, provided the strategic basis for British foreign policy between 1930 and 1937. Five politicians served as foreign secretary at this time: Henderson (January 1930–August 1931), Lord Reading (August–October 1931), Sir John Simon (October 1931–June 1935), Sir Samuel Hoare (June–December 1935) and Eden (December 1935–December 1937). By mid-1930, after initial misgivings caused by an anti-French bias prevalent in the upper echelons of the Labour Party, Henderson and Dalton accepted the experts' view that it would aid Britain's cause to work with France in international arms limitation negotiations and over resolving the seemingly interminable reparations and war debts question.[101] By finding common ground, the two leading powers in Europe could force the pace over these issues. This

---

[98] For instance, FO memorandum (CID 1056 B), 'The Basis of Service Estimates', 25 June 1931, CAB 4/21; FO 'Memorandum on the Foreign Policy of His Majesty's Government in the United Kingdom' (CID 112B), 19 May 1933, CAB 4/22; Vansittart memorandum (on German rearmament) (CP183 (33)), 14 July 1933, CAB 24/242; 'Minute by Sir R. Vansittart' (DC(M) (32) 117), 2 June 1934, CAB 27/510.

[99] For an idea, see G. W. Baer, *The Coming of the Italo-Ethiopian War* (Cambridge, MA, 1967); E.W. Bennett, *German Rearmament and the West, 1932–1933* (Princeton, 1979); C. Thorne, *The Limits of Foreign Policy: The West, the League and the Far Eastern Crisis of 1931–1933* (London, 1972).

[100] B.J.C. McKercher, *Transition: Britain's Loss of Global Preeminence to the United States, 1930–1945* (Cambridge, forthcoming), chapters 5–6.

[101] In FO memorandum (approved by Henderson) in 'Papers Prepared for the Use of the Chiefs of Staff in their Fifth Annual Review of Imperial Defence (1930)' (CID 1008-B), 29 July 1930, CAB 4/20.

transition can be seen in the criticism heaped on Vansittart by Cecil and Philip Noel-Baker, another staunch believer in the League, both of whom received junior political posts in the Foreign Office in June 1929.[102] Bypassed in policy-making by Henderson and Vansittart, they saw an Anglo-French alignment, especially over disarmament, as undermining Britain's supposed fidelity to the internationalism of the League. As a caretaker foreign secretary between the formation of the National Government and its confirmation in the general election of October 1931, Reading spent much of his time out of London attending League meetings dealing with the initial phases of the Manchurian crisis. Despite holding office for almost four years, Simon quickly lost the respect of his leading Cabinet colleagues like MacDonald, the premier of the National Government until June 1935, and Neville Chamberlain, the chancellor of the exchequer.[103] A lawyer by training, he could dissect a problem, offer alternative policies, but prove unable to decide which solution might be most profitable. Thus, MacDonald increasingly relied on Vansittart to guide foreign policy. He had Vansittart meet foreign leaders without Simon present; and he even discussed privately with the PUS how to resolve political problems that he had in Cabinet with Simon and other ministers.[104] Hoare came to the Foreign Office on the eve of the Abyssinian crisis. Whilst the National Government prepared for an Autumn election, he followed Vansittart's lead to keep Italy in the balance to contain Germany.[105] This took the form of a secret Anglo-French agreement – the Hoare–Laval pact; it accepted Italy's East African conquest whilst providing the Abyssinian emperor with the face-saving device of having some of his former territory under his control. Made public through a leak in the French Foreign Office before the ground could be prepared for its acceptance, parliamentary criticism in Britain, importantly amongst Conservative backbenchers, including Austen Chamberlain,[106] forced Hoare's resignation.

---

[102] W.R. Tucker, *The Attitude of the British Labour Party Towards European and Collective Security Problems, 1920–1939* (Geneva, 1950), pp. 244–6. Cf. R. Cecil, *A Great Experiment* (London, 1941), pp. 212–13; P. J. Noel-Baker, *The First World Disarmament Conference 1932–33 And Why It Failed* (Oxford, NY, 1979), pp. 47–9.

[103] MacDonald diary, 17, 22 Nov., 11, 17 Dec. 1933, 27 Jan., 4 Mar. 1934, MacDonald PRO 30/69/1753; Neville Chamberlain to Hilda, his sister, 17 Nov. 1934, NC 18/1/896. Cf. D. Dutton, *Simon. A Political Biography of Sir John Simon* (London, 1992), pp. 120–1.

[104] On meeting foreign statesmen, see Simon to MacDonald, 10 June 1932, Simon FO 800/287; MacDonald to Simon, 23 June 1933, ibid., 800/288. On discussing Cabinet politics, Vansittart to MacDonald, n.d. (but Nov. 1933; the first pages of this letter are missing), MacDonald PRO 30/69/1767. With regard to the latter, Vansittart did the same with Curzon, see Vansittart to Curzon, 30 Mar. 1921, Curzon MSS F 112/22(B).

[105] Neville Chamberlain 'thought that the Foreign Secretary had been greatly misled by his Staff'; for this and general Cabinet criticism (but not from MacDonald and Baldwin), see CC 56(35), CAB 23/90B. Cf. Vansittart to Hoare, 10 July 1935, Templewood MSS (University Library, Cambridge) VIII/I; Hoare to Neville Chamberlain, 17 Mar. 1937, NC 7/11/30/74.

[106] Chamberlain to Ida, his sister, 15 Dec. 1935, AC 5/1/717.

Coupled with Cabinet displeasure at the domestic political cost of the Hoare-Laval pact, Eden's selection to succeed Hoare proved to be the beginning of the end of 'Edwardian' primacy in the interwar Foreign Office. Eden was just thirty-eight when he became foreign secretary, he had served in the Great War, and became an MP in 1923. His entire time at the Cabinet level had centred on foreign policy – parliamentary secretary to Austen Chamberlain, 1926–9; under-secretary for foreign affairs, 1931–3; minister responsible for disarmament, 1934–5; and minister without portfolio responsible for League affairs, 1935. Representative of the generation who achieved political maturity during and after the war, he had a profoundly different perception of how best to protect British interests: believing in collective rather than unilateral means of ensuring international peace and security.[107] In his early work, he came into contact with younger men like Oliver Stanley and William Ormsby-Gore, who shared his general political views;[108] and, importantly, with older ones like Cadogan, whose ten years as the Foreign Office official responsible for League affairs led him to support cooperative efforts in foreign policy.[109] Although Eden and Vansittart worked well together at first, the younger man's *amour propre* soon chafed at the fact that his principal adviser had more influence with Baldwin and MacDonald; and, as time went on, he deprecated Vansittart's strategic vision for British foreign policy. By January 1937, he tried unsuccessfully to shift Vansittart to the Paris Embassy;[110] only when Neville Chamberlain became prime minister did Eden find an ally powerful enough to dislodge Vansittart. To entrench his vision of how best to meet the threats posed by Nazi Germany, fascist Italy and militaristic Japan, Eden helped Cadogan's successful candidacy as PUS.

Foreign Office influence in policy-making between the fall of Lloyd George and Vansittart's removal as PUS lay in the confluence of a series of senior officials, on one hand, and prime ministers and foreign secretaries, on the other, who shared the 'Edwardian' world view. Admittedly, the interwar Foreign Office was not a power unto itself within government – but neither was any department of state before 1914 or after 1918, including the Treasury, the service ministries and others. Accordingly, the interwar Foreign Office failed sometimes to get its way; and on particular international questions, like Treasury handling of war debts and reparations, other ministries held responsibility for making and executing policy. With regard to the latter point, this only conformed to the

---

[107] For instance, A. Eden, *Foreign Affairs* (London, 1939).
[108] Stanley entered parliament in 1924 and had junior Cabinet positions until holding a series of ministerial posts beginning in 1933; Ormsby-Gore entered parliament in 1910 and the Cabinet in 1931.
[109] Dilks, *Cadogan Diaries*, pp. 4–8.
[110] D. Carlton, *Anthony Eden* (London, 1981), p. 105; Rose, *Vansittart*, pp. 200–2.

long-established tradition in the administration of British external relations. On the whole, however, successive PUSs and foreign secretaries were able to use their political strength in inter-departmental debates in specialist committees, the CID and the Cabinet to fashion bureaucratic alliances to shape policy in a way that reflected 'Edwardian' responses to potential threat. Few historians have appreciated the ability of the interwar Foreign Office to assert its authority over British foreign-policy-making. For instance, the notion that the Treasury had disproportionate influence over British external policy after 1919 has long been argued: that the failure of British diplomacy to prevent the outbreak of war in 1939 can be found in the inability of Vansittart and other professionals to overcome meddling by Fisher and, after the National Government took office in 1931, the chancellor of the exchequer, Neville Chamberlain.[111] Much of this comes from Selby. Annoyed at being passed over as Lindsay's successor and then shunted off to head the legation at Vienna – thus, not getting an ambassadorship at a major Embassy – he charged in his memoirs that Fisher engineered Vansittart's appointment as PUS and then, using his position as head of the civil service, neutered Foreign Office contributions to policy-making.[112] Apart from considering suing Selby for libel over some of his more ludicrous and untrue charges, Vansittart's response was 'that the Treasury and Warren Fisher were never a kind of octopus which paralysed our foreign policy'.[113]

Lately, the criticism has been made that Foreign Office effectiveness in the mid-1930s was blunted by the committee system through which the Cabinet and CID examined foreign and defence problems and then made policy. A plethora of committees, offering contradictory solutions, clogged the decision-making process and prevented expert assessments from reaching the highest levels of government.[114] Although a compelling thesis – brilliantly presented – this argument sidesteps the fact that the Foreign Office, especially Vansittart and his most trusted subordinates like Sargent, never wavered in the general strategies they advocated. Indeed, Vansittart's doggedness in identifying the German threat, in seeking to establish a group of anti-German powers, and in pushing his political masters to use British resources and this countervailing group to contain German ambitions led Chamberlain and Eden to remove him in

---

[111] For instance, L. Namier, *Diplomatic Prelude, 1938–1939* (London, 1948).

[112] W. Selby, *Diplomatic Twilight* (London, 1953). Selby also attempted to be a new Crowe with a major memorandum on the balance of power in the 1930s; it was ignored by the Foreign Office establishment. See Selby 'Note as regards Anglo-German Relations. Sir Eyre Crowe's Memorandum of January 1st, 1907', 7 Dec. 1931, Simon FO 800/285.

[113] Vansittart to Bridges (former Cabinet secretary), 20 May 1953, VNST II/1/50. For his consideration of libel charges, Butler (Vansittart's lawyer) to Vansittart, 11 May 1953, with enclosure, ibid.

[114] G. Post, Jr, *Dilemmas of Appeasement. British Deterrence and Defense, 1934–1937* (Ithaca, 1993).

December 1937. Moreover, what Vansittart, Sargent and other 'Edwardians' did was consistent with what Grey, Hardinge, Curzon, Crowe and those before them had argued about immutable interests and mutable friendships.

Nowhere is this clearer than in British policy concerning arms limitation and security, the *sine qua non* of British foreign policy throughout the interwar period. After the Paris Peace Conference, British foreign policy faced problems of the first rank in Europe (the Franco-German cold war), the Mediterranean (in Morocco and along the eastern littoral) and the Far East (Chinese nationalism and American pressures on the Anglo-Japanese alliance). In each of these regions, the Foreign Office advocated strategies that sought to find a *modus vivendi* with like-minded powers that balanced their competing interests and ensured stability. Thus, during the Washington conference, Foreign Office advisers like Crowe and Wellesley saw the utility of the nine-power and four-power treaties, tied to the naval settlement, in protecting British commercial investments in China whilst providing a strategic basis for imperial and trade defence.[115] This does not mean that the Foreign Office abdicated its responsibilities in the Far East – the sending of the marines to the Yangtse Valley in 1927 on Lampson's recommendation is indicative of the will to protect Britain's Chinese holdings;[116] rather, it showed the 'secular policy' of preventing a potential rival from dominating in the region. The same thinking animated Curzon and Crowe during the negotiation of the Treaty of Lausanne and the search for a working arrangement with the French over Morocco. And as noted earlier, Foreign Office acceptance of Stresemann's proposal for a 'Rhineland pact' had at its base a recognition that British security would be enhanced by giving London a voice in restructured Franco-German relations.

In all of these initiatives, interwar Foreign Office advisers, and through them, their foreign secretaries, argued for the pursuit of a global balance of power to safeguard British security. This can be seen in the 1920s in Crowe's opposition to the universal implications of the 'Draft Treaty' and the 'Protocol', Tyrrell's support for a firm Anglo-French axis within Locarno, and Wellesley's defence of the Washington treaties as means to maintain good Anglo-Japanese relations.[117] British diplomatic and armed

---

[115] Crowe minute on Alston (British ambassador, Peking) memorandum, 1 Aug. 1920, *DBFP* I, XIV, 86; Wellesley memorandum, 'General Survey of Political Situation in Pacific and Far East with Reference to the Forthcoming Washington Conference', 20 Oct. 1921, FO Far Eastern Department, 'British Commitments in the Pacific Ocean', 10 Oct. 1921, Wellesley memorandum, 'Japanese Spheres of Interest', 10 Oct. 1921, all FO 412/118

[116] B.J.C. McKercher, 'A Sane and Sensible Diplomacy: Austen Chamberlain, Japan, and the Naval Balance of Power in the Pacific Ocean, 1924–29'. *Canadian Journal of History*, 21 (1986), 187–213.

[117] Cf. Crowe memorandum, 24 June 1923, FO 371/9419/5047/30; Crowe memorandum, 2 Jan. 1925, CAB 16/56; Tyrrell memorandum (of a conversation with the French ambassador), 28 Oct. 1927, *DBFP IA*, IV, 72–3; Tyrrell to Chamberlain, 11 Feb. 1929,

resources should be directed to specific areas with the potential for trouble; Britain should work with those powers sharing its interests; and adherence to the League should occur only in so far as doing so did not imperil Britain's ability to protect itself and the Empire. Naturally, if powers pursued policies that endangered regional balances or threatened Britain's position, they had to be opposed. Meeting the American threat to British naval supremacy and future belligerent rights can be seen in this context. Importantly, Foreign Office determination of friends and adversaries occurred in coldly realistic terms. Shared political or cultural values had nothing to do with whether Britain should align with particular powers. During the Moroccan crisis in 1922, even Crowe needed reminding:

> you do not wish to appear to 'encourage or bolster up [Spain's] administration which is a byword for cruelty, incompetence and corruption'. As to the latter, I would only remark *en passant* that we have had sometimes to do this in the past, for the sake of larger and wider purposes of policy, e.g. as regards Turkey in the Near East ... It is not agreeable, but occasionally, in order to avoid greater evils, it has to be done.[118]

And what was true of Spain or France or Japan was doubly so concerning that international pariah of the interwar period, Bolshevik Russia. When Chamberlain and Tyrrell assessed the potential 'Russian' threat to India and British Far Eastern holdings, ideological considerations were absent from their submission. 'In the Far East', Tyrrell told the CID in July 1926, 'we have a Bolshevist Russia pursuing the same aims as the Czarist Russia, the main difference being that the Bolshevists are far more efficient and unscrupulous in the pursuit of that policy than their predecessors ever were.'[119] Although such equanimity evaded Baldwin's Cabinet and Conservative backbenchers – leading to a rupture in Anglo-Bolshevik relations in 1927[120] – 'Edwardian' professionals understood that other powers' external interests, despite their societal and internal political differences, were just as eternal as British ones.

Rather than basing policy on moral judgements about particular issues or the internal affairs of particular powers, it was the context of international politics and the cold calculation of national interest within those politics that brought forth Foreign Office counsel. In the latter half of the 1920s, a period of relative international economic and political stability thanks to the Washington and Locarno treaties, the lack of urgent threats saw the Foreign Office promote policies designed to buttress the status

---

AC 55/504; Wellesley memorandum 'The Improbability of War in the Pacific', 1 Jan. 1925, FO 371/10958/27/9; Wellesley minute, 4 July 1927, FO 371/12407/5531/2.

[118] Howard to Crowe, 5 Feb. 1922, FO 371/8394/1666/1666.

[119] Tyrrell memorandum, 26 July 1926, enclosed in Chamberlain minute, 28 July 1926 (CP 303(26)), CAB 24/181.

[120] McKercher, 'Chamberlain's Control', 588–60.

quo. Thwarting American naval pretensions, continuing to entrench a British presence in the European balance, and keeping Anglo-Japanese relations on an even keel were all parts of this endeavour. Indeed, in those League-sponsored arms limitation discussions, designed to produce a basis for a World Disarmament Conference, Foreign Office experts consistently connected arms limitation with security.[121] In this context, security involved having adequate forces to defend imperial frontiers, safeguard sea routes to the Empire and overseas markets, and maintain British treaty commitments. Pressures for reducing arms arose from three sources: the fact that because the 'war to end all wars' had ended in 1918, British public opinion saw no need to maintain large armed forces; the desire of successive governments to retrench; and the apparent willingness of other powers to reduce their national armouries.[122] Since British arms limitation policy involved political and strategic considerations as much as financial ones, it evolved in government through debate by the politicians and amongst officials from the Foreign Office, the Treasury and the service ministries. As recent work shows, foreign secretaries and their advisers proved adept at forming bureaucratic alliances with the other ministries to fashion bargaining strategies that looked to reduce the British armed forces in a way that did not leave Britain and the Empire vulnerable to attack.[123] That preparatory discussions for the World Disarmament Conference, which convened in February 1932, stretched from the spring of 1926 to the autumn of 1931 indicates the difficulties in arriving at arms limitation *formulae* that met the desire to limit arms whilst ensuring that the global balance of power was not upset to British disadvantage.

By 1933, however, the international order constructed in the 1920s began unravelling. The onset of global depression created economic, political and social pressures within every power that led to a questioning of existing international agreements – war debts, for instance – and, for opportunistic men like Hitler and Japanese militarists, an opening to reshape regional balances in their favour. The weakening of the Washington treaty system with Japan's invasion of Manchuria in 1931, the virtual collapse of the war debt and reparations agreements in 1932, and Hitler's decision to take Germany out of the League and the World

---

[121] FO memorandum (RLA (26)53), 'Possibility of Regional Agreements between Foreign Powers', Aug. 1926, CAB 16/74; R.H. Campbell's comments in RLA (26) 19th Meeting, 1 Apr. 1927, CAB 16/72; FO memorandum (RA 2), 'The Model Treaty to Strengthen the Means of Preventing War', 17 Dec. 1929 (RA 3), 'Draft Treaty of Financial Assistance', 18 Dec. 1929, both CAB 16/98; Cadogan minute, 18 Dec. 1929, Craigie minute, 23 Dec. 1929, both FO 371/14256/130/1.

[122] R. Boyce, *British Capitalism at the Crossroads, 1919–1932: A Study in Politics, Economics, and International Relations* (London, 1987); M. Ceadl, *Pacifism in Britain, 1914–1945: The Defining of a Faith* (London, 1980); G.C. Peden, *British Rearmament and the Treasury, 1932–1939* (Edinburgh, 1979).

[123] Ferris, *Men, Money*, pp. 1–14; D. French, *The British Way in Warfare, 1688–200* (London, 1990), pp. 175–201; McKercher, *Transition*, chapters 1, 3.

Disarmament Conference in 1933 provided stark testimony to changing circumstances. For Vansittart and his subordinates, British foreign policy had to be modified to meet new international conditions.[124] Since essential British interests had not altered, the ends of policy remained the same as they had been since 1919: maintaining the global balance of power. But whereas in the 1920s, policy centred on maintaining the international status quo, after 1933 it entailed ensuring that any changes to the status quo occurred in ways short of war. The difficulty involved how that policy should be pursued.

In May 1932, Vansittart joined with Fisher and the Chiefs of Staff Committee to pressure the National Government to undertake arms spending to meet the emerging German and Japanese threats.[125] By November, they were constituted as the Defence Requirements Sub-committee (the DRC) of the CID. Reporting three months later, this group made specific recommendations to improve British armed strength by 1939, the date when war seemed probable – crucially, its purpose was not rearmament so much as meeting deficiencies in existing programmes delayed by retrenchment and the anticipation that the World Conference would have some success. Although the Cabinet reduced DRC-proposed spending by 30 per cent later in the year, the more important result of DRC deliberations was the emergence of a new strategy for British foreign policy that lasted until Neville Chamberlain became prime minister. It was not altered at the Cabinet level and resulted mainly from Vansittart.

In discussions in the DRC with Fisher that out-flanked the service chiefs – an alliance of the Foreign Office and Treasury – Vansittart got the DRC Report to identify Germany as Britain's 'ultimate potential enemy'. The Treasury was more concerned about the Japanese threat, which meant increased naval spending and building up Singapore. Although agreeing with Fisher about the need to 'show a tooth' in the Far East, Vansittart made the convincing point: 'The order of priorities which put Japan first pre-supposed that Japan would attack us after we had got into difficulties elsewhere. "Elsewhere" therefore came first, not second; and elsewhere could only mean Europe, and Europe could only mean Germany.'[126] Pressing successfully for an expeditionary force to be sent to the Low Countries in the event of a crisis, as well as Royal Air Force units to support it, he won the point in the DRC that British foreign

---

[124] Vansittart memoranda, 'The United Kingdom and Europe' (CP 4(32)), 1 Jan. 1932, CAB 24/227; 'The Crisis in Europe' (CP 52(33)), CAB 24/239; '... on the Present and Future Position in Europe' (212 (33), CAB 24/243; Sargent to Vansittart, 2 Sept. 1932, Sargent MSS FO 800/275/Ger/32/4; Lindley (British ambassador, Tokyo) memorandum (CP 145 (33)), 20 May 1933, CAB 24/241.

[125] Cf. N. Gibbs, *Grand Strategy*, I (London, 1976), pp. 93–9; C. Morrisey and M. Ramsay, ' "Giving a lead in the right direction": Sir Robert Vansittart and the DRC', *Diplomacy and Statecraft*, 6 (1993), 39–60.

[126] DRC Meeting 3, 4 Dec. 1933, CAB 16/109.

policy had simultaneously to work to deter future German and Japanese attempts to alter the European and Far Eastern balances in a way that would diminish London's ability to protect its formal and informal empires until the deficiencies in British armed strength were rectified. His efforts did not end there. In the Cabinet committee evaluating the DRC report, Neville Chamberlain argued for strength in the Far East and a concentration on home defence; hence, he opposed the despatch of ground and air forces to the Low Countries.[127] Vansittart then lobbied Baldwin and MacDonald to support a continental commitment to balance British strengthening in the Far East.[128] He encased his argument in a paper based on a classic exposition of the 'Crowe doctrine':

Not only did we keep everyone guessing [in 1914], until Germany guessed wrong but there was thought in Europe to be little deterrent on our path to a gamble. Europe remains in equal doubt both as to our policy and to our capacity. The results are already – or perhaps I should say at last – becoming manifest. Italy, Poland, Yugoslavia, Roumania, are all at varying degrees tending to be drawn into the German orbit; and on Italy's inconstancies now largely depend Austria, Hungary and Bulgaria ... The political map of Europe is, in fact, altering under our eyes and to our disadvantage, if we must look upon Germany as the eventual enemy.[129]

Foreign Office counsel was accepted by the Cabinet committee when it endorsed the DRC report in July.[130]

For the next two and one-half years, British foreign policy followed the strategic lines articulated by Vansittart between November 1933 and June 1934: the maintenance of a global balance of power.[131] This was the great achievement of Vansittart and 'Edwardian' thinking about foreign policy and national strategy in the 1930s and, ironically, its undoing. As Vansittart had told the DRC and Cabinet, an intimate connection existed between the balances of power in the Far East and Europe. A crisis in either sphere which weakened Britain's position would provide the Germans and the Japanese with the opportunity to tip the balances in their favour. This

---

[127] See his remarks in DC(M) (32) meetings 41–50, CAB 27/505; cf. 'Note by the Chancellor of the Exchequer on the Report of the Defence Requirements Committee' (DC(M) (32) 120), CAB 27/511.

[128] Simon memorandum (DC (M) (32) 118), 14 June 1934, CAB 27/510; Simon memorandum (DC (M) (32) 119), 14 June 1934, CAB 27/511. MacDonald and Baldwin's comments in DC (M) (32) 50th meeting, 25 June 1934, CAB 27/507.

[129] 'Minute by Sir R. Vansittart' (DC (M) (32) 117), 2 June 1934, CAB 27/510.

[130] Report on Defence Requirements (CP 204 (34)), 31 July 1934, CAB 16/110.

[131] Except where noted, the next two paragraphs are based on S. Bourette-Knowles, 'The Global Micawber: Sir Robert Vansittart, the Treasury and the Global Balance of Power, 1933-1935', and M. L. Roi, 'From the Stresa Front to the Triple Entente: Sir Robert Vansittart, the Abyssinian Crisis and the Containment of Germany', both *Diplomacy and Statecraft*, 6 (1995); 61-90, 91-121; J. Ferris, 'Worthy of Some Better Enemy? The British Estimate of the Imperial Japanese Army, 1919-41, and the Fall of Singapore', and K. E. Neilson, ' "Pursued by a Bear": British Estimates of Soviet Military Strength and Anglo-Soviet Relations, 1922-1939', both *Canadian Journal of History*, 28 (1993), 189-256.

belief was shared in varying degrees by Vansittart's chief associates in the Foreign Office: Lawrence Collier, Alan Leeper, Charles Orde and Ralph Wigram, respectively, the heads of the Northern, Western, Far Eastern, and Central departments. Thus, the question became how best to use political means to maintain a global equilibrium until British defence deficiencies were met. In the Far East, Vansittart and the Foreign Office experts looked to keep as free a hand as possible: finding a *modus vivendi* with the Japanese and Chinese in China whilst avoiding a formal agreement with Japan. This translated into resisting pressures from Neville Chamberlain and Fisher about concluding an Anglo-Japanese non-aggression pact – such an agreement would only make Japan more adventurous, antagonise the Americans and alienate the Bolshevik Russians.[132] Whilst United States involvement in Far Eastern affairs was more potential than real, a result of American isolationism, Vansittart and his colleagues saw Bolshevik Russia as a counter-weight to Japanese pretensions on continental East Asia. 'I feel that we must take facts as we find them,' wrote Collier in February 1934, 'and that, since we live among a number of Powers, few of whom really wish us well but some of whom have the same interests as ourselves, we should, whenever possible, encourage the latter to join with us in defending the *status quo* against those whose interests (in their own view) demand its overthrow.'[133]

It became British policy to balance between Japan and Bolshevik Russia in the Far East, tacking this way and that to avoid strengthening one or the other, though seeking to prevent an overt Russian weakening which might rebound unfavourably on the use of a Russian counter-weight against Germany in Europe. For the Foreign Office after early 1934, the maintenance of the European balance involved firm ties with France and Italy, both of which opposed German revisionism; this explains Foreign Office support for the Hoare–Laval pact. Moreover, containing Germany meant depriving Hitler of allies; and, in this regard, Vansittart was willing to work with Bolshevik Russia, for instance, supporting its entry into the League of Nations in 1934, to prevent a Russo-German rapprochement. Because of ideological opposition in the Conservative Party – an echo of the politics that had led to the Anglo-Russian rupture in 1927 – a formal agreement was impossible. However, Paris concluded a mutual defensive alliance with Moscow in May 1935, which the Foreign Office saw as holding the potential for keeping the Russians in the anti-German grouping of Powers. And even after Anglo-Italian estrangement following the mis-

---

[132] See Chamberlain to Simon, 10 Sept 1934, Simon to MacDonald, 3 Oct. 1934, both Simon FO 800/291; Chamberlain to Simon, 1 Sept. 1934, *DBFP II*, XIII, 24–5; Simon – Chamberlain memorandum (CP 223 (34)), 16 Oct. 1934, CAB 24/250. Cf. Dutton, *Simon*, pp. 192–3; A. Trotter, 'Tentative Steps for an Anglo-Japanese Rapprochement in 1934', *Modern Asian Studies*, 8 (1974), 59–83.

[133] Collier minute, 16 Feb. 1934, FO 371/18176/823/316. I would like to thank Simon Bourette-Knowles for directing me to this file.

fortune of Hoare–Laval – the parliamentary reaction to its premature announcement – the possibility of Britain finding common ground with France and Russia remained; in Michael Roi's words, this tended towards reviving the pre-1914 'Triple Entente'.[134] In the context of the time, gravitating towards 'Russia' offered expedient means to preserve the global balance of power. This does not mean that Vansittart and other Foreign Office 'professionals' opposed making concessions to the Germans. The 1935 Anglo-German naval agreement is a case in point, although it created problems with the French who argued correctly that Britain had helped Germany break the disarmament provisions of the Treaty of Versailles. However, as Hitler had already announced German rearmament, a naval deal would only help Britain's global strategic position.[135] Concessions like the Anglo-German naval agreement were seen in the Foreign Office as means by which the international status quo could be modified peacefully and in a way that did not weaken British strength.[136] Coupled with the difficult diplomacy that looked to preserve the European and Far Eastern balances – and following the Abyssinian crisis, that in the Mediterranean – the Foreign Office did much with foreign policy to gird Britain's position as the greatest of the great powers.

However, the Foreign Office, and Vansittart, in particular, had critics within the government. Neville Chamberlain and Fisher were especially harsh, especially after their vision for closer Anglo-Japanese relations proved untenable as much from Foreign Office effectiveness in bureaucratic wrangling as from the actions of Tokyo.[137] After the Hoare–Laval failure, Foreign Office critics increased, especially in the Cabinet.[138] And the advent of Eden as foreign secretary saw the gradual division between him and Vansittart that led to those efforts in January 1937 to have Vansittart succeed Clerk as the ambassador at Paris. Once Chamberlain became prime minister, it was simply a matter of time before Vansittart was pushed out. Anxious to avoid war – the implicit result of the failure of the balance of power – and believing that international conferences solved nothing, Chamberlain and his supporters believed that bilateral settlements with British adversaries could better preserve international peace.[139]

---

[134] See Collier minute, 29 June 1936, FO 371/20348/751/287; cf. Roi, 'Stresa Front'.
[135] H. H. Hall III, 'The Foreign Policy-Making Process in Britain, 1934–1935, and the Origins of the Anglo-German Naval Agreement', *Historical Journal*, 19 (1976), 477–99. Cf. the insightful D. C. Watt, 'The Anglo-German Naval Agreement of 1935: An Interim Judgement', *Journal of Modern History*, 28 (1956), 155–76.
[136] Craigie minute, 17 Jan 1935, FO 371/18731/901/22; Craigie minute, 29 Mar. 1935, FO 371/18732/3190/22; Craigie memorandum, 4 June 1935, FO 371/18733/5214/22.
[137] Chamberlain to Hilda, his sister, 15 Dec. 1935, 12 Sept., 14 Nov. 1937, NC 18/1/942, 18/1/1020, 18/1/1028; Fisher to Chamberlain, 15 Sept. 1936, NC 7/11/29/19.
[138] See the special Cabinet on Hoare-Laval, CC 56(35), CAB 23/90B.
[139] Eden to Chamberlain, 9 Nov. 1936, NC 7/11/29/16; Hoare to Chamberlain, 17 Mar. 1937, NC 7/11/30/74; Chatfield (first sea lord) to Backhouse (commander-in-chief, Home Fleet), 27 Mar. 1936, CHT (Chatfield MSS, National Maritime Museum, Greenwich)

This reflected on a larger scale the arguments Chamberlain propounded about Anglo-Japanese conciliation in 1934 and, once Vansittart was removed, formed the basis of the variant of appeasement diplomacy practised by his government until March 1939. As Cadogan said even in the middle of the second world war, 'the grand fault of our policy' between 1933 and 1938 was that Britain failed to 'open up with friend or foe'. The 'Edwardian' view was that granting major concessions to uncompromising powers would achieve nothing but strengthen those powers at British expense. After May 1937, Neville Chamberlain's new view prevailed. When Eden resigned as foreign secretary in February 1938 over a dispute with Chamberlain about how to handle the Italians,[140] the new prime minister controlled foreign policy. Lacking a grounding in *realpolitik*, this policy began the fruitless search for compromises that were not there, and which by September 1939 led to Britain's weakening in the Far East, the Mediterranean and continental Europe.

For most of the interwar period, the Foreign Office had decided authority in the process that made British foreign policy. Whilst it had less influence after 1919 than before 1914, between the premierships of Lloyd George and Neville Chamberlain it certainly existed as *primus inter pares* amongst the departments of state concerned with Britain's external position: national security, imperial defence and the protection of trade routes and markets. Much of this derived from a succession of politically powerful foreign secretaries and permanent Foreign Office officials who had the support of MacDonald and Baldwin. More important, it also derived from the ability of these men to see the world and Britain's position in that world for what it was, not what it should be. British resources were not inexhaustible. Britain could not go it alone. Thus, the generational belief, formed before 1914, that Britain had to combine with those powers that shared its interests to maintain the balances of power in Europe and the wider world crucial to British interests. But as Lloyd George before 1922 and Neville Chamberlain after mid-1937 demonstrated, 'old diplomacy' worked only as long as the political will to utilise it existed. Different ideas about the nature and purpose of diplomacy – new ideas – abounded in the interwar period; only the 'Edwardian' Foreign Office and its supporters produced realistic policies able to protect adequately British global interests.

4/1; Jones (former Downing Street private secretary) to Lady Grigg, 21 Feb. 1936, in T. Jones, *A Diary with Letters, 1931–1950* (Oxford, 1954), p. 176.
[140] Carlton, *Eden*, pp. 124–33; Rhodes James, *Eden*, pp. 193–4.

ERIK GOLDSTEIN

CHAPTER 6

The evolution of British diplomatic strategy for the Locarno Pact, 1924–1925

Introduction

The Locarno Pact of 1925 was the result of the convergence of several factors occurring simultaneously between November 1924 and March 1925, events which made Britain the diplomatic pivot of Europe. This period coincided with the beginning of Austen Chamberlain's tenure as foreign secretary, as well as the last months of Sir Eyre Crowe's career as permanent under-secretary at the Foreign Office. These events acted as the catalyst for a resurgence in Foreign Office influence, after more than a decade in the doldrums. First was a renewed German attempt at international rehabilitation through an offer, initially to Britain, of a reguarantee of the western European territorial status quo; second was the desire of France to reinsure its security *vis-à-vis* Germany through a security pact with Britain; and third was the decision of the new Conservative government in Britain to refuse to ratify the Geneva Protocol. The result would be the Locarno Pact, but underlying that achievement can be discerned fundamental shifts in the location of foreign policy formulation, and in Britain's assessment of its international role.[1]

For Britain 1919 had marked the apogee of empire, the end of the age of expansion and the beginning of a period of consolidation. A debate ensued as to what Britain should do in response to the international problems which abounded in the post Great War era. The years 1919–25 saw

[1] The British role in Locarno has formed part of a number of studies, among which the most important are Keith Middlemas and John Barnes, *Baldwin: A Biography* (London, 1969), pp. 42–58; Sibyl Crowe, 'Sir Eyre Crowe and the Locarno Pact', *English Historical Review*, 87 (1972), 49–74; Jon Jacobson, *Locarno Diplomacy: Germany and the West, 1925–1929* (Princeton, 1972); Anne Orde, *Great Britain and International Security* (London, 1978), pp. 68–154; David Dutton, *Austen Chamberlain: Gentleman in Politics* (Bolton, 1985).

a slow drift in the maintenance of a coherent diplomatic strategy. Britain's international, and European, role was in need of clearer definition. By 1925, with the advent of Stanley Baldwin's second government, Britain was in urgent need of considering its relationship to Europe, the Empire, and the United States. Its assessment of these concerns would be based on apprehension of the prevalent state of fear and anxiety evident in the international system, the still powerful sense of a special British mission, and traditional British thinking about the balance of power. The move to develop a focused and coherent foreign policy was driven by the combined forces of the new foreign secretary, Austen Chamberlain, and his dying permanent under-secretary, Sir Eyre Crowe.

Fear and foreign policy

The year 1925 dawned in Europe with a palpable atmosphere of fear hanging over the continent. Austen Chamberlain had warned the Committee of Imperial Defence (CID) in December 1924 that this was the dominant sentiment in Europe, and that another war was inevitable unless Britain could give Europe a sense of security.[2] Chamberlain reiterated this view in a meeting with Edouard Herriot, the French premier, stating that, 'the biggest factor in the world today was fear, and this fear was not confined to Europe.'[3] Churchill confirmed Chamberlain's assessment to the Cabinet on returning from a visit to Paris in January 1925, causing Chamberlain to inform Crowe that, 'Mr Churchill brought back from his Paris talks the impression of brooding fear which I reported to the CID.'[4] This sense of the psychological condition of world affairs permeated official thinking. Harold Nicolson in an important overview memorandum on the European situation at the beginning of 1925 noted that:

One-half of Europe is dangerously angry; the other half is dangerously afraid. The friction between these inflamed emotions is incessant, and acts as some septic irritant, poisoning the wounds which are yet unhealed. Fear begets provocation, armaments, secret alliances, ill-treatment of minorities; these in turn beget a greater hatred and stimulate a desire for revenge, whereby fear is intensified, and its consequences are enhanced. The vicious circle is thus established.[5]

[2] CAB 2/4/CID 192, meeting of 16 Dec. 1924, Cabinet Papers, PRO, London.
[3] *DBFP* 1/27/251, 'Memorandum by Mr Chamberlain of a conversation with M. Herriot', 16 Mar. 1925, *Documents on British Foreign Policy, 1919–1939*, 1st ser., vol. 27 (London, 1986) (hereinafter cited as *DBFP*).
[4] FO 371/10726/C459/459/18, Chamberlain to Crowe, 16 Jan. 1925, Foreign Office Papers, PRO, London. Churchill told the Cabinet on 15 Jan. that, 'The outstanding feature was the anxiety of France as to her security, in view of the probable revival of Germany within the next five to ten years and the bad relations still existing between the two countries.' CAB 23/49, also in Martin Gilbert, *Winston S. Churchill*, V, pt. 1, *The Exchequer Years, 1922–1929* (London, 1979), p. 343.
[5] FO 371/11065/W2035/9/98, Nicolson, 'Present Condition in Europe', 23 Jan. 1925. The final version dated 20 Feb. 1925 is in C2201/459/18 and is reprinted in *DBFP* 1/27/205, and is also in the Confidential Print.

The concept of fear was particularly associated with French motivations. Miles Lampson, head of the Foreign Office's Central Department, commented on 13 January that, 'it is not so much *truth* as *fear* that we have to contend with. France has twice passed through the ordeal of German aggression: her people are saturated, from the highest to the lowest, with fear of a similar experience. Perhaps they exaggerate the danger – but their feelings are at least intelligible.'[6] Crowe agreed with Lampson that the reality of French fear could not be denied.[7]

Sir William Tyrrell, assistant under-secretary at the Foreign Office, saw the situation as one which had remained unresolved since the end of the war, 'because we have neglected the psychological factor which dominates the situation. We have failed to remove the feeling of fear from our chief ally, France, who came out of the war a victor mainly in a technical sense. Her victory did not enable her to provide for her own security.'[8] These assessments of French concerns were borne out in meetings with leading French figures. Eric Phipps, minister in Paris, reporting a meeting with Marshal Foch, noted that the victorious Allied commander of the first world war, 'Many times in the course of our conversation ... started up from his chair and led me to a large-sized map of Europe hanging on the wall, pointing fearfully to the German monster, which, indeed, is always a somewhat terrifying spectacle on the map, and to the strangely-shaped countries which flank it on the east and south.'[9] Chamberlain as part of his effort to improve international relations sought to eradicate one of the prime causes of this fear, hoping that, 'by giving our guarantee to this Western frontier we should remove the acute fears which distort French policy and which prevent any improvement in Franco-German relations and threaten, unless removed, to make those relations steadily worse'.[10] Chamberlain informed the palace that, 'I believe the key to the solution is to be found in allaying French fears.'[11]

Some officials, however, saw an element of fear in French psychology as useful to British policy. Sir Maurice Hankey, in a memorandum circulated to the most senior ministers, suggested that if a guarantee treaty were concluded then 'by removing the restraint of fear, a pact might encourage France to maintain an overbearing and unaccommodating attitude towards Germany, thereby sowing the seeds of future wars'.[12] Amery, one of the leading opponents of further commitments to France, strongly

[6] FO 371/10726/C459/459/18, minute by Lampson, 13 Jan. 1925. Also *DBFP* 1/27/181.
[7] Ibid., minute by Crowe, 14 Jan. 1925.
[8] FO 371/11066/W6497/9/98, minute by Tyrrell, 18 Mar. 1925, in response to a proposal by Cecil for a general arms reduction scheme.
[9] *DBFP* 1/27/238, 'Record by Mr Phipps of a conversation with Marshal Foch', 11 Mar. 1925.
[10] *DBFP* 1/27/255, Chamberlain to D'Abernon (Berlin), 18 Mar. 1925.
[11] FO 800/257, Chamberlain to Stamfordham, 9 Feb. 1925.
[12] *DBFP* 1/27/191, memorandum by Hankey, 23 Jan. 1925. Since the war Hankey had consistently been dubious of any British guarantee commitments to France.

opposed the view that French anxiety should motivate British policy, and he contested in Cabinet the view that Britain should enter, 'into a definite commitment to defend France on the ground that she would never behave rationally till we relieved her fears of what may happen twenty years hence'.[13] James Headlam-Morley, the Foreign Office historical adviser, in a calm historical overview, did suggest that, 'if we look at Europe as a whole, is not the present state of anxiety, though natural enough, much exaggerated? We are still too much under the impressions of the late war. There are too many alarmists in the world.'[14] Nevertheless there was a definite sense that there were problems in Europe, problems which perhaps Britain alone could resolve.

British particularism

The concept of particularism is one often used by historians to denote certain strands in American diplomatic thinking. The same concept applies equally well to Britain. There is a distinct sense of mission in much of the thinking about Britain's international role, which is particularly evident in the aftermath of the Armageddon of the first world war. None could perhaps exceed the views of Arthur Hirtzel of the India Office who wrote in 1919, 'The Empire ... has been given to us as a means to that great end for which Christ came into the world, the redemption of the human race.'[15] At the 1921 Imperial Conference Lord Curzon, then foreign secretary, had expressed the belief that, 'The British Empire is a saving fact in a very distracted world. It is the most hopeful experiment in human organisation which the world has yet seen.'[16] Chamberlain wrote in March 1925 that:

I am not without hope that the influence of Great Britain may still be made the decisive factor in restoring the comity of nations. With America withdrawn, or taking part only where her interests are directly concerned in the collection of money, Great Britain is the one possible influence for peace and stabilisation. Without our help things will go from bad to worse.[17]

Britain then was seen as having a special role, and therefore an obligation to maintain order. Zara Steiner has observed that, 'Crowe thought almost exclusively in terms of the balance of power and saw in England the policeman of Europe, a moral force among the European nations'.[18] Chamber-

---

[13] John Barnes and David Nicholson, *The Leo Amery Diaries*, I, *1896–1929* (London, 1980), p. 399, 4 Mar. 1925.

[14] FO 371/11064/W1252/9/98.

[15] Sir Arthur Hirtzel, *The Church, The Empire, and The World* (London, 1919).

[16] CAB 32/2, Imperial Conference, 1st meeting, 20 June 1921.

[17] *DBFP* 1/27/256, Chamberlain to Howard (Washington), 18 Mar. 1925.

[18] Zara Steiner, *The Foreign Office and Foreign Policy, 1898–1914* (Cambridge, 1969), p. 113.

lain and Crowe were certainly not imbued with the Christian zeal of those like Hirtzel, but they had a strong secular faith in Britain. It was perceived that Europe, indeed the whole international system, was ill and weakened by anxiety and fear. It was therefore the first task of British diplomacy to find some emollient for those ills, which would in turn improve the general health of the international system, making it possible to address in a more rational way other irritants. It was commonly agreed that the country most afflicted with anxiety, and therefore the patient most in need of British ministration, was France.

France

The French desire for an association with Britain can be seen stretching from the Anglo-French Entente of 1904, through the joint military planning commenced in 1906, the Anglo-French Naval Accord of 1912, the wartime collaboration, and the abortive Anglo-American Guarantee of 1919. France, still in a state of anxiety about its own security *vis-à-vis* Germany, wanted to include Britain as an element in its security system. British attitudes towards France though were ambivalent, alternating between two considerations. On the one hand, France was Britain's best potential military ally on the continent, with the bonds strengthened by the four years of wartime alliance. On the other hand, France was Britain's centuries-old traditional rival, which now seemed to be attempting once again to exert its hegemony over Europe in the wake of Germany's defeat. British attitudes towards France wavered between the policy requirements of these two positions, and the British official mind remained very suspicious of French intentions.

Baldwin, on forming his first ministry, had a meeting with Raymond Poincaré, during which he informed the French premier that he was, 'struck by the absence of that confidence and close harmony so necessary between the two countries if the Entente were to be preserved'.[19] It was indeed an accurate description of the situation. Crowe observed to Phipps a few weeks after this meeting, 'The whole game as played by France is sickening and revolting. But we ought to be gradually getting accustomed to it.'[20] Phipps reported to Crowe from Paris that, 'The whole atmosphere of the Quai d'Orsay is, as you so well know, totally uncharged with "honesty". Indeed it is impossible to keep up with all the lies they churn out.'[21] As the moves towards the Locarno settlement began Sterndale Bennett warned that, 'The French are putting the onus upon us, i.e. they

[19] Baldwin 108. 'Note on a Conversation with M. Poincaré 19th September 1923', Baldwin of Bewdley papers (University Library, Cambridge).

[20] PHPP 2/3. Crowe to Phipps, 24 Nov. 1923, Phipps papers (Churchill College Archive Centre, Cambridge).

[21] PHPP 2/3, Phipps to Crowe, 27 Feb. 1924.

are refusing to make any concessions to Germany unless we pay the price by guaranteeing French security. From the French point of view this is very good policy, and it rests on sounder bases then their reparation policy, but all the same it is a little awkward for us.'[22]

The atmosphere in London was not helped by the presence there as French ambassador of the Comte de St Aulaire, who was not held in high regard. Curzon at one point avoided seeing the French diplomat, telling his wife, 'I am not going to see so venomous a snake.'[23] Curzon was not alone in his opinion. George V disliked him intensely, and signalled his desire that St Aulaire be succeeded by Fleuriau.[24] It is notable that when this did occur, Anglo-French tension eased. Crowe, always alert to the dynamics of diplomacy, observed about appointments at the French embassy, 'I believe that if there is to be a great effort to get Anglo-French relations definitely put on a better footing – and there is every desire here – nothing should be left undone to strengthen the "imponderabilia" of personal contacts between those of both sides who want to be really friendly.'[25]

Nicolson, while understanding of France's position, also shared the concerns of the those who worried about the threat that a confident France could pose. He argued that current French concerns

are the root cause of the present insecurity of Europe. They constitute for every Frenchman an increasing nervous ordeal, a persistent obsession, which while it colours the whole attitude of France towards Europe, renders her incapable of understanding the less concentrated policies of securer countries. The French dread of Germany is hereditary and inevitable, nor would we wish to see it entirely removed. Within limits, it serves as a corrective to the enterprising vanity of the French character which, if unchecked, would undoubtedly bring our two countries into conflict.[26]

Chamberlain too was worried about the loss of influence over France, if in rejecting the Geneva Protocol no alternative reassurance to France was forthcoming. He observed that 'we shall lose all influence over French policy. Do what we may, we shall win no gratitude from Germany. We shall be dragged along, unwilling, impotent, protesting, in the wake of France towards the new Armageddon. For we cannot afford to see France crushed.'[27] Even as negotiations towards the Locarno Pact progressed Lord Crewe felt the need to encourage London to persevere in its dealings with Paris, cabling Chamberlain with the message, 'I earnestly trust that His Majesty's Government will continue to show patience in dealing with

[22] FO 371/10727/C1319/459/18, minute by Bennett, 29 Jan. 1925.
[23] Marchioness Curzon of Kedleston, *Reminiscences* (London, 1955).
[24] PHPP 2/2, Phipps to Crewe, 17 Oct. 1924.
[25] PHPP 2/3, Crowe to Phipps, 28 Jan. 1924.
[26] FO 371/11065/W2035/9/98.
[27] FO 371/11064/W362/2/98, minute by Chamberlain, 4 Jan. 1925. Also in *DBFP* 1/27/120.

the sometimes exasperating attitude assumed by this country.'[28] If Britain though was turning its focus onto European affairs, it would have to consider the impact of this on its links to the Dominions.

The Dominions dimension

Britain had been grappling since the turn of the century with the bifurcated nature of its identity, imperial or European. Headlam-Morley summed up the difficulty aptly, 'This country has a double status. In the first place it is an integral part of Europe, a European state just as much as is France or Germany; secondly it is the centre and nucleus of a worldwide confederation, the other members of which are the Dominions.'[29] Nicolson took it as axiomatic that, 'it would be unsound for the Governments of the Empire to commit Great Britain and the Dominions to responsibilities which are not direct necessities of Imperial defence, and of which the people of the Empire would not approve.'[30] The need for Dominions support was strongly felt, as Miles Lampson observed: 'Do not let us forget Chanak. Mr Lloyd George discovered to his cost what it meant to move without the Dominions.'[31] Obviously the memory of Chanak loomed large, as Lampson reminded Hankey that, 'after Chanak we know that the opinion of the [Dominions] cannot be overlooked with impunity.'[32] Lampson was one of the strongest advocates within the Foreign Office for the closest cooperation with the Dominions, seeing it as the ultimate basis for British security. He noted that:

The United Kingdom cannot go to war alone: it is the British Empire which goes to war as a whole. This makes it all the more essential that the policy which we adopt is a truly *Imperial* policy and one to which the Dominions can subscribe and which they will loyally support when the time for action comes – if it ever does.[33]

Chamberlain found the Dominions dimension a convenient excuse with which to explain to Herriot why Britain could not enter into an Anglo-French security pact.[34]

The bonds of empire though can be seen to be have been rapidly loosening by 1925. Baldwin unsuccessfully attempted to hold an Imperial Conference to discuss the Geneva Protocol and alternative arrangements, with the Dominions replying that they were too busy to attend. Britain's European concerns were not the Dominions', and the reality of the gradual

[28] *DBFP* 1/27/233, Crewe (Paris) to Chamberlain, 9 Mar. 1925.
[29] FO 371/11064/W1252/9/98.
[30] FO 371/11065/W2035/9/98.
[31] FO 371/11065/W2035/9/98, minute by Lampson, 29 Jan. 1925.
[32] FO 371/10727/C1218/459/18, Lampson to Hankey, 27 Jan. 1925.
[33] FO 371/10727/C1493/459/18, minute by Lampson, 29 Jan. 1925.
[34] *DBFP* 1/27/224, Chamberlain (Paris) to Crowe, 7 Mar. 1925.

dissolution of Joseph Chamberlain's imperial ideal must have been all too evident to his son. In retrospect this nonchalant response on the part of the Dominions is the backdrop to the Balfour Report of 1926 and the subsequent Statute of Westminster, which formally cut the Dominions free from London, and vice versa. The decisions taken in early 1925 can be seen, in retrospect, as the turning point in London's relations with its self-governing Dominions. The creation of a separate Dominions Office in 1925, far from representing an institutional attempt to tighten the bonds of empire, was a recognition of the growing divergence of their foreign and defence concerns.

The United States of America

Even as the Dominions sank in importance to London, so Washington remained a constant, if baffling factor. As Lord Balfour told the CID, 'One of our difficulties in our foreign policy at this moment is that we have to deal with the United States, and it is very hard to know how to deal with it.'[35] The United States had proved an elusive partner, and any hope of utilising the new world as a counterweight in the old had faded. Disillusionment followed Wilson's failure to bring the United States into the League and through the security guarantee into European affairs. Attempts to revive cooperation through the Washington and Lausanne conferences had failed. Crowe was clear that attempts to appease the United States should stop, noting in March 1925, 'I hope we may cease to be obsessed by the idea of "placating" the United States.'[36] Elaborating on this view he observed:

I have never believed in the policy of dragging the United States into our European affairs. They are supposed to be helpful but in fact they rarely are except where their pocket is concerned – as in the case of they Dawes Report which we now know they supported because they wanted to claim reparations for themselves. In most cases American intervention and American 'observers' do nothing but mischief and cause endless complications. I should not go out of our way to bring them in.[37]

But if the United States was not going to be a player in the European arena, and the Dominions were equally wary, Britain would have to reassess its own involvement in Europe.

Balance of power

The 1919 settlement had been meant to establish a new international order replacing the old Concert of Europe and the balance of power. Even

[35] CAB 2/4/CID 195, 13 Feb. 1925.
[36] FO 371/10728/C3629/459/18, minute by Crowe, 13 Mar. 1925.
[37] FO 371/10728/C3628/459/18, minute by Crowe, 13 Mar. 1925.

at the time many were doubtful that such fundamentals were capable of substitution, and the period after 1919 saw a painful attempt to return to the best of the old order. Headlam-Morley had observed at the time of the peace settlement that, 'It is to be regretted that public opinion appears to countenance the view that the doctrine of the Balance of Power can be neglected. It is, and will remain, a fundamental point just as much after the establishment of a League of Nations as it has been before.'[38] Nicolson later recalled of this period that, 'Benes taught me that the Balance of Power was not necessarily a shameful, but possibly a scientific, thing. He showed me that only on the firm basis of such a balance could the fluids of European amity pass and repass without interruption.'[39] By 1925 Nicolson was advising that some modification in the Paris settlement would be beneficial if the old Concert of Europe spirit could be recreated, observing in January that, 'Although in the present mood of Europe it would be useless even to mention the revision of the peace treaties, yet if the concert of Europe can thus gradually be recreated saner councils will prevail.'[40]

Headlam-Morley had continued to advise of the durability and utility of the Concert system. He carried on a brisk correspondence with Lord d'Abernon, the ambassador in Berlin, during 1924–5 on the balance of power, and in an influential memorandum in February 1925 Headlam-Morley argued forcefully for the benefits of utilising the best elements of the old system.[41] He restated the common rationale for British involvement with the Continent, 'Our island is so close to the continent that we cannot afford to ignore what goes on there, and so we get the next fundamental requirement, that the opposite shores of the Channel and North Sea should never be brought under the control of a single great military and naval power.'[42] In his argument he drew a particular analogy between current needs of British diplomacy and the foreign policy of Castlereagh after the Napoleonic wars.

Headlam-Morley's ideas appealed to Chamberlain, who admitted to being, 'much struck with an observation made by Mr Headlam-Morley . . . that the first thought of Castlereagh after 1815 was to restore the Concert of Europe & that the more ambitious peacemakers of Versailles when they framed the Covenant, still left a gap which only a new Concert of Europe can fill.'[43] Indeed so taken was Chamberlain with this analogy that by May he was recommending to the German ambassador C.K. Webster's new book on *The Foreign Policy of Castlereagh*, telling him that his policy

[38] FO 371/4353/f23/PC55.
[39] Harold Nicolson, *Peacemaking 1919* (Boston, 1933), p. 210.
[40] FO 371/11065/W2035/9/98.
[41] HDLM, Acc 727, boxes 38–39, Headlam-Morley papers (Churchill College Archive Centre, Cambridge).
[42] FO 371/11064/W1252/9/98.
[43] FO 371/11064/W1252/9/98, minute by Chamberlain, 21 Feb. 1925.

followed the same lines.[44] Later he would have Castlereagh's portrait hung in the room where the Locarno treaties were signed, no doubt as the presiding deity.[45] In the old traditions of British diplomacy, so lucidly explained in Headlam-Morley's internal Foreign Office tutelary memoranda, Chamberlain saw Britain as the manager of the European balance, writing to d'Abernon of, 'the constant risk that either France or Germany may upset the apple-cart'.[46] The European apple-cart though had some species in it that Chamberlain found preferable to others.

Britain and Europe

British foreign policy can be seen as traditionally following a course of aloofness from continental affairs, intervening only from time to time to assure a balance of power. In applied terms, for Britain a balance of power system was one which prevented any one power from dominating western Europe and thus posing an invasion threat. Britain was far less concerned about balance in the east, where stability was the key, its part being to remain stable and thereby avoid causing consequential disturbances to the western European balance. Britain's policy towards western Europe was therefore guided by basic security precautions. If western Europe were properly in equilibrium any threat to Britain would be much reduced. Headlam-Morley advised that, 'for more than 500 years our statesmen and rulers have always held that we had a predominant interest in this part of the Continent of Europe'.[47] The current map of western Europe had been designed in 1919 at the Paris Peace Conference, and met the British specification of neatly balancing France and Germany. The French though were continually threatening to put it out of balance by instigating separatist movements in the Rhineland, occupying the Ruhr, or refusing to evacuate Cologne. The Germans likewise threatened the region's stability, as having accepted the settlement under the duress of defeat, they might in the future attempt revision. Not surprisingly much British diplomatic energy was expended in finding a way to stabilise the situation. Chamberlain on taking office explored various solutions, including a security pact with France and Belgium, in order to calm their security fears, and to

---

[44] *DBFP* 1/27/325, Chamberlain to d'Abernon (Berlin), 15 May 1925. Webster's book had just been published that January. Charles Webster, *The Foreign Policy of Castlereagh* (London, 1925).

[45] Sir Charles Petrie, *The Life and Letters of the Right Hon. Sir Austen Chamberlain*, II (London, 1940), pp. 154–5.

[46] *DBFP* 1/27/283, A. Chamberlain to d'Abernon (Berlin), 2 Apr. 1925. Also in FO 800/127, and in part in Petrie, *Chamberlain*, II, pp. 271–2.

[47] FO 371/11065/W2070/9/98, Headlam-Morley, 'The Problem of Security: England and the Low Countries', 10 Mar. 1925. Reprinted in Headlam-Morley, *Studies in Diplomatic History* (London, 1930), pp. 156–71.

make clear to Germany that revision of western European borders was not an option.

There were those who preferred to avoid entangling alliances with volatile continental states. Hankey summed up this school of thought in a memorandum sent to senior ministers, 'I have always felt that the utmost difficulty would be encountered in overcoming the average Britisher's instinctive dislike of any Continental commitment (which I share) ...'[48] Nicolson countered this argument, writing at the same time as Hankey,

the policy known as 'splendid isolation' is not today a practicable policy. For America, powerful and aloof, such a course is still, perhaps, a possibility. For the British Empire no such escape is feasible. History and economics show that isolation in present conditions spells danger, vulnerability and impotence. Geography and aeronautics show that isolation is not in our case a scientific fact.[49]

If Britain were to eschew the ostrich approach, could it afford to limit its interest solely to western Europe? At the Paris Peace Conference several members of the British delegation associated with the New Europe group had argued, with some success, that given the complexities and interlocking nature of the European balance the continent had to be seen as a whole, that any settlement of western Europe had to take account of eastern Europe. Several New Europe supporters were still in the Foreign Office and continued to argue this case, in particular Headlam-Morley and Nicolson.

Eastern Europe's place on the British mental map of Europe, even in the post First World War era, was still very much *terra incognita*. The eastern Europe of 1925 had only been invented a few years earlier at the Paris Peace Conference, and Britain was still uncertain as to whether these newly created states would survive. Both their political stability and their close links to France were matters for concern. Eastern Europe had traditionally played a secondary role to western Europe. At the Congress of Vienna in 1815 Britain had only been interested in eastern Europe to the extent it could be used as a source of territorial compensations to facilitate the construction of a western European balance of power. This idea of eastern Europe providing the *quid pro quo* for stability in areas of more immediate concern to Britain was a durable one, with its influence running through Locarno, the Munich settlement, the percentages agreement, Yalta and the acquiescence in a divided Europe.

Austen Chamberlain's own view of eastern Europe's role and its importance to Britain remained consistent throughout his period at the Foreign Office. He saw the eastern European situation as unstable,[50] and that Britain

---

[48] *DBFP* 1/27/191, memorandum by Hankey, 23 Jan. 1925.
[49] FO 371/11065/W2035/9/98.
[50] FO 371/11064/W362/2/98, minute by Chamberlain, 4 Jan. 1925. Also in *DBFP* 1/27/180.

had very different interests in a Europe he divided neatly between east and west, observing, 'that in Western Europe we are a partner ... in Eastern Europe our role should be that of a disinterested amicus curiae'.[51] The potential explosiveness of eastern Europe worried him, and he famously told Lord Crewe that, 'no British Government ever will or ever can risk the bones of a British grenadier', for the Polish corridor.[52] He acknowledged to d'Abernon that 'in obtaining additional security in the West, I think we do not in fact lessen the danger of war in the East.'[53] Nonetheless a policy of out of sight out of mind was to be followed, with Chamberlain telling d'Abernon that, 'for the moment I think the less that is said about the east the better it will be'.[54] Chamberlain remained adamant that it was contrary to British policy to become involved in any new arrangements or guarantees in eastern Europe.[55] When Balfour in a Cabinet committee discussion included among the territorial issues of concern the eastern frontier of Poland, Chamberlain ignored this point in his reply.[56]

There were those within the Foreign Office who were concerned that ignoring eastern Europe in the lead up to Locarno was similar to doing an equation with some of the figures missing. These views were put cogently by Headlam-Morley in his background memorandum for Chamberlain, in which he proposed that, 'the danger point in Europe is not the Rhine, but the Vistula, not Alsace-Lorraine, but the Polish corridor and Upper Silesia'. He argued that, 'It is the real interest of this country to prevent a new alliance between Germany and Russia, an alliance which would no doubt be cemented by an attack on Poland.' Headlam-Morley was able to see that any increase in German strength in the east would eventually be brought to bear upon the Rhine. He was a stout advocate of the concept of balance of power and equilibrium, and did not see how east and west Europe could be artificially decoupled. Even in 1925 Headlam-Morley could discern the scenario which might lead to the outbreak of war in the future, with the greatest prescience suggesting as an 'improbable' situation, 'Austria rejoined Germany; that Germany, using the discontented minority in Bohemia, demanded a new frontier far over the mountains, including Carlsbad and Pilsen, and at the same time, in alliance with Germany, the Hungarians recovered the southern slopes of the Carpathians'.[57] He warned that, 'in the past our diplomacy has always failed

---

[51] FO 371/11064/W1252/9/98, minute by A. Chamberlain, 21 Feb. 1925.
[52] *DBFP* 1/27/200, Chamberlain to Crewe, 16 Feb. 1925. Also reprinted Petrie, *Chamberlain*, II, pp. 358–60.
[53] *DBFP* 1/27/255, Chamberlain to D'Abernon (Berlin), 18 Mar. 1925.
[54] *DBFP* 1/27/283, A. Chamberlain to d'Abernon (Berlin), 2 Apr. 1925. Also in FO 800/127, and reprinted in part in Petrie, *Chamberlain*, II, pp. 271–2.
[55] *DBFP* 1/27/321, 'Memorandum by Chamberlain for the Cabinet', 14 May 1925.
[56] *DBFP* 1/27/343, notes on meeting of Committee of the Cabinet held in the prime minister's room at House of Commons, 26 May 1926.
[57] FO 371/11064/W1252/9/98.

when it was confronted by problems arising in the east of Europe'. Indeed so it would prove in 1939. Austen Chamberlain's tentative approach to Europe in 1925 would confirm Britain's traditional reluctance to see Europe as a whole, and it is hardly surprising to find his brother later saying of the Czech crisis that it was 'a quarrel in a faraway country between people of whom we know nothing'.[58]

The Chamberlain–Crowe alliance

The British Foreign Office before the First World War had been the driving force in shaping foreign policy, but during the Lloyd George government it witnessed an alarming erosion of its influence.[59] The professional Foreign Office staff fought back against Downing Street's growing interference, but the permanent under-secretary, Lord Hardinge, although he proved to be a skilful bureaucratic infighter, never overcame the critical handicap of the prime minister's dislike. Sir Eyre Crowe succeeded Hardinge in 1920, and in the years that followed he worked assiduously to restore the Office to the preeminence it had enjoyed when he first joined it. His course was not made the easier by difficult political masters, first Lord Curzon and then Ramsay Macdonald. Curzon under Lloyd George was hardly a free agent, and, subsequently when freed from those constraints, displayed a worrying tendency to rely on his own infallibility, while under the short-lived Labour government the Foreign Office was effectively merged in Downing Street through Macdonald's decision to hold both portfolios. The appointment of Chamberlain as foreign secretary in November 1924 gave Crowe the opportunity he had been waiting for, a foreign secretary he could collaborate with. The synergy Chamberlain and Crowe produced would become a powerful, if all too short-lived, force in foreign policy. Chamberlain, on Crowe's death, would observe that he 'could not have believed that in so short a time, friendship had taken such deep roots'.[60] A key element in the resurgence of Foreign Office influence was Crowe's ability to work with his political masters, in particular gaining the confidence of Baldwin and Chamberlain, even in the few months he had occasion to work with them. Baldwin would eulogise Crowe as, 'the ablest public servant of the Crown'.[61]

These were in fact the last months of Crowe's life, he went on leave at the end of March and died at the end of April 1925. One of the greatest diplomatists Britain ever produced, he was during his career the intellectual

---

[58] *Documents on International Affairs 1938*, II, pp. 270–1.
[59] Roberta Warman, 'The Erosion of Foreign Office Influence in the Making of Foreign Policy, 1916–1918', *Historical Journal*, 15:1 (1972), 133–59.
[60] Chamberlain to Lady Crowe, 29 Apr. 1925, quoted in Sibyl Crowe and Edward Corp, *Our Ablest Public Servant: Sir Eyre Crowe* (Braunton, Devon, 1993), p. 489.
[61] Quoted in S. Wilkinson, 'Eyre Crowe', *Dictionary of National Biography*, ed. J.R.H. Weaver (London, 1937).

dynamo of British foreign policy. Very much an independent thinker, Zara Steiner has observed of him that he was the author of what was, 'perhaps the only Foreign Office memorandum to have become a classic state paper', the famous 1907 'Memorandum on the present state of relations with France and Germany.'[62] Even on the eve of his death it remained the problem which still dominated his mind. The memory of Crowe and his intimate connection with the origins of the policy planning which would result in Locarno was still powerful enough for the Foreign Office to hold in 1994 a commemorative lecture on his contribution to foreign policy, appropriately enough in the resplendent Locarno Room.

Chamberlain's career was marked by a number of disappointments, and although he had only reluctantly accepted the foreign secretaryship, he was determined to show he could make a success of it. Chamberlain had been contemptuous of Curzon's inability to establish his ascendency in foreign policy, telling Lord Derby that Curzon had, 'no weight with Lloyd George in Foreign Affairs,' and he condemned Curzon for not bringing matters to a head in Cabinet.[63] Chamberlain undoubtedly recalled by way of comparison Grey's mastery of foreign policy, and he was determined to establish his own ascendency in this field.[64]

Some of Chamberlain's Cabinet colleagues clearly felt that he had all too readily been captured by his civil servants, in particular by Crowe. Lord Cecil told Churchill that, 'Austen seems to have become a mere phonograph of Crowe.'[65] Such a view is unduly harsh on Chamberlain's essential intellectual independence. Undoubtedly though such forceful thinkers on foreign policy as Crowe, and his close friend and successor, Tyrrell, did help inform and shape the policies adopted by Chamberlain, policies so acclaimed in their time that they brought him the Nobel Prize for Peace.

Chamberlain entered office determined to elaborate a foreign policy, and, once having evolved a well defined policy, to implement it. He told the CID that, 'I feel every day in the discharge of my work at the Foreign Office the urgent necessity of having at the earliest possible moment a declaration of the policy of the British government in respect of all these questions of security.'[66] He was aware that at some stage he would probably have to establish his authority over foreign affairs in a Cabinet which included several members who themselves held strong views on foreign

---

[62] Steiner, *Foreign Office*, p. 112. The memorandum can be found in G.P. Gooch and H.W.V. Temperley, eds., *British Documents on the Origins of the War, 1898–1914* (London, 1926–38), III, Appendix A.

[63] Randolph Churchill, *Lord Derby 'King of Lancashire'* (London, 1959), pp. 428–9, 488, diary entries for 15 Mar. 1922 and 23 Nov. 1922.

[64] Zara Steiner, 'The Foreign Office and the War', in F.H. Hinsley, ed., *British Foreign Policy under Sir Edward Grey* (Cambridge, 1977), pp. 516–31.

[65] Gilbert, *Exchequer Years, 1922–1929*, pp. 347–8, Cecil to Churchill, 16 Jan. 1925.

[66] CAB 24/4/CID 195, 13 Feb. 1925.

policy, such as Winston Churchill, Lord Curzon, Lord Cecil and Leo Amery.[67] Once the Geneva Protocol was disposed of Chamberlain and the Foreign Office were left with the task of evolving an alternative policy. Chamberlain therefore began his stewardship of foreign policy by inviting his senior officials to a 'symposium' on the European situation. He was clearly impressed by the results, observing in a paper to the Cabinet on their conclusions that, 'it represents not only the personal opinion of the Secretary of State but the considered view of the Foreign Office as a whole and of the very able and experienced body of officials who advise me'.[68] Chamberlain had found in Crowe and the professionals at the Office a team with whom he could work.

From protocol to pact

The first foreign policy decision the new Conservative government had to face on taking office in November 1924 was whether or not to proceed with the ratification of the Geneva Protocol, which had been very much the creation of Ramsay Macdonald and his now defeated Labour government. Under the Protocol signatories agreed not to go to war except with the consent of the Council of the League of Nations, and to compulsory arbitration of disputes. Macdonald, who acted as his own foreign secretary, and his delegates at Geneva, had negotiated the Protocol without the benefit of any preparatory studies by the Foreign Office, and in concert with the French premier, Edouard Herriot. When detailed study of the Protocol began, many concerns emerged.[69] Crowe and the senior members of the Office opposed the Protocol as a poor document from the point of view of British interests. Rejecting the Protocol though would mean an upset in Anglo-French relations, thereby generating a quite unnecessary crisis in Britain's continental relations. The matter was referred to a sub-committee of the CID, while at the same time the Dominions were consulted. Baldwin observed that the Protocol question, 'brings to the forefront far reaching problems affecting the security of the Empire and its future relation to the countries of Europe and the United States of America'.[70] The sub-committee recommended against the protocol on 23 January, a view accepted by the Cabinet on 2 March, with the Dominions concurring.

The CID sub-committee charged with considering the viability of the Protocol consisted of Hankey, Crowe, Hirtzel (India Office) and Lambert

---

[67] Churchill was chancellor of the Exchequer, Curzon was lord president of the Council and chairman of the CID, Cecil was chancellor of the Duchy of Lancaster, and Amery colonial secretary.

[68] *DBFP* 1/27/205, covering note by Chamberlain, 19 Feb. 1925.

[69] Orde, *Great Britain*, p. 69.

[70] *Documents on Canadian External Relations* (Ottawa, 1970), III, document 504.

(acting permanent under-secretary at the Colonial Office).[71] The latter two were clearly inconsequential in such a discussion, even given Hirtzel's messianic view of Britain, as the India Office and Colonial Office were peripheral to European security concerns. The principal members were therefore Crowe and Hankey. Crowe had initially been asked to chair the sub-committee but Chamberlain pleaded his permanent under-secretary's existing heavy burden, and it was decided to give the chair to Hankey.[72] It is hardly creditable that the Cabinet secretary's burdens were viewed as substantially less than those of the permanent under-secretary at the Foreign Office. Certainly if Chamberlain and Crowe were anxious to establish Foreign Office primacy in the arena of foreign policy, ceding the chair of such an important sub-committee was a very curious way of going about it. It was in fact a significant step in this process. Hankey was a key player in Whitehall, and co-opting him in support of the Foreign Office view was vital. Crowe would have remembered all too well how Hankey had side-lined Hardinge at the time of the Paris Peace Conference. Hankey was also one of the most voluble opponents of any further guarantees to France. By placing Hankey in the chair there was therefore first of all a degree of flattery of the powerful Cabinet secretary, while secondly it allowed Crowe full scope as an active participant to advocate a line of policy, while Hankey would be somewhat circumscribed by his presiding role. The tactic worked, with Hankey agreeing that the committee should recommend a suggestion by Crowe for an Anglo-French-Belgian security pact.[73] Crowe also suggested leaving open the possibility of German adhesion, but fear of French reaction prevented this being proposed.[74] Hankey now wrote to Baldwin, Chamberlain, Curzon and Balfour that in his view, 'that we should orient our policy so as to remain, so far as possible, on such close and cordial terms with France that there is no risk of hostilities with that country,' and specifically advocated the Crowe line.[75]

Events now began to overtake the CID sub-committee's proposal. Germany's offer of 20 January 1925 opened new possibilities, and reopened Crowe's idea of including Germany in the proposed pact.[76] Crowe advised on 22 January that the German offer was, 'a move in the right direction and ought not to be discouraged'.[77] Lord d'Abernon had been manoeuvring in Berlin to prompt Germany towards such a suggestion. He was not acting, as has often been stated, independently of London. He had been in

---

[71] CAB 16/56.

[72] CAB 16/56/4657, CID minutes, 16 Dec. 1924.

[73] FO 800/257, Hankey to Chamberlain,

[74] CAB 16/56/G.P.(24)8.

[75] *DBFP* 1/27/191.

[76] Orde accurately observed that, 'The German proposals of 20 January initially cut across the policy which Chamberlain was trying to get his colleagues to adopt, but in the end provided a way out of the impasse.' Orde, *Great Britain*, p. 83.

[77] FO 371/10726/C980/459/18, minute by Crowe, 22 Jan. 1925.

London during late November and early December for consultations with the new government, and his correspondence with Headlam-Morley shows that he was not in ignorance of thinking in the Office on the security problems of Europe. Indeed he asked Headlam-Morley to comment on his memorandum on Security and the Maintenance of European Peace before it was submitted, a memorandum intended to open the way for a new western European relationship.[78]

Chamberlain had not arrived at the Foreign Office with set views, but through the period from December 1924 to March 1925 he and the Office, in particular Crowe, synthesised the various western European concerns into a projected pact which would become the basis for the Locarno agreements. Chamberlain had initially favoured a pact with France, and possibly Belgium, as the optimum solution, but as the implications of the German offer became apparent, new options were considered and he began to move towards Crowe's idea of including Germany in some form. The shift in Chamberlain's thinking can be seen by 9 February when he informed the king's private secretary that it was, 'the first task of statesmanship to set to work to make the new position of Germany tolerable to the German people in the hope that as they regain prosperity under it they may become reconciled to it and be unwilling to put their fortunes again to the desperate hazard of war'.[79] At some time between 26 February and 1 March Chamberlain moved decisively from the idea of an Anglo-French-Belgian pact to a four power pact including Germany. He wrote on 1 March: 'I have now got my policy clear and definite in my own mind; but can I carry the Cabinet? It is an awful fight and adds tremendously to my labours and anxieties. The policy is not an easy one, may meet with much opposition inside and outside the Government and deals with fundamental and tremendous issues – and time is of the essence of success.'[80] Before the Cabinet met on 2 March Crowe and Tyrrell saw Baldwin and obtained his support for the policy Chamberlain would present to the Cabinet.[81] At this Cabinet session the Protocol was definitely rejected and Chamberlain, with Baldwin's support, was authorised to explore the possibility of a four power pact at his meeting with Herriot scheduled for 6 March in Paris.

Hankey, although he had accepted the original Crowe formulation, was horrified by what he saw as the possibility of a pandora's box of continental commitments being opened by allowing Chamberlain out, unchaperoned, to negotiate with the French. Hankey spent 3 March attempting to limit Chamberlain's freedom of action, seeing in succession Baldwin, Curzon

---

[78] HDLM Acc 727, Box 39, d'Abernon to Headlam-Morley, 13 Nov. 1924. Also in BL Add. MS 48927, D'Abernon Papers (British Library, London).
[79] FO 800/257, Chamberlain to Stamfordham, 9 Feb. 1925.
[80] AC 5/1/347, Chamberlain to Ida Chamberlain, 1 Mar. 1925, Austen Chamberlain Papers (University of Birmingham).
[81] AC 52/240, Crowe to Chamberlain, 12 Mar. 1925.

and Balfour. This resulted in Curzon, with a reluctant Balfour in tow, calling upon Chamberlain on the evening of 3 March to object to the policy adopted.[82] It was agreed to discuss the issue the next day in Cabinet.

The Cabinet met again on 4 March to clarify the formula Chamberlain would use when seeing Herriot. Baldwin however had rushed off to the bedside of his ailing mother, and was therefore unable to back the foreign secretary. A powerful coalition of Curzon, Balfour, Amery, Churchill and Birkenhead, all of whom wanted no continental commitments, moved in to circumscribe Chamberlain's freedom of action. Not even the possibility of a four power guarantee pact was to be suggested to the French. Amery was delighted, noting in his diary the complete defeat of, 'the FO scheme (which captured Austen) for rushing the country (forgetting the Empire) into a definite commitment to defend France on the ground that she would never behave rationally till we relieved her fears of what may happen twenty years hence'.[83] Hankey congratulated himself that, 'Chamberlain had to go to Paris and to Geneva to meet Herriot with instructions severely limiting his initiative and power in the matter of the four-power pact.'[84] With Baldwin away Chamberlain was forced to bide his time.

Some events could not wait. Chamberlain was due in Geneva to announce publicly the British decision on the pact, and he was expected to call on Herriot as he passed through Paris. His meeting with Herriot on 6 March was not a pleasant experience, and confirmed Chamberlain's view that unless French anxiety was assuaged a major crisis loomed. There followed the most crucial days of Chamberlain's period in office. As Chamberlain's comments about Curzon's foreign secretaryship make clear, he knew that at some point he would have to test his authority in Cabinet. Ironically it was now Curzon who was the chief obstacle to the foreign secretary's control of foreign policy. The confrontation came sooner than he can have expected, and he was forced to conduct much of the confrontation at long distance. Chamberlain on 7 March cabled Crowe to request Baldwin to allow him to make a more substantive offer to the French, in effect the action Chamberlain had failed to get the Cabinet to support in Baldwin's absence.[85] Crowe saw the prime minister, briefly, over lunch on 11 March, and told him that the French had, not surprisingly, reacted poorly to Chamberlain's delivery of the British decision and the absence of a substantive alternative. Crowe reinforced

---

[82] HNKY 1/7, Hankey diary, 22 Mar. 1925, Hankey Papers (Churchill College Archive Centre, Cambridge). AC 39/118, Chamberlain to d'Abernon, 11 Sept. 1930 and AC 40/123, Chamberlain to Nicolson, 28 May 1934. Chamberlain's account written from memory has minor errors on the timing of meetings.

[83] Amery diary, vol I, p. 389, 4 Mar. 1925.

[84] HNKY 1/7, Hankey diary, 22 Mar. 1925.

[85] DBFP 1/27/227, Chamberlain (Geneva) to Crowe, 8 Mar. 1925. This message was received on 11 Mar., and Crowe went immediately to contact Baldwin.

with Baldwin the view that if France decided to remain intransigent, and therefore in more or less permanent occupation of the Rhineland, they would be faced with France creating, 'the maximum of friction, not only with Germany, but over the whole of Central Europe'.[86] Crowe then confronted Baldwin squarely with the request to, 'use the influence of his position to prevent such a catastrophe, into which his Cabinet were running more or less blindly and for want of understanding'.[87] Crowe proceeded to suggest to Baldwin that Chamberlain should be authorised to tell Herriot that Britain was willing, 'to contemplate the method of separate pacts, so long as the participation of Germany in some form remained assured and the separate pacts were linked together in some formal manner and also in point of time'.[88] It was not logistically possible to summon a special Cabinet in time, so Baldwin summoned an informal meeting of key Cabinet members that same afternoon.

In a two-hour session many of Chamberlain's Cabinet colleagues spoke against any continental commitments. Crowe informed Chamberlain that, 'I cannot describe to you the deplorable impression made upon me by this discussion.' Crowe was eventually asked to leave by Baldwin, who perhaps felt it inappropriate to have a civil servant present while he dealt with his unruly colleagues. Crowe told Chamberlain that he had been so disturbed by the meeting that he had decided, if he were asked to draft a negative cable to Chamberlain, to refuse. Such an action by a senior civil servant was almost unprecedented, and clearly was meant to indicate to Chamberlain the action that he should take. Chamberlain understood and cabled Crowe, in a message flagged to be deciphered personally by the permanent under-secretary, to inform the prime minister that if he did not enjoy the support of the Cabinet he would resign.[89] Chamberlain had taken the action which he once felt Curzon should have taken, and with positive effect. Baldwin had no wish to lose his foreign secretary four months into his new government, and moved to reassure Chamberlain of his personal backing.[90] He summoned Crowe to Chequers on 15 March and instructed him to inform Chamberlain of his full support. Chamberlain returned to Britain and saw the prime minister on 19 March and obtained confirmation of Baldwin's full support. On 20 March Lord Curzon died, and as Hankey noted despairingly in his diary, 'within seven hours of his death the cabinet decided to authorise Austen Chamberlain to announce a policy of aiming at a four-power Pact of Guarantee'.[91] The

[86] AC 52/240, Crowe to A. Chamberlain (Geneva), 12 Mar. 1925.
[87] Ibid.
[88] Ibid.
[89] AC 52/241, Chamberlain to Crowe, 14 Mar. 1925. Reprinted in Petrie, *Chamberlain*, II, p. 264.
[90] AC 52/244, Crowe to Chamberlain, 13 Mar. 1925.
[91] HNKY 1/7, Hankey diary, 22 Mar. 1925.

Cabinet met on the afternoon of Curzon's death and gave its full support to Chamberlain's plan for a four power pact.[92]

What is particularly intriguing about the whole episode is how most of the communications went through Crowe. Certainly ministers of the crown could communicate directly, and did not need the interlocution of their civil servants. It is worth pondering how much Crowe, whose health was rapidly deteriorating, was driving events. Having helped engineer Chamberlain's, and by implication the Foreign Office's, victory over external interference in policy Crowe had achieved one of his great goals. A few days later he went on indefinite sick leave, and Chamberlain went on to negotiate the Locarno Pact.

Conclusion

The year 1925 was a much changed world for the Foreign Office from the doldrum days of Lloyd George. The new Conservative government, led by the semi-detached Stanley Baldwin, was absorbed by domestic concerns, and Baldwin was happy to entrust the general oversight of foreign policy to the care of a parliamentary senior statesman, Austen Chamberlain. Chamberlain was conscious of the need to master the brief which had so unexpectedly been thrust into his hands by Baldwin, and to establish his own primacy in foreign policy. In order to accomplish this he worked closely with his professional staff in a way which had passed out of fashion since the tenure of Edward Grey. His reliance on two of the key figures of the Grey era, Crowe and Tyrrell, is particularly notable.

Among the advice Chamberlain called for in his early days in office was historical advice. In Headlam-Morley, the Foreign Office historical adviser, he had one of the leading diplomatic historians of his time. Lord Hardinge had helped to make historical advice an integral part of the foreign policy process by creating the post of historical adviser in 1918. Headlam-Morley's memoranda as adviser are classic examples not only of diplomatic history but of the elucidation through diplomatic history of contemporary problems. Chamberlain was quite taken with much of what Headlam-Morley presented, and it undoubtedly contributed to Chamberlain's growing attraction to a Castlereaghesque solution to European instability. It is worth noting that in the areas where Headlam-Morley's advice was rejected, particularly over eastern Europe, that difficulties subsequently arose. Clearly diplomatic history did have something to offer the development of foreign policy.

Chamberlain adopted much of the advice he was given, but he rejected that on the significance of eastern Europe as integral to the overall European balance. Strong arguments were made that to have included eastern

[92] CAB 23/49/C17 (25).

Europe in the Locarno arrangement would have prevented any meaningful result being achieved. Eastern Europe was therefore decoupled for later consideration. Chamberlain, however, during his remaining tenure of office never evinced any real interest in moving to the implicit second phase of negotiating an eastern Locarno. Indeed the remaining period of his foreign secretaryship is but a pallid reflection of those first energetic months. Inevitably this raises the question of how far Crowe was, as he so often had been, the real engine. It is of course impossible to say what would have happened had Crowe lived, but it is possible to imagine that he would have acted to deal with the many loose threads left by Locarno.

Chamberlain did succeed in reestablishing the ascendency of the Foreign Office. After his success at Locarno he observed that the conference could not have succeeded except that at the critical moment,

the British Government's policy was found by me, imposed upon the cabinet by me, in face of Curzon's and even Balfour's opposition, before I went to Paris and Geneva in March, re-imposed by my telegram from Geneva to the Prime Minister (when Crowe reported to me that the cabinet committee was going back on me), that I should carry on at Geneva on my way home and in Paris on these lines, but should resign at once on my return if I were not supported, and that it depended for its success on my personal handling of each situation as it arose . . . because I was Foreign Secretary.[93]

Chamberlain had entered a government which was divided between different schools of thought about foreign policy, an imperialist group which saw the empire as the primary focus and Europe as a secondary area, and a little Englander school which paid only marginal attention to the Empire and wished for no binding commitments to Europe. Chamberlain developed the nascent European school which saw Britain as intimately concerned with European affairs, and made this the focal point of foreign policy around which other concerns revolved. In a series of conferences stretching from Paris in 1919 to Locarno in 1925 Britain attempted to address the problems caused by the upheavals of the First World War. There was a core belief that Britain had an important part to play in international affairs, but what that role was had become very blurred. Chamberlain and his Foreign Office advisers wanted to bring policy into clearly defined focus once again. The events of 1925, leading up to the Locarno Pact, show the Foreign Office once again established as the centre point of foreign policy, in great part through the Chamberlain–Crowe partnership.

[93] AC 5/1/370, Austen Chamberlain to Ida Chamberlain, 28 Nov. 1925.

CHAPTER 7

Chamberlain's ambassadors

In the reaction after 1945 against the policy of appeasement, headed in Britain by those leading Tory historians, who had opposed that policy at the time,[1] and in America by those leading members of the Democratic equivalents of the Whig school of history, who had in the main supported Roosevelt and had pressed in the period before Pearl Harbor for American support of Britain, a small group of British ambassadors became the target

---

This chapter is based, in the main, on the work underlying D.C. Watt, *How War Came: the Immediate Origins of the Second World War* (London 1989); on private conversations with the late Sir Robert Craigie and his family, with former junior members of the British Embassy in Berlin under Sir Nevile Henderson and with the late Lady Loraine, widow of Sir Percy Loraine; on the doctoral theses of my former students, in particular on Lord Perth, D.J. Rotunda, 'The Rome Embassy of Sir Eric Drummond, 16th Earl of Perth, 1933–1939' (London 1972), on Sir William Seeds, S. Aster, 'British Policy towards the USSR and the onset of the Second World War, March 1938–September 1939' (London 1969), and on Sir Robert Craigie, the thesis of my colleague at the London School of Economics, Dr A.M. Best, 'Avoiding War: The Diplomacy of Sir Robert Craigie and Shigemitsu Mamoru, 1937–1941' (London 1992); on the draft doctoral thesis of Mr John Herman, my most valued research assistant over many years, 'The Paris Embassy of Sir Eric Phipps, 1937–1939'. I have consulted the papers of Sir Percy Loraine, of Sir Eric Phipps and Sir Hughe Knatchbull-Hugessen. On Sir Nevile Henderson's embassy there is the German doctoral thesis of Dr Rudi Strauch, published as *Sir Nevile Henderson, Britische Botschafter in Berlin* (Bonn 1959). There is a biography of Sir Percy Loraine, Gordon Waterfield, *Professional Diplomat* (London 1973), based on the Loraine papers. There is no proper study of Sir Ronald Lindsay's embassy in Washington known to me; but see Benjamin D. Rhodes, 'Sir Ronald Lindsay and the British view from Washington, 1930–1939' in Clifford L. Egar and Alexander W. Knott (eds.), *Essays in Twentieth Century American Diplomatic History dedicated to Professor Daniel H. Smith* (Washington DC, 1982). I am particularly grateful to Dr Best and to Mr Herman for the help they have given me in my work on this chapter.

[1] They included Sir Lewis Namier, Sir Charles Webster, Sir Llewellyn Woodward, then official historian of the Foreign Office. For a description of their views see D.C. Watt, 'Appeasement. The Rise of a Revisionist School?', *Political Quarterly*, 36:2 (1965); on Sir Lewis Namier see the same, 'Sir Lewis Namier and Contemporary European History', *Cambridge Review* (June 1954).

for obloquy and denunciation.[2] This process was greatly aided, firstly by the publication of the first volume of Churchill's memoir/history of the second world war, *The Gathering Storm*, in 1948, and then by the early publication of Series III of the British Foreign Office Documents for the interwar years, *Documents on British Foreign Policy, 1919–1939*, which covered the years 1938–9. The three western allies engaged in the publication of the captured German diplomatic documents, *Documents on German Foreign Policy, 1918–1945*, had in the same way decided to begin that publication with Series D, the initial volumes of which began at varying dates in 1936–7, the series as a whole covering the period until 7 December 1941.

Behind these decisions by the British, American and French governments lay the advice of their official historians. This advice was determined by the desire to avoid a new War-Guilt controversy; much the same motive lay behind the decision to publish all the documents cited in evidence at the Trial of the Major War Criminals at Nuremberg. British records reveal that the British historians advising the Foreign Office were obsessed by the fear that a version of the events of the 1930s would take hold, in which the guilt for the outbreak of war in 1939 was laid on the British rather than on the German government. They believed that the capture of American opinion in the 1920s by German success in publishing what was eventually proved to be a carefully slanted selection of their diplomatic records for the period 1870–1914, *Die grosse Politik der europäische Mächte*, *before* the British and French records could be published, had operated greatly to Britain's disadvantage in the 1930s and 1940s, since a substantial part of America's university trained elites had absorbed it as part of their education.[3]

The editors of the British documents, Sir Llewellyn Woodward and Rohan Butler, had agreed with the senior Foreign Office officials, that none of the minutes written by officials in Whitehall on the documents they selected for publication should be printed. The effect was to concentrate the attention of those who wished to understand the processes by which British foreign policy was formulated entirely on the reports and letters from the ambassadors in the field and the final versions of the

---

[2] These tended to be historians of Europe, rather than of the United States, and included German *émigrés* such as Felix Gilbert, as well as those who in the 1930s, writing on the war-guilt issue had tended to take the British rather than the German side. They included historians such as Ray Sontag, the first American editor of the allied publication from the captured German archives, *Documents on German Foreign Policy*, or Bernadotte Schmidt, his successor, and their pupils.

[3] For documentation on this point see D.C. Watt, 'British Historians, the War-Guilt Issue and Post-war Germanophobia; A Documentary Note', *Historical Journal*, 36/1 (1993). The doyen of American historians of European diplomacy, Sidney Fay, was widely quoted as having said that none of the documents published since *Die grosse Politik* had afforded him any reason to change the views he had formed on the question of responsibility for the outbreak of the 1914–18 war as a result of the work he had based on that publication.

instructions on which they acted as they were despatched from Whitehall, and in particular on any discrepancies between them. Until his death, Woodward was always defensive when this choice was raised in conversation with him, giving various reasons, which did not always seem consistent with one another. It was in fact abandoned when his successors passed to the publication of the earlier two, or as it was to prove, three series of documents.[4]

Similar criticism could have been aimed at the choice of starting dates for the various topics covered in the volumes, especially the choice not to print any documents dealing with British relations with Italy until October 1938, a choice which left the whole question of Mr Eden's resignation in February 1938 and the negotiation of the Anglo-Italian 'Gentlemen's Agreement' of Easter 1938 to be discussed on the basis of the Italian ambassador, Dino Grandi's, self-glorifying report on his final conversation with Chamberlain and Eden on 15 February 1938,[5] and the similarly self-glorifying version of Roosevelt's famous 'offer/message' to Chamberlain the previous month by the American, Sumner Welles, its original begetter, in the memoirs which he published after his final dismissal as under-secretary of state in the State Department in 1944, picked up by Churchill in *The Gathering Storm*, and confirmed by Eden much later in his own memoirs.[6]

One of the reasons given by Woodward in conversation was that, by contrast with their predecessors, neither Lord Halifax nor Sir Alexander Cadogan, the permanent under-secretary in the Foreign Office from 1938 to 1945, were great writers of minutes. At the time and indeed until after the deaths of Woodward, Halifax and Cadogan, the original records from which he made his selection were closed to research. The reduction of the closed period for government archives to thirty years introduced by the 1967 Public Records Act meant that it was not until 1969–70 that those records were released for independent historical research, and it became possible to judge whether Woodward's stated reasons were valid.

That release showed that there were at least possible grounds for questioning them. It would, perhaps, have been safer for Professor Woodward to have advanced the constitutional argument that the role of officials is confined to giving advice and that responsibility for policy lies with elected

---

[4] The publication of the first series of *Documents on British Foreign Policy, 1919–1939*, was eventually divided into two, with a new Series, IA, beginning in 1925.

[5] Printed in *Ciano's Diplomatic Papers* (Italian original *L'Europa verso la catastrofe*, Rome 1947), Malcolm Muggeridge, ed., London, 1948.

[6] The American historian, Francis Loewenheim, elucidated the processes of misrepresentation by which the myth of the Roosevelt message passed into historiography in a regrettably little known contribution to an American Festschrift. See Francis L. Loewenheim, 'An Illusion which shaped History. New Light on the History and Historiography of American Peace Moves before Munich' in Daniel R. Beaver (ed.) *Some Pathways in American History* (Detroit, 1969).

ministers; identification of the advice given by officials and their consequent politicisation would make it impossible for such advice to be given
freely and frankly. This was in fact the argument advanced both in the
debate which preceded the setting of a fifty-year closed period for the
archives in the 1958 Public Records Act and in that which intervened
before the closed period was reduced to thirty years by the Act of 1967.
It is one familiar to all who have essayed debate since that date on the
introduction into Britain of something resembling the United States Freedom of Information Act. But it is none the less valid, given the very different constitutional environment in Britain by comparison with that in the
United States, where senior officials at the under-secretary and assistant
under-secretary level, let alone ambassadors, may be, and usually are,
political appointments; that this may well permit of its own means of
politicisation of the relationship between officials and ministers will
emerge from the remainder of this chapter.

It has often been pointed out by defenders of the policies followed by
the British government in the 1930s that the decision not to publish
minutes in Series C of the British publication drew a sharp line between
diplomats serving abroad whose views were totally exposed to public censure, and their colleagues in London. The point has a certain abstract
justice; but, the truth is that the British practice of publishing diplomatic
correspondence, which was well established in the nineteenth century,
could not ever have taken place if diplomatists representing Britain abroad
had been treated in the same way as the 'clerks' in the Foreign Office.
Indeed the merger between the diplomatic service and the senior staff of
the Foreign Office was itself a twentieth-century phenomenon, part of the
professionalisation of diplomatic services world-wide which is one of the
most notable phenomena of the interwar years; even in the United States
and the Soviet Union, those bastions of political appointments to major
diplomatic posts, the vast majority of overseas representatives are career
officials. And when Stalin and his minions wiped out much of the pre-1939
Soviet diplomatic service in the purges, he was forced to create a new
career service to replace them.

It is nevertheless true that some of the British ambassadors who served
in the years 1937–9 were singled out for obloquy by the dominant schools
of writers on appeasement in the years after 1950. Those most often
pilloried were Sir Nevile Henderson in Berlin, and Lord Perth in Rome.[7]
Sir Eric Phipps who had preceded Henderson in Berlin, and had been
translated to Paris in 1937, came only second to them as a result of his

---

[7] Most notably Felix Gilbert, 'Two British Ambassadors: Perth and Henderson', in Gordon
Craig and Felix Gilbert (eds.), *The Diplomats, 1919–1939* (New York, 1954). See also Sir
Lewis Namier, *Diplomatic Prelude, 1938–1939* (London, 1948): *Europe in Decline*
(London, 1950), passim.

extraordinary despatches during the month of September 1938.[8] One in particular aroused comment, that of 24 September in which he spoke of a 'small but noisy and corrupt war group' being opposed by 'all that is best in France'.[9] The telegram produced a 'sense of outrage' in the Foreign Office.[10] Lord Perth's successor, Sir Percy Loraine, seems to have largely escaped such censure. Other ambassadors abroad at this time include Sir William Seeds, who arrived in Moscow in January 1939, Sir Robert Craigie in Tokyo, who largely escaped later censure as a result of the concentration on Europe of the critics of appeasement, Sir Ronald Lindsay in Washington, Sir Hughe Knatchbull-Hugessen in Ankara and Britain's first ambassador to the Franco government in Spain, Sir Maurice Peterson. (It has to be remembered that, apart from China, where British representation was raised to the level of an Embassy only in 1935, these were the only British missions abroad who enjoyed the status of an Embassy in the interwar years.)

The policy of 'Appeasement' has been uniquely identified with the prime minister, Neville Chamberlain, his foreign secretary, Lord Halifax, and his private kitchen cabinet at No 10 Downing Street, Sir Horace Wilson, who had succeeded Sir Maurice Hankey as secretary to the Cabinet early in 1938, Sir Joseph Ball and the press secretary to the prime minister, George Steward. Of these Sir Joseph Ball, who headed the Conservative Party's Research Department, and had served in the 1920s in MI5, the British Security Service, is the least possible to fathom. He acted as the British end of the so-called 'secret channel' (*canale segreto*) to the Italian Embassy.[11] He seems to have acted as Downing Street's representative in the preparations for clandestine foreign radio propaganda from 1936 onwards.[12] He maintained close connections with the ultra-right-

---

[8] See for example the reference in Hugh Dalton's memoirs, *The Fateful Years, 1931–1945* (London, 1957), p. 191, The Earl of Birkenhead, *The Life of Lord Halifax* (London, 1965). The view of Phipps as 'defeatist' and a 'nervous little man whose previous tour of duty in Berlin had left him with a mighty fear of Hitler's wrath' was naturally repeated by that master of the unshakeable prejudgement, William Shirer, in his *Collapse of the Third Republic* (London, 1970).

[9] Phipps to London, telegram, 24 Sept. 1938, FO 371/21740, C10602/1941/18, printed in *Documents on British Foreign Policy*, 3rd ser., vol. II, no. 1076.

[10] The phrase is from Lord Strang's memoirs, *At Home and Abroad* (London, 1956), p. 136. William Strang was then coordinating under-secretary for the European Department of the Foreign Office. See also the entries in Sir Alexander Cadogan's diaries for 24 Sept. 1938, in David Dilks (ed.), *The Diaries of Sir Alexander Cadogan, 1938–1945* (London, 1971), and in Sir Oliver Harvey's Diaries for the same date, J. Harvey, ed., *The Diplomatic Diaries of Oliver Harvey, 1937–1940* (London, 1970), and the minute by Sir Orme Sargent on Phipps a/q telegram.

[11] See Rosario Quarteraro, 'Appendice a Inghilterra e Italia' *Storia Contemporanea*, VII: 4 (1976), and *Roma tra Londra e Berlino; Politica Estero Fascista dal 1930 al 1940* (Rome, 1980).

[12] See Nicholas Pronay and Philip M. Taylor, ' "An Improper Use of Broadcasting". The British government and clandestine radio propaganda operations against Germany during the Munich crisis and after', *Journal of Contemporary History*, 18 (1983).

wing weekly, *Truth*, and used it to disparage Churchill in the summer of 1939.[13] Sir Alexander Cadogan's diaries suggest that in his eyes, at least, the staff of No 10 Downing Street needed continuous observation to prevent them from pursuing a different foreign policy, especially in relations with the German Embassy in London, from that advocated by the Foreign Office. The task of observation lay in the hands of the head of MI5, Sir Reginald Kell, who in other respects did nothing to restrain Sir Joseph Ball from presuming on his earlier service in MI5 to hijack the results of its observations.[14]

The real test of the ambassadors on which this chapter proposes to concentrate is the degree to which they were, or made themselves, servants to a foreign policy made in No 10 Downing Street, rather than in the Foreign Office, and to what extent they can be called 'Chamberlain's ambassadors' rather than those of His Britannic Majesty, operating through his principal secretary of state for foreign affairs. One of the tests must be the degree to which they can be revealed as having been in close and regular correspondence with the prime minister or his staff. Such a test reveals that Sir William Seeds and Sir Ronald Lindsay had no known communication of any importance with No 10; this is not surprising given that the countries to which they were accredited played no part in the prime minister's 'peace strategy'. He distrusted the motives as well as the actions of the Soviet Union and the rhetoric and intentions of the United States, both of whom in his view were apt to see themselves as successors to Britain's dominant position in the world.

Nor is there any evidence of Sir Robert Craigie being in regular communication with the prime minister or his personal staff. Like his successor, Winston Churchill, Chamberlain had no 'Far Eastern Policy' separate from that of the foreign secretary and the Foreign Office. Indeed the problem with British policy in the Far East for the period of Sir Robert Craigie's embassy was that the foreign secretary and his senior advisers had no policy either. Policy was set by the Far Eastern Department of the Foreign Office, whose attitudes towards the Far East were incurably racist, who ignored all warnings and evidence as to the military and naval power of Japan, and who were almost to a man supporters of the Chiang Kai-Shek regime in China, irrespective of its dynastic and social corruption, something which in their lordly White Supremacist way they regarded as characteristically oriental.

This had not always been the case. Both Chamberlain in 1934 and Eden in 1936, spurred by the urgings of Sir Warren Fisher in the Treasury and,

---

[13] On this, see especially Richard Cockett, *Twilight of Truth; Chamberlain, Appeasement and the Manipulation of the Press* (London, 1989), esp. pp. 114–15, and Neville to Hilda Chamberlain, 8 July 1939, Chamberlain Papers, University of Birmingham 18/1/1106.

[14] Private information from the late Right Honourable Kenneth Younger, who was at that date serving in MI5.

more intermittently, of Sir Robert Vansittart in the Foreign Office, had attempted to persuade their colleagues in the Cabinet to attempt to revive the Anglo-Japanese alliance of the years 1902–22. In every case however the overriding need for American support in the event of war in Europe, and the opposition from Canadian and South African leaders to anything likely to provoke American hostility led to their defeat. Nor was the evidence of Japanese Anglophiles' ability to deliver on their assurances of Japanese goodwill against the anti-western ideologies of the Japanese military and nationalists all that convincing.[15] Sir Robert Craigie became a close personal friend of Chamberlain's widow, on his return to London in 1943 from internment in Japan, and he and his family remained in contact with her until his death and hers. But there is no evidence extant of any connection between the two men in 1938–9; indeed, the whole course of the Tientsin crisis in 1939 demonstrates that Sir Robert had no other channels of communication with London besides his official links with the Foreign Office. It is significant of his conception of his professional obligations that he had made no effort to circumvent them.

During his tenure of the American department which preceded his posting to Tokyo, he had made a good many enemies both in the Foreign Office and the Admiralty by his relationship with Sir Warren Fisher, the permanent under-secretary to the Treasury. This however stemmed from his role as the government and Foreign Office's principal expert and negotiator in disarmament matters. The official body which advised the Cabinet on disarmament matters was the Committee of Imperial Defence not the Foreign Office *per se* and certainly not any of the three service ministries. Sir Warren Fisher was a leading figure on the various committees of the CID concerned with disarmament, and a main force in the drive to accommodate the defence needs of the country to its economic strengths and financial weaknesses. The failure of the Chiefs of Staff Committee to produce any strategic advice which was more than an amalgam of the separate and often conflicting strategies of the three Services left it to the Treasury under Sir Warren Fisher to impose a solution. If this owed more to outside advisers and theorists such as Admiral Sir Herbert Richmond on the ideal size of capital ships or Captain Sir Basil Liddell Hart on the need to avoid commitments to a continental strategy, the fault lay as much with the so-called joint planning staffs of the Chiefs of Staff Committee as with Fisher, let alone Craigie.

Resentment or misunderstanding of this point, plus a certain desire to turn away possible criticism of their own role led to the post-war myth of Sir Warren Fisher's sinister influence on foreign policy peddled by Mr

---

[15] On this general theme see Ann Trotter, *Britain and East Asia, 1933–1937* (Cambridge, 1975), and the opening papers, especially that by C. Hosoya in Ian Nish, ed., *Anglo-Japanese Alienation, 1919–1952* (Cambridge, 1982).

Ashton-Gwatkin, formerly of the Foreign Office, who had in 1939 played the card of economic appeasement well beyond the bounds of reason, by Lord Perth, by Admiral of the Fleet Lord Chatfield, by Air Chief Marshal Sir John Slessor, by the Master of Elibank, and by the former minister to Lisbon, Sir Walford Selby, whose obsession with Fisher was to be given ample voice in his memoirs.[16] In his retirement Fisher himself regarded his attempt to bring the Foreign Office into a single united Public Service as a failure, epitomised by his inability to influence the appointment of Sir Robert Vansittart's successor as permanent under-secretary.[17] In brief, there was nothing unconstitutional or underhand in Craigie's relationship with Fisher in the period 1929–36, let alone any foreshadowing of a similar relationship with Fisher's successor at the Treasury.

Nor is there any evidence of the prime minister using private intermediaries in relation to the United States. Increasing the influence of the United States in world politics was not consonant with the prime minister's view of the world. He thought the price to be paid for American intervention would be too high. He was *in receipt of* private communications from President Roosevelt, via Lord Runciman and Lord Murray of Elibank, and was also kept informed of Roosevelt's views by the former novelist, John Buchan, who as Lord Tweedsmuir had been appointed governor general of Canada in 1936, and who was a dedicated advocate of an Anglo-American hegemony in world affairs and had been since his connections with that fount of neo-imperialism, Lord Milner's 'Kindergarten' in South Africa in the first decade of the century. But these intermediaries were chosen by the president as a means of evading his ambassador in London, Joseph Kennedy, and to a lesser extent, Sir Ronald Lindsay, who never succeeded in establishing himself with Roosevelt's private court or with either the secretary of state, Cordell Hull, or Roosevelt's protégé, Sumner Welles, neither of whom were natural

---

[16] On Sir Warren Fisher see D.C. Watt, *Personalities and Policies. Studies in the Formulation of British Foreign Policy in the Twentieth Century* (London, 1965), 'Sir Warren Fisher and British Re-armament against Germany'; Eunan O'Halpern, *Sir Warren Fisher, Head of the Civil Service* (London, 1989). For the critics of Fisher see Lord Perth's speech in the House of Lords in 1942, *Hansard's Parliamentary Debates, House of Lords, 1941–1942*, vol. 125, columns 224–232; F. Ashton-Gwatkin, *The British Foreign Service* (Syracuse, 1950); Lord Murray of Elibank, *Some Reflections on Some Aspects of British Foreign Policy between the Wars* (Edinburgh, 1951); G. Legge-Bourke MP, *Master of the Offices* (London, 1949), Sir Walford Selby, *Diplomatic Twilight* (London, 1953).

[17] I am grateful for information on this point from my late colleague Richard Greaves, sometime professor of politics in the London School of Economics, to whom Sir Warren Fisher entrusted the care of his papers (now in the London School of Economics Library). Professor Greaves expressed his views on this issue in a review of D.C. Watt, *Personalities and Policies, Studies in the Formulation of British Foreign Policy in the Twentieth Century* (London, 1965) which included an essay on 'Sir Warren Fisher and British Rearmament', in the *Political Quarterly*, 37 (1966).

Anglophiles.[18] The impeccable Republican connections of his second wife, a Colville Hoyt from New York, may have had something to do with this.

Nor did either Turkey or, once Franco's victory in the Spanish Civil War was secured, Spain, figure in any way in Mr Chamberlain's foreign policy, concerned as it was with the attempt to limit or reduce the threat of Britain being involved in a major war in Europe or the Mediterranean. (This is not to say that Chamberlain was sympathetically disposed towards the Spanish Republican government. Far from it. But Spain only figured as part of his attempts to woo Mussolini into reducing the commitment of Italian forces to intervention in Spain.) One would not therefore expect to find either Peterson or Knatchbull-Hugessen involved in any irregular contacts with Downing Street, any more than Loraine, Knatchbull-Hugessen's predecessor in Ankara. We do not have any Peterson papers. But neither Loraine's papers (which the author of this piece was allowed to see while they were still in the late Lady Loraine's possession), nor Knatchbull-Hugessen's handwritten diaries carry any hint of such contacts as may have existed between Downing Street and Sir Nevile Henderson, and as can be proven to have existed between Downing Street and Sir Eric Phipps.

We are left with Perth and Loraine in Rome, Henderson in Berlin and Phipps in Paris. There is no evidence of private communications between Downing Street and the British Embassy in Rome. Loraine was in any case far from being the kind of man who would lend himself to such irregularities. He came from the English borders with Scotland, from an area that had produced in turn ferocious and bloodthirsty reivers and equally ferocious rugby forwards. He had served as a volunteer in the Imperial Yeomanry in South Africa in 1901–2. His years in the Diplomatic Service had been spent in the Middle East in areas where British imperial interests required that 'face' be maintained and British prestige be upheld. Before moving to Rome he had served as British ambassador to Ankara where his remark to a fellow diplomat that 'when Britain was ready she would quickly destroy Italy and smash the Duce' had reached Mussolini's ears and infuriated him into arranging, a characteristically Mussolini-esque touch, for Loraine to be sent various anonymous insulting letters.[19] Loraine's first interview with Mussolini left him with the conclusion that 'the visibility of overwhelming strength' was the only language Mussolini respected.[20] He was, however, so to work with Lord Halifax that, by August 1939, Count Ciano, Mussolini's son-in-law and foreign minister, had come

---

[18] For Roosevelt's relations with Chamberlain see D.C. Watt. 'Roosevelt and Chamberlain; Two Appeasers', *International Journal*, 28: 2 (1973).

[19] Ciano diaries entry of 22 Dec. 1938. On Loraine in general see Watt, *How War Came*, especially pp. 412–16.

[20] Loraine to Halifax, *Documents on British Foreign Policy, 1919–1939* (hereinafter *DBFP*), 3rd ser., vol. VI, doc. no. 353.

to trust him to the point where he took his advice and acted upon it while Loraine was still sitting in his office. Loraine's papers, as mentioned above, show no signs of any communication with Sir Joseph Ball, George Steward or Sir Horace Wilson, who were the main agents in the Downing Street kitchen cabinet.

Where Perth is concerned we have no direct equivalent of the Loraine papers. What we do have however is the negative proof provided by the Italian sources. The open and defenceless state of the British Embassy's records against the Italian secret service under Perth and Loraine is notorious; the diaries of Count Ciano are full of titbits gleaned from their regular pillaging of the Embassy's safe. As we shall see below, the Italians passed on some of these titbits to Hitler whenever they felt it would be to their advantage. It is virtually impossible that any private political correspondence between the ambassador and Downing Street, such as is preserved in Sir Eric Phipps' papers, could have escaped their attention or mention in the Italian sources.

Chamberlain and his intimates did not use the British Embassy for an additional reason. Chamberlain did not trust the members of the Foreign Office under Eden, and preferred to make his approaches to Mussolini by other channels. These included his brother's widow, Lady Austen Chamberlain. But the most regular channel was that which led via Sir Joseph Ball and the Maltese-born legal adviser to the Italian Embassy in London, Adrian Dingli, whose diary, preserved in Italian hands, is the only source for these contacts.[21] This source largely ceased to be an effective point of contact after it had been used to deliver Chamberlain's furious remonstrances after the Italian annexation of Albania on Good Friday 1939.[22]

Which leaves the analyst of Chamberlain's private foreign policy with two figures alone. (We shall return to Craigie later.) These are Sir Nevile Henderson and Sir Eric Phipps. Sir Nevile's embassy, and his private correspondence from his days in Berlin, was most probably incinerated, together with the archives of the British Embassy in Berlin, at the outbreak of war.[23] We know from the files of the Foreign Office that he was a

---

[21] It is analysed in Quartararo, 'canale segreto', and extensively quoted in the same author's *Roma tra Londra e Berlino*. See Introductory Note on sources.

[22] Quartararo, *Roma*, pp. 452–3.

[23] According to the Library and Records Department of the Foreign Office, Henderson's belongings, which included four volumes of diaries, were packed by the American chargé d'affaires' office in Berlin in September 1939 into four vans, to be transported to Switzerland for internment until the end of the war. When the cases were opened after the war (and Henderson's death) the diaries could not be found. It would seem that they were removed before the vans were sealed, possibly by the Embassy butler who actually packed them. Detailed enquiries in Berlin after the war by the British Military Government failed to shed any light on their fate. There is no evidence in the German Foreign Office records of their falling into German hands. If they had, one would have expected the propaganda section of the Foreign Ministry to have exploited them as they did the Czech, Polish,

compulsive correspondent. Sir Llewellyn Woodward printed a copious selection of his letters from the years 1938–9 in the various appendices to the volumes of the third series of *Documents on British Foreign Policy, 1919–1939*. His successor, Professor W.N. Medlicott, a man less inclined to make of the publication of Foreign Office Documents a *roman à clef*, printed a similar wealth in the volumes of the second series, published in the early 1970s. He wrote to his contemporaries, he wrote to the foreign secretary, he wrote to Sir Orme Sargent, the avuncular figure who served as deputy to the permanent under-secretary; it is by no means unlikely that he wrote to Sir Horace Wilson. It is an unhappy coincidence that, upset, it is said, by the failure of his one attempt to open himself to a younger generation of historians, Sir Horace Wilson destroyed his private papers before his death. There is, however, no evidence that Henderson wrote to Mr Chamberlain, whose papers are open to historical investigation in Birmingham University Library, and which show no evidence of any selective destruction.

In his memoir of his Berlin Embassy, *Failure of a Mission*, Henderson claimed that he regarded himself as the prime minister's personal agent. The prime minister had outlined his policy to him on his appointment to Berlin. He, Henderson, considered himself less as a subordinate of the Foreign Office than as a personal agent of the prime minister whose policy he was appointed to carry out. He remained in constant contact with Sir Horace Wilson, to whom he directed appeals whenever he disapproved of the instructions which reached him from the Foreign Office.[24] He also told Professor Conwell-Evans, a curious figure who held a chair in English literature at the university of Königsberg, and acted as translator for Mr Lloyd George, a fellow Welshman, on the latter's visit to Hitler in 1937, that he 'based his policy on instructions continuously received from 10 Downing Street'.[25] It is highly probable that these claims apply to the period during which Chamberlain was prime minister and Eden foreign secretary. Once Lord Halifax had succeeded to Eden, the degree both of Halifax's initial commitment to the appeasement of Germany, and Chamberlain's respect for and friendship with Halifax, would have made such underhand behaviour on Chamberlain's part both undesirable and

Belgian and French records. Vaughn A. Baker, 'Nevile Henderson in Berlin', *Red River Valley Historical Journal*, 2:4 (1977) at footnote 54, has the story.

[24] *Failure of a Mission*, pp. 16–17.

[25] T.P. Conwell Evans, *None So Blind* (London, privately printed, 1947) p. 72. Professor Conwell-Evans' status is curiously ambivalent. To the Germans, and to some of his contemporaries, he appeared as one of the small band of dedicated Germanophiles (many of them active members of minority Christian sects), who were prepared to go to almost any length to avoid another Anglo-German war. On the other hand he was certainly one of the contacts employed for purposes of gathering political intelligence for Sir Robert Vansittart's private intelligence service organised by Group Captain Christie, a former assistant air attaché in Berlin. Christie's papers are preserved in the Library of Churchill College, Cambridge, together with a copy of Conwell-Evans' memoirs.

unthinkable as well as unnecessary. Halifax's turn against Chamberlain's policy began only in the Cabinet debate on the proposals Chamberlain brought back from his second meeting with Hitler at Bad Godesberg. Thereafter the deviation between the two men can be traced in Chamberlain's letters to his sisters, as well as in the support Halifax came to enjoy from a majority of the Cabinet, for example, for the approaches to the Soviet Union from April 1939 onwards, approaches which Chamberlain disliked and opposed.

Henderson's position after Munich was greatly weakened by his absence from Berlin from November 1938 to February 1939, while he was undergoing treatment in London for the cancer of the jaw which eventually killed him. Unofficial approaches, by self-appointed English intermediaries on the one hand, and by German or European emissaries who claimed that General Goering was their backer on the other, continued throughout the spring and summer of 1939. The usual members of Chamberlain's private circle figure in them, although they seem from the records to have adopted a much more cautious and passive role than in the period before Munich. But Henderson himself seems to have lost his credibility in both London and Berlin, both with Downing Street and with von Ribbentrop, whose Anglophobia after Munich grew by leaps and bounds.

There are, then, two distinct periods in Henderson's career in Berlin, those in which British foreign policy was in dispute between Chamberlain and Eden (and German foreign policy was still managed by Baron von Neurath, a former professional German diplomat who had served in London in the 1920s), and that in which British foreign policy was dominated by Lord Halifax (and German by the increasingly Anglophobe von Ribbentrop, intent on avenging the 'failure of a mission', his mission, as German ambassador in London). It is to this division that we must now briefly return.

Neville Chamberlain took up office as prime minister on 27 May 1937. By that date Sir Nevile Henderson was already in Berlin. It is interesting to note that, if there is any truth in the claim made by him that he acted on instructions from Downing Street, he must have conferred with and agreed his instructions with Chamberlain before the latter kissed hands, in fact while he was still chancelllor of the exchequer. On 10 May, Henderson drafted a lengthy memorandum of which he subsequently sent a copy to Orme Sargent, presumably to defend himself against the criticisms raised in the Foreign Office by his reports of conversations with, among others, General Goering.[26]

The actual date of drafting is in dispute. William Strang, who sent a copy to Lord Halifax, as part of his briefing for his visit to Germany in November 1937, wrote that the memorandum was drafted by Henderson

[26] The memorandum is printed in *DBFP*, 2/19, 53, as sent to Sargent on 20 July 1937.

'before he took up his post in Berlin'.[27] It is more than possible that the document fell into German hands as did other British documents in this period, most probably via the Italian Embassy in Berlin, as part of the Italian secret service's regular plunder from the British Embassy in Rome.[28]

There is not room to discuss the contents of this lengthy memorandum in detail. It argued that France, whose alliance and independence in western Europe was defined as an essential aim of British foreign policy, should be persuaded or pressed to abandon 'her quasi-protectorship over Poland and the Little Entente'. It maintained that Britain should assure Germany of her desire to preserve her neutrality 'in a Russo-German conflict'. It recommended that Britain could accept the absorption of Austria by Germany, and that of the Sudetenland as well, and the recovery by Germany of her colonies. 'None of these aims should injure purely British national interests.'

It provoked the most severe criticism from the senior figures in the Foreign Office as going far beyond official British policy, and indulging in a dangerous vagueness of phraseology. 'What', wrote Sir Robert Vansittart, 'does German political predominance in Eastern Europe mean? ...' and again, 'Britain cannot disinterest herself in the course of events in Central Europe.' Most of all, the kind of changes which Sir Nevile Henderson 'envisaged so blithely were impossible to imagine without the use of force'. Sir Robert was inclined to see in this the hand of Lord Lothian, formerly, as Philip Kerr, secretary and secret go-between for Lloyd George in 1919–22, and now a member of the 'Cliveden Set' centred around the Astor family's country house at Cliveden, secretary of the Rhodes Trust and an interminably active and self-appointed intermediary in both Anglo-German and Anglo-American differences.

The 'Cliveden Set', as an active and conspiratorial Mafia within and around the Chamberlain–Halifax axis, was largely invented by the egregious Claud Cockburn, and publicised through his widely read and quoted

[27] Strang to Halifax, 13 Nov. 1937, *DBFP* 2/19, 319.

[28] There are three such documents printed in *Documents on German Foreign Policy, 1918–1945*, Ser. C, vol. VI. They are nos. 344, an incomplete record of a memorandum by Mr Eden of a conversation of 29 Apr. 1937 with the Belgian premier, M. van Zeeland, in Brussels, of which the full text is printed in *DBFP*, 2/18, as no. 453; a report by Henderson to Eden, of 20 July 1937, C3314/270/18, which included a note sent by Henderson to Goering; and a copy of a letter from Mr Ogilvie Forbes, then counsellor at the Berlin Embassy, to Mr Strang of 21 July 1937. In each case the document was found in the records of Goering's personal staff office, and was a photostat of an office copy made in London and bearing the stamp 'This document is the property of His Majesty's government', something which suggests that the originals had been distributed to embassies abroad by the device of the Foreign Office Confidential Print. The second of these documents bears a marginal comment in Goering's handwriting dated 15 October 1937. The third carries a notation indicating that it was passed to Goering's office by Signor Magistrati, then counsellor of the Italian Embassy in Berlin, and, coincidentally, son-in-law to Count Ciano.

newsletter, *The Week*. Its existence was largely taken for granted by opinion around President Roosevelt, and in Soviet and Sovietophile circles where conspiratorial theories of British society fitted only too easily into their respective political matrices. Unfortunately for those who still profess to admire Cockburn, who doubled as assistant editor of the official organ of the Communist Party of Great Britain, the *Daily Worker*, under the *nom-de-plume* of Frank Pitcairn, belief in the seminal role of the garrulous but largely powerless *habitués* of Cliveden does not survive the examination of the private papers of either Chamberlain or Lord Halifax, to whom the Astors and their Christian Science ilk, were simply one among a number of groups and individuals who offered them hospitality and sought to impress their opinions upon them. Neither the prime minister nor his foreign secretary were anybody's catchpaw. Such theories belong to the mental ambience of those who sought to explain British foreign policy as the product of a combination of ignorance, if not innocence, abroad and wimpishness, of the 'good Lord Mayor of Birmingham in a bad year' kind of put-down of Chamberlain, or of his manipulation by sinister capitalist influences in the City of London, 'economic royalists' in President Roosevelt's phrase.

Vansittart, who had known and loathed Lothian from 1919 onwards, was misled. What is so striking about Henderson's memorandum is its closeness to the position which Lord Halifax was to take in his meeting with Hitler in November 1937. It certainly went much further than official British policy was prepared to go in the summer of 1937. But by November the prime minister's opinions had already developed to the point where the French ministers who came to London at the end of November to hear Lord Halifax's report on his meeting with Hitler found themselves put under the strongest pressure either to renounce or to exercise much more strongly their 'quasi-protectorship' over Czechoslovakia so as to nip in the bud the much feared and anticipated confrontation between the Czech government and Berlin arising out of the dispute between the Sudeten Germans and the Czech state. There is no evidence as to where Chamberlain imbibed these ideas. But they were a logical development of British views of Czechoslovakia, already well established in the 1920s in the Foreign Office as well as in the wider foreign policy community in Britain.[29] Czechophiles were a small, active and vociferous body, whom the Czech mission in Britain did its best to encourage by financial subsidy, where necessary. But against similar efforts exerted by the German 'grey'

---

[29] On this see Mark Cornwall, 'A Fluctuating Barometer: British Diplomatic Views of the Czech–German Relationship in Czechoslovakia, 1918–1938', in Eva Schmidt-Hartmann and Stanley B. Winters, eds., *Great Britain, the United States and the Bohemian Lands, 1848–1938. Vorträge der Tagung des Collegium Carolinum in Bad Wiessee vom 2. bis 6. November 1988* (Munich, 1991); and 'The Rise and Fall of a "Special Relationship"?: Britain and Czechoslovakia, 1930–48', in Brian Brivati and Harriet Jones, eds., *What Difference did the War make?* (Leicester, 1993).

propaganda agency, the *Wirtschaftspolitische Gesellschaft*, whose director, Marguerite Gärtner, had cut her teeth as a propagandist for the Reichsmarine during the 1914–18 war, the Czechs had an uphill task, one which they made infinitely more difficult by the indifference they showed to the issue of Austrian independence, when Britain was casting around for a substitute for Mussolini as a protector for Austria against German pressure, or to the non- and anti-Nazi elements among the Sudeten Germans.

The majority opinion among the Czech Agrarian Party matched German racist attitudes towards the Czechs with an equal hostility towards all Germans, no matter what their politics. Indeed in the secret negotiations for a modus vivendi between Czechoslovakia and Nazi Germany in the winter of 1936–7, President Benes showed that he was quite ready to abandon the German anti-Nazi political organisations which operated against Hitler's control of German politics from bases on Czech soil as part of a settlement.[30]

Efforts have been made over the years to identify various journalists, including Geoffrey Dawson of *The Times*, as Chamberlain's guru/mentor in foreign affairs. These are based on the same misunderstanding of Chamberlain's personality as that displayed by those whose credulity led them into accepting the alleged role of the Cliveden Set. Chamberlain took his ideas from a variety of sources; as most people do. What was particular to his personality was that they were adopted as instruments towards his conviction that another European war should be averted, if possible, that traditional methods and diplomacy increased rather than managed the hazards out of which such a war might come (in this his hostility to traditional diplomacy hardly differed from that of the radical left wing of the Union of Democratic Control during and after the 1914–18 war), and that he had been given the ineluctable responsibility, at whatever cost to himself, of averting war. To this he added a distrust of public opinion, which he regarded as capable of irrational and irresistible movements, if not rigidly controlled and starved of reportage of an 'irresponsible' kind, and of the rhetoric of national or personal honour. Henderson's 'instructions', whether self-drafted or dictated by Chamberlain, reflect his narrow view of Britain's interests.

They do not reflect Chamberlain's determination to maintain the cause of peace in Europe as a European equivalent of the Italian-Americans' *cosa nostra*, something to be settled by the leading powers of Europe, from which the future superpowers of the periphery should be kept well away, to be settled by the four European powers who were to meet in Munich on 29–30 September, 1938. If he failed, and this was always some-

---

[30] On these negotiations see Gerhard Weinberg, 'The Secret Hitler–Benes Negotiations in 1936–37', *Journal of Central European Affairs*, 19:4 (1960); and, *The Foreign Policy of Hitler's Germany; Diplomatic Revolution in Europe, 1933–1936* (Chicago, 1970, pp. 317–20; J.W. Brügel, *Tschechen und Deutsche, 1918–1939* (Munich, 1967), pp. 255–61.

thing which he thought to be much more than a mere possibility, then the United States would have to be brought in. From the summer of 1938, if not earlier, avoiding action which might strengthen the Anglophobes and isolationists across the Atlantic was one of the factors limiting his freedom of action.[31] Given his scepticism that America could be persuaded to do anything more than refrain from action likely to make the protection of British interests in Europe and on the oceans impossible, it is easy to depict him as totally hostile to any American help. But that would be an overstatement of the issue, and would not explain the effort which he and Halifax put into cultivating Joseph Kennedy, whom they wrongly conceived to be in the president's confidence. (As a figure possessing substantial political influence in America, Joseph Kennedy represented a considerable advance on his predecessor as American ambassador in London, an obscure southern judge, Mr Bingham.)

These considerations have taken us some way from Sir Nevile Henderson. In discussing his embassy a distinction needs to be drawn between the period before the Anschluss of Austria, when the policy followed by Chamberlain and his government was in effect intended to anticipate and prevent an Anglo-German clash developing out of the conflict between German revisionism and the status quo, and the period following in which British policy began by attempting to 'manage' the conflicts that seemed to threaten in the summer of 1938 and moved in the winter of that year and the first months of 1939 towards a policy of deterrence by declaration.

The last move in what jargonists of today would call the 'proactive' phase in British appeasement of Germany was the 'colonial' offer which was overtaken and rendered outdated by the Anschluss. Henderson's difficulty was that he carried over into the next phase, that when Lord Halifax and Chamberlain were attempting to 'manage' the incipient Czech–German conflict, the attitudes he had brought to the previous phase. He was unable to play the warning and restraining role with his German contacts this new phase of British foreign policy demanded. He had no sympathy with the Czechs, only impatience. He felt that the Sudetens were not worth the bones of a single British soldier. He thought Czechoslovakia an artificial creation dominated by a people who were collectively not worth the candle and had exaggerated notions of their international status. And he made no secret of his views, not only in London, where they were not unknown, only largely regarded by his colleagues as irrelevant to the main issue, but, unforgivably in Berlin. British attempts to exercise restraint in Berlin by a variety of the uncertainty principle reminiscent of John Foster Dulles' 'brinkmanship' twenty years or so later, failed completely for want of an ambassador who was capable of instilling doubt and uncertainty into

---

[31] On British concern for American opinion and on Chamberlain's somewhat ambivalent attitude see Nicholas John Cull, *Selling War; The British Propaganda Campaign against American 'Neutrality' in World War II* (New York, 1994), especially pp. 13–32.

the minds of those on whom it might have been effective. He had too long played an ingratiating role with the Nazi *Prominenten*, for the role of Cassandra to carry much force with them, even if he had tried to play it.

In part this was because, having met Hitler, he spotted earlier than most the degree to which Hitler was liable to be driven to more extreme action by overt attempts to put pressure upon him, still more by press claims that he had yielded to such pressure. In this his judgement was excellent. It was vitiated, however, by the perception which took root in London and Paris, as a result of the knowledge of conflict between Goering and von Neurath on the one side, not to mention Hjalmar Schacht, the banker who held the position of minister of economics until the winter of 1937–8, and the so-called extremists, Goebbels, Himmler and the SS, and increasingly, von Ribbentrop, on the other.[32] But, given his unquestioning commitment to the view that a war with Germany was the ultimate disaster, to be avoided at all costs, the effect of his realisation was to make him feel that all attempts to deter Hitler would be self-defeating, that they would, rather than give him pause, impel him more swiftly and completely into the hands of the radical nihilists whom Henderson rightly recognised in Goebbels and the SS.

This Henderson made no effort to explain in London. Presumably he still felt that he and the prime minister were of one mind, and that the protests he received from London were *pro forma* complaints from office-bound diplomats who were not properly in the picture. Whether he received any intimations from Sir Horace Wilson or any other member of the Downing Street staff remains unknown. It is known that George Steward and others were attempting to convey messages to the German 'moderates' through the staff of the German Embassy in London and individual German press representatives who represented themselves as being able to influence elements in Hitler's entourage.[33] Significantly or not, these attempts were most apparent during the period in which Henderson was absent from Berlin. It is therefore altogether possible that at least before his return to London in November 1938 he received messages from London which have not survived. It is certainly possible that he sought and received some such assurances in the period *before* Munich. But there is again no hard evidence on which to base any conclusions. Whatever the reasons the evidence shows that as a restraint on Hitler he was worse than useless because of the degree to which he was inclined to water down the warnings he was supposed to transmit. As a result, it was not until

[32] On Hitler's reaction to external crises which portrayed him as yielding to foreign pressure see D.C. Watt, 'Hitler's Visit to Rome and the May Week-end Crisis; A Study in Hitler's Response to External Stimuli', *JCH*, 9: 1 (1974); on the belief that Hitler's entourage was divided in to 'moderates' and extremists, see C.A. Macdonald, 'Economic Appeasement and the German "Moderates", 1937–1939; An Introductory Essay', *Past and Present*, 56 (1972).

[33] Cf. Watt, *How War Came*, p. 86 and the sources there cited.

Sir Horace Wilson, that most improbable of Nelsonic figures, fired a meta-
phorical gun across Hitler's bows and managed, on 27 September 1938,
to convey to him that Britain was about to go to war, that Hitler realised
what he was up against.

Shortly thereafter Sir Nevile Henderson disappeared from the scene for
a vital four months. The reportage from the Berlin Embassy was freed
from his constant efforts to conceal or belittle the evidence of his own
ineffectiveness. That reportage had exercised a kind of echo effect on
British policy by feeding and satisfying the anxieties of the Dominions
who, for different reasons, arising out of their own individual strategic
worries, feared British involvement in the defence of the status quo in
Europe. His reports were, as a matter of routine, printed and circulated
to the Dominions high commissioners in London, that bunch of nervous
Nellies, who reinforced all the anxieties and misgivings in Whitehall and
Westminster. Now it had ceased.

Sir George Ogilvie Forbes, the chargé d'affaires in Berlin, was not himself a 'toughie'; but he had none of Henderson's desperate willingness to
ingratiate himself, to substitute optimism for observation, nor his fear of
failure. He was a professional of the second rank and a realist where the
powers of diplomacy to avert conflict were concerned; and he does not
seem to have been plugged into that curious conspiracy for peace which
linked State Secretary von Weizsäcker of the German Foreign Ministry
with Henderson, André François-Poncet, the French ambassador until
October 1938 (his successor, Robert Coulondre, was much less
sympathetic) and Bernardo Attolico, the Italian ambassador.[34] Ogilvie
Forbes made no effort to lessen the impact in London of events in Berlin
or elsewhere. He reported the growing militarisation of German life after
Munich as he and his colleagues in the Embassy saw it – earning for them
all a stinging rebuke from Sir Nevile Henderson when he returned to
Berlin for a last fortnight or so of euphoria before the German march into
Prague destroyed his idyll for ever.

His return to Berlin in February 1939 coincided with Chamberlain's
unhappy burst of euphoria, when, partly as a result of the failure of the
'war-scare' of the third week in January 1939 to eventuate, the prime minister had concluded that the policy of quiet deterrence was beginning to
produce results, and probably fed it. The events of 15 March dispelled
that illusion forever.

Henderson was not the man to handle the months of alarums which
were to follow. He lived on his nerves, which betrayed him badly on various
occasions, especially in confrontations with von Ribbentrop, whom he

[34] Cf. Leonidas Hill, ed., *Die Weizsäcker-papiere, 1938–1950* (Frankfurt/M, 1974); Werner
Blasius, *Für Grossdeutschland – gegen den grossen Krieg; Staatssekretär Ernst Freiherr
von Weizsäcker in den Krisen um die Tschechoslowakei und Polen 1938/39* (Cologne,
1981).

came to loathe as much as Ribbentrop loathed him. He took pressure and crisis very badly, losing both his self-control and his professional skills. His reportage in the crises of August 1939 was confused, delayed and incompetent. Never very careful of security matters, he was indiscreet to the point of treason on the telephone. To his fellow diplomatists, especially Jozef Lipski, the Polish ambassador in Berlin, he showed his most hysterical and uncaring face. Stiffness of the upper lip, steadiness under fire, coolness of judgement were virtues conspicuous in him by their absence. He shocked Robert Coulondre, the French ambassador. His colleagues and masters in London behaved admirably in their efforts to reassure him, and to restore his professional judgement, summoning him to London, consulting him before Cabinet meetings; but they may equally have felt that by exhibiting him in all his nervous febrile state of panic they would discredit whatever credibility the doves in the Cabinet and among the high commissioners still placed in his views. Reading the diaries of Sir Alexander Cadogan one can detect in his sheer absence of comment a feeling that Henderson had placed himself beyond any position of usefulness. The role of intermediary passed from him to people such as the Tory MP, Henry Drummond-Wolf, Lord Brocket and others who touched base with the increasingly sceptical Sir Horace Wilson before launching their individual attempts to derail or stop the run-away train of impending war.

The case for arguing that Henderson can be seen as an instrument of Downing Street's alternative policy is essentially a negative one. We have very little beyond the *post facto* claims and justifications of a self-confessed 'Failure' who knew himself to be under sentence of death. His end was sad, even though he was a man promoted well beyond his capabilities. One can only speculate how any of the alternative candidates for his post would have coped.

When one turns to the figure of Sir Eric Phipps, one moves on to much surer ground. Not only, thanks to Sir Eric's training as a typist, do we have carbon copies of all his letters to the powers before and behind the throne, so to speak. We can see in him a man who, with his close friend-ship with Sir Maurice Hankey, carried a good deal of clout behind the scenes, in a way poor Sir Nevile never did. Like Craigie he was also a friend of Sir Warren Fisher. He was the son of a professional diplomatist, Sir Esmond Constantine Phipps, who never won ambassadorial status. He was educated privately in Dresden, Vienna and Paris. In 1933 he intrigued with Fisher and Sir John Simon to get the Paris Embassy, only to find that his brother-in-law, Sir Robert Vansittart, had secured his posting to Berlin. He found it as difficult to forgive Vansittart for this as Vansittart did to excuse his lobbying them.[35] He loathed Berlin, distinguishing himself

---

[35] Vansittart to Sir John Simon, 'strictly personal', n.d. FO 794/16. For this, as for many other references of this kind I am indebted to Mr John Herman.

by a form of reportage which made such ludicrous mockery of the Nazi
leadership, that, to avoid the best of his *bon mots* finding their way out of
London society to the disapproving ears of the German Embassy, the
Foreign Office ceased to give them circulation outside the office. Hitler
thought him 'a thug'. He loathed Henderson, who repaid his loathing
warmly. Like Henderson he corresponded regularly with Orme Sargent.
He had not an ounce of Germanophilia in his body despite, or perhaps
because of, his education in Dresden.

Phipps suffered in an extreme form from that most English of diseases
(Arthur Koestler called it the 'French 'flu'), Francophilia. He served in
Paris from 1922 to 1928, when he was in his late twenties, before going
on to Vienna and Berlin. His appointment to Paris as ambassador scandal-
ised his predecessor, Sir George Clerk, forced to retire on grounds of age,
in favour of a man who was a mere eleven months younger. But he was
able to mobilise his friends in London, most notably Hankey, to keep
himself ambassador until early in 1940, three years beyond what should
have been the date of his retirement.

The country to which he was posted was one teetering on the edge of
civil war. Under the Popular Front government of Leon Blum, a man with
whom Phipps personally maintained friendly relations, its political system
required the most careful management to avoid its disintegration into rival
warring camps. In the autumn of 1937, shortly after Phipps' arrival in
Paris, the Cagoulard conspiracy was uncovered, before its plans for a *coup
d'état* could be realised. Its support reached into the senior ranks of the
armed forces. The year had seen the French rearmament programme totally disrupted by the left-wing campaign for a forty-hour week. German
and Italian money and influence penetrated deep into the French,
especially the Parisian, press. The international left by contrast were pros-
trated by the effect of the purges and the general incompetence of the
Moscow-trained bureaucrats who were replacing the revolutionary generation of European Comintern leaders which had congregated in Paris after
Hitler had driven them out of Germany. The Spanish tragedy was wending
its weary and blood-stained way downwards to defeat, with the representatives of Yezhov, Yagoda and Beria doing their little bit to destroy any signs
of competent, let alone independent, leadership among the various Republican factions.

The Quai d'Orsay, like the deputies of the Assemblée Nationale, were
divided between those who saw in the alliance with Britain the only chance
of survival for France, but found it difficult to discover a British policy
and advocates in power with whom they could ally themselves, and those
who thought a proclamation of neutralism or perhaps a link with Mussolini's Italy in a pan-Latin Anglophobe Alliance was the best way for France
to follow. The views of the neutralists unfortunately for the Anglophiles
most closely fitted with those of Chamberlain and the appeasers, with
their terror that Britain might be dragged into a European war at the heels

of French advocates of an independent great power policy based, as in the 1920s, on alliance with the powers of the Little Entente and Poland. French neutralists feared war even more than did the appeasers in Britain, though for rather different reasons. Patriotism in France had been captured by the non-communist left.

Phipps' hostility towards Germany, his extreme pessimism as to the likelihood of any government headed by Hitler being persuaded by the British government's policy of attempting to lull Hitler by judicious concessions to German revisionism emerge clearly from American sources soon after Phipps' arrival in Paris. William Bullitt, the American ambassador in Paris, reported him on 30 April 1937, as calling Hitler 'a fanatic who would be satisfied with nothing less than the domination of Europe', and saying that he 'did not see the faintest possibility of coming to any kind of agreement with Hitler', his experience in Berlin having shown him that

the only thing which would impress the Germans today was military force . . . any negotiations which might be begun today with Germany . . . would end in failure unless France and England should be prepared to accord Germany absolute domination of the international scene . . . It was his opinion and that of his government that the only chance of preserving peace was for Great Britain to re-arm as fast as possible and during the period of rearmament try to keep Germany as quiet as possible.[36]

On 1 July 1937, William Dodd, the American ambassador in Berlin, his former colleague, wrote to Phipps in alarm about the kind of remarks Sir Nevile Henderson was making to senior Germans, and asking if Henderson's views represented those of the British government.

Your Ambassador [Dodd wrote], has said more than once to me that English public opinion for such 'Bismarkian' expansion [i.e. German control, and actual annexation, of the Danube-Balkans zone [(a most un-Bismarckian policy, D.C.W.)] is the proper thing and even asked if the United States would approve such a move and join a moral triple alliance.[37]

A reply to Dodd's letter was concocted in the Foreign Office, assuring him that this was *not* British policy, Vansittart adding, 'It is a melancholy reflection that we should have to spend any time in thinking how to protect ourselves against our own ambassador.'

Phipps' gradual defection to the Downing Street camp began in the winter of 1937. The issue was that of Chamberlain's attempt to detach Italy from Germany at a time when the French government was under

---

[36] Bullitt to Hull, 30 Apr. 1937, *Foreign Relations of the United States, 1937*, I, nos. 556–7, pp. 84–5.

[37] Phipps sent a copy of Dodd's letter privately to Vansittart, on 11 Aug. 1937, having consulted him in person a week earlier. Phipps to Vansittart, FO 371/20711, C5541/3/18, 11 Aug. 1937.

great pressure to break the Non-Intervention Agreement in Spain, and open the Franco-Spanish frontier to arms deliveries to the Spanish government. Phipps was kept well informed of the conflict between Chamberlain and the pro-Italian element in the Cabinet and Eden by Hankey, himself a strong supporter on strategic grounds of the folly of antagonising Mussolini when Britain was under such pressure in the Far East and might at any time have to face the necessity of transferring the major part of the British battle fleet through the Mediterranean to Singapore. That Phipps was still emotionally tied to Eden is shown by the personal note struck in his letter of regret to the outgoing foreign secretary at the time of Eden's resignation; he had equally been able to persuade Vansittart not to follow his appointment as 'chief diplomatic adviser' to the prime minister, an event which baffled observers then as much as it is still misunderstood today, with a visit to Paris. Vansittart's acceptance of Phipps' advice was friendly and in no sense reflected the antagonism which was to develop in September 1938 and persist thereafter.

This defection was encouraged by Phipps' own political orientation in terms of French politics. Although he remained on friendly terms with Léon Blum and with Delbos, whom Chautemps retained as foreign minister after the fall of the Popular Front government, he was forming ever closer relations with Caillaux, Flandin and others of the future *capitulards*, on the parliamentary right, in opposition to the general line pursued by successive French governments. Originally these relationships were purely social; but they moved into the political sphere over the issue of the improvement of relations between France and Italy and the increasing activation of Phipps' hatred of communist influence in France. He was persuaded that this influence had engulfed some of the prominent opponents of appeasement in the Quai d'Orsay, most notably Alexis Léger, the secretary-general at the Quai d'Orsay.[38] He was however still a long way from the position he was to come to occupy, as is shown by his telegraphing the Foreign Office at the end of February 1938 after London had announced the opening of talks with the Italians, without first consulting the French government at all, 'the approval of M. Flandin would therefore be small compensation for creating distrust in moderate French Left circles'.[39]

Phipps really began to reveal his true defeatist colours during the month of September 1938, when it began to look as if the British 'management' of the Czech crisis was failing to prevent the onset of war. His infamous telegram of 24 September had already been preceded by numerous messages suggesting that he accepted the views of Flandin, Caillaux and others of the right-wing opposition to the Daladier government that there was a

[38] Phipps to Eden, 'personal and secret', 6 Oct. 1937, Phipps Papers.
[39] Phipps to Halifax, telegram by telephone, 25 Feb 1938, FO 371/22404 (R1784/23/22).

'war party' in the French Cabinet and in the Assembly who were far from representative of French opinion. He had moreover reported in detail on Bonnet's collapse into defeatism on 13 September, reports which had played a crucial part in precipitating Chamberlain into his first visit to Germany to see Hitler at Berchtesgaden.[40] But the real break seems to have come with the reactions of his colleagues in the Foreign Office to the 'All that is best in France' telegram. This was read by Chamberlain to the Cabinet on 25 September, the meeting to which he was reporting his meeting with Hitler at Bad Godesberg, and his reactions to this experience.

The evidence we have as to the views of the senior officials in the Foreign Office, from Cadogan, Sargent, Harvey and Strang downwards, suggests that they had already reconciled themselves to the idea that war with Germany was close to being made inevitable by the behaviour of the German government. Cadogan, in fact, persuaded Halifax into reversing his original acceptance of Chamberlain's recommendation that the Godesberg proposals should be accepted. He was now to instruct Phipps to ascertain the opinions of a range of French military and political figures, including the head of the Catholic Church in France, Cardinal Verdier, and to require British consuls in France to furnish direct reports to the Foreign Office on the state of opinion in their various consular districts.[41] The suggestion inherent in these instructions that if they were sent via the Embassy they would be liable to be 'doctored', would not have escaped Phipps.

In the event, Phipps' pessimistic view of French opinion and of French readiness for war was probably not all that wide of the mark, given that, on 24 September, war seemed inevitable. After the news of British rejection of Hitler's demands and of the mobilisation of the Czech forces became known on 25 September, Phipps himself reported a 'complete swing-over' (the phrase was Herriot's), in French opinion. What stuck in the throat of his colleagues was his characterisation of the elements who were resolute as a 'small, noisy and corrupt war party' and his identification of Bonnet, Flandin and Caillaux, as 'all that was best in France'. Sargent seems to have struck him off his list of correspondents, and, with Hankey's retirement as Cabinet secretary earlier in 1938, Phipps lost any private sources of guidance from within the inner circles of foreign-policy-makers. It is interesting and significant that it was at this moment that he began to communicate directly with the prime minister, albeit through the Foreign Office. On 28 September he sent a telegram to Chamberlain

---

[40] See Phipps to Halifax, 2 Sept. 1938, FO 371/21734 (C9064/1941/18); his eight telegrams to London of 13 Sept. 1938, all in FO 371/21737; Cab 23/95, Cab 38(38), meeting of 14 Sept. 1938; Cadogan diaries, entries of 13, 14 Sept. 1938.

[41] Cadogan to Phipps, 25 Sept. 1938, FO 371/21740 (C1062/1941/18); Cadogan diaries, entries for 25, 26 Sept. 1938.

giving his 'considered view' of French opinion, that it was against being led into war on what at that date looked like 'a mere question of procedure'. He continued to provide evidence of French opposition to war right up to the opening of the Munich conference. And on 30 September, forwarding a letter from ex-President Millerand to Chamberlain, Phipps made his declaration of loyalty to the prime minister, denouncing the 'sad and criminal war party' around Daladier, the 'evil forces working for war combined with foolish and misguided but perhaps patriotic forces' which, he said, he had 'the distinct impression were working their hardest ... both here and in England ... to undermine your efforts'.

After Munich, Phipps' own resentment of his treatment by the Foreign Office was to emerge in a series of bitter complaints to Hankey, whom he saw in Paris on 1–3 October and wrote to on 6 October. Vansittart, he said, on the basis of private information from the political director of the official French News Agency, *Havas*, had 'stabbed him in the back' by leaking his telegrams of 13 September to the French journalist, Pertinax, and telling him that Phipps did not properly report British official views to the French government and that British public opinion was hostile to Mr Chamberlain, who 'would soon be overthrown'.[42] (The story of Phipps' reports had appeared in the French left-wing newspaper *L'Epoque* and the communist *L'Humanité*.) He seems to have suggested to Hankey the existence of a conspiratorial relationship between dissidents in the Foreign Office led by Vansittart and their equivalents in the Quai d'Orsay led by Léger who were trying to *saboter* both 'the Chamberlain peace policy and Phipps himself'.[43]

The difficulty with this kind of, at first sight, suspiciously paranoic statement is that it may well have had an element of truth in it. At least one of the private newsletters circulating in London and elsewhere at this date, the *Whitehall Letter*, edited by Victor Gordon-Lennox, then diplomatic correspondent of the anti-appeasement *Daily Telegraph*, was under observation by MI5, for the accuracy of its 'inside information' about government policy. Gordon-Lennox's deputy told me in the 1960s that much of their information came from Vansittart himself or from Rex Leeper, then head of the Foreign Office News Department.[44] There was a debate within the Foreign Office about the problems of serving a foreign policy which many believed for professional rather than ideological reasons to be mistaken.[45]

Phipps felt himself to be particularly vulnerable as he was currently

---

[42] Phipps to Hankey, 6 Oct. 1938, Phipps Papers, PHPP 3/3.
[43] Roskill, *Hankey, Man of Secrets*, vol. 3, p. 90.
[44] Private information from the late Kenneth Younger, PC, who in the 1930s worked in MI5 and from the late Toby O'Brien, deputy editor of the *Whitehall Letter*.
[45] See Donald S. Lammers, 'From Whitehall after Munich; the Foreign Office and the future course of British Foreign Policy', *Historical Journal*, 16 (1974).

engaged in trying to persuade the Foreign Office to extend his tenure of the Paris Embassy. The hostility his behaviour during Munich had aroused in the Foreign Office in general had made many aware that he was already three years over the normal retirement age for public servants. In the event it was Hankey who secured his extension, by representing to Halifax that his removal would be a disaster for the future of Anglo-French relations, given that Halifax was still hoping for a European peace to be assured, as he wrote to Phipps on 1 November, by a 'genuine agreement between Germany, France and Britain. German expansion in Central Europe was', he wrote, a 'normal and natural thing.' The danger, in his view, was that 'France may in certain political circumstances turn so defeatist as to give up the struggle of maintaining adequate defence even for the safety of metropolitan France ... We might have to face alone the full weight of German military power in the West.'[46]

Phipps was able to reassure Halifax on this point, writing on 7 November, of his conviction that 'the French would fight like tigers for their independence'.[47] But it is clear that it had not dawned on Halifax that Phipps' own circle of informants, Flandin and Caillaux, not to mention Bonnet, represented just that defeatist element which most alarmed Halifax. In the meantime Phipps was writing bitterly to the prime minister about the activities of Churchill and his supporters, especially General Spears, in agitating members of the 'war party such as Reynaud, Mandel and co' on their visits to Paris, and bitterly offending Daladier by their remarks. Spears, he added, was a Jew, whose real name was Spiers.[48] One of Phipps' less attractive characteristics was that he had picked up from the self-consciously 'French', English Catholic writer, Hilaire Belloc, the virulent antisemitism of Maurras and the *Action Française*.

Phipps was, in fact, in the process of transforming himself into the prime minister's man in France. His papers are full of correspondence with the prime minister, with Sir Horace Wilson as well as with Halifax. His utility to them was however greatly limited by the eclipse of Chamberlain's attempts to reach a tripartite Anglo-French-German agreement, and to encourage Italy to resume a more independent attitude towards Germany which was to follow. By the end of November 1938, Lord Halifax had swung firmly against Germany as a partner in any settlement. The Franco-German agreement of December 1938 and the prime minister's visit to Rome had produced no pay-off. Italy and France were publicly at loggerheads as a result of Mussolini's ill-advised attempt to exploit the Anglo-Italian Agreement on the Mediterranean, ratified in November, by an overt attack on the French presence in Corsica, Tunis, Nice and Savoy. And the war-scare of the third week in January 1939 had loosened the

[46] Halifax to Phipps, 1 Nov. 1938, FO 800/311.
[47] Phipps to Halifax, 7 Nov. 1938, FO 800/311
[48] Phipps to Chamberlain, 4 Nov. 1938, FO 800/311.

British determination not to commit land forces to the defence of France on any scale.

In this reversal of British policy, Phipps' only role, it emerged, was to take part in an intrigue with Bonnet to press Daladier into a final attempt to appease Italy. His allies, besides Bonnet, included André François-Poncet, his old friend from Berlin days, now French ambassador in Rome. The intrigue led to a personal appeal from Chamberlain to Daladier on 13 July 1939, of which the Italians received prior warning, presumably through a reactivation of the *canale segreto*. Daladier dealt with it with courtesy and resolution. His reply coincided with a series of messages from Sir Percy Loraine in Rome advising Halifax to 'keep Mussolini uncomfortable ... It is best for you to maintain your *silence menaçant* in London and me my *silence souriant* in Rome,' a recommendation which struck the prime minister as 'very sensible'.[49] Germany, in the person of the inimitable von Ribbentrop, duly made the mistake of taking Italy for a satellite, bound obediently to follow every turn and twist of Hitler's foreign policy, and Italian neutrality was assured.

Phipps' behaviour was a product of his conviction that war in Europe would only benefit the Soviet Union, whose influence he saw behind every sign of resolution displayed by the French Cabinet. The 'corrupt war party' was, he was convinced, controlled financially and politically by the French communist leadership using 'Moscow gold'. There certainly was Soviet money active in the French press, just as there was Italian and German. The economics of newspaper production, let alone the standard of living of the major French journalists, required sizable subsidisation. The most sensible comment on his views was contained in a minute by Sargent on the telegram of 27 September in which Phipps had reported the views of Cardinal Verdier, the Archbishop of Paris. When the more junior officials suggested that the cardinal's conviction that the 'war was being worked up by communists was absurd' and an example of the 'Vatican's anti-communist line' Sargent replied 'of course the Communists are working for a war ... that is quite irrelevant to our question which was what French public opinion was to the hateful dilemma of honouring or dishonouring France's treaty obligations'.[50]

Phipps, like his critics, was too apt to see French politics as the product of a multifarious interaction of conflicting conspiratorial groupuscules. In choosing which of these to believe he chose badly and unprofessionally, a prey to his fears and prejudices, rather than the professional judgement he had displayed with such effect in Berlin. This led him into intriguing with the prime minister in the latter's attempts to circumvent and ignore

---

[49] On this whole episode see Watt, *How War Came*, pp. 421–4, and the sources there cited.
[50] FO 371/21741, C10824/1941/18, Phipps to Halifax, 27 Sept. 1938 and minutes by Speaight, Victor Mallet and Sargent, of 27/28 Sept. 1938.

his professional advisers in the field of foreign affairs.[51] Once the prime minister and the Foreign Office had come to occupy positions in which different policies were being advocated by the latter and practised by the former, and factions had developed within Whitehall, it was inevitable that ambassadors, who were themselves of quasi-ministerial status by virtue of the practice of appointing the most senior to the rank of privy council-lor, should be drawn in to the factional conflict, if they were not extremely careful.

Which brings this analysis of Chamberlain's ambassadors back to Sir Robert Craigie. In a sense the most critical part of Sir Robert Craigie's career found him at odds not with Chamberlain, still less Lord Halifax, but with their successors, Churchill and Eden. The issue was Sir Robert Craigie's conviction that the alternative policy he favoured in 1940–1 of postponing a confrontation with Japan until after the war with Germany was over had been prevented by misjudgement in London, a conviction which he was determined to make the burden of the Final Report on his Embassy written on his return from Japanese internment, a report which he assumed would be published as Sir Nevile Henderson's on his Berlin Embassy had been. Churchill took the most violent exception to the report and secured its virtual suppression. The only copies sent outside the office went to Lord Halifax, then ambassador in Washington, and to the king. The Foreign Office, not to be outdone, instructed a junior official, Mr Sterndale Bennett, to write a rebuttal.[52]

It was perhaps injudicious of Craigie to hope that his view, critical as it was of the policy advocated by the prime minister and the foreign sec-retary, could have been published at the time. He could not, of course, have been aware of the possible repercussions in Australia of such a report. And his concern for the disastrous effects of the collapse of the British position in Asia east of the Indo-Burmese frontier could not bal-ance Churchill's overwhelming sense of relief that United States entry into the war had been secured. It is all the same odd that today's Neo-Tory revisionists who criticise Britain's involvement in the European wars of 1914–18 and 1939–41 have never turned their attention to the Craigie thesis, leaving it to the fantasists who seek to involve Churchill in an out-right conspiracy to hide from the United States alleged British knowledge

---

[51] This should not be taken as implying that there is something inherently irregular in the practice of ambassadors writing private letters to their colleagues in the Foreign Office, let alone to ministers. Indeed in 1937 Vansittart advised Phipps that some of his reporting 'would be better contained . . . in a letter to Anthony [Eden] or me' (Vansittart to Phipps, 29 Sept. 1937, PHPP 2/18). Both Austen Chamberlain's and Halifax's private papers are filled with letters from British ambassadors abroad.

[52] On this episode see Best, 'Sir Robert Craigie'. See also my own article 'Senso kaihi wa kano de atta ke: Kure-gi-hokokhu to seisaku kettei erito no Hanno' (Could War in the Far East have been prevented in November 1941? Sir Robert Craigie's Final Report on his Embassy to Japan and the Reactions of the British Foreign Policy Making Elite), in A. Iriye and T. Aruga, eds., *Senkanki no Nihon gaiko* (Tokio, 1984).

of the Japanese plans to attack Pearl Harbor,[53] an accusation once levelled by the American extreme right against President Roosevelt. It is the odder when it is considered that the burden of the Neo-Tories complaint is that Britain was too ready to risk her world position to intervene against a potential European enemy; one would have expected them in their efforts to chip away at the massive reputation of Churchill and the continuing popular acceptance of his version of history to turn to the real period in which the losses were made. But it is a truism that they share with their gigantic bugbear, a total ignorance of the real elements of the imperial strategy abandoned by the British government in 1933–9, and a racism which assumes that international politics east of Suez could have been taken care of with much the same ease and much the same employment of handfuls of troops and ships not required elsewhere that Napier employed against King Menelik of Abyssinia or Kitchener against the 'fuzzy-wuzzies' of the Sudan.

Craigie had no such illusions. What he did have, unfortunately for him, was a black mark in Churchill's memory which dated back to the aftermath of the collapse of the Geneva Three-Power Conference of 1927 on naval arms limitation, in a welter of Anglophobia in the United States and anti-Americanism in the British Cabinet. Churchill, then chancellor of the exchequer, had formed the view that Craigie was an appeaser rather than a patriot and had been insultingly critical of a memorandum written by Craigie, in his capacity as head of the American Department in the Foreign Office, exploring the alternatives and costs of attempting to reach a settlement with the United States which would defuse the crisis and make the resumption of progress in Anglo-American negotiations possible.[54]

It is particularly ironic that on this issue Churchill was playing his anti-American role of British patriot, a role which was echoed by the home secretary, Joynson-Hicks and the first lord of the Admiralty, Sir William Bridgeman, who confided to his journal that the senior figures of the Foreign Office's willingness to sacrifice British interests in the maintenance of the right to blockade in war resulted from their unwillingness to confront their American wives across the breakfast table. (At that time, the permanent under-secretary, Sir Ronald Lindsay, his successor, Sir Robert Vansittart, and Craigie himself were all married to American-born wives.) Churchill did not forget or forgive. And, as already remarked, Craigie's role in the continuing negotiations on naval arms control, which included

---

[53] Cf. James Rusbridger and E. Nave, *Betrayal at Pearl Harbor; How Churchill Lured Roosevelt into War* (London, 1991).

[54] On this episode cf. B.J.C. McKercher, *The Second Baldwin Government and the United States, 1924–1929* (Cambridge, 1984). Craigie's offending memorandum of 12 Nov. 1928 and Churchill's insulting commentary of 19 Nov. 1928 upon it are printed in *DBFP*, Series 1A, vol. V. The relevant correspondence and minutes are in FO 371/12812 and 12813. See also Martin Gilbert, *Churchill*, pp. 307–8.

the negotiation of the Anglo–German Naval Agreement of 18 June 1935, associated him in the eyes of many with the notion of appeasement.

Craigie's sheer success as a negotiator and the feeling that he 'fraternised' too closely with elements outside the Foreign Office, almost schoolboyish as they were with the suggestion that he spent his time 'sucking up' to Baldwin, Chamberlain, Warren Fisher and Simon, made him enemies among both his contemporaries and his juniors in the Foreign Office. The fact that he was personally shy and found all the satisfaction human company could offer in his wife, who accompanied him everywhere he went at home or abroad, meant that he formed few of the intra-service friendships normal among his contemporaries. His own papers were virtually all destroyed in Tokio when war broke out. But there is very little correspondence from him in those collections of private papers which have survived. He is celebrated in the *Dictionary of National Biography*, but the notice of his career is, even by contrast with that of Sir Nevile Henderson, cold and distant.[55]

His posting to Tokio was ascribed by the more hostile of his contemporaries to his political ties rather than any suitability for the job. He had never, it was pointed out, had any service in the Far Eastern Department of the Foreign Office or in any diplomatic mission in a Far Eastern capital. The criticism is very revealing. Foreign Ministries generally try to keep the *déformation professionnelle* to which diplomats are peculiarly prone, that of confusing the maintenance of good relations between their own state and that to which they are posted with the best interests of their country, by regularly bringing them home and changing their postings at three-yearly intervals. This policy fails in its purpose if, as so often happens, postings abroad and appointments at home are confined to one major geographical area, as it might be the Arab-language, or Spanish-speaking areas, or, as in this case, the Far East. Within the ministry devoted to the furtherance of British interests, including, if unavoidable, by conflict with inimical regimes, there can, under these conditions, develop a sub-culture exhibiting the same *déformation professionnelle* as the professional advocate of the protection of Anglo-Ruritanian friendship against all comers.

The Foreign Office has long exhibited this phenomenon in its Near and Middle Eastern Departments. In the 1930s the Far Eastern Department was in a similar state. I have written elsewhere of the extraordinary behaviour of its members in May–June 1939, when they came within a whisker of involving Britain in the war in the Far East for which Hitler and Ribbentrop had been scheming for the past ten months in the hope of winning themselves a clear hand for the subjection of Poland and

---

[55] The author was Sir Joseph Dodds, who had served as counsellor under him at the British Embassy in Tokio.

France, on which Hitler had set his heart after Munich. This was after the British guarantees for Poland, Romania, Greece and Turkey, the German denunciation of the Anglo-German Naval Agreement, and a first-class war scare over the last week-end in May over a possible German *coup de main* in Danzig.[56] One can only wonder at the near-criminal myopia of the officials concerned. Part of this myopia was due to universal hostility to the Japanese and a dismissal of their military strength which sprang from deep-rooted white supremacist assumptions.

Craigie had, in fact, been at the centre of policy-making towards East Asia ever since his involvement in the naval arms negotiations. He had been the principal Foreign Office negotiator at the London Naval Conference of 1930. He had taken part in the preliminary naval conversations of 1934 as part of the preparations for the London Naval Conference of 1935–6. He had taken part in that conference. He was one of the inner circle who had access to the 'product' of the various British intelligence agencies. He worked very closely, even though not always in sympathy with, the first sea lord and the naval planners of the Admiralty. From Fisher and the Treasury he knew as closely as anyone the limitations on expenditure within which a politico-military strategy had to be conducted. Nor was he anti-American, although the Americans did not always appreciate this.

His main faults, in the eyes of the Foreign Office's Far Eastern Department, were that he did not share their commitment to the China of Chiang Kai-Shek, and that he felt that a viable diplomatic strategy could be built on co-operation with the Japanese Anglophiles and the so-called 'moderates' with whom he had excellent relations. His main weakness was that his hopes of a policy which would alternate displays of firmness and suavity failed on the total absence of any strength to display.

Dealing as we are [he wrote on March 6, 1937 on arrival in Tokio], with a militarist element in Japan whose worship of force is second only to the militant Nazis, we shall produce the maximum effect on the Japanese mind if we can leave the Japanese government in no doubt as to our determination to restore our armaments to their former relative position in the world balance.[57]

This effort to support the Admiralty's bid for a New Standard was in vain. And his belief in the possibility of building a policy on the Japanese 'moderates' was at odds with the views of the long-serving commercial counsellor, Sir George Sansom, who, on his return to London, joined the Far Eastern Department in an advisory capacity, becoming their 'guru' on matters Japanese. Having watched the political eclipse of his friends since the early 1930s, Sansom thought the power of the moderates a 'myth' and Craigie a 'fool', thus reinforcing the anti-Japanese prejudices of the Far Eastern Department, all but a handful of whose Far Eastern experience

[56] Watt, *How War Came*, pp. 349–59.
[57] Craigie to Eden, 6 Mar. 1937, FO 371/20549, A5459/6/45.

had been with China rather than the vulgar imitative Japanese as they were then represented. Sansom's views were shared by other members of the British Embassy in Japan. They were supported, much to Craigie's disadvantage, by the military attaché, Major General Piggott, so crude a Japanophile, that 'Piggotry' was a word of abuse in Far Eastern Department minutes. There is no greater disadvantage to having one's views taken seriously than their support by the club buffoon.

Craigie's position was so isolated that he was driven to write to Mr Howe of the Far Eastern Department that

I am left here with the feeling that such efforts as we are able to make here to prevent the state of our relations with Japan from going from bad to worse are viewed with suspicion and misgiving by the Far Eastern Department and that only when we are engaged in our normal duty of protesting and recriminating can you sleep comfortably in your beds.[58]

The letter can be read as a bitter protest or a mild satire. But placed alongside Craigie's later reference to 'the Far Eastern Department's Bourbon-like inability to learn from past events',[59] the former interpretation seems the more likely. This is strengthened by his comment elsewhere that 'my advice on these points and others has been neglected because it would have compromised not so much the strictness of our neutrality as its excessive benevolence towards China'.[60]

The Tientsin crisis confirmed Chamberlain's view of the Foreign Office's inability to do their job, and led him to one of his characteristic private denunciations of its 'ineptitude' in his letters to his sisters.

Thanks to the ineptitude of the Foreign Office we have been manoeuvred into a false position where we are single-handed and yet are being attacked over a policy as essential for America, France and Germany as ourselves ... The only thing that gives me any confidence is Craigie's attitude ... He always seems to preserve his calm and never to get rattled ... Only the anti-Japanese bias of the Foreign Office in the past have never given him a chance.[61]

It seems a familiar note, what with the prime minister railing against the Foreign Office and an ambassador at odds with them receiving his praise. The difference however is that Chamberlain had long abandoned his hopes of an Anglo-Japanese rapprochement. He had been as much in the dark as had Halifax and Cadogan about the onset of the Tientsin crisis, which was not one provoked and managed by an enemy of Britain with a view to her humiliation, but one provoked as much by the blind intransigence of the Foreign Office's Far Eastern Department as anything. The Japanese general in command on the spot, General Homma, was an Anglo-

[58] Craigie to Howe, 30 June 1939, FO 371/23485, F8566/372/10.
[59] Craigie to Ronald, 9 Aug. 1939, FO 371/23529, F8489/6457/10.
[60] Craigie to Halifax, *DBFP* 3/IX, no. 227, 18 June 1939.
[61] Neville to Hilda Chamberlain, 15 July 1939, Chamberlain Papers, NC 18/1/1107.

phile and a moderate, for whatever that was worth, and not inclined, as his deputy was, to force matters to a confrontation.

Chamberlain, like Craigie's critics later, tried to force the Tientsin crisis into the pattern of 'appeasement'. Soviet critics, mindful of the concurrent Soviet–Japanese conflict over Nomonhan in Mongolia, have been particularly critical. But the Soviets had a land frontier, superior forces both numerically and technically, and evaded war in Europe by concluding the Nazi–Soviet Non-Aggression Pact, clearing the way for the German attack on Poland and absorbing the eastern half of the country when the Germans had defeated the Polish army. By comparison, the British evasion of a conflict over an enclave surrounded by Japanese troops, unreachable by sea, when confronted with a possible war in the Mediterranean and on France's eastern frontier, seems only military common sense.

This was not a view shared by the Far Eastern Department, whose Mr Dening had commented in June on a chiefs of staff report that 'all that is required is some degree of firmness in order to make the Japanese desist'. Japan, in Sir George Sansom's view, was so weakened economically by the war in China, that she could not afford to go to war. One must, in parentheses, marvel at a man so dismissive of the Japanese moderates as Sansom, and with such a reputation for understanding the Japanese scene, so lacking in knowledge and understanding of how the Manchurian crisis or the Marco Polo Bridge incident had been used by the ultra-nationalists of the Japanese officer corps to involve their country in conflict, that he could maintain so impersonal and rationally Marxist an analysis of Japanese politics. Sansom could write with great distinction and sophistication about Japanese culture. As a political analyst he was a dangerous and dogmatic failure. Nor was Craigie politically naïve in Japanese or any other terms. His one fault was over-optimism. His own *déformation professionnelle* was his confidence in his own powers as a negotiator. Where the alternative policy outlined in his Final Report is concerned, he was arguing on the basis of a policy he was never allowed to apply and a negotiating strategy from which he was ordered to exclude himself.

The case of Sir Robert Craigie does not really match those of Perth, Phipps or Henderson. He had no intellectual or ideological commitment to the avoidance of conflict, only a hardnosed conviction that the state of Britain's armaments and economy made it essential. His diplomatic strategy was based on the conclusions of the Treasury and the chiefs of staff. His views on the possibilities of an alternative policy towards Japan were matched by those of his American colleague, Joseph Grew. Grew was, if anything, more of a mandarin than Craigie, a man intimately involved in the American 'old money' East Coast establishment with its instinctive dedication to public service. It was he who carried the professionalisation of the American Foreign Service through a Republican Congress under Calvin Coolidge. He was appointed ambassador by the Republican,

Hoover, and reappointed by the Democrat, Roosevelt, something almost unheard of in American practice.

The main difference between Grew's outlook and that of Craigie was that he understood populist politics. An accommodation with Japanese militarist objectives was not something that could be reconciled with public opinion and a free press, or not for long enough for it to be practicable politics. The tide of opinion in both Britain and America was setting towards a kind of Wilsonian para-ideology. It could be held at bay, as it was in the 1930s where Germany was concerned, by a form of isolationism, or in the earlier 1940s, where the Soviet Union was concerned, by a self-deceiving, self-censoring press. But the hard realism, preached, for example by E.H. Carr vis-à-vis Nazi Germany in the 1930s and the Soviet Union thereafter, was not one which fitted the self-images of the two countries entertained by their respective public opinions. Realism for Grew was something to govern tactics. He did not expect an ambassador's advice regularly to overcome opinion in Congress, let alone, unless it were confused and divided, opinion in the country.

By contrast Craigie was not a political animal but a professional diplomatist to his fingers' ends. Parliamentary politics was to him largely a closed book, something that was the responsibility of the political leaders. He was a humane man with feelings and sensibilities. But he was so 'inner-directed', so absorbed in his private relationship with his formidable wife, that the inexorable movement of British public opinion into the quasi-ideological set of attitudes which led to, or rather preceded, the decision of the British government to go to war in 1939, largely escaped him. He was enough of a man of his time to feel that where Germany was concerned war was unavoidable; though he was one of those who was excessive in his favourable judgement of the ethically somewhat dubious procedures that led to Munich.[62] But his final report reveals him to be a man who had lost touch with the inevitable movement of public opinion in Britain once war had broken out, still more after Dunkirk. It is inconceivable that he could have been a *capitulard*; his roots were securely fixed in the golden last quarter of Queen Victoria's 'sixty glorious years'. His kind of 'flexibility' was itself tactical, something necessary while Britain's strength was rebuilt. The notion that it could never be rebuilt would have struck him as defeatist and disloyal.

Although the burden of this argument is that Craigie was not one of 'Chamberlain's ambassadors' in the sense that Phipps certainly and Henderson most probably were, it has to be said that no more than Craigie was Chamberlain a potential capitulationist or defeatist. He believed Britain should be prepared to make some hard and realistic adjustments to the decline in her power. He was prepared to manage both the demo-

---

[62] FO 262/1978 8/234/38, Craigie memorandum 5 Oct. 1938.

cratic process and public opinion for reasons of state in the service of making these adjustments. But he never concealed his willingness to face the possibility of war should he fail; and the image of war he entertained was possibly worse for Britain than the reality, at least in terms of the destruction of Britain's cities and the decimation of Britain's youth. The indictment of Chamberlain, for those, probably still the majority, for whom the study of history is inseparable from the process of pronouncing condemnatory judgements, must rest on his willingness to take on his own shoulders the responsibility for deceiving and misleading the majority of those in whose name he exercised power, and on his determination to assume responsibility for imposing sacrifices on the publics of countries who had looked to Britain as a model and a protector. The immorality of appeasement is that it became the securing of peace of mind for the appeasers at the expense of the sacrifice of the interests and well-being if not the independence of others not their fellow citizens. The process could be justified, as Henderson justified it, by arguing that the victims of appeasement were in some way guilty and therefore deserved their fate; an unpleasant argument. But then there is much that was unpleasant about Henderson. Of all the appeasers he most merits a reassessment; but it would be a very ignorant or very unusual historian who could argue convincingly that he was of adequate quality for the task that was set him.

Chamberlain saw, however, no objection to subverting the loyalties or the chain of command of the Diplomatic Service. Ambassadors were to him instruments of the government as a whole, and of government policy as he, rather than the foreign secretary, or the senior advisers of the Foreign Office saw it. (Much the same attitude was to be displayed by Eden during the conspiratorial period of his relations with the French government in October 1956, and, more recently, by Mrs Thatcher, so it is said.) If the Cabinet was divided on the issues of policy, this attitude inevitably involved either the total circumvention of the members of the Diplomatic Service who happened to be *en poste* in the relevant foreign capitals or the 'politicisation' of individual members of the service by making them instruments of the policy of a faction within government and Cabinet. The evidence surveyed in this chapter suggests that Chamberlain employed both methods, both unofficial private emissaries and factionally inclined diplomatists; the only clear evidence of the latter phenomenon is provided by the case of Sir Eric Phipps, although there is strong circumstantial evidence in the case of Sir Nevile Henderson. The other ambassadors who represented the Chamberlain government in the period 1937–40 are not, so far as the evidence goes, in any way implicated in the constitutionally dubious practices of the prime minister, driven, as he was, by the conviction that God or history had laid upon his particular shoulders and conscience the duty and responsibility of avoiding, averting or preventing a second European-wide Anglo-German war in his lifetime, and he has earned the permanent disapproval of his people and of historians for the moral and ethical judgements he made and the things he did in consequence in attempting to fulfil that duty.

CHAPTER 8

The Foreign Office and France during the Phoney War, September 1939–May 1940

Before 1939 Britain, in her search for an accommodation with Nazi Germany, had tended to ignore and disparage France, complaining of the corruption and weakness of the Third Republic, doubting the potential steadfastness in war of the French army and paying little attention to France's security concerns in Europe.[1] However, in 1939 the British, faced with the growing prospect of war with Germany and aware of increasing French demoralisation, turned once again to their ally and attempted, somewhat belatedly, to stiffen her resistance to Germany by embarking on full military collaboration with France. This appeared to have some effect: in March the British ambassador to France, Sir Eric Phipps, reported to London that

an observant visitor to France to-day will find an atmosphere very different from that of 1936, or even of last autumn . . . To-day there is a feeling that good progress has been made towards a solution of both the financial and economic problem. Although the international situation is full of danger, and weighs heavily on the budget, the market and public opinion, the country is now more united to meet a menace from abroad than for many years past . . . Finally a most important factor in the revival of confidence has been the steadily growing feeling of the force of Great Britain and of her friendship and loyalty to France.[2]

The reluctance of France to declare war immediately after the German

---

[1] For Britain's military policy towards France after 1936 see Brian Bond, *British Military Policy between the Two World Wars* (Oxford, 1980), pp. 214ff; for British disparagement of France see Correlli Barnett, *The Collapse of British Power* (Gloucester, 1984), pp. 325–7, 329–30. See also John C. Cairns, 'A Nation of Shopkeepers in Search of a Suitable France, 1919–1940', *American Historical Review*, 79:3 (June 1974). For an excellent study of French foreign policy before 1939 see Anthony Adamthwaite, *France and the Coming of the Second World War*, 1936–1939 (London, 1977).
[2] Phipps, desp. 311, 13 Mar. 1939, FO 371/22909.

invasion of Poland on 1 September 1939 was not an auspicious beginning to the war-time relationship.[3] This was the first of a series of controversies between the two countries during the ten months of 'Phoney War'. However, on the civilian side of the relationship the Foreign Office did all it could to conciliate the French, a welcome change from Britain's pre-Munich attitude towards that country.[4]

In the economic field a reasonable degree of collaboration was achieved between the two countries in areas such as the procurement of raw materials and overseas purchases. In December 1939 an Anglo-French Co-ordinating Committee was set up chaired by the French financial expert, Jean Monnet, to oversee the ten Anglo-French executive committees which had been established to organise Anglo-French resources.[5] Early in January the Board of Trade concluded that 'by means of these arrangements a degree of coordination of the economic war efforts of the two countries, which in the last war was reached only at the end of the third year, has been attained'.[6]

There was, however, no overall Anglo-French ministerial body to oversee the civilian agencies, for which the Monnet had pressed, nor was a supreme economic council created.[7] The Supreme War Council, the first of whose occasional meetings was held at Abbeville on Tuesday 12 September 1939, was not intended to fulfil this task and was mostly concerned with military issues. Its revival, in conscious imitation of its first world war predecessor, had been agreed by the two governments in August and the Abbeville meeting was proposed by the prime minister, Neville Chamberlain, to his French counterpart, Edouard Daladier, as an opportunity to exchange views on the current situation and on future developments and to demonstrate to the public that the two governments were in active consultation.[8]

At the 12 September meeting both sides gave an optimistic account of the Entente's military position. Chamberlain had 'heard' that the German people were not enthusiastic about the war in the west. 'It had been, as it were, amusing to indulge in hostilities with Poland but the testing time would come when Germany had to fight France and the United Kingdom.' He then embarked on a theme which, while comforting to British listeners, was not welcomed by the economically hard pressed French: that time was on the side of the Entente and that, therefore, Britain was pre-

[3] Adamthwaite, France, p. 358.
[4] For the military side of the relationship see Eleanor M. Gates, End of the Affair: The Collapse of the Anglo-French Alliance, 1939–1940 (London, 1981); Martin S. Alexander, The Republic in Danger: General Maurice Gamelin and the Politics of French Defence, 1933–1940 (Cambridge, 1992).
[5] See W.K. Hancock and M.M. Gowing, British War Economy (London, 1949), pp. 184–90; J. Hurstfield, The Control of Raw Materials (London, 1953), pp. 246–7, 251; Gates, End of the Affair, p. 60.
[6] Board of Trade memorandum, 4 Jan. 1940, FO 371/24293.
[7] Hancock and Gowing, British War Economy, p. 186.
[8] Foreign Office (from prime minister) to Phipps, tel. 337, 11 Sept. 1939, FO 371/22926.

paring for a three-year war which would enable her to mobilise her full industrial, military and air strength. He added that Britain would not discuss any peace settlement with Germany except with a German government upon whose word reliance could be placed and which shared the ideals of the western democracies.[9]

In his speech the prime minister had addressed a number of sensitive issues which were to disturb Anglo-French relations down to the fall of France and whose constant repetition by British ministers was likely, in the eyes of the Foreign Office, to have detrimental effects on French morale. During the Phoney War the British Embassy in Paris and the Central Department monitored French public and political opinion carefully to detect any signs either of defeatism or loss of confidence in Britain's steadfastness and determination. Foreign Office nervousness about the stability of French morale reflected its assumptions about the volatile nature of the Gallic temperament, and the knowledge that a clique of French politicians, led by Pierre Laval, a former prime minister, Paul Etienne Flandin, a former foreign minister and Jean Mistler, president of the Foreign Affairs Committee in the Chamber, were, according to Phipps, conducting 'an insidious propaganda campaign on the lines that we dragged France into war ... They think this will make them popular if things go badly militarily wrong.'[10]

Nevertheless Phipps was convinced that this 'week-kneed' 'peace at the first opportunity' group 'were not dangerous', and that, 'the great majority of the people realise the real issue of the war and what an unbeaten or insufficiently beaten Germany must mean for the future of France and for themselves as individuals'.[11] The Foreign Office's fears were only partially allayed by Phipps's reassurances since, at the same time, the ambassador was reporting that the views of the French defeatists might, in the future, appeal to a wider audience in France if they were able to convince French public opinion that Britain was not pulling her weight within the alliance. From the outset of the war German radio broadcasts to France emphasised the limited contribution the British were making towards the Entente war effort. This propaganda was causing the French Information Service anxiety since it reflected, according to Phipps, 'the wide-spread feeling in France that the British Expeditionary Force is slow in arriving and in taking part in operations ... and that Britain will fight to the last French soldier'.[12]

---

[9] Minutes of the Supreme War Council, 1st meeting, Abbeville, SWC(39), 12 Sept. 1939, FO 371/24296.

[10] Phipps, tel. 786S, 12 Oct. 1939, FO 371/22910.

[11] Phipps, tel. 735S, 3 Oct. 1939, FO 371/22913; see also Phipps, tel. 648S, 10 Sept. 1939, FO 371/22913.

[12] Phipps tel. 651S, 11 Sept. 1939, FO 371/22913; Phipps to Halifax, desp. 1249, 14 Sept. 1939, FO 371/22920; for further information about alleged French dissatisfaction with Britain's war effort and her war aims see, 'Memorandum on the French attitude towards Great Britain and the British effort', by Somerset Maugham, communicated by Lord

As a result of Phipps's warnings, the Foreign Office asked the British Ministry of Information to undertake more publicity in France about the arrival of British forces there in order to demonstrate to the French people that Britain was determined to make the maximum contribution to the war. However the War Office and the other service departments had insisted that 'nothing must be published which will jeopardize or eliminate the element of surprise inherent in a swift and early entry of the British Army into the field'. This edict effectively prevented any information being given out to the French press about the British Army and the Royal Air Force in France and a War Office suggestion that 'good feeling' might be cemented by reminding the French 'of the now historical good relations and camaraderie existing between French and British troops', was not thought likely by the Foreign Office to have much effect.[13]

A Central Department official, Ivone Kirkpatrick, observed that:

It is no answer to say that the greater the secrecy the better. What we have to balance is the advantage of secrecy on the one hand and the imperative necessity from the point of view of public opinion in France, America and in a number of other countries of publicity for the war effort we are making.[14]

The foreign secretary, Lord Halifax, raised the issue at the War Cabinet on 16 September and convinced the service departments of 'the importance of giving maximum, if innocuous, "colour" information' to the French press about Britain's armed forces in France.[15] Thereafter the French press was provided with more copy: Phipps reported on 13 October that French newspaper correspondents had been allowed to visit British General Headquarters and the Advance Air Striking Force bases and to publish carefully censored accounts of what they had seen there.[16] However the ambassador was concerned that, when the French learned that Britain had sent only 158,000 troops to France, this might have a discouraging effect on them given that there were 3.5 million Frenchmen under arms. He hoped that the British would declare emphatically that the British contingent was an advance guard and that reinforcements were being despatched to France at high speed.[17]

British publicity dwelling on the positive aspects of the Anglo-French

---

Maugham to Halifax, 24 Oct. 1939, and 'Further Memorandum on the French attitude towards Great Britain', by Somerset Maugham, 5 Nov. 1939, communicated by Campbell, desp. 1531, 14 Nov. 1939, FO 371/22927.

[13] Foreign Office to Phipps, tel. 338, FO 371/22925; H.G. Cready, War Office to Foreign Office, 21 Sept. 1939, FO 371/22926.

[14] Kirkpatrick minute, 17 Sept. 1939, FO 371/22926.

[15] Halifax minute, 17 Sept. 1939, FO 371/22926.

[16] Foreign Office to Phipps (by telephone) tel. 348, 21 Sept. 1939, FO 371//22926.

[17] Phipps, tel 289S, 13 Oct, 1939, FO 371/22926; Leslie Hore-Belisha, the war secretary, in a radio broadcast on 21 Oct. attempted to reassure French opinion on this point by declaring that the Field Force was merely the vanguard of a much larger force, Strang to Ronald Campbell, 25 Oct. 1939, FO 371/25296.

relationship was regarded as crucial by the Foreign Office as a means of countering German propaganda and of boosting French morale. When the British press failed to report favourably on French affairs or, worse, ignored the French altogether in its reporting, the Foreign Office immediately took action to try to improve the situation.[18] For example, Sir Ronald Campbell, soon after he replaced Phipps as ambassador to France on 1 November 1939, warned the Foreign Office that French officials and journalists were complaining of the paucity of articles in the British press about France. He pointed out that even the few that did appear in British newspapers were likely to offend the French reader,

alleging, for instance, that the Englishman in France must be severe with begging children, and must be prepared to find the French mean and grasping. Many articles appear to be based on ignorant and outworn conceptions of the French character ... In meeting the German attempt to divide the two countries, it is of first importance that the interpretation of France in the English press should be as sympathetic and warm-hearted as that of Great Britain in the French press.

The Foreign Office duly appealed to the Ministry of Information to use its contacts in the British press to improve matters.[19]

When, in December 1939, the Ministry of Information reported 'a growing inclination' in France 'to lukewarmness about the prosecution of the war', and an increasing tendency to minimise Britain's contribution, a conference of officials from the Ministry of Information, the Service departments and the Foreign Office was convened to see what measures could be taken to improve publicity in France about Britain's war effort.[20] The Foreign Office also welcomed close collaboration between British and French trade unions in the hope that these would strengthen the position of the pro-war section of the French labour movement against right-wing, pacifist and communist elements.[21]

The Office was also closely involved in the issue of Anglo-French war and peace aims and in mounting pressure on both sides of the Channel as the war dragged on for a 'no separate peace' declaration as a means of convincing the French that Britain was determined to fight to the finish. Such a declaration was first mentioned in an article on 11 September in the semi-official *Le Petit Parisien*, which suggested that the best response

---

[18] For the attitude of British public opinion towards France see P.M.H. Bell, 'L'Évolution de l'opinion publique anglaise à propos de la guerre et de l'alliance avec la France (septembre 1939 –mai 1940)', in *Comité d'Histoire de la 2e Guerre Mondiale: François et Britanniques dans la drole de Guerre: Actes du Colloque franco-britannique tenu à Paris de 8 au 12 Decembre 1975* (Paris, 1979), pp. 51ff.

[19] Campbell tel. 850S 14 Nov. 1939, Barclay minute, 16 Nov. 1939, FO 371/22927.

[20] E.H. Carr, Ministry of Information, to Foreign Office, 27 Dec. 1939, FO 371/22915.

[21] Barclay minute, 18 Sept. 1939, on Phipps, desp. 1257, 16 Sept. 1939, FO 371/22913; on the formation of an Anglo-French Trade Union Council, see Sir Walter Citrine, general secretary of the Trade Union Council, to Halifax, 21 Dec. 1939; Halifax minute, 3 Jan. 1940, FO 371/22928.

to German efforts to divide the Entente was for both countries to agree not to sign a separate peace with Germany.[22] The permament under-secretary, Sir Alexander Cadogan, was 'doubtful of its value ... Aren't we and the French committed up to the hilt – fighting for our lives – and will any scrap of paper make any difference?' Halifax decided that 'the conclusion is to do nothing'.[23]

The Foreign Office was also anxious to pre-empt French demands that the two countries should formulate the measures they would need to take at the end of the war to prevent the revival of German aggression.[24] The British did not want this potentially divisive issue to be raised so early in the war, and while initially opposed to the 'no separate peace' declaration, later adopted it in the hope that it would reassure the French that 'after victory, the conflicts which had plagued Britain and France between the wars would not recur'.[25] Furthermore, Chamberlain's insistence that the war was being fought against Hitlerism and not the German people alarmed the French, since it suggested that Britain might be willing to make peace with a non-Hitler Germany, which was not far from the truth at that time.[26] Given these French suspicions the Foreign Office was hardly surprised when, in mid-October, Daladier asked Charles Corbin, the French ambassador to Britain, in mid-October to suggest an exchange of views on war aims with the British.[27] On 23 October the French govern-ment presented an *aide-mémoire* to Halifax on this subject.[28] While the British remained reluctant to enter into such discussions, Phipps warned London in telegrams and despatches written shortly before he retired, about the dangers of giving the French any reason to suppose that Ger-many would be treated leniently after her defeat: 'I must point out that if a premature and inconclusive peace were concluded it is highly doubtful whether France would again face further and inevitable attempts at German expansion.' Britain would then have to fight alone.[29] Phipps

---

[22] Phipps tel. 649S, 11 Sept. 1939, FO 371/22913.

[23] Cadogan minute, 18 Sept. 1939; Halifax minute, 16 Oct. 1939, FO 371/22926.

[24] For the wider political ramifications of the war aims issue in Britain see P. Ludlow, 'Le débat sur les buts de paix', in *Français et Britanniques dans la drôle de Guerre*, pp. 93ff.

[25] P.M.H. Bell, *A Certain Eventuality: Britain and the Fall of France* (London: Saxon House, 1974), p. 6.

[26] See reports from British consuls in France on French suspicions of Britain's war aims: Phipps, tel. 285 S 21 Sept. 1939; Phipps desp. 1447, 23 Oct. 1939, FO 371/229426. For the 'Venlo incident' see Christopher Andrew, *Secret Service: The Making of the British Intelligence Community* (London, 1985), pp. 434–9; Winston Churchill, the first lord of the Admiralty, opposed such secret Anglo-German contacts on the grounds of the devas-tating effect they would have on French opinion should they be publicly disclosed. See Peter Hoffmann, 'The Question of Western Allied Co-operation with the German anti-Nazi Conspiracy', *The Historical Journal*, 34:2 (1991).

[27] Cadogan minute, 18 Oct. 1939, FO 371/22946.

[28] Halifax to R.I. Campbell, Paris, desp. 2603, 23 Oct. 1939, FO 371/22946; see also Hoffmann, 'Western Allied Co-operation'.

[29] Phipps, tel. 810S, 23 Oct. 1939, FO 371/22913.

repeated that anxiety about Britain's post-war intentions was widespread among Frenchmen 'of every political colour and in all parts of France', and continued:

[T]he dangers involved in a divergence of view of this nature are obvious. Not only would a rift between our two countries, at a time when the closest cooperation is vital in the pursuit of our common task, be intolerable and it might lead to a lowering of French morale: the French soldier might well ask why he should fight when Great Britain, after Hitlerism has been destroyed, may wish to be kind once more to their defeated foe? The French ... are now engaged in a further struggle for their existence ... Is it unnatural that they should hope that now Great Britain has ceased to be an island in relation to Europe and that her frontier is on the Rhine, she should share that estimate of the essential German character which contact with the Germans over two centuries has made second nature to the Frenchman? ... I hope I have said enough to illustrate the argument that there are not two Germanies but one Germany and that that Germany, whether Imperial, Democratic or National Socialist, is at heart inspired by hatred of Great Britain and France. In this, the last political despatch I shall have the honour of writing after forty years of service, I have felt it my duty to lay the above considerations before your Lordship and to urge that they should constantly be borne in mind by His Majesty's Government.[30]

Roger Makins, a first secretary in the Central Department, agreed that

there is here a real divergence between us and the French, which has its roots in the essential difference between the Anglo-Saxon and the Latin mentality and outlook. It is useless to talk to the French about 'the fight against evil' ... They do not understand this sort of talk, which they are apt to consider hypocritical. The French are fighting as, fundamentally, we are also fighting, for their own security, and nothing else.

He suggested that Britain should reassure the French that after the war Britain would agree that effective material guarantees would be imposed on Germany. Meanwhile, the French must accept that the Entente's main war aim was the defeat of Germany and that only when Germany had been defeated could Britain consider the outlines of a territorial settlement. He added that

Since one of the Entente's declared war aims was that the liberties of the European peoples must be secured, they could hardly deny this to the German people. Allied guarantees must ensure that Germany can never again build up a preponderance of armed force and that in future a watertight system of international supervision of arms production must be established.[31]

William Strang, the superintending under-secretary of the Central Department, and Cadogan both addressed this subject in minutes on 31 October and 1 November respectively. Their arguments suggested that some of

[30] Phipps, desp. 1442, 23 Oct. 1939, FO 371/22946.
[31] Ibid., Makins minute, 28 Oct. 1939, FO 371/22946.

the French fears about Britain's post-war intentions were not entirely groundless. Strang remarked that

we are fighting to preserve our position in the world against the German challenge; to establish peace and freedom in Europe; and to safeguard Western civilisation ... We must ... try to convince the German people that war is not a paying proposition, and it is in their interest to re-enter the Western European system.[32]

Cadogan was disturbed that the French appeared to be united in wanting to crush Germany:

Anyone can sympathise with the French in the ordeals that they have been through. But to what conclusions do these French feelings lead? We must put aside the extermination of the German people, which is impossible. There remains, in the French view, 'the destruction of German unity.' ... I believe it to be a fallacy that such dismemberment can be imposed from without: it can only come from within. If imposed it becomes merely the root of further trouble. We are evidently going to have a great deal of difficulty with the French before we have finished. I agree that it is necessary above all things to put off that difficulty until it is necessary to face up to it – which I hope will not be until Germany has been broken up or has collapsed.[33]

However this issue could not be so easily disposed of. Campbell repeated Phipps's warning that to refuse a private discussion with the French might 'convince them that their worst fears are justified',[34] but he was equally concerned that, 'at the present moment, when France finds herself closely united to Britain in sympathy and destiny ... the principal danger to French morale ... seems to lie in a divergence on the question of war aims'. He urged the Foreign Office to persuade the British press to refrain from discussing war aims on lines which might alarm the French and thus weaken French morale.[35] Sir Robert Vansittart, the chief diplomatic adviser, who fully supported the French on this issue, agreed:

a hint might be dropped to *The Times* to refrain from opening its columns to every woolly amateur who constantly desires to rush into them ... There is certainly a grave danger of a split between us and the French if the latter think they have any ground for the idea that we would fall on the neck of a regenerated Germany. They are wise enough to see that we should be committing suicide if we do. It is abundantly clear that we are fighting not only Hitlerism; we are fighting Germany. We are fighting a country which has already cost the world a great deal more than it is worth, and not only our cooperation with France but our own security and existence make it imperative that we should have better security for the future this time than the last. I am sure that public canvassing and above all *definition*

[32] Ibid., Strang memorandum, 31 Oct. 1939, FO 371/22946.
[33] Ibid., Cadogan minute, 1 Nov. 1939, FO 371/22946.
[34] Campbell, desp. 1518, 9 Nov. 1939, FO 371/22946.
[35] Campbell, tel. 833S, 6 Nov. 1939, FO 371/22946.

of war aims while we are still at the beginning of a life and death struggle is terribly dangerous.[36]

Corbin returned to the subject again during a meeting with Halifax on 30 November. The French ambassador insisted that it would be impossible after the war 'to treat Germany as a trustworthy member of European society, except after a transitional period, during which special provisions might be in operation ... The French had no desire for conquest, but they wished the Germans to stay where they were.' Halifax replied that he hoped to find a balance between what he described as 'two lines of thought':

The one that might be called the negative line of treatment, by which I meant whatever measures might be thought wise, to make aggression by Germany difficult, and the other the positive line of thought, by which I meant all measures that we could take to convince the German people by wise treatment of economic problems and the like, that peace was to be preferred to war.[37]

Frank Roberts, an official in the Central Department, was convinced that, despite Corbin's disclaimer that French public opinion had any fixed ideas about how permanent European security could be achieved, 'the Rhine frontier, or some alternative which gives them equivalent security, must be the main French aim'.[38]

The Foreign Office had already produced a draft reply to the French *aide-mémoire* on war aims at the end of October. This repeated the by now familiar British view that, while there must be guarantees against future German aggression and also close Anglo-French cooperation after the defeat of Germany, the defeat of Germany must remain the Entente's only major war aim at present since territorial questions could only be determined in the light of the circumstances prevailing after this defeat. The British government now claimed that it accepted that Hitler's removal would not be a sufficient remedy against the reemergence of German militarism and expansionism. However, any statement that Germany would be dismembered on her defeat would unite all Germans behind Hitler. While the British government was prepared to discuss the subject with the French, Britain would prefer to wait on events before entering into any definite commitments about Germany's future.[39] The Foreign Office was anxious that this should be despatched to Paris at the earliest possible opportunity in order to quieten French fears about British

[36] Ibid., Vansittart minute, 7 Nov. 1939, FO 371/22946; following this, Cadogan tried to discourage *The Times* from discussing war aims in its columns. Cadogan minute, 15 Nov. 1939, FO 371/22946.
[37] Halifax to Campbell, desp. 2881, 30 Nov. 1939, FO 371/229467.
[38] Ibid., Roberts minute, 1 Dec. 1940, FO 371/22946.
[39] Foreign Office draft reply to French memorandum of 23 Oct. 1939, initialled by Cadogan and Halifax, 31 Oct. 1939 and 1 Nov. 1939, FO 371/22946; see also Hoffmann, 'Western Allied Co-operation'.

intentions,[40] but the War Cabinet wanted the Dominions' governments to be consulted about its contents first.

Although Halifax remained reluctant to pursue a 'no separate peace' declaration,[41] the prime minister was converted to the idea in mid-November. As a result, the War Cabinet placed it on the agenda of the fourth Supreme War Council meeting in Paris on Tuesday 19 December.[42] At that meeting, Chamberlain stated that, while it was unthinkable that either of the two countries should ever sign a separate peace with Germany, he now supported such a declaration for its psychological effect. Daladier thought that it might help to counter divisive German propaganda. The French prime minister said that a declaration would require careful study as it involved the vast question of allied war aims into which he had no wish to go at this stage. He pointed out that France opposed both what Chamberlain had referred to as 'Generous Utopias' and drastic and illusory solutions such as the dismemberment of Germany. However, France did not believe that Hitler's downfall would justify making peace with Germany since another 'Hitler' might soon emerge in his stead. Personally Daladier believed that 'no guarantee could replace a strategic and military but not territorial frontier running along the left bank of the Rhine'. Chamberlain agreed that the downfall of Hitler would not be a guarantee of lasting peace but he thought it an essential prerequisite. Britain too wanted lasting guarantees against Germany's resurgence and 'could he be convinced that the particular guarantee suggested by the latter would assure what they both desired, he would examine its implications with the greatest interest'. He was only too willing to accept Daladier's suggestion that detailed discussions of joint war aims should be left for a later stage and that only the 'no separate peace' declaration should be studied at present.[43]

The Foreign Office was also relieved by Daladier's remarks and hoped that the declaration would serve to divert French attention from war aims discussions. Hence the relatively innocuous and non-committal draft Foreign Office reply to the French memorandum was finally approved by

---

[40] Makins minute, 7 Nov. 1939, Strang minute 7 Nov. 1939 on Ronald Campbell, tel. 833 S, 6 Nov. 1939, FO 371/22946.

[41] Cadogan thought that 'It might be better to keep it [the no separate peace declaration] as a manifestation after some disaster. Or it might be better after some success.' Cadogan minute, 9 Dec. 1939, FO 371/22939.

[42] Major-General Sir Edward Spears, an MP and liaison officer to French general headquarters in the first world war, raised the issue with Halifax in mid-November, after returning from a visit to France: Sir Edward Spears, *Assignment to Catastrophe, Vol 1, Prelude to Dunkirk July 1939–May 1940* (London, 1954), p. 65; Gates, *End of the Affair*, p. 63; Lawford minute to Halifax, 16 Nov. 1939, Halifax minute, 18 Nov. 1939, FO 371/2298; Cadogan minute, 9 Dec. 1939; FO minute, Central Department brief for Supreme War Council meeting on 19 Dec. 1939, 16 Dec. 1939, FO 371/22928.

[43] Sir Edward Bridges to Cadogan, 21 Dec. 1939, enclosing draft minutes of the Supreme War Council meeting, FO 371/24297; minutes of the 4th meeting of the Supreme War Council, 19 Dec. 1939, FO 371/22928.

the War Cabinet on 20 December[44] and presented to the French government on the 22nd.[45] At the same time the Foreign Office reversed itself
on the subject of the discussion of war aims in the press. R.E. Barclay of
the Central Department explained to a somewhat perplexed Paris
Embassy official that it had become

undesirable to pursue an ostrich-like policy as regards French war aims, and the
sooner people over here realise the French standpoint in this problem, the less
danger there will be of sudden disillusionment in the future. It is no use trying
to conceal the fact that differences in outlook do exist, and if this is appreciated
before public opinion in this country takes on too definite shape, it might be easier
to reach some agreement on essentials.[46]

Little progress was made with the no separate peace declaration during
January and February, although the Foreign Office drafted a statement by
the end of January that the two governments 'mutually undertake that
during the present war they will neither negotiate nor conclude an armistice or a treaty of peace except by mutual agreement'.[47] The secretary
general of the French Foreign Office, Alexis Léger, told Campbell on 7
February that, as far as the French were concerned, there was no immediate hurry to conclude the declaration.[48] The refusal of the Dominions to
become signatories to such a declaration was responsible for much of the
delay: indeed their objections led Anthony Eden, the Dominions secretary,
to call for its abandonment.[49] However, towards the end of February, both
Léger and Georges Mandel, the French colonial minister, urged Campbell
that both countries should now sign the declaration. Mandel thought that,
if Daladier fell from power, the declaration would make it virtually impossible for a new government to repudiate such a binding instrument, while
Campbell believed that Mandel's real motive was to outmanoeuvre those
French politicians who were working to oust Daladier and seek an accommodation with Germany.[50]
Campbell suggested to the Foreign Office that the declaration be widened and reinforced to provide some contractual form to the continuation
of economic collaboration and for a military alliance for a specified period
after the war, both as a means of lowering German morale and encouraging the French. A pledge of post-war collaboration might also reduce
French pressure for the imposition of post-war material guarantees on
Germany. The Foreign Office legal adviser, Sir William Malkin, was

[44] War Cabinet conclusions, 120 (39), 20 Dec. 1939, FO 371/22948.
[45] See Gates, *End of the Affair*, p. 61.
[46] Barclay minute, 10 Jan. 1940, FO 371/34362.
[47] Kirkpatrick minute 31 Jan. 1940, FO 371/24297.
[48] Cadogan minute, 7 Feb. 1940, FO 371/24297. For a sympathetic portrait of Léger see
Elizabeth R. Cameron, 'Alexis Saint-Léger Léger', in Gordon A. Craig and Felix Gilbert,
eds., *The Diplomats 1919–1939* (New York, 2 vols., 1965), II, pp. 378–405.
[49] Cadogan to Campbell, 21 Feb. 1940, FO 371/24297; Gates, *End of the Affair*, p. 64.
[50] Campbell to Cadogan, 23 Feb. 1940, FO 371/4024287; Gates, *End of the Affair*, p. 64.

enthusiastic, especially as it might overcome the problem of Dominions abstention since they were not parties to existing Anglo-French economic and financial agreements. 'Moreover it could be argued that whatever the Dominions do or do not do the fortunes of England and France are inextricably linked.' He suggested the addition of a clause that 'the two Governments declare their intention to continue the fullest cooperation in their financial, economic and defence policy after the conclusion of peace'.[51] Halifax approved this,[52] and the draft declaration was circulated to the Board of Trade and the Treasury for their comments before it was presented to, and approved by, the War Cabinet on 21 March.[53] On the same day Paul Reynaud replaced Daladier as president of the French Council of Ministers – much to the distress of the Foreign Office, who neither trusted Reynaud nor thought he would long survive in office[54] – but it was Reynaud who signed the declaration on 28 March.[55]

Financial and trade issues also caused considerable dissension between the two countries.[56] When war was declared the British government imposed restrictions on imports of luxury goods into Britain and some were banned altogether. These restrictions were intended to conserve foreign exchange for a long war and to reduce unnecessary consumption at home. France immediately protested that they would have a deleterious effect on French producers of silk goods, textiles, wines and liqueurs. Indeed the French demanded that there should be greater liberalisation of trade between the two allies.[57] The Treasury argued that Britain could ill afford the outflow of francs the lifting of such restrictions would entail, especially as the British had to provide scarce francs for the upkeep of the British Expeditionary Force (BEF) in France. Furthermore if Britain gave concessions to the French on luxury goods, other countries, like Canada, who were similarly affected, would demand similar treatment.[58]

The French countered that while Britain regarded such imports as luxuries, they were produced in France by Frenchwomen or by men who were not eligible for service with the colours and who would otherwise be

---

[51] Campbell to Cadogan, 29 Feb. 1940, Malkin minute, 28 Feb. 1940, FO 371/24297.

[52] Ibid., Halifax minute, 1 Mar. 1940, FO 371/24297.

[53] Halifax to Campbell, desp. 658, 21 Mar. 1940, FO 371/24298.

[54] Campbell, desp. 356, 27 Mar. 1940; Campbell, tel. 232S, 22 Mar. 1940, FO 371/24308; Roberts minute, 1 Apr. 1940, FO 371/24308; Makins minute, 1 Apr. 1940, FO 371/24308; Gates, *End of the Affair*, pp. 41–2. See Bell, *A Certain Eventuality*, pp. 8–9 for further details about the Foreign Office view of Reynaud.

[55] Supreme War Council conclusions, 6th meeting, Tuesday 28 Mar., 10 Downing Street; Campbell, telephone, to FO, 29 Mar. 1940, FO 371/24299. For the full text of the declaration see Gates, *End of the Affair*, p. 65.

[56] See also Robert Frankenstein, 'Le financement français de la guerre et les accords avec les Britanniques, (1939–1940)', pp. 461 ff. and L.S. Pressnell, 'Les finances de guerre Britanniques et la coopération Franco-Britannique, 1939 et 1940', *Français et Britanniques dans la drole de Guerre*, pp. 489ff.

[57] Phipps tel. 639 S, 7 Sept. 1939, FO 22929.

[58] Stacy, Board of Trade to Kirkpatrick, 19 Oct. 1939, FO 371/22929.

unemployed. These people would not understand why Britain was trying to destroy their livelihood.[59] On 30 October, Corbin told Cadogan that the matter was likely to have 'political implications'.[60] John Watson, a third secretary in the Central Department, minuted that 'all this is very characteristic of France, and contrasts poorly with Canada, whom we are treating more severely'. R. E. Barclay, a second secretary in the Central Department, while admitting that 'most of the articles' the French wanted to import 'are luxury products which we can well do without', had some sympathy with the French case.[61] The Board of Trade were also sympathetic, suggesting that 'we go a little further to remove the sense of grievance which they seem to be suffering'.[62] However, the Treasury was not prepared to make any concessions unless these were linked to French agreement to help Britain meet the outflow of francs to the BEF.[63] The French threatened to retaliate by imposing duties on British imports into France or by refusing licences for such imports: indeed by November British firms trading with France were complaining that the French authorities had stopped issuing import licences.[64]

The Foreign Office became increasingly concerned when Hervé Alphand, the director of the Trade Agreement Division of the French Ministry of Commerce, warned Campbell on 7 November that the issue was having a harmful influence on French opinion, and that German propaganda was beginning to exploit it.[65] On the same day an official of the French Economic Mission to the United Kingdom told A.J. Shackle of the Board of Trade that 'No French soldier would be able to understand that the United Kingdom Government were not prepared to lend a helping hand to French industry . . . This was inviting the break up of the French economy and would begin to sap the basis of the Alliance.'[66]

Despite Kirkpatrick's insistence that 'we must be firm with the Treasury, who are determined to lose the war',[67] and statistics drawn up by Shackle which showed that 'our restrictions were bearing more hardly on France than her's on us',[68] the chancellor of the exchequer, Sir John Simon, was not prepared to make any concessions unless France agreed to provide Britain with a loan to 'help us with the very large sums we shall require for our troops in France'.[69] Paul Reynaud, the French minister of

---

[59] Stacy, Board of Trade to Kirkpatrick, 13 Oct. 1939, FO 371/22929.
[60] Cadogan minute, 30 Oct. 1939, FO 371/22929.
[61] Watson minute, 24 Oct.; Barclay minutes, 28 and 31 Oct. 1939, FO 371/22929.
[62] R.J. Shackle, Board of Trade, to T.K. Bewley, Treasury, 31 Oct. 1939, FO 371/22929.
[63] Barclay minute 31 Oct. 1939, FO 371/22929.
[64] Strang to Cadogan, 31 Oct. 1939; Stacy to Barclay, 23 Nov. 1939, FO 371/22929.
[65] Campbell, desp. 1510E, 7 Nov. 1939, FO 371/22929.
[66] Board of Trade minute, 7 Nov. 1939, FO 371/22929.
[67] Kirkpatrick minute, 9 Nov. 1939, FO 371/22929.
[68] Shackle, Board of Trade to A.S. Hoskin, Export Licensing Department, 8 Nov. 1939, FO 371/22929.
[69] Simon to Reynaud, 23 Nov. 1939, FO 371/22929.

finance, visited London on 11 November in an attempt to reach a settlement of these issues in direct talks with Simon. Barclay pointed out that 'the problem is causing an increasing stir, in this country, as well as in France. Something ought to be done without further delay.'[70] On 27 November the Treasury finally agreed to relax some of restrictions on imports of French foodstuffs, textiles and clothing. Kirkpatrick thought that 'these concessions represent a very great effort on our part and have been made to no other Power', but the French were still not entirely satisfied.[71]

No agreement could be reached on the financial questions which were dealt with during a further round of talks between Reynaud and Simon and their respective officials in Paris in December. The French then agreed to place 2 million francs into the Anglo-French exchange equalisation account to cover the sums spent by the British army in France and to make available £85 million of France's sterling balance for purchases in the British Empire. An Anglo-French financial agreement was signed on 12 December 1939,[72] which included an article whereby both countries promised not to impose restrictions on trade between them to protect home industries or for foreign exchange reasons.[73]

At the end of January 1940 the French minister of commerce, Fernand Gentin, visited London for trade talks. At the Board of Trade on the 22nd he surprised British officials by calling for the complete liberalisation of Anglo-French trade and a common export policy and by complaining that the import concessions Britain had made on 27 November had not gone far enough since considerable French trade remained shut out of the British market.[74] As a result of this pressure, Anglo-French economic experts in London reached an agreement on 10 February 1940 on the removal of import restrictions on a wide range of goods traded between France and Britain.[75] This agreement was signed by French and British commercial representatives in London on 16 February 1940.

Related to the controversy over British restrictions on French trade with Britain were French complaints about the prohibitions the British government had imposed after the outbreak of war on British nationals wishing

---

[70] Barclay minute, 12 Nov. 1939, FO 371/22929; see also FO memorandum, 'Notes for M. Reynaud's Visit', 9 Nov. 1939, FO 371/22928.

[71] Kirkpatrick minute, 25 Nov. 1939, FO 371/22929.

[72] For details see, 'Record of Discussion between Sir John Simon and M. Paul Reynaud at the Ministry of Finance, Paris, 11.00 a.m. Monday 4 Dec. 1939'; Neville Chamberlain to Edouard Daladier, 7 Dec. 1939; Halifax to Lord Lothian, Washington, tel. 893, 12 Dec. 1939, FO 371/22930; Hurstfield, *Raw Materials*, p. 250; Hancock and Gowing, *British War Economy*, p. 190.

[73] Hurstfield, *Raw Materials*, p. 248.

[74] 'Précis of Statement made by M. Gentin at the Board of Trade', 22 Jan. 1939, Makins minute, 23 Jan. 1940, FO 371/24293.

[75] R.J.W. Stacy, Board of Trade to Foreign Office, 12 Feb. 1940, Makins minute, 14 Feb. 1940, FO 371/24294.

to visit France. The French were anxious to encourage British tourism in the Riviera and in French winter sports centres outside the war zone. The economic well-being of these areas before the war had depended on the tourist industry but with the advent of war tourism had collapsed. This had led to considerable hardship and British consuls in these areas reported that the local people were blaming Britain for dragging France into a war which had resulted in their impoverishment.[76] The Foreign Office wanted to encourage British tourists to go to the South of France in the hope that the money they spent there would combat anti-war sentiments there, but the Treasury was unwilling to provide British visitors with francs for this purpose. Makins warned the Treasury on 11 January that this was 'a matter of life or death to the French tourist industry'.[77]

Foreign Office pressure eventually persuaded the Treasury to relent[78] but the Home Office Aliens Department and the Foreign Office Passport Control Department objected to the resulting liberalisation on travel restrictions on British nationals which had been imposed at the beginning of the war to assist the work of the British Security Services. The Passport Control Department protested that the removal of such restrictions

would ... be criminal ... I think we all realise that the French Government are all out to attract British people to go to France *because they want our money*, but on the other hand, nobody seems to have pointed out ... that it is because His Majesty's Government want to keep British money in this country as far as possible that a limitation exists upon joy rides to France.[79]

Makins responded that, while he appreciated the importance of security,

from every other point of view, intercourse between this country and France is in quite a different category from that with other countries, in view of our special relationship ... From the point of view of Anglo-French relations it is really urgent that restrictions be, if not removed, but [sic] simplified and reduced to the lowest possible minimum consistent with security.[80]

On 27 February, after several meetings, an inter-departmental overseas travel committee drafted a 'Franco-British Agreement on Travel between the Two Countries' designed to protect the security interests of both countries. The details were then worked out by Anglo-French officials but, when the final agreement was ready for signature on 22 May, John Ward of the Central Department commented that given 'recent "events"

[76] Hopkinson, Anglo-French Liaison Section, War Cabinet Offices to Kirkpatrick, 30 Dec. 1939; Hugh Dodds, consul general, Nice to British Embassy, Paris, desp. 82, 22 Dec. 1939, FO 371/24307.
[77] Makins to J.I. Cook, Treasury, 11 Jan. 1940, FO 371/24307.
[78] Treasury to Foreign Office, 19 Jan. 1940, FO 371/24307.
[79] R.T. Parkins minute, 17 Jan. 1940, FO 371/24296.
[80] Makins minute, 24 Jan. 1940, FO 371/24296.

private travel on any scale is likely to be at a discount for some considerable time'.[81]

By the end of 1939 the Foreign Office was moving towards much closer
ties between Britain and France as a means of convincing the French that
Britain intended to fight to the finish. On 1 December, R.W.A. Leeper,
the head of the Foreign Office Political Intelligence Department, sent a
long memorandum to Strang on 'Peace Aims' which concluded that closer
union was the only means of sustaining French determination to continue
in the fight. He was convinced that the influence of 'Utopianism' on British foreign policy since 1918 had blighted Anglo-French relations and
enabled Germany to exploit the differences between the two countries.
As a result,

we were so anxious to make friends with Germany that we underestimated the
importance of remaining friends with France, forgetting the simple fact that our
own interests were so closely interlocked with those of France that if we were to
be friends of Germany it had to be an Anglo-French friendship with Germany on
terms which were as acceptable to France as to ourselves. In other words the
maintenance of Anglo-French cooperation was the only foundation for peace in
Europe.

He continued, that while the rise of Nazi Germany and the ensuing war
'shattered the hopes of a Utopian Europe ... almost as soon as the struggle was engaged, the Utopians in our midst reared their heads and began
piping all the old outworn phrases which contained all the dangerous
illusions of the past and brought nothing that was really new or constructive for the future.' Utopians were already talking of a new Europe

in which the 'good German people', as apart from Hitler, will be equal partners,
in which there will be disarmament and free exchange of goods and in which the
lion will lie down with the lamb of a federated Europe. This makes no appeal to
the sceptical French mind ... The French ... are determined to enforce such
guarantees as will compel them ['good Germans'] to be 'good'.

Both countries wanted 'a peaceful Europe made secure against
aggression', and this could only be achieved through Anglo-French cooperation after the war:

Already at the beginning of the war this cooperation is making rapid strides and
it is fairly clear that by the end of the war we shall be acting as a solid unit. That
unit may well be the only stable element in Europe, the only element in fact to
which America will lend money for the reconstruction of Europe.[82]

On 28 February, Orme Sargent, the superintending under-secretary of the

[81] Minutes of eight meetings of the Overseas Travel Committee, Feb.–Apr. 1940; J.G. Ward
to F.A. Newsam, Home Office, 22 May 1940, FO 371/24307.
[82] R.W.A. Leeper memorandum, 'War Aims', 30 Nov. 1939; Leeper to Strang, 1 Dec. 1939,
FO 371/22947.

General Department, who became a leading exponent of such a union, minuted that,

there can be no doubt as to the great importance of the British public being brought to realise that a permanent system of close co-operation with France is the contribution we must be ready to make in the interests of a stable peace after the war . . . as will for all international purposes make of the two countries a single unit in post-war Europe.

This would, he thought, constitute an effective counterweight to the eighty million Germans in central Europe. If the French public were convinced that Britain genuinely wanted post-war unity of action it ought to be possible to persuade them 'that the cooperation which we are prepared to offer them would constitute a far surer and more lasting guarantee than any occupation of German territory, which is what they will certainly press for – much to our embarrassment'. He admitted that

the idea of the Federation of Europe can make its appeal to [British] public sentiment so long as it appears only as a vague Eldorado about the details of which we need not bother our heads at present. But the application of this idea of confederation to the concrete case of Great Britain and France is quite another matter and it will need a considerable amount of education before the British public will get accustomed to the notion of their having made this unpalatable and unprecedented sacrifice on the altar of European peace.[83]

This pressure for closer Anglo-French relations continued when, after visiting Paris early in March, Arnold Toynbee, of the Foreign Press and Research Service at the Royal Institute of International Affairs, and Sir Alfred Zimmern of Chatham House, warned the Foreign Office that while French morale was at present excellent, their conversations with prominent Frenchmen convinced them that this might not last indefinitely and that Britain should take some initiative to bind the two countries closer together in the face of the likely tribulations ahead. For instance, I.-F. Aubert, the chargé de mission au cabinet de Daladier, had informed them that 'there is a definite limit to the time for which the French morale can stand a general mobilisation unaccompanied by military activity'. The withdrawal of active men from civil life, he said, had produced 'a state of high psychological tension' which could not be maintained indefinitely. 'The men had little to think about except their neglected fields and the wives were writing to them begging them to come back and do sowing.' Nor did the French share Britain's confidence that time was on the side of the Allies. A former minister of education, Senator Honnorat, subsequently suggested to them that the immediate conclusion of a treaty of perpetual association between Britain and France might help to calm some of these worries. He proposed a brief and simple document which would

[83] Sargent minute, to Cadogan, 28 Feb. 1940, FO 371/24298.

provide for a combined defence and foreign policy and the pooling of the economic resources of the two Empires, together with a degree of common citizenship and the encouragement of the elites in the two countries to become bilingual. Such an association would stimulate the morale of the French by convincing them that Britain was prepared to make common cause with them for the duration of the war and thereafter. Toynbee, on his return from France, suggested to Cadogan that such an association might solve the problem of the divergence of Britain and France over peace aims which 'has been one of the causes of such friction as there has been in Anglo-French relations since the beginning of the war'.[84]

As a result of this report, the Foreign Office parliamentary undersecretary, R.A. Butler, wrote to Halifax about the need to do something immediately to interest the French in the future after the war. He had asked Toynbee and Zimmern 'to develop their thoughts during their leisure hours at Chatham House'. Butler wanted the Entente to build up a Europe 'within the fortress of civilisation, that is, this side of the Maginot Line'.[85] Halifax had read Sargent's 28 February minute and supported efforts to promote a closer Anglo-French union, telling the prime minister that 'I don't think Sir O. Sargent exaggerates its importance.'[86]

Leeper, who was supervising Butler's Chatham House study, agreed that something should be done 'to stir the imagination of two peoples who do not easily understand or appreciate each other'. He recommended that the study of the English and French languages should be made compulsory in every British and French school and that closer cultural contacts between the two countries should be encouraged. 'If we are looking to the future we have to get together the young people in both countries.'[87]

On the question of closer intra-government cooperation, Halifax persuaded the former Cabinet secretary, Lord Hankey, now minister without portfolio in Chamberlain's War Cabinet, to chair a committee of experts from the Foreign Office, the Treasury and the Board of Trade to examine the administrative and procedural aspects of the subject.[88] The terms of reference of Hankey's committee were,

to examine the question of post-war Anglo-French collaboration with the following

[84] Arnold Toynbee to Gladwyn Jebb, private secretary to Cadogan, 13 Mar. 1940, enclosing a note on 'Some French views on Franco-British Relations and the Time Factor in the War', FO 371/27288.

[85] Butler to Halifax, 13 Mar. 1940, FO 371/24288.

[86] Halifax to Chamberlain, 29 Feb. 1940, FO 371/24298. Chamberlain replied that 'I entirely agree with this [Strang's] memorandum and shall be glad if [the] M/Information can do something to draw attention to the subject.' Prime minister to Halifax, 1 Mar. 1940, FO 371/24298.

[87] Leeper minute, 9 Apr. 1940, FO 371/24298.

[88] Hankey to Halifax, 9 Apr. 1940, FO 371/24299.

terms of reference: To examine the purely administrative implications of post-war Anglo-French collaboration; to select the fields where, after the war, the experiment of Anglo-French union can best be made; to enumerate the difficulties and limitations of an administrative nature that would stand in the way; and to devise means of circumventing them.[89]

At the same time various government departments were also approached by the Foreign Office to see what measures they could take to secure closer relations between the French and British peoples. As a result of this appeal, the president of the Board of Education, Earl de la Warr, informed the Foreign Office that, while the Board could not insist on the compulsory teaching of French in British schools, he would ask school inspectors to impress upon the teachers the need to give greater emphasis to France in future when teaching history and geography. The Board would concentrate on encouraging out of school activities such as the showing of French plays and films and, 'amongst other things they might learn something about French food, and I believe there are a number of unemployed French chefs in London whom we might get to go round the schools and cook French meals'.

Roberts minuted that 'these schemes only touch the fringe of the problem. The goal must be the compulsory teaching of each others' language. This cannot be done by out of class activities.' However Makins felt that 'we must not force the pace if this is going to "catch on" '.[90] Ward suggested the rewriting of school history textbooks in both countries so that future generations would become imbued with 'the real community of ideals and interests which united the two countries' and would learn how the only basis for the future was lasting friendship and close connection between them. 'We can now see that the fatal inability of each country to understand the other's point of view in the years after the war led to the political estrangement that is directly responsible for the failure to cope in time with the menace of a renascent Germany.'[91]

When the Supreme War Council on 28 March agreed that its meetings should be held regularly and that a permanent secretariat should be created, Strang was delighted, since this would 'lay the foundation for the intimate association between the two Governments which it is hoped will be one of the abiding results of the war'. Sargent agreed that 'it is of great psychological importance from the point of view of accustoming the British

---

[89] 'Inter-Departmental Committee on Post-War Anglo-French Collaboration: Composition and Terms of Reference', note by the secretary, H.L. d'A. Hopkinson, 20 Apr. 1940, FO 371/24200.

[90] Earl de la Warr to Halifax, 15 Mar. 1940, Roberts minute, 29 Mar. 1940, Makins minute, 30 Mar. 1940, FO 371/24298.

[91] Ward memorandum, 'Anglo-French Educational Co-operation', 9 Apr. 1940, FO 371/24299.

and French nations to the idea of permanent collaboration not merely during and for the purpose of the war, but after the war for purposes of ensuring a common policy and a common action in peace time'.[92]

Butler's Chatham House study group produced a 'Draft Act of Perpetual Association between the United Kingdom and France', drafted by Zimmern in consultation with Leeper and Toynbee.[93] Leeper told Sargent that 'we felt that a short and striking document summing up a scheme for Anglo-French co-operation might be the best answer to Hitler's claim that he is establishing a new order in Central and Eastern Europe. Our new order, if it embraces the British and French Empires, would have far wider scope and would provide a real peace aim for the youth of England and France.' Butler wrote that 'this has my warm support', while Cadogan told Halifax that it 'contains much that is useful and suggestive and even, I think, practical'. Halifax thought it 'interesting – and a valuable start in the business of translating general aspirations into more concrete form'.[94]

The memorandum began by explaining that the word 'Act' had been chosen in preference to 'Pact' 'Treaty' 'Convention' or 'Covenant',

all of which call up associations which it is desirable to avoid. 'Act' is a solemn term of domestic politics and its French counterpart is equally suitable. 'Association' is half way between 'Cooperation' and 'Union'. It implies an organic connection which stops short of complete fusion ... What is proposed is in form a treaty, to be adopted by the two parliaments. But in fact it provides a framework for a process of integration which has already begun in the sphere of war-time cooperation between the two governments and has reached a point where it is ripe for embodiment in permanent institutions. These in their turn will require to be underpinned by a solid foundation in the public mind of the two peoples ... 'Perpetual' provides the assurance that there will be time for the process of growth ...

Under Article 1 of the Zimmern draft, 'the Two Powers pledge themselves to pursue a common Policy in all their External Relations, and to maintain a Common Organ for that purpose'. Zimmern presumed that 'the Common Organ' would be the Supreme (War) Council. Articles 2 to 5 followed a similar phraseology in calling for close military, defence, economic and financial relations between the two powers and for an agreement not to treat each other's nationals as aliens. Finally under Article 6, 'the two Powers pledge themselves to develop Mutual Comprehension between their Peoples by all the means at their disposal, and to maintain a Common Organ for that Purpose'. Zimmern commented that

---

[92] Supreme War Council Conclusions, SWC (940), 28 Mar. 1940; 'Meetings of the Supreme War Council and the Formation of a Permanent Secretariat', memorandum by the secretary of state; War Cabinet conclusions, 29 Mar. and 6 Apr. 1940; Strang minute 28 Mar. 1940; Sargent minute, 29 Mar. 1940, FO 371/24298.

[93] Note by H.L. d'A. Hopkinson, 26 Apr. 1940, FO 371/24299.

[94] Leeper to Sargent, 26 Mar. 1940, Cadogan to Halifax, 27 Mar. 1940, Halifax minute, 28 Mar. 1940, Butler minute 29 Mar. 1940 FO 371//24299.

the deeper understanding aimed at is the only sure foundation for the proposed political, economic and social superstructure, which will be a house built upon the sands unless and until its foundations are carried down to the bedrock of community feeling. This implies systematic action in the field of education and culture.

The first essential would be to make each nation as far as possible bilingual, with French and English compulsory subjects in each other's schools. 'Equally essential is the sympathetic presentation to young people of the moral and practical principles common to both countries in their unity-in-diversity, as opposed to the traditional treatment of "French and English" as rivals and opposites.'[95]

The Foreign Office placed Zimmern's memorandum on the agenda of the first meeting of the Hankey Committee on 30 April. This was attended by Sargent and T.K. Bewley from the Treasury. The Board of Trade representative, Sir Arnold Overton, was absent. The Zimmern memorandum was not universally welcomed:

Some discussion took place as to whether it was really necessary to have a comprehensive document of this nature, which was somewhat academic. It was suggested that in the first instance it might be better to consider the actual spheres in which collaboration might be elaborated.

It was, however, finally agreed that Zimmern's document 'formed a convenient basis for discussion'.

Hankey liked the term ' "Association", which seemed to represent accurately the goal at which we were aiming'. Sargent said that a continuous Anglo-French association to set up a bloc of 85 million people in western Europe to withstand German pressure would be an alternative to the French demand for the left bank of the Rhine which, if granted, would result in a German desire for revenge and a further war. Hankey 'realised that the association would not necessarily be based on feelings of sympathy between the two peoples, but upon their common fear of Germany'.

In examining the individual articles the Committee made considerable modifications to Zimmern's proposals. On Article 1 the Committee decided that, since both countries possessed sovereign parliaments, it would be impossible for them to pursue a common foreign policy but agreed that the closest cooperation between the two countries could be achieved through the Supreme Council, which 'would not only deal with foreign policy but would be the court of appeal on all Anglo-French military, economic, financial and other questions under the ultimate control of the respective Parliaments'. The Committee agreed to close cooperation in military planning, in intelligence and in supply but on the question of a common currency the Treasury doubted that either country would

---

[95] 'Memorandum by Sir A. Zimmern on a Proposed Act of Perpetual Union between the United Kingdom and France' (undated but late Apr. 1940) FO 371/24298.

be prepared indefinitely to support the value of the franc or the pound respectively.[96] After this somewhat inauspicious beginning, the Committee fixed its next meeting for 21 May, in which a paper by Sir Arnold Overton, on an Anglo-French customs union, was to be considered.[97]

Overton rejected most of Zimmern's recommendations for closer cooperation between Britain and France in trade and raw material allocation. He was particularly critical of the proposed Customs Union which 'would be beset with many and serious political, practical and administrative difficulties'. Its success would require 'a fusion' of financial and political relations between the two countries while the abolition of customs duties would damage the domestic economies of both – with France suffering the worse. 'These [obstacles] may not be insuperable, but they would call for a very full and careful study.'[98]

At the meeting of his committee on 21 May, Hankey described this as a 'negative' and yet 'very convincing' paper. Overton repeated his doubts that France would be prepared to sacrifice her economic sovereignty in a Customs Union, while Bewley of the Treasury added that 'a common currency had never been possible historically without a common government'.

The Committee then stated that its planning was based on the assumption that the post-war situation would be one of armed truce in which the Entente would have to organise and utilise its resources for the next war. Despite this unpromising outlook, Hankey opposed any Anglo-French arrangement which would reduce British sovereignty. In his view the Committee should seek to create machinery for Anglo-French coordination at least as close as or possibly closer than that which Britain enjoyed with the Dominions. He concluded that the most Britain could commit herself to after the war was the development of the closest possible economic and financial cooperation and leave it to whatever organ was set up to interpret these in practice. Sargent drew the Committee's attention to a paper by Lionel Curtis of the Royal Institute of International Affairs on 'The Stabilisation of Peace on the Basis of a Permanent Franco-British Alliance'. Curtis had little patience with federalist solutions to the German and European problem or of an international government with wide ranging powers which were currently being ventilated in the press. He wanted a more restricted and practical alternative for public consumption so that the British public would not be led astray by idealistic concepts. The

[96] 'Inter-Departmental Committee: Post-War Anglo-French Collaboration: Minutes of the 1st Meeting held in Lord Hankey's Room, Treasury, on Tuesday 30 Apr. 1940 at 3.00 p.m.' FO 371/24299.

[97] Ibid.

[98] Memorandum by Sir Arnold Overton, Board of Trade, 'Implications of the Proposed "Act of Association" between the United Kingdom and France, with particular reference to a Customs Union', 9 May 1940, FO 371//24300.

theme of his paper was that firm and solid Anglo-French cooperation required joint executive and legislative bodies which must be limited to dealing with security and foreign affairs only: social and economic questions must remain the province of the national governments. For his part, Sargent considered that the military alliance was the only effective basis for mutual cooperation.

The Committee concluded by agreeing that the proposal not to treat the French as aliens in the United Kingdom would be discussed with the Foreign Office legal adviser while Sargent suggested that at its next meeting the Committee might also discuss closer Anglo-French cooperation in areas like transport and communications, cable and wireless, shipping, cartels and civil aviation.[99] The next meeting was set for 28 May but, as Sargent reported on 22 June, recent events had made the whole project 'academic' and the Committee was now 'in suspense'.[100] Nor was Hankey's committee consulted when Churchill offered France a close Anglo-French union on 16 June.[101] There is some evidence that before the débâcle in Belgium in mid-May, Halifax was becoming alarmed that even the limited proposals that had been put forward by Curtis and the Committee might be going too far. He minuted on Curtis's paper 'that I have read and re-read his paper with great interest ... It is a pretty far-reaching idea but I find it difficult to believe it's practical politics. But I may be too timid.'[102]

The fall of France has been the subject of numerous studies.[103] With her collapse, the British reverted to the neo-isolationism which had characterised their policy towards France before 1939, only now their attitude towards the French was one of downright contempt and hostility. Hankey, for instance, stated that all his experience since 1919 had taught him that 'the French have been our evil genius'.[104] After 1940 Britain would seek both her salvation and ultimate victory in cooperation with her

---

[99] 'Inter-Departmental Committee: Post-War Anglo-French Collaboration, 2nd meeting, minutes', Tuesday 21 May 1940; memorandum by Curtis, 'The Stabilisation of Peace on the basis of a Permanent Franco-British Alliance', 22 Apr. 1940 and circulated to Hankey's Committee on 21 May 1940; see also Christopher Warner minute, 25 Apr. 1940, FO 371/24300.

[100] Sargent to Lord Perth, Ministry of Information, 22 June 1940, FO 371/24298. Stephen Roskill in his *Hankey: Man of Secrets, Vol. III 1931–1963* (London, 1974) states erroneously that 'the committee held its only meeting' on 30 Apr. p. 460. In July Hankey was informed officially by Halifax that his committee was dissolved. David Reynolds, '1940: Fulcrum of the Twentieth Century?' *International Affairs*, 66:1 (Jan. 1990), 325–50.

[101] Hankey protested, in vain, to Halifax when he found out about the proposed union. Roskill, *Hankey*, p. 478.

[102] Halifax minute, 9 May 1940, Halifax to Curtis, 13 May 1940, FO 371/24300. The Labour Party was also dubious about such an association, see Bell, 'L'Évolution', p. 7.

[103] For a relatively recent account see Gates, *End of the Affair*, and bibliography.

[104] Roskill, *Hankey*, p. 478. For further comments by Hankey see Gates, *End of the Affair*, p. 381.

Empire and in a 'special association' with the United States, for which the Foreign Office began planning in July.[105]

The 'honeymoon', if it can be thus described, between Britain and France had been of short duration. Nevertheless, despite the legacy of suspicion which had clouded Anglo-French relations since the first world war, the two countries had made a serious attempt in 1939 and 1940 to bury many of their differences and to collaborate in the face of a powerful enemy. While Britain's ten divisions (by May 1940) on the Western Front were totally inadequate as a means either of assisting the French militarily or of moulding the alliance into a genuine collaboration of military equals, economically and politically the short-lived association between the two countries had been relatively successful.

Much of this success was due to the efforts of the Foreign Office and of the foreign secretary, with, on occasions, the support of Neville Chamberlain, in the face of much scepticism and foot-dragging on the part of other departments, and particularly by the Treasury. One of the Foreign Office's main weapons in its efforts to forge closer Anglo-French relations was publicity, in both the United Kingdom and in France, to encourage the politicians and peoples of both countries to see each other in a new and more favourable light, although in this respect it is doubtful if its efforts met with much success. As the British consul general in Marseilles, Sir Norman King, put it: 'All other propaganda, explaining what nice and interesting people the English are is a waste of time. The French are not interested in Great Britain or the British Empire except as allies to help them beat the Germans.'[106] Nevertheless the need to maintain a climate of optimism as far as the French were concerned prompted many officials to dismiss negative reports about the malign influence of defeatist French politicians[107] and to ensure that, at least, 'outward appearances were well maintained'.[108] It also entailed trying to prevent potentially unfavourable publicity in Britain which might undermine the Entente. For instance Halifax interceded with the vice-chancellor of Oxford University in January 1940 to prevent the Oxford Union from holding a debate on the desirability or otherwise of Anglo-French cooperation.[109] The Foreign Office also attempted to justify Daladier's persecution of French communists after 2 September, a flagrant violation of civil liberties by a supposedly democratic government. Indeed some Central Department officials wanted the British government

---

[105] See Reynolds, '1940: Fulcrum of the Twentieth Century'.
[106] Bell, 'L'Évolution', p. 7. Campbell, desp. 1476, enclosing memorandum by King, 31 Oct 1939, FO 371/22914.
[107] For one example see Bell, 'L'Évolution', 9–10
[108] Ibid. 9.
[109] Halifax wrote that he could 'imagine the delight of Dr Goebbels at being provided' with criticisms of France during such a debate by 'young Englishmen'. Halifax to vice chancellor, Oxford University, 4 Jan. 1940, FO 371/24296.

to act against 'left-wing organisations' in Britain who were campaigning against Daladier's decrees. Frank Roberts managed to prevent these illiberal notions from being put into effect.[110]

The idea of a closer association with France, which was first articulated extensively by Sargent in his memorandum of 28 February, was taken up by the Foreign Office for a variety of motives: to distract the French from discussions about war aims, in the hope of sustaining French morale in a long war in which questions were being asked in France about the likelihood of ultimate success in such a sanguinary struggle and because many officials, and Sargent in particular, supported such an association.[111] Here they found themselves pitted against the Treasury and Board of Trade officials on Hankey's committee who were sceptical about the practicality of the financial and trade recommendations. Hankey shared their doubts: devoted to the British Empire and a fervent navalist, he was unlikely to share the vision of an Anglo-French union in which both submerged their sovereignties to the possible detriment of close relations between the Dominions and Britain. It was Sargent who provided Hankey's committee with such momentum as it generated.

Indeed the sceptics might ultimately have been correct in their assumptions about the likely frailty of any closer Anglo-French association. Reynaud put his finger on one of the impediments during his talks with Simon in November 1939, when he recited a list of figures intended to demonstrate how much poorer the French Empire was in raw materials, population and wealth than the British Empire, in effect demanding that Britain would need to pull more than her weight if the alliance was to survive.[112] The Foreign Office was bombarded with French complaints that Britain was not producing sufficient munitions, that she was failing to provide France with promised supplies of raw materials and fuel and that British workers were not working long enough hours. Many French manufacturers suspected that Britain was taking advantage of the concentration of French resources on armaments production to consolidate its world trade and expand its exports.[113] Whether these and similar French grievances would have mounted in volume in the years ahead cannot be answered: much would have depended on Britain's ability to despatch to the Western Front its promised thirty-two divisions at the end of the

---

[110] Millard minute, 25 Apr. 1940, Roberts minute, 1 May 1940, FO 371/24299. See Gates, *End of the Affair*, pp. 30–2

[111] On one occasion Sargent emphasised the crucial importance of 'getting the ordinary citizen in both countries, as contrasted with the officials, interested in the idea of post-war collaboration between Great Britain and France ...' Sargent minute, 8 May 1940, FO 371/24299.

[112] 'Note of Meeting between M. Paul Reynaud and Sir John Simon at the Treasury', 20 Nov. 1939, FO 371/23298.

[113] Campbell, tel. 955S, 23 Dec. 1939, FO 371/22930; Col. D.W. Graham, military attaché, Paris to Campbell, desp. no. 18, 6 Jan. 1940, FO 371/24293.

second year of the war,[114] the *sine qua non* of continued French confidence in the alliance, and to expand its military industrial production significantly. Britain did expand both the size of her army and air forces and her military production after 1941, and there is no reason why she should not have done the same if France had survived. What would have been the ultimate outcome if France had managed to defeat the German offensive in May 1940 is, of course, an unanwerable question.

[114] Gates, *End of the Affair*, p. 27.

CHAPTER 9

Churchill the appeaser?
Between Hitler, Roosevelt and
Stalin in World War Two

On Bonfire Night, 5 November 1944, a German V-1 'flying bomb' landed in Sussex. Nothing surprising in that: southern England had been under fire since June. But this V-1 carried propaganda not explosives. Its four-page leaflet explaining why Britain should sue for peace ended with a V-1 shaped crossword. The clues and answers included the following:

He is your enemy, too. *Bolshevik.*
He wants all you have got. *Roosevelt.*
Britain has none at inter-Allied conferences. *Voice.*
At Tehran, Churchill practically did this before Stalin. *Knelt.*[1]

The claim that Churchill had sold out Britain to America and Russia was a staple of Nazi wartime propaganda. As the Yalta conference was beginning in February 1945, Hitler denounced Churchill for living in the past:

The crucial new factor is the existence of these two giants, the United States and Russia. Pitt's England ensured the balance of world power by preventing the hegemony of Europe – by preventing Napoleon, that is, from attaining his goal. . . . If fate had granted to an ageing and enfeebled Britain a new Pitt instead of this Jew-ridden, half-American drunkard, the new Pitt would at once have recognised that Britain's traditional policy of balance of power would now have to be applied on a different scale, and this time on a world scale. Instead of maintaining, creating and adding fuel to European rivalries Britain ought to do her utmost to encourage and bring about a unification of Europe.

In these final outpourings, Hitler argued that he had given Churchill

---

The author is grateful to Professor Peter Clarke and Dr Michael Dockrill for their comments on a draft version.
[1] Public Record Office, Kew, PRO CAB 66/57, WP (44) 642; cf. *Sunday Dispatch*, 13 Jan. 1945, p. 4.

plenty of opportunity for 'grasping the truth of this great policy' and allowing Germany a free hand on the Continent. Britain 'could have pulled her chestnuts out of the fire' after the defeat of Poland or the fall of France. 'At the beginning of 1941,' Hitler claimed, 'after her success in North Africa had re-established her prestige, she had an even more favourable opportunity of withdrawing from the game and concluding a negotiated peace with us.' But instead she preferred 'to obey the orders of her Jewish and American allies, people, indeed, who were more voracious than even the worst of her enemies'.[2]

Accusations similar in substance, if not tone, were also voiced at times in wartime London, especially in 1944–5. It was, for instance, a widespread feeling in the Foreign Office in December 1944 that Churchill was erroneously pursuing a 'policy of appeasement' towards Moscow and Washington. This was a time of acute transatlantic friction and even the normally pro-American weekly *The Economist* demanded publicly: 'let an end be put to the policy of appeasement which, at Mr Churchill's personal bidding, has been followed, with all the humiliations and abasements it has brought in its train, ever since Pearl Harbor removed the need for it'. On the political right, there were many who viewed Churchill's policy towards Stalin in the same light by 1945. The Yalta agreement on Poland prompted four government ministers to abstain in the Commons. Two resigned their posts. Ironically, some of the sternest critics of Poland's treatment were men such as Lord Dunglass (later Lord Home) who had been Chamberlain loyalists in 1938. And Churchill himself sounded distinctly like Chamberlain when he told the Commons that he returned from Yalta with the impression that Stalin wished 'to live in honourable friendship and equality with the Western democracies' and added: 'I know of no Goverment which stands to its obligations, even in its own despite, more solidly than the Russian Soviet Government.' It seemed that the wheel had come full circle. To quote MP and diarist Harold Nicolson, 'the warmongers of the Munich period have now become the appeasers, while the appeasers have become the warmongers'.[3]

After the archives were opened, some historians and commentators developed these wartime criticisms. At the end of his book *The Collapse of British Power* (1972), Correlli Barnett argued that in 1940 'Churchill and his government quite deliberately, if in their view inevitably, chose to sacrifice England's existence as an independent power, a power living and

---

[2] François Genoud, ed., *The Testament of Adolf Hitler*, trans. R.H. Stevens (London, 1961), pp. 30–5.

[3] Basil Liddell Hart Papers, LH 11/1944/65 (Liddell Hart Centre for Military Archives, King's College, London) (henceforth KCL); *Economist*, 30 Dec. 1944, p. 858; Commons, *Debates*, 408: 1284, 27 Feb. 1945; Churchill to Roosevelt, 10 Mar. 1945, in Warren F. Kimball, ed., *Churchill and Roosevelt: Their Complete Correspondence*, 3 vols. (Princeton, 1985), III, p. 552 (henceforth C–R); Harold Nicolson, *Diaries and Letters, 1939–1945*, ed. Nigel Nicolson (London, 1967), p. 437.

waging war on her resources, for the sake of "victory".' The options of peace with Hitler or a limited war to hold the Axis at bay were dismissed, Barnett argued, in favour of a quixotic policy of 'victory at all costs' which ran down Britain's wealth and made her dependent on the United States. Thus 'Lend-Lease gradually consummated the policy that Churchill had begun of transforming England into an American satellite warrior-state.'[4]

In 1993, biographer John Charmley fused the wartime grumblings of left and right to suggest that Churchill overestimated both the altruism of America and the fidelity of Russia, thereby sacrificing what was left of British power and independence. He implies that Chamberlain's own, derided version of appeasement – aimed at Germany – in fact 'offered the only way of preserving what was left of British power; if 1945 represented "victory", it was, as Chamberlain had foreseen, for the Soviets and the Americans'. Turning Charmley's insinuations into verities, former Tory government minister Alan Clark claimed in *The Times* that, but for Churchill, peace could have been obtained on 'reasonable' terms in 1940 and on 'excellent' terms in 1941. This piece was perhaps a midwinter *jeu d'esprit*, by an ex-politician whose generous sense of mischief was matched by a certain stinginess with the *actualité*. But it (and a bad week for serious news) helped make Charmley's book a *cause célèbre*. The extent to which such assertions have solidified as certitudes is suggested by a *Guardian* columnist who wrote in 1994 that Churchill 'sold every stick of family silver to his American cousins along with his beloved empire, class and party. All went bust in 1945. Oh yes, and the Russians ended up with half Europe, as Churchill spotted too late.' Despite the flippant tone, these are presented as matters of fact.[5]

But *are* they true? Even in the more scholarly books, where not delivered tongue in cheek, they are offered more as lament than argument. At root, they seem to rest on an implicit syllogism. In 1945 Britain was weaker than in 1940. Churchill was leader from 1940 to 1945. Ergo, Churchill was the guilty man. The alternatives are not seriously examined: indeed they cannot be from the limited vantage point of biography. Like most swings of the historiographical pendulum, Churchillian revisionism is a reaction to the heroic orthodoxy that prevailed for so long. It is, up to a point, much needed because that orthodoxy, pioneered in Churchill's own war memoirs, has often been fawningly claustrophobic. It requires little time in the archives and diaries of the war to discover that Churchill's self-portrait was not a snapshot of real life. But to replace a hero with an anti-hero, or at least a more recognisably flawed figure, is of limited utility. The approach is still biographical: one man fills the picture, the

[4] Correlli Barnett, *The Collapse of British Power* (London, 1972), pp. 588, 592.
[5] John Charmley, *Churchill: The End of Glory. A Political Biography* (London, 1993), pp. 2, 559–61; *The Times*, 2 Jan. 1993, p. 12; *The Guardian*, 24 Mar. 1994, sec. 2, p. 11. See also John Charmley, 'The Price of Victory', *Times Literary Supplement*, 13 May 1994, p. 8.

background is obscured. It is certainly ironic that Churchill, of all people, presided over a decline in British power. But irony is not causality; *post hoc* does not mean *propter hoc*.

The issues involved here are large and intricate, far beyond the compass of a short essay. But, as a contribution to an important debate, I offer some reflections on three central questions. Was there any hope of a viable modus vivendi with Hitler in 1940–1? What did Britain *gain* from its alliance with the Soviet Union and the United States? And what exactly was Britain's strategy during the dark middle of the war from the fall of France to the dawning of D-Day? Only with these issues in mind can Churchill's wartime diplomacy be justly evaluated.

First, then, what should be made of claims, or insinuations, that Britain could have reached a modus vivendi with Hitler in 1940–1 – either through a negotiated peace or a war of limited liability that would have kept the Nazis at bay across the Channel? To respond, we must examine German intentions and capabilities, a move rarely made by proponents of these arguments.

Some scholars of Nazi foreign policy, such as Gerhard Weinberg, have insisted that Britain was a prime target of Hitler's malevolence and that the Führer showed no readiness to take account of British interests. Certainly Hitler sometimes spoke in this way – 'I want to beat England whatever it costs,' he told Goebbels in December 1939. But most authorities take the view that Hitler's oft-stated animosity towards Bolshevik Russia should be considered the lode-star of his policies and that, at least in the medium term, he sought an accommodation (*Ausgleich*) with Britain that would have given him a 'free hand' on the Continent. Germany's failure to do this in the decade before 1914 was Hitler's fundamental criticism of the Kaiser's foreign policy, set out at length in his so-called Second Book of 1928. There is little doubt that Hitler tried to avoid this error after he came to power or that, by 1939, he had actually repeated it. The result was a war in the west that he had neither expected nor wanted at this stage. His famous remark to the Swiss diplomat, Carl Burckhardt, in August 1939 can probably be taken at face value: 'Everything I undertake is directed against Russia; if the West is too stupid and blind to grasp this, I shall be forced to reach an understanding with the Russians to defeat the West and then, after its downfall, turn with all my concerted forces against the Soviet Union.'[6]

After the defeat of Poland and the fall of France Hitler made speeches

---

[6] Gerhard L. Weinberg, 'Hitler and England, 1933–1945: Pretense and Reality', *German Studies Review*, 8 (1985), 299–309; *Hitler's Secret Book*, trans. Salvator Attanasio (New York, 1961), chapter 14; Andreas Hillgruber, *Hitlers Strategie: Politik und Kriegführung, 1940–1941* (Frankfurt a.M., 1965), p. 29. For a recent survey of the literature see Marie-Luise Recker, *Die Aussenpolitik des Dritten Reiches* (Munich, 1990).

in the Reichstag offering peace to Britain, on 6 October 1939 and 19 July 1940. Both were aimed at least partly at domestic opinion, but the British Foreign Office judged that 'these offers were seriously meant' and that 'Hitler was disappointed at the decisive manner in which they were rejected.' Certainly there is little doubt that Hitler was surprised and perplexed at British intransigence in mid-1940. He had assumed that victory in the west would end the war with Britain as well as France, leaving Germany free to turn east with impunity. When these hopes proved wrong, the *Wehrmacht* hastily improvised attempts to force Britain to make peace, by bombing or invasion, but, to quote historian Williamson Murray, 'the task facing the Germans in the summer of 1940 was beyond their capabilities'. The Army High Command was preoccupied with Eastern Europe and the Mediterranean; the *Luftwaffe* lacked both doctrine and aircraft for strategic bombing; and the Navy warned that lack of air supremacy meant that any landing must be regarded as a 'last resort'. As the summer wore on, the general hope in Berlin was that bombing would force the British to their senses, perhaps via a change of government. In the words of the German official military historians, 'the preparations for landing were predominantly an instrument of psychological warfare; at times Hitler did not rule out the operation ... but soon he again lost interest in an enterprise for which the indispensable prerequisites seemed unattainable'.[7]

As is well known, some British Government ministers in mid-1940 wanted at least to find out what Hitler's terms would be, notably Lord Halifax, the foreign secretary, and his parliamentary under-secretary R.A. Butler. The most intense debate occurred at the end of May, before the 'miracle' of Dunkirk was assured, but Halifax and Butler remained of this view throughout the summer. As we shall see, Churchill's vision of the future war was more complex than mythology suggests, but on the immediate issue that summer he was stereotypically pugnacious. The Cabinet debate centred on the chance of securing terms that would preserve Britain's 'independence' – Halifax's key word. In his view, that ruled out, for instance, 'surrender of the Fleet or Air Force, which would leave this country entirely at his [Hitler's] mercy', but not territorial concessions in the British Empire. Malta, Gibraltar and some African colonies were mentioned. Churchill defined independence more rigorously, insisting, to quote the Cabinet minutes, that it was 'impossible to imagine that Herr Hitler would be so foolish as to let us continue our rearmament'. This he regarded as essential. He was willing to concede 'the restoration of German colonies and the overlordship of Central Europe' but would

---

[7] PRO PREM 4/100/8: FO memo on peace feelers, 1 July 1942, para. 2; Williamson Murray, *Luftwaffe: Strategy for Defeat, 1933–1945* (London, 1988), p. 81; Hans Umbreit in K. A. Maier, H. Rohde, B. Stegemann and H. Umbreit, *Germany and the Second World War, II* (Oxford, 1991), p. 369.

'never accept' that 'peace and security might be achieved under a German domination of Europe' as a whole. Churchill did not rule out an eventual peace treaty, but argued that 'we should get no worse terms if we went on fighting' and that 'the position would be entirely different when Germany had made an unsuccessful attempt to invade this country'.[8]

Such remarks shift the debate on to early 1941 which, in retrospect, both Adolf Hitler and Alan Clark regarded as the critical moment. By then the Battle of Britain had been won and the Italian assault on Egypt decisively repulsed. By this time, too, Hitler's plans for invading Russia were well advanced. Hence the continuing fascination with the dramatic arrival in Britain of Hitler's deputy Rudolf Hess on 11 May 1941 and his proposals for a compromise peace. Thanks to the sustained disingenuousness of the British government, the full story of the 'Hess Mission' remains to be told. But whether it was sanctioned by Hitler or, as is more probable, a lone mission by a deranged man, is not material here.[9] Two points *are* germane to our argument. On the one hand, what Hess proposed was broadly what his leader had long desired. On the other hand, in May 1941, as a year before, a viable compromise peace was, *for Britain*, still unobtainable.

One reason, quite obviously, was the difficulty of taking Hitler at his word. Here the takeover of Bohemia and Moravia in 10 March 1939 had been a watershed. Previously it had been possible to believe Hitler's protestations that he was only redressing the inequities of Versailles and bringing all Germans within the Reich. But Munich was a bilateral agreement with the British prime minister; Prague was its brutal revocation and a clear step beyond *Grossdeutsch* limits. British perceptions of Hitler changed fundamentally. When the government officially rejected his peace offer of October 1939, a central argument was that 'assurances given by the German Government in the past have on so many occasions proved worthless that something more than words will be required today to establish confidence which must be the essential basis of peace'. And henceforth, although Chamberlain and Halifax equivocated at times, most British policy-makers felt that 'something more than words' entailed at the very least a new German government. As Sir Alexander Cadogan, permanent under-secretary at the Foreign Office, put it in October 1939, the

---

[8] Halifax, draft message to FDR, c. 25 May 1940, Hickleton Papers, A4.410.4.1 (Churchill College Archives, Cambridge); Churchill quoted from PRO CAB 65/13, ff. 141, 180, 184. See generally, e.g. Christopher Hill, *Cabinet Decisions on Foreign Policy: The British Experience, October 1938–June 1941* (Cambridge, 1991), chapter 6; Thomas Munch-Petersen, ' "Common Sense not Bravado": The Butler-Prytz Interview of 17 June 1940', *Scandia*, 52: 1 (1986), 73–114. On Churchill's first ten months in office see also Sheila Lawlor, *Churchill and the Politics of War, 1940–1941* (Cambridge, 1994).

[9] Bernd Martin, *Friedensinitiativen und Machtpolitik im Zweiten Weltkrieg, 1939–1942* (Düsseldorf, 1974), pp. 425–47; John Costello, *Ten Days to Destiny* (New York, 1991), chapters 1, 16–17; Ulrich Schlie, *Kein Friede mit Deutschland: Die geheimen Gespräche im Zweiten Weltkrieg, 1939–1941* (Munich, 1994), pp. 290–324.

line should be 'that *we won't make peace with Hitler*. Get rid of Hitler: that is my *war* aim – not peace aim. Do that first: then you will win the war.'[10]

Aside from the basic question of trust, it is also clear now that Hitler's desire for accommodation with Britain was a tactical expedient. His larger aims remain the subject of controversy. Did he want world domination (*Weltherrschaft*) or 'merely' world power status (*Weltmachtstellung*)? Did he have a coherent *Programm* or phased *Stufenplan*? These debates, which still revolve around the 1960s work of Günter Moltmann, Andreas Hillgruber and Klaus Hildebrand, are beyond our compass here, but three points may be made. First, most of Hitler's statements on these matters were at the level of what Ian Kershaw calls 'vague and visionary orientations for action'. When Hitler talked of a global conflict with America, for instance, this was usually identified as a task for his successors. But, secondly, at moments of triumph in 1940–1 they assumed greater priority. After France fell and again on the eve of *Barbarossa*, Hitler sanctioned major naval building programmes aimed at control of the Atlantic. The fact that these plans were subsequently reversed does not undermine the basic point: when Hitler *thought* he had a free hand on the Continent, he started flexing his muscles on the world stage. On 14 July 1941, for instance, he urged the Japanese ambassador that, with Russia apparently routed, their two countries should combine to 'destroy' America as well as Britain. At other times, admittedly, he spoke of Britain as (junior) partner in the struggle with America, and that may have remained his hope. But, thirdly, there is no doubt that his larger aspirations included colonial territories for Germany as well as an Atlantic imperium. And it is hard to see how Britain could have remained indifferent (let alone independent) as these developed. In May 1940 General Franz Halder, chief of the army general staff, noted in his diary: 'We are seeking contact with Britain on the basis of partitioning the world.'[11] Given Hitler's larger aims, that partition was likely to be as temporary as the Nazi–Soviet pact.

In considering the prospects for an Anglo-German modus vivendi in 1940–1, it is also worth noting the voices around Hitler clamouring for a *more* anti-British policy. Another feature of recent historiography has been the attack on a classic totalitarian image of Nazi Germany, in which all policy supposedly emanated from one man. Instead, scholars have talked of a Nazi 'polycracy' with bureaucratic rivalries inadequately restrained by

[10] Lothar Kettenacker, ed., *Das 'Andere Deutschland' im Zweiten Weltkrieg* (Stuttgart, 1977), p. 144; David Dilks, ed., *The Diaries of Sir Alexander Cadogan, OM, 1938–1945* (London, 1971), p. 221.
[11] Ian Kershaw, *The Nazi Dictatorship: Problems and Perspectives of Interpretation* (3rd edn, London, 1993), p. 129; Klaus Hildebrand, *The Foreign Policy of the Third Reich, 1933–1945* (London, 1973), pp. 96, 100, 109, 112–13; Meir Michaelis, 'World Power Status or World Dominion?', *Historical Journal*, 15 (1972), 331–60; Milan Hauner, 'Did Hitler Want a World Dominion?', *Journal of Contemporary History*, 13 (1978), 15–32.

the Führer and of a 'plurality of conceptions' in foreign policy. One such historian, Wolfgang Michalka, notes that the 'wooing of Great Britain, which for Hitler was of central importance for future German policy, was viewed by conservative politicians with much more sceptical and dubious eyes'. Within the German Foreign Office and among economic policy-makers, notably Hjalmar Schacht before the war, colonial and commercial expansion were priorities, while Admiral Raeder and the Navy entertained Tirpitzian aspirations for Germany as a naval world power. For both groups, Britain was a major and immediate threat. Their ideas were given coherence and weight by Joachim von Ribbentrop, Nazi foreign minister from 1938, who envisaged a tripartite Axis alliance aimed at Britain. To this end he masterminded the pact with Russia in 1939. Now it remains true that the crucial foreign policy decisions of the Third Reich were Hitler's: the totalitarian thesis is not completely without foundation. But the *Konzeption-Pluralismus* underlying German foreign policy is relevant when we recall the hopeful British scenario of negotiating with a non-Hitler German government. Some of those around the Führer regarded Britain as a more immediate enemy than did their leader.[12]

The Raeder–Ribbentrop anti-British policy is particularly relevant to our thinking about 1940–1. When the Wehrmacht started improvising military plans to make Britain seek peace in June 1940, General Alfred Jodl, chief of its operations staff, outlined two possible strategies. One was the direct approach of bombing and eventual landing, the other was an indirect strategy to seal off the Mediterranean, including capture of Gibraltar and the Suez Canal. Underlying both was the idea of long-term pressure through blockade of Britain's imports. This policy was warmly supported by the Navy who also hoped to enhance its reach by acquiring bases on Spanish and Portuguese islands in the Atlantic. Hitler toyed with this strategy in the autumn of 1940, courting Franco and Pétain, before confirming plans to attack Russia in 1941. But he justified that decision (which reflected his own deepest desires) by insisting that Britain was placing its remaining hopes in Russia and so a successful war in the east would end the war in the west as well. It seems reasonable to suppose, therefore, that, had Hitler vanquished Russia in 1941, he would have resumed the endgame against Britain. And the indirect strategy of demolishing Britain's empire and strangling her supply routes offered an attractive alternative to the hazards of direct assault by air and land.[13]

To sense what might have happened, we need only look at the evolution

---

[12] Wolfgang Michalka, 'Conflicts within the German Leadership on the Objectives and Tactics of German Foreign Policy, 1933–9', in Wolfgang J. Mommsen and Lothar Kettenacker, eds., *The Fascist Challenge and the Policy of Appeasement* (London, 1983), p. 52; Hildebrand, *Foreign Policy of the Third Reich*, pp. 58–9, 96–9.

[13] Maier, *Germany and the Second World War*, II, pp. 367, 404–15, 419; G. Schreiber, B. Stegemann and D. Vogel, *Das Deutsche Reich und der Zweite Weltkrieg*, III (Stuttgart, 1984), pp. 178–222.

of the Battle of the Atlantic in 1941–2. This, it should be noted, was waged by a German navy that had not begun preparing for war with Britain until 1938, which lacked its own reconnaissance aircraft, and whose resources were split between surface raiders (Hitler's obsession) and submarines (the preference of Raeder and Dönitz, the U-boat commander). Despite these weaknesses, in 1942 Nazi depredations neared the 700,000 tons a month target that Dönitz claimed would offset new construction by the Allies and force Britain to sue for peace. In November 1942, U-boats alone destroyed 729,000 tons of shipping – their best month of the war. The 1942 crisis coincided with (and was partly caused by) the German addition of a fourth wheel to their Enigma coding machines, rendering them unbreakable by the Allies between February and December. Only the codebreakers' success in regaining the initiative (and the introduction of High Frequency Direction Finders on Allied vessels from the summer) prevented the crisis from becoming a catastrophe. As it was, victory over the U-boat was not secured until the summer of 1943. Historian John Keegan suggests that if each U-boat had sunk only one more merchant ship in the summer of 1942, when losses already exceeded launchings by 10 per cent, 'the course, perhaps even the outcome, of the Second World War would have been entirely otherwise'.[14]

Even so, the consequences for Britain were grave. Imports in the first year of war were 44.2 million tons, compared with 50–60 million in the last years of peace. By calendar year 1942 they had dropped to 22.9 million tons. (The figure for 1917, with a smaller population to support, had been 29.8 million.) Churchill never forgot the import crisis. He claimed in his memoirs that he had been basically optimistic about invasion and the air threat and that the 'only thing that ever really frightened me during the war was the U-boat peril'. His writings at the time bear out this claim. His long letter to Roosevelt on 8 December 1940 is usually cited as the stimulus for Lend-Lease. In fact, finance took up only about one-tenth of this 4,000-word letter. 'I wish to focus on shipping', Churchill insisted to advisers, and he devoted over half the letter, plus a long appendix, to the problem. He told the president that it was 'in shipping and in the power to transport across the oceans, particularly the Atlantic Ocean, that in 1941 the crunch of the whole war will be found'. In a similar strategic *tour d'horizon* dated 31 October 1942, Churchill told Roosevelt: 'First of all, I put the U-boat menace', insisting 'I cannot cut the food consumption here beyond its present level.' At the Casablanca conference the following January, the combined chiefs of staff stated: 'The defeat of the U-boat must remain a first charge on the resources of the United Nations.' They

[14] S.W. Roskill, *The War at Sea, 1939–1945*, II (London, 1956), pp. 94, 218, 485–6; H. Boog, W. Rahn, R. Stumpf and B. Wagner, *Das Deutsche Reich und der Zweite Weltkrieg*, VI (Stuttgart, 1990), III/2–3, esp. p. 301; John Keegan, *The Second World War* (London, 1989), p. 123.

placed this ahead of all other desiderata: aiding Russia, invading Sicily, bombing Germany and liberating France.[15]

Of course, Britain's exact import requirements are hard to establish. What constituted an essential minimum was keenly debated in Whitehall and, in fact, belt-tightening went much further than the prophets of doom believed possible. Moreover, some of the imports were required for offensive action, or to free British industry for war production, and this might not have been needed on such a scale if the fortress-Britain or limited-war scenarios had been adopted. It is also true that some of the losses of 1942 were due to the bloody minded slowness of (anglophobe) US Admiral Ernest R. King in adopting a (British) convoy policy for merchantmen in American waters.[16] None of these qualifications, however, invalidates the basic point: Britain was an island geographically but not economically. Its 'independence' could be threatened indirectly as well as directly. Even if the British could have resisted direct assault, by air or land, they were acutely vulnerable to blockade, particularly after 1940 when Germany acquired bases along the north and west coasts of France. In estimating the chances of the British reaching a viable peace or at least an armed modus vivendi with Hitler, one must take account of the Battle of the Atlantic as well as the Battle of Britain.

There are, then, cogent reasons for believing that Britain's 'independence' could not have been preserved, except in the very short term, while Hitler dominated continental Europe. Even if direct invasion had been repulsed or deterred, even if the Luftwaffe had been neutralised by successful defence and the threat of massive retaliation on Germany, there still remained the danger of death by strangulation. It is against this background that we must ponder Churchill's aphorism that 'there is only one thing worse than fighting with allies, and that is fighting without them!'[17]

The year 1940 had ended in stalemate. The British had been evicted from the Continent and the Germans held at bay above and around the British Isles. But the British military faced the spring of 1941 with new anxiety. During his visit to London in April 1941, General 'Hap' Arnold, head of the US Army Air Corps, found many British policy-makers admitting that the Germans could establish a beachhead on the south coast any time they were willing to make the sacrifice. He noted: 'Dill, Beaverbrook, Freeman and Sinclair all believe it can be done and will be tried.' Sir John Dill, chief of the imperial general staff, went so far as to send Churchill

---

[15] C.B.A. Behrens, *Merchant Shipping and the Demands of War* (2nd edn, London, 1978), pp. 37–8, 190, 201; Winston S. Churchill, *The Second World War*, 6 vols. (London, 1948–54), II, p. 529; David Reynolds, *Lord Lothian and Anglo-American Relations, 1939–1940* (Philadelphia, 1983), pp. 46–7; Kimball, ed., *C–R*, II, pp. 103, 648, 650; Michael Howard, *Grand Strategy*, IV (London, 1970), p. 621.

[16] For a more sympathetic view of Admiral King see Eliot A. Cohen and John Gooch, *Military Misfortunes: The Anatomy of Failure in War* (New York, 1991), chapter 4.

[17] E.g. Alanbrooke diaries, 5/10, 1 Apr. 1945 (KCL).

a formal memo on 6 May, warning against further diversion of troops to the Middle East. He argued that Germany could concentrate resources fairly quickly for an invasion and claimed that 'we have gone to the limit, if not beyond it, in respect of the security of Great Britain'. It was not until early June that British intelligence concluded that an attack on the Soviet Union was imminent, but, even then, most British policy-makers reckoned that Germany would win in three to six weeks. On 22 June *Barbarossa* began with devastating effect. On 1 July Churchill told Roosevelt: 'I am asking that everything here shall be at concert pitch for invasion from September 1st'.[18]

We know now that the Russians survived and eventually reversed the German onslaught, in a struggle that ended four years later amid the ruins of Berlin. But in 1941 Churchill and his colleagues would have needed a crystal ball (and one of particularly roseate hue) to foresee such an outcome. The stubborn Russian resistance in July 1941 enabled relaxation of anti-invasion plans on 2 August, when the British armed forces were told they would have one month's notice of any renewed threat. The Red Army's counter-attack in midwinter 1941–2 was heartening, but the new German offensive of June 1942 revived the previous year's anxieties, particularly in the Joint Planning Staff, who on 17 July were talking of 'the possibility of Russian defeat'. Much of the debate about Anglo-American strategy in mid-1942 revolved around this issue. By September the mood was more optimistic and in 1943, after the Russian victory at Stalingrad, the Joint Intelligence Committee advised that 'the prospect of a German defeat of Russia has receded to vanishing point'.[19]

On the other hand, the danger of another Nazi–Soviet pact seemed greater. At the end of January 1943, for example, the British ambassador in Moscow, Sir Archibald Clark Kerr, thought 'Stalin may make a separate peace if we do not help him.' We now know that the Soviet–German peace feelers via Stockholm were at their most active in the first half of 1943 and it seems likely that, at this stage, they reflected genuine interest on Stalin's part. After all, Russia was safe from defeat, but the Red Army was 1,000 miles from Berlin and Anglo-American commitment to invading France was still uncertain. The details of these contacts remain unclear but they exercised British and US intelligence during the summer, at a time when Stalin was venting his fury at the May 1943 decision to defer a cross-Channel attack until the following year.[20]

[18] Gen. H.H. Arnold, diary of visit to England, 21, 24 Apr. 1941, Arnold papers, box 271, Library of Congress, Washington DC; PRO WO 216/5: Dill to Churchill, 6 May 1941; F.H. Hinsley et al., *British Intelligence in the Second World War* (4 vols., London, 1979–88), I, pp. 470–83; Churchill to Roosevelt, 1 July 1941, in Kimball, ed., *C-R*, I, p. 216.
[19] Hinsley et al., *British Intelligence*, II, pp. 78–9, 101, 105, 615.
[20] Clark Kerr is quoted in Harold Nicolson, *Diaries and Letters, 1939–1945* (London, 1967), p. 277. See generally Vojtech Mastny, *Russia's Road to the Cold War* (New York, 1979), pp. 73–85; Bernd Martin, 'Deutsch-sowjetische Sondierungen über einen separaten Friedensschluss im Zweiten Weltkrieg', in I. Auerbach, A. Hillgruber and G. Schramm, eds.,

For at least two years after *Barbarossa*, therefore, the possibility could not be ruled out of Hitler turning back to intensify the war against Britain and its sea lanes. During this period, too, the British had become dependent on the United States for economic survival against the German blockade. The most celebrated feature was Lend-Lease, in March 1941, when America was still neutral, under which Britain could receive essential goods and materials without need for immediate payment. This was not pure altruism – Roosevelt considered Britain to be America's front line of defence, giving his country time to rearm – and Churchill's description of Lend-Lease as 'the most unsordid act in history of any nation' was for public consumption. But the more sordid bargaining in private should not detract from the essential point. Even allowing for British reciprocal aid, Lend-Lease covered a staggering 54 per cent of the British balance of payments deficit in the war years 1939–45. A second facet of American aid, though less well known, was the president's commitment in November 1942 to alleviate Britain's supply crisis by promising that in 1943 7 million tons of imports (a quarter of the estimated total) would be carried in US vessels. He told his advisers: 'If we are going to keep England in the war at anything like this maximum capacity, we must consider the supplementing of their merchant fleet as one of the top military necessities of the war.' Although Roosevelt, characteristically, had made the promise without squaring his own bureaucracy, causing a messy squabble in Washington, he did honour his commitment. What the US official historians called the 'gamble' of this 'massive shift of American shipping into British services' eventually paid off, because of victory in the Atlantic (and in the shipyards), but at the time it was a real gamble.[21]

Roosevelt's support for Britain was sustained against considerable domestic opposition. Lend-Lease required a bruising two-month battle in Congress – one of the longest legislative struggles of his whole presidency and as bitter as the Supreme Court furore of 1937. Even after America entered the war, priority for Britain remained controversial. The humiliations of Pearl Harbor and the Philippines left Americans most concerned for revenge against Japan. Polls in 1942 indicated that about 30 per cent of the American population favoured a compromise peace with Germany. Even in April 1944, after the campaigns in Tunisia and Italy, 20 per cent were willing to discuss peace with Hitler. And, among policy-makers, the 'Pacific First' strategy was consistently advanced by the US Navy and by some interested generals such as MacArthur. Their bureaucratic clout

Felder und Vorfelder Russischer Geschichte (Freiburg, 1985), esp. pp. 281, 284–7; Ingeborg Fleischhauer, *Die Chance des Sonderfriedens: Deutsch-sowjetische Geheimgespräche, 1941–1945* (Berlin, 1986), esp. pp. 286–7.
[21] R.S. Sayers, *Financial Policy, 1939–1945* (London, 1956), p. 498; Richard M. Leighton and Robert W. Coakley, *Global Logistics and Strategy, 1940–1943* (Washington DC, 1955), pp. 679, 702.

was evident in late summer 1942, during the policy deadlock about operations in Europe, as they swung idle manpower and resources into the Pacific war. At the end of the year more American troops were deployed against Japan than against Germany and Italy. Little wonder that Roosevelt was so anxious to get US troops into action in Europe in 1942. Otherwise the political and bureaucratic pressures against the 'Germany First' policy might have become overwhelming.[22]

For three years from June 1941, the Russians bore the brunt of the war against Germany. At the same time, Britain's economic survival came to depend heavily on American finance, shipping and supplies. The Russians diverted the Nazi threat away from Britain; the Americans sustained the British against the German blockade. Whether or not Churchill paid too high a price at times, whether Britain had leverage of its own that could have been used more effectively, are important issues, but they require case-by-case analysis on a scale beyond the scope of a short essay. What I am emphasizing here is simply that Russian and American aid was vital to Britain in the dark middle years of the war. And it could not be taken for granted.

There was a third benefit of 'fighting with allies' that should also be noted. Russia and America were, in their separate ways, important for Britain's survival in 1940–3; jointly they were also essential to ensure victory in 1944–5. No separate peace had occurred. Nor had Germany collapsed. The battle had to be carried right into Berlin. The Russian contribution to victory was, of course, overwhelmingly the greatest. Between June 1941 and June 1944, 93 per cent of German Army battle casualties (4.2 million men) were inflicted by the Red Army. Even after D-Day, the Russians were facing about two-thirds of the *Wehrmacht*, except during the Battle of the Bulge. But the American contribution in Europe was significant in the last nine months of the war. Although only 43 per cent of the troops who hit the Normandy beaches on D-Day were American, the proportion grew inexorably over the ensuing months. At the end of the war 65 per cent of the 4 million Allied soldiers in Western Europe were American, only 20 per cent were British. Not surprisingly, the British Army Group in northern Germany became, by the spring of 1945, a marginal factor in the strategy and conduct of the final campaign.[23]

I have suggested so far that a compromise peace (or limited war) with a Hitler-dominated European continent would have been neither tenable

[22] Richard W. Steele, 'American Popular Opinion and the War against Germany: The Issue of a Negotiated Peace, 1942', *Journal of American History*, 65 (1978), esp. 705, 709, 722; Mark A. Stoler, 'The "Pacific First" Alternative in American World War II Strategy', *International History Review*, 2 (1980), 432–52; Leighton and Coakley, *Global Logistics*, p. 662.
[23] Jonathan R. Adelman, *Prelude to the Cold War: The Tsarist, Soviet, and US Armies in the Two World Wars* (London, 1988), pp. 128, 176, 180; L.F. Ellis, *Victory in the West*, 2 vols. (London, 1962–8), II, p. 406.

nor desirable for Britain in the long run. I have also argued that Russian and American help was significant in averting British defeat and ensuring eventual victory. These were tasks that Britain could not achieve alone, as is clear if we look at the evolution of British strategy after 1940.

What must be emphasised is that Britain alone never had a credible policy for defeating Nazi Germany. It was assumed, when war began in September 1939, that Britain probably faced a long conflict, to be waged in the manner of the Hanoverians in the eighteenth and nineteenth centuries. That meant relying on Britain's economic, financial and naval strength in conjunction with the manpower of continental allies – or, as the French put it, 'the British would fight to the last Frenchman'. Planning papers in 1939 envisaged that the French army, plus a token British Expeditionary Force, would resist the initial German onslaught. Then Germany's economy and morale would be undermined by blockade, bombing and intensive propaganda, until the time was ripe for the final offensive.[24] The scenario was not dissimilar to that of 1914–18 – a war of attrition which would end in the enemy's political and economic collapse, not a war of manoeuvre culminating in Germany's military defeat.

Even in 1939 this scenario was optimistic. The naval blockade had been of limited utility against Napoleonic France, a country significantly reliant on maritime trade. It was much less credible against Nazi Germany, which could draw on the resources of hinterland Central and Eastern Europe. And by the 1930s Britain itself was newly vulnerable to direct attack because, in the age of airpower, an enemy could leapfrog the 'moat defensive' and menace London – centre of government, commerce and finance and home to one-fifth of the country's population. When Britain started to rearm in 1934, the government concentrated on creating a bombing force to match Germany's. After his famous warning that 'the bomber will always get through', Baldwin added that 'the only defence is in offence, which means that you have to kill more women and children more quickly than the enemy if you want to save yourselves'.[25] Although chances of defence against the bomber improved in the late 1930s, with fast monoplane fighters and the advent of radar, Britain's defence spending all through the war was shaped by this commitment to the bomber from the early 1930s. Equally important, during this time the army remained of minor concern. Unlike the continental powers since Bismarck's era, Britain had always eschewed peacetime conscription, counting on its empire (especially India) for global military manpower and on the French army nearer home. Fitting out a BEF was the lowest priority for defence spend-

---

[24] PRO CAB 16/183A, DP(P) 44: COS sub-commt., 'European Appreciation', 20 Feb. 1939, esp. paras 27–37, 267–8.

[25] Keith Middlemas and John Barnes, *Baldwin: A Biography* (London, 1969), p. 735; for the argument in this para. see generally David Reynolds, *Britannia Overruled: British Policy and World Power in the 20th Century* (London, 1991), chapter 5.

ing in the late 1930s and in May 1940 Britain had only 10 divisions on the Western Front, compared with 104 French, 22 Belgian and 8 Dutch.

The debacle of 1940 exposed and exacerbated the weaknesses of this strategy. Hitler's lightning conquests of Scandinavia and western Europe, coupled with his economic pact with Russia, made nonsense of any naval blockade. Italy's entry into the war opened up new dangers in the Mediterranean, at a time when France's collapse left the Royal Navy to face them alone. And Britain had only a tiny army (nearly lost at Dunkirk) with which to plan reentry on to the continent of Europe, always assuming it could survive Nazi bombing, invasion or blockade. Yet Churchill believed (rightly, I have argued) that a modus vivendi with Hitler would not guarantee security. How, after June 1940, did he expect to win the war?

Here historians have been too ready to take at face value his oratory, such as the famous words on 13 May 1940 about 'victory at all costs'. For traditionalists, they epitomise his 'indomitable stoutness'; for revisionists, they are proof of his self-delusion.[26] Both take them as a statement of policy. It would be more accurate, I think, to consider his words on 13 May as a rhetorical trope, designed to hearten Commons and country in his first speech as prime minister. Churchill knew that talk of victory was essential to head off talk of defeat. But total military victory over Germany had never been a British aim in 1939, let alone after France fell. We need to look more closely at Churchill's war aims and strategy as they evolved in the middle of the war.

Taking war aims first: left to itself in 1939–40, the British government assumed some kind of eventual negotiated peace. This was clearly Churchill's position, though Establishment figures now ridicule such suggestions as 'rubbish'. In the Cabinet discussions during the Dunkirk crisis, Churchill left open the possibility of future negotiations: 'A time might come when we felt that we had to put an end to the struggle, but the terms would not then be more mortal than those offered to us now.' While this was partly intended to disabuse Halifax of the idea that he was a diehard, it reflects his position at other times. In August 1940 (as in October 1939) he argued that firm rejection of Hitler's peace offers was 'the only chance of extorting from Germany any offers which are not fantastic'.[27]

The British position in mid-1940 can be discerned more clearly in the light of discussions a year later. In a speech on 5 July 1941 Anthony Eden, the foreign secretary, stated that 'we were not prepared to negotiate with

---

[26] Cf. Isaiah Berlin, *Mr Churchill in 1940* (London, 1964), pp. 15, 26; Charmley, *Churchill*, pp. 401–2, 465–8, 596.

[27] David Reynolds, 'Churchill and the British "Decision" to Fight On in 1940: Right Policy, Wrong Reasons', in Richard Langhorne, ed., *Diplomacy and Intelligence during the Second World War* (Cambridge, 1985), esp. pp. 152–4; cf. Lord Annan in *London Review of Books*, 1 Aug. 1985, p. 5.

Hitler at any time on any subject'. (The previous December the Foreign Office had baulked at such a categorical statement. Frank Roberts of the Central Department had advised against a public commitment about 'never undertaking negotiations in any circumstances with Herr Hitler'.) On 7 July 1941 Churchill drew the War Cabinet's attention to Eden's words: 'While this statement expressed the opinion of the whole War Cabinet, it was perhaps the most explicit public declaration on the subject that had been made. Such a declaration had been necessary at this moment in order to forestall any peace offensive by Hitler in the near future.' The Cabinet minute concluded: 'The War Cabinet took note, with approval, of this declaration.'[28] Churchill's remarks (and the care taken to record Cabinet approval) suggest awareness that this was a significant policy step.

This firming up of policy reflected the need to reassure the Soviet Union, where London's secrecy about the Hess mission had strengthened fears of an Anglo-German deal against Russia. One of Stalin's first demands from his new British ally was a pledge not to sign a separate peace with Germany. But Russia's own resistance could not be guaranteed and Churchill told the Cabinet on 5 September that he 'had the feeling that the possibility of a separate peace by Stalin could not be altogether excluded'. By then Churchill also had America to consider, having agreed what became known as the Atlantic Charter at his meeting with Roosevelt in August. Although he had hoped for a declaration of war not of war aims, the moral identification of America with the Allied cause was significant. The Charter did, however, allude to 'the final destruction of the Nazi tyranny' and, more generally, implied that British diplomacy towards Germany would henceforth take account of America as well as Russia. Churchill's frame of reference by the autumn of 1941 is shown by his insistence on 10 September that there should not be 'the slightest contact' with any German peace feelers. 'Nothing would be more disturbing to our friends in the United States or more dangerous with our new ally, Russia, than the suggestion that we were entertaining such ideas.'[29]

Yet this did not mean that an eventual negotiated peace had now been ruled out. In November 1941 Eden was keen about 'exorcising certain suspicions in Stalin's mind', including the idea that Britain would 'be prepared to make peace with a Germany controlled by the Army, if they were to overthrow the Party'. It is interesting to note that Churchill did

---

[28] PRO CAB 65/19, WM 66 (41) 5, 7 July 1941; cf. PRO FO 371/24362, C13729/7/62, minute by Roberts, 18 Dec. 1940, noted without contradiction by Strang and Cadogan.

[29] PRO CAB 65/23, WM 90 (41) 3 CA, 5 Sept. 1941; PRO PREM 4/100/8: Churchill to Eden, M888/1, 10 Sept. 1941. Cf. Gabriel Gorodetsky, 'The Hess Affair and Anglo-Soviet Relations on the Eve of "Barbarossa" ', *English Historical Review*, 101 (1986), 405–20; and David Reynolds, 'The Atlantic "Flop": British Foreign Policy and the Churchill-Roosevelt Meeting of August 1941', in Douglas Brinkley and David Facey-Crowther, eds., *The Atlantic Charter* (New York, 1994), pp. 129–50.

not rule out this idea. According to the Cabinet minutes for 27 November 1941, he said that

> we had made a public statement that we would not negotiate with Hitler or with the Nazi *regime*; but he thought it would be going too far to say that we would not negotiate with a Germany controlled by the Army. It was impossible to forecast what form of Government there might be in Germany at a time when their resistance weakened and they wished to negotiate.[30]

How was this eventual negotiated peace to be achieved? Not, it should be stressed, by invading the Continent and smashing a way to Berlin. This was even less likely after the fall of France than it had been in 1939: the Allies no longer had even a beachhead on the Continent. As befitted a state that had consistently placed its army last in defence priorities, Churchill's government always assumed that invading Fortress Europe would be the final *coup de grâce* rather than the central *coup de main*. To quote the Chiefs of Staff in September 1940:

> It is not our policy to attempt to raise, and land on the continent, an army comparable in size to that of Germany. We should aim nevertheless, as soon as the action of the blockade and the air offensive have secured conditions when numerically inferior forces can be employed with good chance of success, to re-establish a striking force on the Continent with which we can enter Germany and impose our terms.

Churchill certainly saw the army in this essentially auxiliary role. The humiliating disasters of 1940–2 – from Norway and Dunkirk to Singapore and Tobruk – cast a permanent shadow over his evaluation of German and British military capabilities. 'I am ashamed. I cannot understand why Tobruk gave in,' he told his physician in June 1942. 'More than 30,000 of our men put their hands up. If they won't fight . . .' He stopped, abruptly. Reviewing the war situation the following month, he placed first among its 'salient features' what he called 'the immense power of the German military machine'. Bearing in mind what two panzer divisions and one light division had done in North Africa 'against our greatly superior numbers and resources,' he wrote, 'we have no excuse for underrating German military power in 1943 and 1944. It will always be possible for them to set up a holding front against Russia and bring back fifty or sixty, or even more, divisions to the West.'[31] This was why he adamantly opposed plans for invading France before German power was broken.

How, then, did Churchill imagine that Germans would be brought to

---

[30] PRO CAB 65/24, WM 120 (41) 5 CA, 27 Nov. 1941; cf. Eden's paper printed as CAB 66/20, WP (41) 288.

[31] PRO CAB 80/17, COS (40) 683, 4 Sept. 1940, para 214; Lord Moran, *Churchill: The Struggle for Survival, 1940–1965* (London, 1968), 21 June 1942, p. 55; PRO CAB 66/26, WP (42) 311, 21 July 1942; cf. Joseph L. Strange, 'The British Rejection of Operation SLEDGEHAMMER, An Alternative Motive', *Military Affairs*, 46: 1 (Feb. 1982), 6–14.

overthrow Nazism and seek peace? Frankly, he was not sure, but, like most strategists, he looked back to the last war. In a neglected part of his 'finest hour' speech to the Commons on 18 June 1940, he reminded his countryman, shocked by France's capitulation, that:

During the first four years of the last war, the Allies experienced nothing but disaster and disappointment ... During that war we repeatedly asked ourselves the question, 'How are we going to win?' and no one was able ever to answer it with much precision, until, at the end, quite suddenly, quite unexpectedly, our terrible foe collapsed before us, and [he could not resist adding] we were so glutted with victory that in our folly we threw it away.

The 1918 scenario underlies British strategic thinking in the middle part of the war, as evidenced by the steady flow of reports to the Cabinet and chiefs of staff on the state of economy and morale, both in Germany and the extended Reich. In these the prediction of a 1918-style collapse of 'startling rapidity' recurred at times of particular optimism.[32]

The disintegration of 1918 had begun with Germany's allies and this is one reason why Churchill was so keen to support subversion within the Third Reich. The Special Operations Executive that he created in the summer of 1940 was intended to help 'set Europe ablaze', exploding timely 'detonators' to set off resistance movements across Europe. His celebrated 'peripheral strategy' into the Baltic and the Mediterranean always had this in mind. Invasion of Italy in 1943, for example, was predicated on the (eventually erroneous) assumption that Hitler would evacuate most of the peninsula up to the Alps. This campaign was therefore expected to knock one member of the Axis out of the war quickly, at little cost. It would also allow the Allies to aid the partisan struggles in Greece and Yugoslavia. Churchill told Eisenhower in July 1943, 'if we can get hold of the mouth of the Adriatic so as to be able to run even a few ships into Dalmatian and Greek ports, the whole of the Western Balkans might flare up with far-reaching results'.[33]

The main assumption behind British hopes of a Nazi collapse lay in the supposed tautness of Germany's economy and morale. In a typical appraisal, the Ministry of Economic Warfare claimed in September 1940:

the Nazi economy is much more brittle than the Germany economy of 1914–18 which was not so highly integrated. It is not impossible that an acute shortage of oil or a tie-up of the transport system might cause a breakdown of the closely-knit Nazi system with repercussions throughout Germany and German Europe of the utmost importance.

[32] Commons, *Debates*, 5s, 362: 59–60, 18 June 1940; cf. Hinsley et al., *British Intelligence*, II, pp. 98, 114, 159.

[33] David Stafford, 'The Detonator Concept: British Strategy, SOE and European Resistance after the Fall of France', *Journal of Contemporary History*, 10 (1975), 185–212; Hinsley et al., *British Intelligence*, 3/1, pp. 5, 14; Michael Howard, *Grand Strategy* IV (London, 1970), p. 501.

This was an axiom of British thinking in 1940–2, reflecting the erroneous belief that Germany's economy was already fully mobilised for war, and it gave apparent credibility to the strategy of maintaining economic pressure on the enemy. The problem was how to keep up that pressure, given Hitler's vast conquests in 1940. Although the MEW talked in September 1940 of the blockade henceforth as 'a stiletto rather than a bludgeon', Churchill himself had no doubt that the blockade had been 'blunted and rendered largely ineffectual'.[34] *Faute de mieux*, he looked to the skies not the seas.

On 3 September 1940, the first anniversary of the outbreak of war, Churchill told the Cabinet: 'The Navy can lose us the war, but only the Air Force can win it.' He went on:

The Fighters are our salvation, but the Bombers alone provide the means of victory. We must therefore develop the power to carry an ever-increasing volume of explosives to Germany, so as to pulverise the entire industry and scientific structure on which the war effort and economic life of the enemy depend, while holding him at arm's length from our Island. In no other way at present visible can we hope to overcome the immense military power of Germany ...

Throughout the winter of 1940–1 he threw resources into bomber production, describing it as 'one of the greatest military objectives now before us'. And on 12 July 1941, he ordered that 'we must aim at nothing less than having an air force twice as strong as the German Air Force by the end of 1942'. This was, he said, 'the very least that can be contemplated, since no other way of winning the war has yet been proposed'.[35]

During 1942, any hope of an alternative German government faded. In part, this reflected a hardening of opinion in Whitehall as Nazi atrocities became evident and convictions strengthened about the incorrigibility of Germany as a whole. Over the 'last 70 years', Eden told the Commons in December 1942, 'successive German Governments have consciously and consistently pursued a policy of world domination' and it would therefore be 'sheer folly to allow some non-Nazi German Government to be set up, and then, so to speak, to trust to luck'. Although the term 'unconditional surrender' was only unveiled publicly by Roosevelt and Churchill at Casablanca in January 1943, it had been circulating privately in Whitehall for some months before. Equally significant in the hardening of attitudes were the constraints of alliance politics, once both Russia and America were formally in the war. As early as January 1942, the United Nations declaration pledged signatories to 'complete victory over their enemies'. Sensitivity to the views of Washington and Moscow (and also of the minor European allies) dictated a continued policy of 'absolute silence' to peace

---

[34] PRO CAB 79/6, COS (40) 295th mtg., 5 Sept. 1940, esp. item 2, annex and appendix.
[35] PRO CAB 66/11, WP (40) 352; PRO AVIA 9/5, esp. Churchill minutes M485, 30 Dec. 1940, and M740/1, 12 July 1941.

feelers and encouraged the preference for a blank-slate approach to peace-making rather than haggling with numerous allies over possible terms. Moreover, the entry of Russia and America now made military victory more likely. Unconditional surrender therefore seemed both desirable and possible – the two aspects were reciprocally related.[36]

Although Britain's prospects and goals were gradually transformed during 1942, it is noteworthy that Churchill's strategic framework remained essentially the same: the new wine was poured into old bottles. For instance, in his paper on 'The Campaign of 1943', written in December 1941 after Pearl Harbor, Churchill suggested that, as the growing power of the three allies was brought to bear on Germany, 'an internal collapse is always possible, but we must not count on this'. The alternative scenario was therefore 'the defeat in Europe of the German armies'. But 'it need not be assumed that great numbers of men would be required'; rather 'armies of liberation', spearheaded by 'armoured and mechanised forces', in conjunction with popular revolt. 'We have therefore to prepare for the liberation of the captive countries of Western and Southern Europe by the landing at suitable points, successively or simultaneously, of British and American armies strong enough to enable the conquered populations to revolt.'[37]

Reviewing the war position on 21 July 1942, Churchill appeared to recognise the dubiousness of strategic bombing and the new stategic position following American entry. He wrote:

In the days when we were fighting alone, we answered the question: 'How are you going to win the war?' by saying: 'We will shatter Germany by bombing.' Since then the enormous injuries inflicted on the German Army and man-power by the Russians, and the accession of the man-power and munitions of the United States, have rendered other possibilities open.

But these 'other possibilities' were actually variations on the old theme: 'We look forward to mass invasion of the Continent by liberating armies, and the general revolt of the populations against the Hitler tyranny.' Moreover, he added,

it would be a mistake to cast aside our original thought which, it may be mentioned, is also strong in American minds, namely, that the severe ruthless bombing of Germany on an ever-increasing scale will not only cripple her war effort including U-boat and aircraft production, but will also create conditions intolerable to the mass of the German population.

---

[36] Commons, *Debates*, 5s, 385: 1238, 2 Dec. 1942; Rainer A. Blasius, 'Waiting for Action: The Debate on the "Other Germany" in Great Britain and the Reaction of the Foreign Office to German "Peace-Feelers", 1942', in Francis R. Nicosia and Lawrence D. Stokes, eds., *Germans against Nazism: Nonconformity, Opposition and Resistance in the Third Reich* (New York, 1990), esp. pp. 296–300.

[37] J.R.M. Butler, *Grand Stategy*, III, part 1 (London, 1964), pp. 334–5.

This memo was intended for widespread official consumption, in Washington as well as London. In private, Churchill was even more categorical. He told Clement Attlee, the deputy prime minister, on 29 July 1942:

Continuous reflection leaves me with the conclusion that, upon the whole, our best chance of winning the war is with the big Bombers. It certainly will be several years before British and American land forces will be capable of beating the Germans on even terms in the open field.[38]

Even in 1942–3 British policy continued to hope for a German internal collapse. In June 1942, with the Nazis' Russian offensive in full cry, the Cabinet's Joint Intelligence Committee advised that, between August and October, 'events may move to a climax ... and it may be touch and go which of the two adversaries collapses first'. The JIC acknowledged that 'we cannot rule out the possibility of Russia collapsing', but was more hopeful about the Axis crumbling first. 'If the Germans realise that they cannot avoid another winter campaign in Russia and are faced with the threat of Anglo-American invasion in the West, they may collapse with unprecedented rapidity as they did in 1918.' The Chiefs of Staff thought that the picture was 'painted in rather too rosy a hue for Russia'. But Churchill considered it 'a very good appreciation'. Perhaps the high-water mark of the 1918 scenario came in September 1943. On the day after the Italian surrender, the JIC produced a paper which it went so far as to entitle 'Probabilities of a German Collapse'. This was a historical comparison between the current situation and the dramatic finale of the Great War. The JIC concluded that 'Germany is if anything, in a worse position to-day than she was in the same period of 1918.' But for the fact that the country was this time under a brutal, totalitarian regime, 'we should unhesitatingly predict that Germany would sue for an armistice before the end of the year'. In this connection, the JIC noted, 'great weight must again attach to the view taken by Germany's Allies'. Churchill had the paper circulated to the War Cabinet.[39]

At the same time, he still had not modified his opposition to a premature invasion of the Continent. He told Roosevelt in October 1943: 'Unless there is a German collapse the campaign of 1944 will be far the most dangerous we have undertaken and personally I am more anxious about its success that I was about 1941, 1942 or 1943.' By implication, this put 1944 on a par with 1940, and that indeed was Churchill's worst nightmare. Although he occasionally spoke in lurid terms about the Channel running with blood, his real fear was not another Dieppe but a second Dunkirk.

---

[38] PRO CAB 66/26, WP (42) 311, memo of 21 July 1942, para 6; PRO PREM 3/499/9: Churchill to Attlee, 29 July 1942. A copy of WP 311 was passed, for instance, to the US War Dept. – see George C. Marshall Library, Lexington, VA: Verifax 1278.

[39] PRO PREM 3/395/13: JIC (42) 200, 1 June 1942, paras 69–71; Hollis to Churchill, 5 June 1942; Churchill to Ismay, 7 June; PRO CAB 66/42, WP (43) 479, JIC (43) 367, 9 Sept. 1943.

According to minutes of a meeting with the Chiefs of Staff in October 1943: 'He felt that we should probably effect a lodgement and in the first instance we might make progress. It was the later stages of the operation which worried him,' fearing, as before, that the Germans might transfer troops rapidly across the Continent and 'inflict on us a military disaster greater than that of Dunkirk' which would lead to 'the resuscitation of Hitler and the Nazi regime'.[40]

But Churchill was no longer able to shape Allied strategy. This was demonstrated by his coerced commitment at Teheran in November 1943 to invade France the following spring. American military planners (outside the Army Air Force) had never shared the British concept of a war of attrition, using the army only for the knock-out blow when Germany was about to collapse. They saw this as 'a confession of bankruptcy', a strategy 'derived from British weakness'.[41] More exactly, it was derived from general weakness and specific strengths, particularly the 1930s concentration on the bomber. If not quite a case of making bricks without straw, certainly grasping at whatever straws were blowing in the wind, such as the persistent hope that Germany was over-stretched.

By the autumn of 1943, the bankruptcy of British strategy was evident. Churchill had lost faith in strategic bombing, as photographic and economic intelligence cast doubts on the RAF's claims. Even in December 1942 he was speaking of the bombing offensive not as the winning weapon but only as 'our principal effort in the air'. Meanwhile, the peripheral approach had resulted in lengthy wars of attrition in Tunisia and Italy, in which it was far from clear whether the Allies were pinning down the Germans or vice versa. Nor had European resistance been detonated; instead, notes David Stafford, the dynamite proved 'a rather damp squib'. Robert Keyserlingk observes that this whole strategy rested on a misplaced faith in the 'essential decency (*Anständigkeit*) and power of historic European nationalism' and yielded 'no tangible results'. In fact, after the JIC's heady optimism of September 1943 evaporated, Churchill became increasingly sceptical about a German collapse. On 5 January 1944, he expected Hitler still to be in power on the fifth anniversary of the war, 3 September 1944. A few days later, the JIC admitted in response to Churchill's questioning that they now saw no prospect of Germany crumbling from within and acknowledged that the Russian advance into the Balkans would probably prompt Nazi occupation rather than Axis collapse.[42]

---

[40] Churchill to Roosevelt, 17 Oct. 1943, in Kimball, ed., *C-R*, II, pp. 541; PRO CAB 79/66, COS (43) 254(0), item 4, 19 Oct. 1943.

[41] Leighton and Coakley, *Global Logistics*, p. 119; Theodore A. Wilson, *The First Summit: Roosevelt and Churchill at Placentia Bay, 1941*, 2nd edn (Lawrence KS, 1991), p. 122.

[42] PRO CAB 66/32, WP (42) 580: Churchill, note on 'Air Policy', 16 Dec. 1942; Stafford, 'The Detonator Concept', p. 210; Robert H. Keyserlingk, 'Die Deutsche Komponente in Churchills Strategie der Nationalen Erhebungen, 1940–1942', *Vierteljahrshefte für Zeitgeschichte*, 31 (1983), 625, 634; John Colville, *The Fringes of Power: Downing Street Diaries*,

At the same time, however, the idea of a compromise peace with Hitler remained unacceptable. The threat, direct and indirect, remained. There was the looming menace of Nazi V-weapons, eventually unleashed in June 1944 and developed by Hitler at great expense to the strained Nazi war economy as terror weapons against Britain, Moreover, the battle of the Atlantic had only just been turned and Raeder made a new effort with modernised U-boats in 1944. Here we have reached the heart of Churchill's strategic dilemma. Britain was right to fight on in 1940 but, alone, she had no viable strategy for eliminating the Hitler threat. Churchill complained privately in April 1944 that *Overlord* had been 'forced upon us by the Russians and the United States military authorities'.[43] But D-Day was also tacit recognition that British strategy had reached the end of the road. Only military victory would force a German collapse – not blockade, bombing, subversion or peripheral operations. And this victory could only be won by Russian and American arms.

The last year of the war saw the marginalisation of Churchill in Allied grand strategy.[44] What some critics, then and later, saw as his growing 'appeasement' of America and Russia was the diplomatic consequence of that strategic reality. This is not to suggest that Churchill had absolutely no room for manoeuvre – as indicated by his occasional disputes with Eden, particularly over France. Nor is it to imply that his vision was unclouded by sentiment. Today his talk in September 1943 about 'common citizenship' between the United States and the United Kingdom seems utopian, as do his remarks to Eden in January 1944 about 'the deep-seated changes which have taken place in the character of the Russian State and Government' and 'the new confidence which has grown in our hearts towards Stalin'. But Churchill's differences with Eden were matters of emphasis not substance: the foreign secretary's francophilia hardly offered the prospect of 'some control for Britain over an independent foreign policy'. And while it is neat and, up to a point, apt, to compare Churchill and Chamberlain as 'appeasers', the 'man of Yalta' and the 'man of Munich' – one writing off the Poles, the other sacrificing the Czechs – there remains a fundamental difference.[45] Churchill had his blind spots about Roosevelt and Stalin, whereas Chamberlain's vision was clouded

---

1939–1955 (London, 1985), p. 433; PRO PREM 3/396/10: esp. JIC interim report in Ismay to Hollis, 14 Jan. 1944. See also the insightful discussion in Tuvia Ben-Moshe, *Churchill: Strategy and History* (Boulder, CO, 1992), chapter 9.

[43] PRO PREM 3/197/2: Churchill to Cadogan, 19 Apr. 1944.

[44] A theme explored in David Reynolds, 'Churchill and Allied Grand Strategy in Europe, 1944–1945: The Limits of British Influence', in Charles F. Brower, ed., *World War II in Europe: The Final Year* (New York, forthcoming).

[45] Charmley, *Churchill*, pp. 541, 551, 556, 561, 612; cf. David Reynolds, 'Great Britain: Imperial Diplomacy', in Reynolds, W.F. Kimball and A.O. Churbarian, eds., *Allies at War: The Soviet, American, and British Experience, 1939–1945* (New York, 1994), pp. 333–53.

about Hitler. Misjudging one's allies is dangerous, but misjudging one's enemies can be fatal.

Churchill's 'policy' was not 'glory'. It was not even 'victory at all costs'. Less elegantly but more accurately his aim is encapsulated in his private motto of 1940–1: 'KBO' or 'Keep Buggering On.'[46] He was right that Britain could not be secure as long as Nazi Germany controlled continental Europe, but his strategy for security was largely wishful thinking. Ultimately, this is not a comment on Churchill's mind but on Britain's power. The country never had a capacity alone for waging a continental war, in the nineteenth century let alone the twentieth. Its global power had assumed a continental balance maintained by other means. In defeating Hitler – as with Napoleon and the kaiser, not to mention Philip II of Spain or Louis XIV – allies were needed to enhance Britain's strength. And, where these were lacking, appeasement was a long-standing method of adjusting policy to the limits of power – 'in a sense,' Paul Kennedy has observed, 'the "natural" policy for a small island state gradually losing its place in world affairs'.[47]

This reminds us also of the limits of biography. Although there has not been space here for detailed examination of Churchill's wartime diplomacy, I have argued that it must be set in its proper context. That means not only the international situation and the strategic calculus, but also the long-term dilemmas of British power. Near the end of her classic study of *Britain and the Origins of the First World War*, Zara Steiner quoted Lord Salisbury's observation of 1895: 'Power has passed from the hands of Statesmen, but I should be very much puzzled to say into whose hands it has passed.'[48] Half a century later, Churchill would have understood. He *is* open to the label of appeaser, particularly when taken in its historical context. But one could equally remark on the power he was able to conjure out of impotence – how much he made out of so little for so long.

---

[46] Charmley, *Churchill*, p. 560; M. Gilbert, *Churchill*, VII, p. 1273.

[47] Paul Kennedy, *Strategy and Diplomacy, 1870–1945* (London, 1984), p. 38; Reynolds, *Britannia Overruled*, pp. 19–25, 61–2.

[48] Zara S. Steiner, *Britain and the Origins of the First World War* (London, 1977), p. 250.

CHAPTER 10

From ally to enemy: Britain's relations with the Soviet Union, 1941–1948

When Nazi Germany invaded the Soviet Union on 22 June 1941 it also threw the latter into a temporary alliance with Britain. The implication in this sentence that the alliance was accidental is intentional. Certainly no one would have confidently predicted it even a matter of weeks before the German attack. Anglo-Soviet relations since the Russian revolution of 1917 had never been good, let alone close. Britain had taken a leading part in the futile and misguided allied intervention on the side of the 'Whites' in the Russian civil war; diplomatic relations, opened in 1924, were broken off by the British government in 1927 on the grounds of Russian inter-ference in Britain's domestic affairs; and although these relations were restored in 1929, the Soviet Union continued to be the object of suspicion and barely disguised hostility on the part of the right-wing governments which ruled Britain in the 1930s. Russian attempts to build an anti-fascist coalition from 1935 onwards were never taken seriously by these govern-ments, partly because the Red Army was deemed to be capable only of defensive operations – a sentiment heightened by the Stalinist purges of 1936–8 – and partly because it was feared that Russia's Communist rulers were anxious to embroil Britain in a war for their own selfish purposes.

The events of 1939–41 did nothing to modify these sentiments. Indeed, there were now fresh grounds for suspicion and hostility: the Molotov–Ribbentrop non-aggression pact of August 1939 itself, the Soviet occu-pation of eastern Poland (a corollary of the pact), its invasion of Finland,

This chapter was originally presented as a paper at the international conference on 'The Soviet Union and Europe in the Cold War, 1943–1953', held in Cortona, Italy, on 23–24 Sept. 1994 under the auspices of the Institute of Universal History (Moscow), the Feltrinelli Foundation (Milan) and the Gramsci Institute (Rome). As such, the essay is being published by the Feltrinelli Foundation in its edition of the proceedings of the conference and the Foundation's kind permission to reproduce it here is gratefully acknowledged.

its annexation of the Baltic States and its supply of raw materials to Nazi Germany. Although Britain was never as enthusiastic as its French ally to send troops to help the Finns or to bomb the Russian oil fields in the Caucasus, plans to do both were seriously examined and might have been implemented but for Finland's collapse in March 1940, the disastrous Norwegian expedition in April and the German offensive in the west in May. Even as the German onslaught upon the Soviet Union was clearly looming in the summer of 1941, the opinion in the Foreign Office was that any resultant pressure to treat the latter as an ally should be resisted.[1]

It was too much to expect this atmosphere of suspicion to vanish overnight. Although Winston Churchill's famous broadcast speech on the day of the German invasion proclaimed that: 'Any man or state who fights on against Nazidom will have our aid,' and that 'It follows therefore that we shall give whatever help we can to Russia and the Russian people,'[2] Gabriel Gorodetsky has pointed out that the prime minister – in accordance with the Foreign Office's attitude – 'refrained from using the term "ally" throughout the speech' and that assistance was offered in qualified terms.[3] Churchill's fierce anti-Communism – he had denounced the ideology in 1920 as 'a pestilence more destructive of life than the Black Death or the Spotted Typhus'[4] and had been the leading advocate inside the government of intervention to destroy it – was never far below the surface. At the end of August 1941 he asked his minister of information, Brendan Bracken, to consider what action was needed 'to counter the present tendency of the British public to forget the dangers of Communism in their enthusiasm over the resistance of Russia'[5] and told his foreign secretary, Anthony Eden, on 14 November 1941 that when he became prime minister, he could do as he liked about relations with the Soviet Union, 'But while I am here we fight strictly on [the] basis of two people who have come together just to do this job.'[6]

Churchill was not the only member of the government who gave vent to anti-Communism in this period. Colonel Moore-Brabazon, the minister for aircraft production, was reported as having said in early September 1941 'that he hoped the Russians and Germans would exterminate each

[1] Martin Kitchen, *British Policy towards the Soviet Union during the Second World War* (London, 1986), p. 53.

[2] Martin Gilbert, *Finest Hour: Winston S. Churchill 1939–1941* (London, 1983), p. 1121.

[3] Gabriel Gorodetsky, *Stafford Cripps' Mission to Moscow 1940–42* (Cambridge, 1984), p. 176.

[4] Robin Edmonds, 'Churchill and Stalin', in Robert Blake and William Roger Louis, eds., *Churchill: A Major New Assessment of his Life in Peace and War* (Oxford, 1993), p. 311.

[5] Philip M.H. Bell, *John Bull and The Bear: British Public Opinion, Foreign Policy and the Soviet Union 1941–1945* (London, 1990), p. 43.

[6] John Colville, *The Fringes of Power: Downing Street Diaries 1939–1955* (London, 1985), p. 436.

other'.[7] The British military, too, were deeply suspicious of the Russians. The chiefs of staff observed on 8 July 1941 that 'we are not allied with Russia nor do we entirely trust that country',[8] while Lieutenant-General Sir Henry Pownall, the deputy chief of the army staff, went even further in the privacy of his diary, writing on 29 October, 'Would that the two loathsome monsters, Germany and Russia, drown together in a death grip in the winter mud.'[9]

These sentiments closely paralleled those expressed by the future US president, Harry Truman, in the aftermath of the German invasion of the Soviet Union, but while Truman's comments have been made much of by former Soviet and western 'revisionist' historians, the British statements cited in the previous paragraph have been largely ignored. This is curious to say the least, because in 1941 Truman was a relatively obscure senator in a neutral country. Moore-Brabazon and Pownall on the other hand were, respectively, a minister and a senior military officer specifically charged with implementing their government's declared policy of military aid to a fellow belligerent. Nevertheless too much should not be made of these remarks, which could doubtless be paralleled on the Russian side. They are important only in so far as they illustrate the important fact that there was a deep legacy of mistrust of the Soviet Union in Britain which meant that, even when relations between the two countries seemed to have improved, it did not take much to persuade British policy-makers to jump to the most pessimistic conclusions about Russian motives.

Things were not improved by the Russian diplomatic style, which thoroughly exasperated and annoyed the British. A comment by Eden's private secretary, Oliver Harvey, in his diary for 10 February 1943 expressed a common reaction: 'The Russians are very tiresome allies, importunate, graceless, ungrateful, secretive, suspicious, [and] ever asking for more', although he graciously added that in military terms they were 'delivering the goods'.[10] It was thought, no doubt with some justification, that one reason for the Russian attitude was the nature of the Soviet political system, which left individual diplomats and soldiers with little room for manoeuvre. Churchill, for one, was therefore always pleased to deal with Stalin directly. 'If only I could dine with Stalin once a week,' he said in January 1944, 'there would be no trouble at all. We get on like a house on fire.'[11] To be fair, the Russians were not the only ones at fault. The three heads of the British military mission in Moscow, for example, were

---

[7] Anthony Eden diary, 14 Nov. 1941, AP20/1/21, Avon Papers (Birmingham University Library). Cited by permission of the Countess of Avon.

[8] Gorodetsky, *Stafford Cripps' Mission to Moscow*, p. 188.

[9] Brian Bond, ed., *Chief of Staff: The Diaries of Lieutenant-General Sir Henry Pownall, II, 1940–1944* (London, 1974), p. 50.

[10] John Harvey, ed., *The War Diaries of Oliver Harvey 1941–1945* (London, 1978), p. 219.

[11] Martin Gilbert, *Road to Victory: Winston S. Churchill 1941–1945* (London, 1986), p. 664.

all disasters and Stalin complained personally to the British ambassador
in September 1944 about the last of them. The officer in question, he
said, 'had no respect for the Russian leaders or for the Red Army, and
they had none for him'.[12] The fact remains that the degree of cooperation
between Britain and the Soviet Union never even remotely approached
that between Britain and the United States, before or after the latter
entered the war in December 1941. If the late Christopher Thorne could
describe the British and the Americans between 1941 and 1945 as 'Allies
of a Kind',[13] how then should we refer to the British and the Russians?

Between 1941 and 1944 there were two main issues between Britain
and the Soviet Union: the 'second front' and post-war Russian objectives
in Europe. I shall say very little about the first because I believe it was
more significant in relation to Russian perceptions of Britain than vice
versa. There is no evidence that the British deliberately delayed the opening of the 'second front' in order to bleed the Soviet Union white, and
the principal consequence of continual Russian pressure upon Britain's
perception of the Soviet Union was to heighten that feeling of exasperation
and annoyance to which reference has already been made. The British
could not understand why the Russians did not appear to comprehend
the military problems involved. They also felt that it was hypocritical of
the Soviet Union to complain about being left to face the Germans alone
when, largely as a result of Russian policy, Britain had been in exactly the
same position between 1940 and 1941. As Churchill put it to the British
ambassador in Moscow on 28 October 1941, the Russians had 'brought
their own fate upon themselves' when they signed their pact with Nazi
Germany in August 1939 and had 'cut themselves off from an effective
second front when they let the French army be destroyed'. 'We did not
... know till Hitler attacked them', the prime minister continued,
'whether they would fight or what side they would be on. We were left
alone for a whole year while every Communist in England, under orders
from Moscow, did his best to hamper our war effort. If we had been
invaded and destroyed in July or August 1940, or starved out this year in
the Battle of the Atlantic, they would have remained utterly indifferent.'
In the circumstances, Churchill said, he was left 'quite cool' by Russian
reproaches.[14]

Post-war Russian objectives in Europe were much more influential in
moulding British perceptions of the Soviet Union than the 'second front'.
When Stalin first set them out in conversations with Eden in Moscow in
December 1941, the British foreign secretary was clearly impressed by his
relative moderation. He told the editor of the *Manchester Guardian* on 15

---

[12] Clark Kerr to Foreign Office, 25 Sept. 1944, Avon Papers, FO 954/26/461–62.
[13] Christopher Thorne, *Allies of a Kind: The United States, Britain, and the War against
Japan, 1941–1945* (London, 1978).
[14] Gilbert, *Finest Hour*, pp. 1227–8.

January 1942 that people had to make up their minds whether Russia was motivated by Communist ideology or by the ideas of Peter the Great. 'Personally he was convinced that Stalin's policy was that of a Peter-the-Great Russia and that we could, and therefore must, live with her in Europe.' When the editor wondered how far a Peter the Great's ambitions might extend, Eden said that 'Stalin had convinced him that Russia was, and would be, reasonable in her aims.'[15] That these were not merely soothing words for the benefit of public opinion is shown by the fact that he took a virtually identical line in a contemporary letter to the British ambassador to Washington.[16]

At the same time Eden was well aware that a Russian victory on the eastern front would put temptation in Stalin's way and he therefore wished to commit him as far as possible in advance. As he put it on 8 February 1942, 'German collapse this year will be an exclusively Soviet victory with all that implies. Therefore clearly we must do all in our power to lessen grievances and come to terms with him for the future. This may not prevent him from double-crossing us, but it will at least lessen pretexts. He has them now.'[17]

Stalin had insisted that any treaty with Britain must include, as a minimum, British recognition of the annexation of the Baltic States by the Soviet Union, together with the modifications in the Russo-Finnish border following the 'Winter War' of 1939–40. Beyond that the Russian leader had made it clear that his ultimate objective was the restoration of the entire western frontier of the Soviet Union at the time of the German invasion, i.e. including eastern Poland, Bessarabia and northern Bukovina. Initially, Churchill was totally opposed to Soviet incorporation of these territories. 'They were acquired', he reminded Eden on 8 January 1942, 'by acts of aggression in shameful collusion with Hitler.'[18] Eden eventually won him and the rest of the Cabinet round to accepting Stalin's minimum demands, but then the Russians introduced a new condition which set off the alarm bell of mistrust: a secret protocol authorising treaties of guarantee between the Soviet Union and Finland and Romania which would permit the Russians to station troops on their territories. Even Oliver Harvey, who was relatively sympathetic to the security needs of the Soviet Union, jibbed at this. On 21 May 1942, the day the Soviet foreign minister, Vyacheslav Molotov, arrived in London to complete the negotiation of the proposed Anglo-Soviet treaty, Harvey noted in his diary that 'we cannot possibly give way over Finland and Roumania. To acquiesce in these

[15] A.J.P. Taylor, *Off the Record: Political Interviews of W.P. Crozier 1933–43* (London, 1973), p. 266.
[16] Eden to Halifax, 22 Jan. 1942, Avon Papers, FO 954/29/360–62.
[17] Graham Ross, ed., *The Foreign Office and the Kremlin: British Documents on Anglo-Soviet Relations 1941–45* (Cambridge, 1984), pp. 89–90.
[18] Winston S. Churchill, *The Second World War*, IV, *The Hinge of Fate* (Boston, 1950), p. 695.

guarantee pacts would be tantamount to handing them over body and soul to Russia.' As he pointed out, the absorption of the Baltic States had begun with just such pacts.[19]

Whether a satisfactory compromise could have been reached is a matter for speculation, since Molotov finally dropped his insistence upon a treaty incorporating territorial provisions in favour of an alternative draft put forward by the British which established a twenty-year alliance between Britain and the Soviet Union but contained no mention of frontiers. It is sometimes argued that it was American opposition to any commitment over frontiers which was behind the British counter-draft,[20] but domestic politics also played a part. According to Churchill, in October 1943, the reason why Britain abandoned the attempt to reach an agreement on frontiers 'was the perfectly clear menace of very considerable division of opinion in the House of Commons'.[21] In other words, British suspicion of Soviet motives was still very much alive in the summer of 1942.

British ambassadors to the European governments-in-exile in London during the second world war tended to share the fears of those to whom they were accredited concerning post-war Soviet expansionism. In a despatch at the end of 1942 George Rendel, the ambassador to the Jugoslav government-in-exile, raised the spectre of Russian domination of the Balkans after the war, and especially the key importance in this of Bulgaria, where he had also been British ambassador between 1938 and 1941. Sir Orme Sargent, the No. 2 official in the Foreign Office, commented on 11 January 1943 that there was 'no doubt a good deal of foundation for Mr Rendel's fears, and the Russians would be more than human if they did not attempt to turn to their own advantage any developments in the Balkans favourable to themselves'. However, he was 'not convinced that the Soviet Government are consciously planning to dominate the Balkans by means either of Bolshevisation or Pan-Slavism'. Indeed, 'the present trend of Soviet policy, as far as one can judge, appears to be against unlimited expansion'. It was nevertheless possible that the Balkan states would 'collapse into Communism' at the end of the war as a result of economic chaos and he thought that the best way of avoiding this was to enter into direct negotiations with the Russians about an agreed policy in the area. He assumed, he added, that the government was 'definitely opposed' to the policy of leaving this part of Europe exclusively to the Russians as was consistently advocated by – among others – the historian E.H. Carr in leading articles in *The Times*.[22]

Eden agreed with Sargent's conclusions. He had been trying, unsuc-

[19] Harvey, *War Diaries*, p. 126.
[20] E.g. Steven Merritt Miner, *Between Churchill and Stalin: The Soviet Union, Great Britain and the Origins of the Grand Alliance* (Chapel Hill, NC, 1988), pp. 248–9.
[21] Gilbert, *Road to Victory*, pp. 518–19.
[22] Ross, *Foreign Office and the Kremlin*, pp. 119–20.

cessfully, for some time to interest the prime minister in post-war planning. He now resolved to press forward on his own initiative and instructed the British ambassador in Moscow to sound out the Russians about their own ideas. It was not until 16 June 1943, however, that the British Cabinet gave the foreign secretary authorisation to approach both the Soviet and American governments with the concrete proposal that those enemy countries which fell away from the Axis alliance should be controlled on a tripartite basis under the aegis of a tripartite 'United Nations for Europe'. Eden explained that the reason for this proposal was to avoid the creation of an exclusive Soviet sphere of influence in eastern Europe.[23] The Russians did in fact accept the proposal, although its rationale was obviously not put to them, and it was the British and the Americans who almost immediately reneged on it in practice if not in theory in the case of Italy for what appear to have been purely operational reasons.

By the time the British foreign secretary had put forward his proposal the problem of Russian ambitions in eastern Europe had of course become more acute as a result of the break in diplomatic relations between the Soviet Union and the Polish government-in-exile over the Katyn massacre. Eden, as his private secretary recorded at the time, was 'at a loss to know what Stalin is up to',[24] but that did not lessen the need for an agreement with him. Quite the reverse. The British government's attitude to Katyn was in fact extremely muted.[25] Although there was little doubt in London that the Russians were responsible for the killings, *raison d'état* dictated the need not to split the anti-German alliance. Press and radio were asked to play the issue down and the Foreign Office was strengthened in its belief that the Poles should be compelled to accept the Curzon Line as their eastern frontier, in their own best interests as well as those of the British government. As Bell has noted, however, Katyn did mark an important step in the evolution of British public opinion. During the preceding year the latter was dominated by what he calls 'Russomania', an atmosphere in which no one could doubt 'the extent and intensity of admiration for the Soviet Union, concentrated primarily upon its military performance, and rubbing off on the regime and the personal reputation of Stalin'. Katyn precipitated a division in public opinion and although the majority supported the Russian position, a sizeable minority took the side of the Poles and the crisis fuelled anxieties about post-war relations.[26]

Although they did not resolve the Russo-Polish problem, the tripartite foreign ministers' meeting in Moscow in October 1943 and the subsequent 'summit' conference in Teheran in December led to an

[23] Sir Llewellyn Woodward, *British Foreign Policy in the Second World War*, V (London, 1976), pp. 46–50.
[24] Harvey, *War Diaries*, p. 251.
[25] Bell, *John Bull and the Bear*, Chapter 4.
[26] Ibid., pp. 96, 99.

improvement in Anglo-Russian relations. Eden reported to Churchill from Moscow on 29 October 1943 that: There have been many signs during our Conference that the members of the Soviet Government are sincere in their desire to establish relations with ourselves and the United States on a footing of permanent friendship.'[27] The previously cited remark of Churchill's that he got on with Stalin 'like a house on fire' was made in the aftermath of the Teheran conference, and in an exchange of minutes with Eden in January 1944 both men agreed that the Russians should have their 1941 frontiers in Europe, which in fact fell short of those of the Russian empire of 1914.[28] During the course of their exchanges the prime minister admitted that his own feelings had changed since Stalin first raised the matter with Eden in December 1941. 'The tremendous victories of the Russian armies,' he wrote, 'the deep-seated changes which have taken place in the character of the Russian State and Government, the new confidence which has grown in our hearts towards Stalin – these have all had their effect.'[29]

At the same time Churchill admitted that the principal motive for acceding to Soviet demands was one of *Realpolitik*: the Red Army would soon be moving into these disputed areas and there was no means of getting them out. The real issue was how much farther the Russians would go. Alarmed by the Soviet Union's recognition of the government of Italy, from which country's control it had been effectively excluded by the British and the Americans, he asked on 3 April 1944:

Why are they [i.e. the Russians] gate-crashing in Italy in this way? Their conduct could be explained as a calculated attempt to smash all left parties and centre parties save the Communists ... I confess to growing apprehension that Russia has vast aims, and that these may include the domination of Eastern Europe and even the Mediterranean and the 'communising' of much that remains.[30]

A month later Churchill called for a paper on 'the brute issues between us and the Soviet Government which are developing in Italy, in Roumania, in Bulgaria, in Yugoslavia, and above all in Greece ... Broadly speaking the issue is: are we going to acquiesce in the Communisation of the Balkans and perhaps of Italy?'[31]

Both Churchill and Eden were reflecting the importance of the Mediterranean in British policy. It had long been regarded as crucial to Britain's position in the Middle East and India. It had been the principal theatre of operations for the British during the war so far and much effort had

[27] Eden to Churchill, 29 Oct. 1943, Avon Papers, FO 954/26/187.
[28] Sir Llewellyn Woodward, *British Foreign Policy in the Second World War*, III (London, 1971), pp. 112–15.
[29] Gilbert, *Road to Victory*, p. 652.
[30] Victor Rothwell, *Britain and the Cold War 1941–1947* (London, 1982), p. 125; Woodward, *British Foreign Policy*, III, p. 109.
[31] Woodward, *British Foreign Policy*, III, p. 320.

been expended to prevent the Axis powers from extending their control from its northern to its southern shore. The British government had no intention of permitting any other power to threaten its hegemony in the Mediterranean at the end of the war. As Churchill indicated, the danger seemed most acute in Greece. In common with his political masters a Foreign Office official like Oliver Harvey was perfectly willing to grant the Soviet Union its 1941 frontiers, but would have no truck with Communism in Greece. The Communists in the Greek resistance, he wrote in his diary on 7 November 1943, 'are a virulent minority of brigands [and] anti-British'. They were not fighting the Germans, but their moderate fellow countrymen, while at the same time 'accumulating the arms to seize Athens when the day comes and to set up a Communist dictatorship'. British policy must be to prevent this from happening.[32] His successor as Eden's private secretary, Pierson Dixon, wrote on 14 February 1944 that the British were not so attached to Poland as they were to Greece.[33] The Foreign Office certainly was not, which as well as the geographical considerations involved goes a long way towards explaining why the British government intervened with force to prevent a Communist takeover in Greece but eventually abandoned the Poles to their fate.

The problem in the case of Yugoslavia was different. It could not be argued, as in Greece, that the Communist partisans were not killing Germans. Indeed, it was precisely because they seemed much better at it than their non-Communist rivals that the British government threw its weight behind them at the end of 1943. But what of the situation after the war? Fitzroy Maclean, one of Churchill's envoys to Jugoslavia, was 'sure that Tito represents the future government of Yugoslavia, whether we like it or not, a sort of peasant communism, and we should be wise to come to terms and try to guide them'.[34]

In the light of these considerations the genesis and content of the notorious 'percentages agreement' of October 1944 become clear. In Romania – some of which had formerly been part of Russia and which was an Axis power to boot – the Soviet Union would enjoy 90 per cent predominance and 'the others' only 10 per cent. In Greece the percentages were reversed, except that there was no doubt about who 'the others' were: Britain received the 90 per cent. In Bulgaria, which bordered on Greece and on whose territory British post-war planners had pointed out the Russians could 'establish airfields within 100 miles of the Straits',[35] the Soviet Union would obtain 75 per cent and 'the others' 25 per cent, i.e. a significantly more important stake than in Romania. In Yugoslavia – and also in

[32] Harvey, *War Diaries*, p. 320.
[33] Pierson Dixon diary, 14 Feb. 1944, Pierson Dixon Papers in the possession of Mr Piers Dixon and cited with his permission.
[34] Harvey, *War Diaries*, p. 320.
[35] Ross, *Foreign Office and the Kremlin*, p. 143.

Hungary – the division of responsibility would be half and half. Stalin accepted the agreement, although Molotov succeeded in raising the Soviet percentages in both Hungary and Bulgaria to 80, and Churchill freely conceded that the Russians scrupulously honoured it in Greece in December 1944, when British troops suppressed the expected Communist revolt.

If a determination to preserve its position in the Mediterranean was one guiding principle of the British government's foreign policy, another was that the ultimate test of Britain's and the Soviet Union's ability to continue their wartime cooperation into the post-war period lay in their treatment of Germany. This is why there was so much concern in the Foreign Office when, during the course of 1944, the post-hostilities planning staff (PHPS) of the Chiefs of Staff put forward the proposal to build up Germany as a potential ally after the war in order to guard against the possibility of a breakdown of the Anglo-Soviet alliance. The rationale behind this view, which was shared by the Chiefs of Staff themselves, is clearly set out in a diary entry of 27 July 1944 by their chairman, Field Marshal Sir Alan Brooke. 'Should Germany be dismembered or gradually converted to an ally to meet the Russian threat of twenty years hence?' Brooke asked, and in answer to his own question 'suggested the latter and feel certain that we must from now onwards regard Germany in a very different light. Germany is no longer the dominating power in Europe – Russia is. Unfortunately Russia is not entirely European. She has, however, vast resources and cannot fail to became the main threat in fifteen years from now. Therefore, foster Germany, gradually build her up and bring her into a Federation of Western Europe.'[36] To the Foreign Office any attempt to implement such a policy, which could hardly remain secret, would bring about the very threat it was designed to forestall. The better policy would be to join with the Soviet Union in holding Germany down.

Much has been made of this disagreement by some historians in order to contrast the prophetic insight of Britain's military as opposed to the purblind 'appeasement' of its diplomats.[37] This is to go too far. As Gladwyn Jebb, the Foreign Office representative on the PHPS, pointed out on 28 July 1944, the Chiefs of Staff 'do not dispute that it would be in our interest to achieve a World Organisation, or anyhow an alliance between the three Great Powers, but they are ... "profoundly sceptical" of a World Organisation ever coming into being and ... of the United States ever coming to our assistance in time if we should get into serious trouble on the continent.'[38] In other words, they did not wish to treat the Soviet Union as an actual enemy, but merely as the only potential one. In practice this was not very different from the Foreign Office's own position.

---

[36] Sir Arthur Bryant, *Triumph in the West* (London, 1959), p. 242.
[37] E.g. Julian Lewis, *Changing Direction: British Military Planning for Post-War Strategic Defence, 1942–47* (London, 1988).
[38] Ross, *Foreign Office and the Kremlin*, p. 160.

As one of the officials most commonly dubbed an appeaser remarked on 10 August 1944, it agreed with the military that the Soviet Union was 'the only power in Europe that can be a danger to our security' and was, as we have seen, resolved to hold the line against the Russians in the Mediterranean. 'The difference between us', this official continued, 'is ... one of method and not of principle, though we may take different views as to the imminence of the Russian danger.'[39]

As far as the treatment of Germany was concerned, considerable agreement was in fact reached during 1944 in the European Advisory Commission, the only relic of Eden's 1943 proposal for a tripartite body to supervise post-war policy in former Axis Europe. In particular, agreements were drawn up on the instrument of German surrender, the machinery for allied control of the occupied country and the boundaries of the zones of occupation themselves. The chief obstacle in the way of these agreements was not Anglo-Soviet antagonism, but the inability of the United States government to get its act together.

Throughout 1944 the British put enormous pressure on the Polish government-in-exile in London to accept the Russian proposals concerning Poland's western frontier in the hope that this concession would dissuade the Soviet Union from imposing a puppet regime on the liberated country. The Poles refused and the Russians recognised the Communist Lublin government on 5 January 1945. Two days later Cadogan told the Polish ambassador that it looked as though the Lublin government would impose the collective farm system among other things. 'Each successive development would make it harder to turn the clock back', he added; 'but he did not see how one could do anything about such events except deplore them, since Britain was in no position to deflect Russia from her course.'[40] The British did try to do something about the situation in Poland at the Yalta conference in February 1945 and the Russians agreed to some concessions. It is difficult to believe, however, that they were regarded by either side as more than cosmetic. The British government was probably more concerned at the possibility of a backlash over Poland from a public opinion already alarmed by the Katyn massacre and the Warsaw uprising. That this was not a figment of its imagination was shown by the Conservative rebellion in the House of Commons over the agreements reached at Yalta. Although small scale it was significant.

Churchill certainly had no illusions about Yalta. In a conversation with the commander-in-chief of the Royal Air Force's Bomber Command, Sir Arthur Harris, on 23 February 1945, he asked, 'What will lie between the white snows of Russia and the white cliffs of Dover' once Harris had finished his destruction of Germany? 'Perhaps, however, the Russians

---

[39] Ibid., p. 161.
[40] Edward Raczynski, *In Allied London: The Wartime Diaries of the Polish Ambassador in London* (London, 1962), p. 262.

would not want to sweep on to the Atlantic', he continued, 'or something might stop them as the accident of Ghenghis Khan's death had stopped the horsed archers of the Mongols.' In any event, the prime minister said, Britain would be weak at the end of the war: 'we should have no money and no strength and we should lie between the two great powers of the USA and the USSR. If he lived, he should concentrate on one thing: the air'.[41]

In their efforts to stem the outflow of Russian power the British vainly urged the Americans to push on as far and as fast as possible into Germany, Austria and Czechoslovakia. The chiefs of staff were even instructed to draw up a military plan for opposing the Soviet Union, but as Brooke commented in his diary for 24 May 1945, 'The idea is, of course, fantastic and the chances of success quite impossible. There is no doubt that from now onwards Russia is all-powerful in Europe.'[42]

By the time the inter-allied conference at Potsdam took place in July 1945 the Soviet Union was pushing for territorial concessions in Turkey, a United Nations trusteeship in north Africa and further improvements to the already substantial gains in east Asia promised to Stalin by President Roosevelt at Yalta in return for Russian entry into the war against Japan – an agreement which Eden had urged Churchill not to sign. 'You mentioned in conversation yesterday', the foreign secretary wrote to the prime minister on 17 July, 'that the Russian policy was one of aggrandisement. This is undoubtedly true.'[43] In view of its waning economic and military strength, what was the British government's response to be?

It fell to a new Labour government, elected by a landslide in July 1945, to solve this problem. Its solution, according to some scholars, was 'to compensate for relative weakness by manoeuvering the USA against the USSR within the "Big Three" framework'.[44] This 'manoeuvering' took the form of enlisting American support for British interests which were felt to be under threat from the Soviet Union. The key figure in this process is seen to be the new foreign secretary, the bluff and belligerent former trade union leader, Ernest Bevin, whose policies led to a degree of reverence among Conservatives for a politician of the opposition party matched only by the contempt of those on the left wing of his own.

It was certainly true that Bevin was greatly concerned by the Russian threat in the Mediterranean and the Middle East. Alluding to the Soviet request for a United Nations trusteeship in Tripolitania, he told the House of Commons on 7 November 1945 that 'one cannot help being a little suspicious if a great Power wants to come right across . . . the throat of the

---

[41] Colville, *Fringes of Power*, pp. 563–64.
[42] Bryant, *Triumph in the West*, pp. 469–70.
[43] The Earl of Avon, *The Eden Memoirs: The Reckoning* (London, 1965), p. 546.
[44] Peter J. Taylor, *Britain and the Cold War: 1945 as Geopolitical Transition* (London, 1990), p. 107.

British Commonwealth'.[45] And referring to the Soviet Union's territorial demands upon Turkey and its apparent attempt to stir up a secessionist movement in northern Iran, he told two influential American Republicans, Senator Arthur Vandenberg and John Foster Dulles, on 24 January 1946, 'how the Russians were trying to wrap one arm to the west round the Straits and the other arm round the eastern end of Turkey by acquiring the provinces of Kars and Ardahan', and that 'after undermining the Persian province of Azerbaijan the Russians hoped to penetrate through Kurdistan and so further wrap the arms of the bear round the eastern end of Turkey, as well as imperilling the oilfields of Mosul [in Iraq]'.[46]

Vandenberg and Dulles were in London as members of the American delegation to the first session of the new United Nations Organisation. This promised to be a lively affair, since the Iranian government had appealed to the Security Council about Russian policy in Azerbaijan and the Soviet Union had retaliated by tabling complaints about the conduct of British troops in Greece and also in Indonesia, where they were helping the Dutch to reestablish control in the face of armed opposition from local nationalists. After a tough session on Indonesia in the Security Council on 10 February 1946, Bevin's principal private secretary recorded, 'Hardly any doubt any longer that Russia is intent on the destruction of the British Empire.'[47]

If this was true, it was very serious. But was it? Hard intelligence on Soviet objectives was scarce. As the Joint Intelligence Committee of the chiefs of staff reported on 1 March 1946, 'We have practically no direct intelligence ... on conditions in the different parts of the Soviet Union, and none at all on the intentions, immediate or ultimate, of the Russian leaders.' This did not, of course, prevent the committee from speculating that the latter 'will consider it important to create and consolidate round the frontier of Russia a "belt" of satellite States with governments subservient to their policy', which would extend into Turkey and 'the major parts of Persia'. Although the Soviet Union would probably seek to avoid major war for at least another five years, a conflict brought about by miscalculation could not be ruled out.[48]

When this report was sent to Moscow for his comments, the British chargé d'affaires Frank Roberts replied, on 21 March, that he was in general agreement with what he described as a 'very well-balanced' document. At the same time, Roberts suggested that the Soviet Union's ambitions were even more extensive than those indicated by the committee. He

[45] Parliamentary Debates, House of Commons, 5th ser., vol. 415, col. 1342.
[46] Roger Bullen and M.E. Pelly, eds., *Documents on British Policy Overseas*, ser. I, vol. IV, *Britain and America: Atomic Energy, Bases and Food 12 December 1945–31 July 1946* (London, 1987), no. 18.
[47] Dixon diary, 10 Feb. 1946, Pierson Dixon Papers.
[48] M.E. Pelly, H.J. Yasamee and K.A. Hamilton (assisted by G. Bennett), *Documents on British Policy Overseas*, ser. I, vol. VI, *Eastern Europe 1945–1946* (London, 1991), no. 78.

thought, for example, that its ultimate objectives included 'a Germany looking East and under Soviet influence', the whole of Iran and the extension of its influence 'throughout [the] Arab world and in [the] Aegean and [the] Eastern Mediterranean'.[49]

Meanwhile, on 5 March 1946, Churchill had made a speech in Fulton in Missouri, which, though he was now in opposition, caused a sensation. 'Nobody knows', he said, 'what Soviet Russia and its Communist international organisation intends to do in the immediate future, or what are the limits, if any, to their expansive or proselytising tendencies.' However, 'an iron curtain' had descended across Europe and to the east of it its population was 'subject in one form or another, not only to Soviet influence but to a very high and increasing measure of control from Moscow'. The region's Communist parties had 'been raised to pre-eminence and power far beyond their numbers', they were 'seeking everywhere to obtain totalitarian control' and the police state had prevailed in almost every case. He went on to draw his audience's attention to the dangers in Turkey and Iran, in Germany, and even in France and Italy with their large Communist parties. Across the globe, indeed, though mercifully not in the British Commonwealth or the United States, 'the Communist parties or fifth columns constitute a growing challenge and peril to Christian civilisation'. In order to combat the threat, Churchill called for 'a special relationship between the British Commonwealth and Empire and the United States', which would include the closest possible military collaboration.[50]

The Fulton speech summed up the growing consensus in the Foreign Office. 'I must say', Pierson Dixon noted in his diary, 'Winston's speech echoes the sentiments of all.'[51] By 2 April 1946, according to one historian, the consensus had jelled sufficiently to justify being seen as the 'precise date' upon which Britain's Cold War policy towards the Soviet Union was born.[52] Two important developments did take place on the date in question. The first was that Christopher Warner, the superintending under-secretary for the northern and southern departments of the Foreign Office (which dealt with the Soviet Union and the Mediterranean), wrote a memorandum entitled 'The Soviet campaign against this country and our response to it'. The second was the first meeting of the so-called 'Russia committee' of Foreign Office officials. In his memorandum, Warner wrote that 'the Soviet Government, both in their recent pronouncements and in their actions have made it clear that they have decided upon an aggressive

[49] Pelly et al., *Eastern Europe 1945–1946*, nos. 84, 85, 86.
[50] Fraser J. Harbutt, *The Iron Curtain: Churchill, America and the Origins of the Cold War* (New York, 1986), pp. 186–7.
[51] Dixon diary, 6 Mar. 1946, Pierson Dixon Papers.
[52] John Zametica, 'Three Letters to Bevin: Frank Roberts at the Moscow Embassy, 1945–46', in John Zametica, ed., *British Officials and Foreign Policy 1945–50* (Leicester, 1990), p. 87.

policy, based upon militant Communism and Russian chauvinism. They have launched an offensive against Social Democracy and against this country.' The reason why Britain had been singled out for attack was not only because it was 'the leader of Social Democracy', but also because it was 'the more vulnerable of the two great Western powers'. In retaliation Warner called for 'a defensive-offensive' campaign which would take the form of attacking and exposing Communism wherever it showed itself.[53] Warner spoke to this memorandum at the meeting of the 'Russia committee', the task of which was, 'to review . . . the development of all aspects of Soviet propaganda and Soviet activities throughout the world, more particularly with reference to the Soviet campaign against this country' and to come up with the necessary counter-measures.[54]

Like Frank Roberts and Churchill before him, Warner mentioned Russian policy in Germany. Under the agreements reached during the war, culminating at the Potsdam conference, Germany was occupied by British, French, Russian and American troops. Each power had its own separate occupation zone, together with its own sector of Berlin, which was situated inside the Soviet zone. At the same time, jointly agreed policies designed to prevent Germany from again becoming a threat to world peace were meant to be implemented throughout the country. In other words, Germany was not to be dismembered, as had been suggested at various stages during the war, but treated as a single country. In practice, however, this did not happen. Initially, the French were mainly to blame. They not only wanted to annex parts of Germany for themselves, but also to break up the rest of the country in order to weaken it, and consequently vetoed every proposal to set up any form of central authority. The Russians were not far behind. First of all they effectively sealed off their zone from contact with the others; and secondly, in February 1946, set about enforcing a merger between the Communist and Socialist parties in their zone.

These developments gave rise to considerable alarm in Britain. There were two main reasons for this. The first was economic and financial. The British zone in Germany was predominantly industrial and it could not feed itself. Food had therefore to be imported and, ideally, much of it should have come from the Soviet zone in exchange for industrial products. But, if the Russians sealed off their zone, this exchange was impossible and the British occupation authorities had to find the food from elsewhere, which added to their already considerable costs. The second reason was political. It was felt that Russian policy was designed not only to consolidate Soviet control in eastern Germany, but to cause problems in the western zones which the newly fused (and Communist-dominated) Socialist Unity Party would exploit in order to take over the rest of the

---

[53] Pelly et al., *Eastern Europe 1945–1946*, no. 88.
[54] R. Merrick, 'The Russia Committee of the British Foreign Office and the Cold War, 1946–7', *Journal of Contemporary History*, 20 (1985), 255.

country. On 23 March 1946, Sir Orme Sargent, who had just taken over from Cadogan as the senior official in the Foreign Office, wrote to Bevin that the time had come to decide what policy to pursue in Germany. 'Should we', he asked, 'proceed on the assumption that we must prepare for a German government which will govern the whole of Germany from Berlin or should we merely concentrate on ensuring that anti-Communist forces are strongly established in our own zone?'[55]

What Sargent was in fact asking was: should Britain, by continuing to support the wartime agreements, run the risk of handing over Germany to Soviet control through the agency of a Communist-dominated central government, or should it try and save as much of Germany as possible by abandoning those agreements and partitioning the country? The issue was discussed at a special meeting chaired by Bevin in the Foreign Office on 3 April 1946, the day after the Warner memorandum was produced. It was decided to draw up a paper for the Cabinet setting out the implications of both courses of action.

Just as Bevin sought to alert the Americans to the Soviet threat in the middle east – as, for example, in his conversation with Dulles and Vandenberg on 24 January 1946 – so he also told his officials on 3 April that 'we must carry the Americans with us' over Germany.[56] The Joint Intelligence Committee, Frank Roberts, Warner and Churchill had all advocated a united front between Britain and the United States to resist Soviet expansion. Without one, it was feared, the Russians might feel less inhibited about challenging an isolated Britain. The argument that Britain sought to engineer a confrontation between the United States and the Soviet Union in order to protect its own interests would therefore seem to be quite plausible.

Unfortunately, it contains two major flaws. The first is that, while a great deal of research on American foreign policy has shown that the United States moved to a position of hostility towards the Soviet Union by the beginning of 1946, it provides no evidence that this movement occurred as a result of British influence. The second major flaw is that while Foreign Office officials (and, of course, the Chiefs of Staff) may have reached a consensus that the Russians not only posed an immediate and serious threat to Britain but must also be resisted in every way possible, their view was by no means shared by the Cabinet. Indeed, at a meeting of the 'Russia Committee' on 14 May 1946, one of the officials present said that he had gained the impression from a recent Cabinet discussion that there was not complete agreement on Russian policy. 'Some ministers, he said, took the line that it would be wrong to consider Russia to be "hostile" to this country, that we should not treat the Soviet Union as

[55] Rolf Steininger, ed., *Die Ruhrfrage 1945/46 und die Entstehung des Landes Nordrhein-Westfalen* (Düsseldorf, 1988), no. 112, n. 1.
[56] Steininger, *Die Ruhrfrage 1945/46*, no. 112.

an "enemy" and so on.'[57] These ministers included, it should be emphasised, such important members of the government as Herbert Morrison and Hugh Dalton, leader of the House of Commons and chancellor of the exchequer respectively.

Even Bevin was not as anti-Soviet as he has sometimes been portrayed. At the meeting in the Foreign Office on 3 April to discuss German policy, his immediate reaction to the proposal to divide Germany was that 'this meant a policy of the Western Bloc and that meant war'.[58] Moreover, when the foreign secretary threatened at the Paris meeting of the council of ministers on 10 July 1946 to go ahead and run the British occupation zone in Germany on its own if agreement could not be reached on treating the country as an economic unit, he did not do so deliberately in order to provoke that division, as some have suggested.[59] This is shown by his response to the proposal which the US secretary of state made on the following day for cooperation between those zones which were willing to work together. He told the Cabinet on 15 July that the Americans wanted to exclude the Russians and he thought 'that it would be a mistake at this stage to commit ourselves irrevocably to a measure which implied a clear division between Western and Eastern Germany'. He only accepted the American proposal, in fact, after he was assured by his officials that it was the only practical solution to the problem of the financial drain caused by the deficit in the British zone – which was the reason for his original threat – and that it did not foreclose the possibility of the eventual unity of Germany.[60]

Similarly, although the Warner memorandum of 2 April 1946, with its call for a 'defensive-offensive' campaign against the Soviet Union, was approved for wider circulation, this did not mean that its contents were wholeheartedly endorsed by the government, and when another Foreign Office official drew up a detailed programme for implementing anti-Communist propaganda along the lines proposed by Warner, Bevin vetoed it. He eventually agreed to a limited operation in Iran, but commented, 'I am not going to commit myself to the whole of ... [this] scheme in order to tackle Persia.'[61] Despite his earlier attempts to frighten Senator Vandenberg and John Foster Dulles about the extent of Soviet ambitions in the middle east, moreover, it was none other than Bevin who panicked in

---

[57] Howe minute, 17 May 1946, Public Records Office, London (hereafter PRO), FO 371/ 56784/N6733/G).
[58] Unsigned 'Notes on Meeting held at the Foreign Office on the 3rd April, 1946', PRO, FO 945/16.
[59] E.g. Anne Deighton, *The Impossible Peace: Britain, the Division of Germany, and the Origins of the Cold War* (Oxford, 1990), pp. 105, 225.
[60] Cabinet minutes, CM (46) 68, 15 July 1946, PRO CAB 128/6; Dean minute, 23 July 1946, PRO FO 371/55589/C8643.
[61] Raymond Smith, 'A Climate of Opinion: British Officials and the Development of British Soviet Policy, 1945–7', *International Affairs*, 64 (1988), 639–41.

March when, in response to Russian troop movements in northern Iran, the Americans took a strong line and the troops were subsequently withdrawn. At the height of the crisis a Cabinet colleague recorded that he found the foreign secretary 'in a great state, saying that the Russians were advancing in full force on Teheran, that "this means war", and that the US were going to send a battle fleet to the Mediterranean'.[62]

Bevin did, in fact, contemplate concessions to the Soviet Union in Iran in order to protect British interests in the country. Alluding to the fear expressed to him by Stalin in a conversation in December 1945, he wrote to Sargent on 5 July 1946 that he had been thinking for some time of asking the Soviet government, 'what do they require of us in order to feel sure that the British are not going to interfere with them in Baku?' He realised that the Russians might interpret such an approach 'as an offer to divide Persia into spheres of influence', but it might be presented in a different way, by 'telling them that we must face facts, and that the facts are that we have no intention of interfering with their commercial interests in north Persia and in return expect a hands-off attitude towards our interests in south Persia'.[63] It was the Americans who encouraged the Iranian government to put an end to Azerbaijani separatism by armed force in December 1946.

At about the same time, Bevin returned from the New York meeting of the council of foreign ministers, which had finally reached agreement on peace treaties with Italy, Romania, Bulgaria, Hungary and Finland. According to Christopher Mayhew, one of his junior ministers, he was 'full of repressed optimism and delight and self-congratulation', cited the remark of the Soviet foreign minister, Vyacheslav Molotov, on the boat back to Europe – 'I think we are learning now to cooperate' – and attributed much of the toughness and bitterness of Russian diplomatic methods to the inexperience of their officials.[64] None of this provides any support for the view that Bevin took the lead in fomenting the Cold War.

If Bevin was less of a Cold War hawk than some have argued, the Labour prime minister, Clement Attlee, was positively doveish. During the first eighteen months of the Labour government the prime minister fought hard for a fundamental revision of British policy which involved nothing less than complete withdrawal from the eastern Mediterranean and the Middle East. His arguments were fourfold. The first was military and based upon his conviction that the British position in the Mediterranean had been based upon sea power and that in an age of air power and the

---

[62] Ben Pimlott, ed., *The Political Diary of Hugh Dalton, 1918–40, 1945–60* (London, 1986), p. 368.

[63] Bevin to Sargent, 5 July 1946, PRO, FO 371/52717/E6460. I owe this reference to Dr Ann Lane of Queen's University, Belfast.

[64] Christopher Mayhew diary, 20 Dec. 1946, Christopher Mayhew Papers, in the possession of Lord Mayhew and cited with his permission.

atomic bomb it was simply not possible to maintain it in wartime. Secondly, he felt that Britain could only rely upon a 'congeries of weak, backward and reactionary States' in order to sustain its present policy.[65] Thirdly, the policy was too expensive anyway; and finally, it was unnecessarily provocative towards the Soviet Union, which must feel threatened by the deployment of British forces so close to its borders. The prime minister's own policy, as summarised by Dalton on 9 March 1946, was that, 'We should pull out ... from all the Middle East, including Egypt and Greece, make a line of defence across Africa from Lagos to Kenya, and concentrate a large part of our forces in the latter ... We should [then] put a wide glacis of desert and Arabs between ourselves and the Russians.'[66] In addition, at the end of 1946, Attlee proposed negotiations with the Russians for the neutralisation of the middle east.

As chancellor of the exchequer, Dalton found Attlee's approach 'very fresh and interesting'. This was due to the huge burden of Britain's defence and overseas expenditure, which he was determined to reduce. 'I am ... resisting suggestions from the F[oreign] O[ffice]', the chancellor wrote on 29 November 1946, 'to spend large sums on Greeks, Turks and Afghans. I sent a minute to the P[rime] M[inister] saying that we have not got the money for this sort of thing and that, even if we had, we should not spend it on *these* people.'[67]

Opposition to Attlee came principally from the Chiefs of Staff and from Bevin. The former regarded the prime minister's attitude as 'past belief' and 'defeatist'.[68] They based their views on the belief set out in a memorandum of 2 April 1946 that '[a] conflict with Russia is the only situation in which it at present seems that the British Commonwealth might again become involved in a major war' and that it was therefore vital to hold the Middle East, not least because it was one of the few areas from which a counter-attack – by bombing Soviet oil fields and industrial centres – could be mounted.[69] Bevin, as we saw earlier, was also concerned about Russian pressure in the Mediterranean and the Middle East. Apart from the economic importance of oil, however, he chose as foreign secretary to emphasise the political importance of holding the area. Abandoning it, he argued, would leave a power vacuum into which the Russians would inevitably move and this would in turn threaten the stability of the whole of southern Europe. Negotiation with the Soviet Union would achieve nothing, but the effect of withdrawal upon the United States would be

---

[65] Ronald Hyam, ed., *British Documents on the End of Empire*, ser. A, II, *The Labour Government and the End of Empire 1945–1951*, part 3, *Strategy, Politics and Constitutional Change* (London, 1992), no. 281.

[66] Hugh Dalton, *Memoirs 1945–1960: High Tide and After* (London, 1960) p. 105.

[67] Ibid., p. 171.

[68] Raymond Smith and John Zametica, 'The Cold Warrior: Clement Attlee Reconsidered, 1945–7', *International Affairs*, 61 (1985), 245–6.

[69] Hyam, *Strategy, Politics and Constitutional Change*, no. 321.

'disastrous', the United Nations would be 'imperilled' and the consequences for the Dominions 'incalculable'.[70]

On 13 January 1947, without prior warning, Attlee capitulated to the opposition, approving an early draft of what was later to become the first of several post-war global strategy papers by the chiefs of staff and which identified as one of the three pillars of British defence policy '[a] firm hold in the Middle East and its development as an offensive base'.[71] What prompted the prime minister's sudden reversal? According to Field Marshal Lord Montgomery, who had succeeded Brooke as chairman in June 1946, it was nothing less than the threat of a mass resignation of the chiefs of staff, organised by Montgomery himself.[72] 'Monty', however, was always prone to exaggerate his own importance and one scholar has argued that the field marshal was in no position to organise anything, being abroad at the time the dispute reached its climax. The same scholar suggests that, in view of the opposition from Bevin and the chiefs of staff to his ideas, 'The only way forward for Attlee would have been to appeal over their heads to the Cabinet' and that he did not wish to take the risk.[73] This is probably as near as we are likely to get to the truth.

Attlee did, however, obtain two important concessions from his opponents: agreement on the need to withdraw British troops from Greece and Palestine. It was as a consequence of this agreement that two notes were presented to the United States government on 21 February 1947 announcing that in view of the country's financial position Britain could no longer provide aid for either Greece or Turkey. This in turn precipitated the formulation and enunciation of the so-called 'Truman doctrine' by the American president in a speech to Congress on 12 March. This speech was undoubtedly another milestone on the road to the Cold War. It was also undoubtedly brought about by British policy. As Robert Frazier has demonstrated, however, the British government did not deliberately set out to provoke a shift in American policy, but was merely responding to Britain's own economic imperatives.[74] Ironically, too, although the number of British troops in Greece was reduced, a sizeable contingent remained at American request until after the Greek government's victory over the Communists in 1949.

The 'Truman doctrine' was proclaimed shortly after the beginning of the Moscow meeting of the council of ministers (10 March–24 April 1947). Not surprisingly, it did little to improve the atmosphere of this meeting,

---

[70] Ibid., no. 282.
[71] Lewis, *Changing Direction*, p. 380.
[72] *The Memoirs of Field-Marshal Montgomery* (London, 1958), p. 436.
[73] John G. Albert, 'Attlee, the Chiefs of Staff and the Restructuring of "Commonwealth Defence" between VJ Day and the Outbreak of the Korean War' (D.Phil., University of Oxford, 1986), pp. 83–5.
[74] Robert Frazier, 'Did Britain Start the Cold War? Bevin and the Truman Doctrine', *Historical Journal*, 27 (1984), 715–27.

which was devoted largely to the quest for a solution to the problem of
Germany, where the British and the Americans had formed their 'bizone',
the French were hesitating and the Russians standing pat. In contrast to
the US secretary of state, George Marshall, who told his official biographer
in 1956 that it was at Moscow that he finally came to the conclusion that
it was impossible to reach a settlement with the Russians,[75] Bevin's attitude was more sanguine. Indeed, he wrote that 'Mr Molotov was beginning
to come to a better understanding of the attitude of His Majesty's Government and to show some sympathy for it.'[76] But his patience was not
inexhaustible and after his return from Moscow he told Christopher
Mayhew – who recorded it in his diary for 26 May 1947 – that Stalin was
'a dreadful fellow' and that if things went on as they were, he would give
up hope of a settlement with the Russians after the next meeting of the
council of foreign ministers in London in November.[77]

This surely implies, however, that – unlike Marshall – he had not given
up hope yet, an interpretation which is supported by his initial reaction
to the latter's famous Harvard speech on 5 June 1947, in which he floated
the idea of an economic recovery programme for Europe to be drawn up by
the European countries themselves with American assistance. The Soviet
Union was invited to take part along with all other European countries,
but it was neither expected nor indeed hoped that it would. When the
Russians agreed to attend the initial conference which Britain and France
had convened in Paris in order to discuss Marshall's offer, however, Bevin
took a completely different view. 'Perhaps they *will* play after all', he opti-
mistically told a ministerial colleague.[78]

They did not. To have accepted American aid or to have permitted their
eastern European satellites to do so would, as Pierson Dixon noted on 2
July 1947, 'introduce western methods and ideas into the Eastern European systems, and thus undermine Soviet influence. It might even undermine the Soviet regime itself.' When Molotov attacked Marshall's proposal,
Bevin murmured to Dixon, 'This really is the birth of the Western bloc.'[79]

As the year progressed east-west relations continued to deteriorate. The
western European countries and the United States sought to put flesh on
the bones of Marshall's original proposal in the shape of the 'Marshall
plan', while the Soviet Union set up the Cominform in reply in September
1947. Finally, the London meeting of the council of foreign ministers
broke down without agreement in December.

Both the speed and nature of Bevin's reaction to this last development
indicate that, in contrast to his position the previous June, he anticipated

[75] Forrest C. Pogue, *George C. Marshall: Statesman 1945–1959* (New York, 1987), p. 196.
[76] Undated Bevin memorandum, PRO, FO 800/447.
[77] Mayhew diary, 26 May 1947, Christopher Mayhew Papers.
[78] Francis Williams, *Ernest Bevin* (London, 1952), p. 265.
[79] Dixon diary, 2 July 1947, Pierson Dixon Papers.

failure and had given a great deal of thought to what should be done next. Early in January 1948 Bevin presented four separate memoranda to the Cabinet in which he set out the nature of the Soviet threat and his proposals for dealing with it. These included the creation of 'some form of union in Western Europe ... backed by the Americas and the Dominions',[80] the establishment of a west German state on democratic lines, which would not only prevent a Soviet takeover of the whole country but also act as a powerful magnet for the Germans in the Russian zone, and an all-out propaganda offensive against Communism, the basis for which should be Britain's social democratic ideology. All his proposals were accepted. Two months later, following the Communist takeover in Czechoslovakia, Bevin informed his Cabinet colleagues that despite all the efforts which had been made since the war to reach an amicable settlement with the Soviet Union.

not only is the Soviet Government not prepared at the present stage to cooperate in any real sense with any non-Communist or non-Communist controlled Government, but it is actively preparing to extend its hold over the remaining part of continental Europe and, subsequently, over the Middle East and no doubt the bulk of the Far East as well. In other words, physical control of the whole World Island is what the Politburo is aiming at – no less a thing than that.[81]

Public opinion was completely behind the government. A poll in August/September 1948, for example, showed that no less than 91 per cent of Britons believed that the Soviet Union wanted to dominate the world, compared with only 38 per cent of Italians and 30 per cent of French people.[82] In so far as these developments marked the abandonment of any hope of an accommodation with the Russians together with the determination to mobilise the 'free world' against the threat of Communist aggression and subversion, they may be said to mark the British government's declaration of the Cold War.

One major American book on the origins of the Cold War is entitled *From Trust to Terror*.[83] This implies that the Cold War was an aberration, the unfortunate outcome of the breakdown of the wartime alliance. It would be more accurate to see the latter as an enforced and uneasy four-year truce in seven decades of suspicion and hostility between the Soviet Union and the capitalist world. As this essay has endeavoured to show, there was not much in the way of 'trust' between Britain and Russia at

---

[80] Ronald Hyam, ed., *British Documents on the End of Empire*, ser. A, vol. II, *The Labour Government and the End of Empire 1945–1951*, Part 2. *Economics and International Relations* (London, 1992), no. 142.

[81] Hyam, *Economics and International Relations*, no. 145.

[82] Geoffrey Warner, 'The United States and France and Italy', in The Open University's Course A324, *Liberation and Reconstruction: Politics, Culture and Society in France and Italy, 1943–1954* (Milton Keynes, 1990), p. 11.

[83] Herbert Feis, *From Trust to Terror: The Origins of the Cold War 1945–1950* (New York, 1970).

any stage during the period it covers. There was always a suspicion on the British side that the Soviet Union represented a threat to Britain's interests and that suspicion progressively hardened into certainty. By 1946 the Foreign Office and the military were united in their view that Soviet hostility was implacable. It was another eighteen months, however, before ministers were entirely persuaded. Suggestions that Britain somehow engineered the Cold War confrontation between the United States and the Soviet Union in order to further its own interests are wide of the mark. Britain was more willing than the United States not only to accept but to endorse an expanded Russian sphere of influence. What it was not prepared to accept was any encroachment upon its own.

Works by Zara Steiner

Books

Steiner, Zara, *The U.S. State Department and the Foreign Service*
(Princeton, 1958)
   Present Problems of the Foreign Service (Princeton, 1961)
   The Foreign Office and Foreign Policy 1898–1914 (Cambridge, 1969)
   Britain and the Origins of the First World War (London, 1977)
   *The Reconstruction of Europe, 1919–1941 (Oxford History of Modern
   Europe Series* (Oxford, forthcoming)
Steiner, Zara (ed.), *The Times Survey of the Foreign Ministries of the
World* (London, 1982) and 'Introduction'

Articles

Cromwell, Valerie, and Steiner, Zara, 'The Foreign Office before 1914: a
study in resistance', in G. Sutherland, ed., *Studies in the Growth of
Nineteenth Century Government* (London, 1972)
'Reform and retrenchment: the Foreign Office between the wars', in
Roger Bullen ed., *The Foreign Office, 1782–1982* (Frederick, MA,
1984)
Dockrill, M.L., and Steiner, Zara, 'The Foreign Office at the Paris Peace
Conference', *International History Review*, 2 (1980)
Eckstein, M.G., and Steiner, Zara, 'The Sarajevo Crisis', in F.H. Hinsley
ed., *British Foreign Policy under Sir Edward Grey* (Cambridge, 1977)
Steiner, Zara, and Dockrill, M.L., 'The Foreign Office reforms, 1919–
1921', *The Historical Journal*, 17 (1974)
Steiner, Zara, 'The Foreign Office and the war', in F.H. Hinsley, ed.,
British Foreign Policy under Sir Edward Grey (Cambridge, 1977)

Steiner, Zara, 'The Foreign Office under Sir Edward Grey', in F.H. Hinsley, ed., *British Foreign Policy under Sir Edward Grey* (Cambridge, 1977)

Steiner, Zara, 'Elitism and foreign policy: the Foreign Office before the Great War', in B.J.C. McKercher and D.J. Moss, eds., *Shadow and Substance in British Foreign Policy 1895–1939. Memorial Essays Honouring C.J. Lowe* (Edmonton, 1984)

Steiner, Zara, 'The diplomatic life: reflections on selected diplomatic memoirs written before and after the Great War', in G. Egerton, ed., *Political Memoir: Essays on the Politics of Memory* (London, 1994)

Select bibliography

Unpublished British government records

Cabinet, CAB 2, CAB 4, CAB 16, CAB 23, CAB 24, CAB 27, CAB 65, CAB
66, CAB 79
Foreign Office, FO 65, FO 262, FO 366, FO 371, FO 412, FO 608,
FO 794, FO 945
Prime Ministers' Papers, PREM 4

Unpublished private papers

Field Marshal Lord Alanbrooke, Liddell Hart Centre for Military Archives,
King's College, London
General H.H. Arnold, Library of Congress, Washington DC
Lord Avon, Birmingham University Library
Arthur Balfour, British Library
Lord Baldwin of Bewdley, Cambridge University Library
Sir Henry Beaumont, Imperial War Museum
Sir Francis Bertie, British Library
Sir Francis Bertie, Public Record Office
Ernest Bevin, Public Record Office
Lord Robert Cecil, British Library
Austen Chamberlain, Birmingham University Library
Austen Chamberlain, Public Record Office
Neville Chamberlain, Birmingham University Library
Lord Chatfield, National Maritime Museum, Greenwich
Group Captain Christie, Churchill College Cambridge
Lord Crewe, Cambridge University Library
Lord Curzon, India Office Library

Lord D'Abernon, British Library
Hugh Dalton, British Library of Economic and Political Science
Sir Pierson Dixon
David Lloyd George, House of Lords Record Office
Lord Granville, Public Record Office
Sir Edward Grey, Public Record Office
Lord Hankey, Churchill College, Cambridge
Lord Hardinge, Cambridge University Library
Sir Basil Liddell Hart, Liddell Hart Centre for Military Archives, King's
    College, London
Sir James Headlam-Morley, Churchill College, Cambridge
Hickleton Papers, Borthwick Institute of Historical Research, University
    of York
Sir Esme Howard, Cumbria County Record Office, Carlisle
Marquess of Lansdowne, Public Record Office
Sir Frank Lascelles, Public Record Office
Lord Lothian, Scottish Record Office
James Ramsay MacDonald, Public Record Office
General George C. Marshall, George C. Marshall Library, Lexington, VA
Christopher Mayhew
Lord Morley, India Office Library
Sir Arthur Nicolson, Public Record Office
Sir Eric Phipps, Churchill College, Cambridge
Earl of Selborne, Bodleian Library, Oxford
Lord Templewood, Cambridge University Library
Sir Robert Vansittart, Churchill College, Cambridge

Newspapers

Economist
The Guardian
London Review of Books
News Chronicle
Review of Reviews
The Times
Material from the *The Daily Mail* and *The News Chronicle* reproduced
    from the British Library Newspaper Library, Colindale

Published documents

British Documents on Foreign Affairs, D. Watt, D. Cameron and K. Bourne,
    eds., Maryland, ongoing
British Documents on the Origins of the War, 1898–1914, G.P. Gooch and
    H. Temperley, eds. (London, 1926–38).

British Documents on the End of Empire
Documents on British Foreign Policy, 1919–1939
Documents on British Policy Overseas 1945–
Documents on Canadian External Relations, Ottawa, 1970
Documents on German Foreign Policy
Foreign Relations of the United States
Parliamentary Debates, House of Commons
Parliamentary Debates, House of Lords
Parliamentary Papers, 1943: HC:Cmd 6420
Review of Overseas Representation: Report by the Central Policy Review Staff, London, 1977

Books

Adamthwaite, A., *France and the Coming of the Second World War, 1936–1939* (London, 1977)

Adelman, Jonathan R., *Prelude to the Cold War: The Tsarist, Soviet and US Armies in the Two World Wars* (London, 1988)

Alexander, Martin S., *The Republic in Danger: Maurice Gamelin and the Politics of French Defence, 1933–1940* (Cambridge, 1992)

Andrew, Christopher, *Secret Service: The Making of the British Intelligence Community* (London, 1985)

Anon., *Essays by the late Marquess of Salisbury, K.G.* (London, 1905)

Ashton-Gwatkin, F., *The British Foreign Service* (Syracuse, 1950)

Auerbach, I., Hillgruber, A., and Schramm, A., eds., *Felder und Vorfelder Russischer Geschichte* (Freiburg, 1985)

Avon, Earl of, *Facing the Dictators* (London, 1963)
  The Eden Memoirs: The Reckoning (London, 1965)

Baldwin, S., *The Torch I Would Hand to You* (London, 1937)

Barnes, J., and Nicholson, D., *The Leo Amery Diaries, 1896–1929*, vol. I (London, 1980)

Barnett, Correlli, *The Collapse of British Power* (Gloucester, 1984)

Beaver, Daniel R., ed., *Some Pathways in American History* (Detroit, 1969)

Behrens, C.B.A., *Merchant Shipping and the Demands of War* (2nd edn, London, 1978)

Bell, P.M.H., *A Certain Eventuality: Britain and the Fall of France* (London, 1974)
  John Bull and the Bear: British Public Opinion, Foreign Policy and the Soviet Union, 1941–1945 (London, 1990)

Ben-Moshe, Tuvia, *Churchill: Strategy and History* (Boulder, CO, 1992)

Bennett, E.W., *German Rearmament and the West, 1932–1933* (Princeton, 1979)

Berlin, I., *Mr Churchill in 1940* (London, 1964)

Birkenhead, Lord, *Halifax: The Life of Lord Halifax* (London, 1965)

Blake, Robert, *Disraeli* (London, 1966)

Blake, Robert, and Louis, William Roger, eds., *Churchill: A Major New Assessment of his Life in Peace and War* (Oxford, 1993)

Blasius, Werner, *Fur Grossdeutschland-gegen den grossen Krieg* (Cologne, 1981)

Bond, Brian, *British Military Policy between the Two World Wars* (Oxford, 1980)

Bond, Brian, ed., *Chief of Staff: The Diaries of Lieutenant-General Sir Henry Pownall, 1940–1944* (2 vols., London, 1974)

Boog, H., Rahn, W., Stumpf, R., and Wagner, B., *Das Deutsche Reich und der Zweite Weltkrieg*, vol. VI (Stuttgart, 1990)

Bourne, K., *Britain and the Balance of Power in North America* (London, 1967)

The Foreign Policy of Victorian England, 1830–1902 (Oxford, 1970)

Boyce, R., *British Capitalism at the Crossroads, 1919–1932: A Study in Politics, Economics and International Relations* (London, 1987)

Brinkley, Douglas, and Facey-Crowther, David, eds., *The Atlantic Charter* (New York, 1994)

Brivati, Brian, and Jones, Harriet, eds., *What Difference did the War Make?* (Leicester, 1993)

Brower, Charles, F., ed., *World War II in Europe: The Final Year* (New York, forthcoming)

Brugel, J.W., *Tschechen und Deutsche, 1918–1939* (Munich, 1967)

Bryant, Sir Arthur, *Triumph in the West* (London, 1959)

Bryce, Viscount, *Memories of Travel* (London, 1923)

Buckley, T.H., *The United States and the Washington Conference, 1921–1922* (Knoxville, TN, 1970)

Burk, Kathleen, *Britain, America and the Sinews of War 1914–1918* (London, 1985)

Burton, D.H., *Cecil Spring Rice: A Diplomat's Life* (London and Toronto, 1990)

Busch, B.C., *Mudros to Lausanne; Britain's Frontier in West Asia, 1918–1923* (Albany NW, 1976)

Hardinge of Penshurst: a Study in the Old Diplomacy (Hamden, 1980)

Butler, J.R.M., *Lord Lothian, 1882–1940* (London, 1960)

Grand Strategy, vol. III, part 1 (London, 1964)

Carlton, D., *MacDonald versus Henderson: The Foreign Policy of the Second Labour Government* (London, 1970)

Anthony Eden (London, 1981)

Ceadl, M., *Pacifism in Britain, 1914–1945: The Defining of a Faith* (London, 1980)

Cecil, Viscount of Chelwood, *The Moral Basis of the League of Nations* (London, 1923)

A Great Experiment (London, 1941)

Chamberlain, Sir Austen, *The League* (Glasgow, 1926)
  Peace in Our Time: Addresses on Europe and the Empire (London, 1928)
  Down the Years (London, 1935)
Charmley, John, *Churchill: The End of Glory. A Political Biography* (London, 1993)
Checkland, Sydney, *The Elgins, 1766–1917: A Tale of Aristocrats, Proconsuls and their Wives* (Aberdeen, 1988)
Cheke, Marcus, *Guidance on Foreign Usages and Ceremony, and Other Matters, for a Member of His Majesty's Foreign Service on his First Appointment to a Post Abroad* (London, 1949)
Churchill, Randolph, *Lord Derby, 'King of Lancashire'* (London, 1959)
Churchill, Winston S., *The Second World War* (6 vols., London, 1948–54)
Cline, C.A., *E.D. Morel 1973–1924. The Strategies of Protest* (Belfast, 1980)
Cockett, Richard, *Twilight of Truth: Chamberlain, Appeasement and the Manipulation of the Press* (London, 1989)
Cohen, Eliot A., and Gooch, John, *Military Misfortunes: The Anatomy of Failure in War* (New York, 1991)
Collier, L., *Flight from Conflict* (London, 1944)
Colville, John, *The Fringes of Power: Downing Street Diaries, 1939–1955* (London, 1985)
Connell, J., *The 'Office': A Study of British Foreign Policy and its Makers, 1919–1951* (London, 1958)
Conwell-Evans, T.P., *None So Blind* (London, private print, 1947)
Conye, G.R., *Woodrow Wilson, British Perspectives, 1912–21* (London, 1992)
Costello, John, *Ten Days to Destiny* (New York, 1991)
Craig, Gordon, and Gilbert, Felix, eds., *The Diplomats, 1919–1939* (New York, 1954)
Cross, J.A., *Sir Samuel Hoare: A Political Biography* (London, 1977)
Crowe, Sibyl, and Corp, Edward, *Our Ablest Public Servant: Sir Eyre Crowe, GCB., CMG., KCB., KCMG., 1864–1925* (Braunton, Devon, 1993)
Cull, N.J., *Spelling War; the British Propaganda Campaign against American 'Neutrality' in World War II* (New York, 1994)
Curzon of Kedlestone, Marchioness, *Reminiscences* (London, 1955)
Dalton, H., *Call Back Yesterday* (London, 1953)
  The Fateful Years, 1931–1945 (London, 1957)
  Memoirs 1945–1960: High Tide and After (London, 1960)
Deighton, Anne, *The Impossible Peace: Britain, the Division of Germany, and the Origins of the Cold War* (Oxford, 1990)
Denholm, A., *Lord Ripon, 1827–1909: A Political Biography* (London, 1982)

Dilks, D., ed., *The Diaries of Sir Alexander Cadogan 1938–1945* (London, 1971)

Neville Chamberlain, vol. 1 (Cambridge, 1984)

Three Visitors to Canada: Baldwin, Chamberlain and Churchill (London, 1985)

Dockrill, M.L., and Goold, J.D., *Peace without Promise: Britain and the Peace Conferences 1919–23* (London, 1981)

Dugdale, Blanche F.E., *Arthur James Balfour*, 2 vols. (London, 1939)

Dutton, David, *Austen Chamberlain: Gentleman in Politics* (Bolton, 1985)

Simon: A Political Biography of Sir John Simon (London, 1992)

Eden, Anthony, *Foreign Affairs* (London, 1939)

Egar, Clifford L., and Knott, Alexander W., *Essays in Twentieth Century Diplomatic History dedicated to Professor Daniel H. Smith* (Washington DC, 1982)

Egerton, G., ed., *Political Memoir: Essays on the Politics of Memory* (London, 1944)

Elcock, H., *Portrait of a Decision: The Council of Four and the Treaty of Versailles* (London, 1972)

Ellis, L.F., *Victory in the West*, 2 vols. (London, 1962–8)

Eubank, K., *The Summit Conferences* (Norman, 1966)

Feis, H., *From Trust to Terror: The Origins of the Cold War, 1945–1950* (New York, 1970)

Ferris, J.R., *Men, Money and Diplomacy: The Evolution of British Strategic Policy, 1919–26* (Ithaca, 1989)

Fleischhauer, Ingeborg, *Die Chance des Sonderfriedens: Deutsch-sowjetische Geheimgesprache, 1941–1945* (Berlin, 1986)

French, David, *British Strategy and War Aims, 1914–16* (Boston, 1986)

The British Way in Warfare, 1688–2000 (London, 1990)

Friedberg, A.L., *The Weary Titan: Britain and the Experience of Relative Decline 1895–1905* (Princeton, 1988)

Fry, M.G., *Illusions of Security, North Atlantic Diplomacy, 1918–1922* (Toronto, 1972)

Gates, Eleanor, M., *End of the Affair: The Collapse of the Anglo-French Alliance, 1939–1940* (London, 1981)

Genoud, Francois, ed., *The Testament of Adolf Hitler* (London, 1961)

Gibbs, N., *Grand Strategy*, vol. I (London, 1976)

Gilbert, M., *Winston S. Churchill*, vol. V, pt. 1, *The Exchequer Years, 1922–1929* (London, 1979)

Finest Hour: Winston Churchill, 1939–1941 (London, 1983)

Road to Victory: Winston S. Churchill 1941–1945 (London, 1986)

Gilbert, M., and Gott, R., *The Appeasers* (London, 1963)

Goldfrank, D.M., *The Origins of the Crimean War* (London, 1894)

Goldstein, E., *Winning the Peace: British Diplomatic Strategy, Peace Planning, and the Paris Peace Conference, 1916–1920* (Oxford, 1991)

Gorodestsy, Gabriel, *Stafford Cripps' Mission to Moscow 1940–42* (Cambridge, 1984)

Grant, J.E., *The Problem of War and its Solution* (London, 1922)

Gregory, J.D., *On the Edge of Diplomacy: Memories and Reflections, 1920–1928* (London, 1929)

Grenville, J.A.S., *Lord Salisbury and Foreign Policy: The Close of the Nineteenth Century* (London, 1970)

Grigg, J., *Lloyd George: The People's Champion, 1902–1911* (London, 1978)

Haldane, R.B., *An Autobiography* (London, 1929)

Hamilton, Keith, *Bertie of Thame: Edwardian Ambassador* (London, 1990)

Hancock, W.K., and Gowing, M.M., *British War Economy* (London, 1949)

Harbutt, Fraser J., *The Iron Curtain: Churchill, America and the Origins of the Cold War* (New York, 1986)

Hardinge of Penshurst, Lord, *Old Diplomacy* (London, 1947)

Harvey, J., ed., *The Diplomatic Diaries of Oliver Harvey 1937–1940.* (London, 1970)

Headlam-Morley, Sir J., *Studies in Diplomatic History* (London, 1930)

Headlam-Morely, A., Bryant, R., and Cienciela, A., eds., *Sir James Headlam-Morley: A Memoir of the Paris Peace Conference* (London, 1972)

Henderson, A., *Labour and Foreign Affairs* (London, 1922)

Henderson, Sir Nevile, *Water under the Bridges* (London, 1945)

Hertslet, Sir Edward, *Recollections of the Old Foreign Office* (London, 1901)

Hildebrand, Klaus, *The Foreign Policy of the Third Reich, 1933–1945* (London, 1973)

Hill, Christopher, *Cabinet Decisions on Foreign Policy: The British Experience, October 1938-June 1941* (Cambridge, 1991)

Hill, L., ed., *Die Weizsacker-papiere, 1938–1950* (Frankfurt/M, 1974)

Hillgruber, Andrea, *Hitler's Strategie: Politik und Kriegfuhrung, 1940–1941* (Frankfurt a.M., 1965)

Hinsley, F.H., *Power and the Pursuit of Peace* (Cambridge, 1963)

Hinsley, F.H., et al., *British Intelligence in the Second World War* (4 vols., London, 1967)

Hinsley, F.H., ed., *British Foreign Policy under Sir Edward Grey* (Cambridge, 1977)

Hirtzel, Sir Arthur, *The Church, The Empire and the World* (London, 1919)

Howard, C.H.D., ed., *The Diary of Edward Goschen, 1990–1914* (London, 1980)

Howard, Michael, *Grand Strategy*, vol. IV (London, 1970)

Hurstfield, J., *The Control of Raw Materials* (London, 1953)
Iriye, A., and Aruga, T., eds., *Senkanki no Nihon gaiko* (Tokio, 1984)
Jacobson, J., *Locarno Diplomacy: Germany and the West, 1925–1929* (Princeton, 1972)
James, Robert Rhodes, *Anthony Eden* (London, 1986)
Jay, R., *Joseph Chamberlain: A Political Study* (Oxford, 1981)
Jenkins, Roy, *Asquith* (London, pbk., 1967)
Jenkins, Simon and Sloman, Anne, *With Respect, Ambassador: an inquiry into the Foreign Office* (London, 1985)
Joll, James, ed., *Britain and Europe: Pitt to Churchill 1793–1940* (Oxford, 1967)
Jones, R.A., *The British Diplomatic Service, 1815–1914* (Ontario, 1983)
Jones, T., *A Diary with Letters, 1931–1950* (Oxford, 1954)
Judd, D., *Lord Reading* (London, 1982)
Keegan, John, *The Second World War* (London, 1989)
Kelly, Sir David, *The Ruling Few* (London, 1952)
Kennedy, P.M., *The Rise and Fall of British Naval Mastery* (London, 1976)
   Strategy and Diplomacy, 1870–1945 (London, 1984)
Kershaw, Ian, *The Nazi Dictatorship: Problems and Perspectives of Interpretation*, (3rd edn, London, 1993)
Kettenacker, Lothar, *Das Andere Deutschland im Zweiten Weltkrieg* (Stuttgart, 1977)
Kimball, Warren F., ed., *Churchill and Roosevelt: Their Complete Correspondence* (3 vols., Princeton, 1985)
Kirkpatrick, Ivone, *The Inner Circle* (London, 1959)
Kitchen, Martin, *British Policy Towards the Soviet Union During the Second World War* (London, 1986)
Kyba, P., *Covenants without the Sword, Public Opinion and British Defence Policy, 1931–1935* (Waterloo, ON, 1983)
Langhorne, R., ed., *British Diplomacy and Intelligence during the Second World War* (Cambridge, 1985)
Lawlor, Sheila, *Churchill and the Politics of War, 1940–1941* (Cambridge, 1994)
Lee, B.A., *Britain and the Sino-Japanese War 1937–1939: A Study in the Dilemmas of British Decline* (Stanford, 1973)
Legge-Bourke, G., *Master of the Offices* (London, 1949)
Leighton, Richard M., and Coakley, Robert W., *Global Logistics and Strategy* (Washington, DC, 1955)
Lentin, A., *Guilt at Versailles: Lloyd George and the Pre-History of Appeasement* (London, 1995)
Lewis, J., *Changing Direction: British Military Planning for Post-War Strategic Defence, 1942–47* (London, 1988)

Lindley, F.O., *A Diplomat off Duty* (London, 1928)

Lowe, C.J., *The Reluctant Imperialists: British Foreign Policy 1878–1902* (2 vols., London, 1967)

Lowe, C.J., and Dockrill, M.L., *The Mirage of Power: British Foreign Policy 1902–1922* (3 vols., London, 1972)

MacDonald, J.R., *The Foreign Policy of the Labour Party* (London, 1972)

Maier, K.A., Rohde, H., Stegemann, B., and Umbreit, H., *Germany and the Second World War*, vol. II (Oxford, 1991)

Manning, W.O., *Commentaries on the Law of Nations* (London, 1975)

Marquand, D., *Ramsay MacDonald* (London, 1977)

Martin, Bernd, *Friedensinitiativen und Machpolitik im Zweiten Weltkrieg, 1939–1942* (Dusseldorf, 1974)

Mastny, V., *Russia's Road to the Cold War* (New York, 1979)

McKercher, B.J.C., *The Second Baldwin Government and the United States, 1914–1929: Attitudes and Diplomacy* (Cambridge, 1984)

Esme Howard: A Diplomatic Biography (Cambridge, 1989)

Transition: Britain's Loss of Global Pre-eminence to the United States, 1930–1945 (Cambridge, forthcoming)

McKercher, B.J.C., and Moss, D.J., eds., *Shadow and Substance in British Foreign Policy, Memorial Essays Honouring C.J. Lowe* (Edmonton, 1984)

Middlemas, K., and Barnes, J., *Baldwin: A Biography* (London, 1969)

Miner, S.M., *Between Churchill and Stalin: The Soviet Union, Great Britain and the Origins of the Grand Alliance* (Chapel Hill, NC, 1988)

Mommsen, Wolfgang J., and Kettenacker, Lothar, eds., *The Fascist Challenge and the Policy of Appeasement* (London, 1983)

Montgomery, Lord, *The Memoirs of Field-Marshal Montgomery* (London, 1958)

Montgomery-Hyde, H., *Neville Chamberlain* (London, 1976)

Moran, Lord, *Churchill: The Struggle for Survival, 1940–1965* (London, 1968)

Morgan, K.O., ed., *Lloyd George Family Letters 1885–1936* (Cardiff/ London, 1973)

Muggeridge, Malcolm, ed., *Ciano's Diplomatic Papers* (London, 1948)

Murray, Williamson, *Luftwaffe: Strategy for Defeat, 1933–1945* (London, 1988)

Murray, Lord of Elibank, *Some Reflections on Some Aspects of British Foreign Policy between the Wars* (Edinburgh, 1951)

Namier, L., *Diplomatic Prelude 1938–1939* (London, 1948)

Europe in Decline (London, 1950)

Neilson, K.E., *Strategy and Supply: The Anglo-Russian Alliance, 1914–17* (London, 1985)

Britain and the Last Tsar: British Policy and Russia 1894–1917 (Oxford, 1995)

Newton, Lord, *Lord Lansdowne* (London, 1929)

Nicolson, Harold, *Peacemaking 1919* (London, 1933)
  Diaries and Letters, 1939–1945 (London, 1967)

Nicosia, F.R., and Stokes, L.D., eds., *Germans against Nazism: Nonconformity, Opposition and Resistance in the Third Reich* (New York, 1990)

Nish, I.H., *The Diplomacy of Two Island Empires* (London, 1966)

Nish, I.H., ed., *Anglo-Japanese Alienation, 1919–1952* (Cambridge, 1982)

Noel-Baker, P.J., *The First World Disarmament Conference: 1932–1933, and Why It Failed* (London, 1979)

Northedge, F.S., *The League of Nations* (Leicester, 1986)

O'Halpin, E., *Head of the Civil Service: A Study of Sir Warren Fisher* (London, 1989)

Olliphant, L., *An Ambassador in Bonds*, 2nd edn. (London, 1947)

O'Malley, O., *The Phantom Caravan* (London, 1954)

Orde, Anne, *Great Britain and International Security, 1920–1926* (London, 1978)

Peden, G.C., *British Rearmament and the Treasury, 1932–1939* (Edinburgh, 1979)

Perkins, B., *The Great Rapprochement. England and the United States, 1895–1914* (London, 1969)

Petrie, Sir Charles, *The Life and Letters of the Right Hon. Sir Austen Chamberlain*, vol. II (London, 1940)

Pimlott, Ben., ed., *The Political Diary of Hugh Dalton, 1918–40, 1945–60* (London, 1986)

Pinto-Duschinsky, M., *The Political Thought of Lord Salisbury* (London, 1967)

Pogue, Forrest C., *George C. Marshall: Statesman 1945–1959* (New York, 1987)

Post, G., Jr, *Dilemmas of Appeasement: British Deterrence and Defense, 1934–1937* (Ithaca, 1993)

Quarteraro, Rosiario, *Roma tra Londra e Berlino; Politica Estrero Fascista dal 1930 al 1940* (Rome, 1980)

Raczynski, Edward, *In Allied London: The War Time Diaries of a Polish Ambassador in London* (London, 1962)

Ralston, J.H., *International Arbitration from Athens to Locarno* (Oxford, 1929)

Recker, Marie-Louise, *Die Aussenpolitik des Dritten Reiches* (Munich, 1990)

Reynolds, David, *Lord Lothian and Anglo-American Relations, 1939–1940* (Philadelphia, 1983)
  Britannia Overruled: British Policy and World Power in the 20th Century (London, 1991)

Reynolds, David, Kimball, W.F., and Churbarian, A.O., eds., *Allies at War: The Soviet, American and British Experience, 1939–1945* (New York, 1994)

Richardson, D., *The Evolution of British Disarmament Policy in the 1920s* (London, 1989)

Robbins, Keith, *Munich 1938* (London, 1968)
  Sir Edward Grey: A Biography of Lord Grey of Fallodon (London, 1971)
  Churchill (London, 1992)
  Politicians, Diplomacy and War in Modern British History (London, 1994)

Roberts, Andrew, *The Holy Fox: A Biography of Lord Halifax* (London, 1991)

Rose, N., *Vansittart: Study of a Diplomat* (London, 1977)

Roskill, S.W., *The War at Sea, 1939–1945*, vol. II (London, 1956)
  Naval Policy between the Wars (2 vols., London, 1968)
  Hankey: Man of Secrets, Vol. III, 1931–1963 (London, 1974)

Ross, Graham, ed., *The Foreign Office and the Kremlin: British Documents on Anglo-Soviet Relations, 1941–5* (Cambridge, 1984)

Rothwell, V., *Britain and the Cold War, 1941–1947* (London, 1982)

Rusbridger, James, and Nave E., *Betrayal at Pearl Harbor; How Churchill Lured Roosevelt into War* (London, 1991)

Sayers, R.S., *Financial Policy, 1939–1945* (London, 1956)

Schlie, Ulrich, *Keine Friede mit Deutschland: die Geheimen Gesprache im Zwiten Weltkrieg, 1939–1941* (Munich, 1944)

Schmidt-Hartmann, Eva and Winters, Stanley B., eds., *Great Britain, the United Stated and the Bohemian Lands* (Munich, 1991)

Schreiber, G., Stegemann, B., and Vogel, D., *Das Deutsche Reich und der Zweite Weltkrieg*, vol. III (Stuttgart, 1984)

Schwarz, T., *Die Reise ins Dritte Reich* (Gottingen, 1993)

Seal, Anil, *The Emergence of Indian Nationalism: Competition and Collaboration in the Later Nineteenth Century* (Cambridge, 1968)

Selby, W., *Diplomatic Twilight* (London, 1953)

Shirer, William, *Collapse of the Third Reich* (London, 1970)

Simon, Viscount, *Retrospect* (London, 1952)

Simpson, J.L. and Fox, Hazel, *International Arbitration, Law and Practice* (London, 1959)

Spears, Sir Edward, *Assignment to Catastrophe, Vol 1, Prelude to Dunkirk, July 1939–May 1940* (London, 1954)

Spender, J.A., *The Life of Sir Henry Campbell-Bannerman* (London, 1923)

Steininger, Rolf, ed., *Die Ruhrfrage 1945/46 und die Entstehung des Landes Nordrhein-Westfallen* (Dusseldorf, 1988)

Strang, Lord, *Home and Abroad* (London, 1956)

Strauch, R., *Sir Nevile Henderson: Britische Botschafter in Berlin* (Bonn, 1959)

Stuyt, A.M., *Survey of International Arbitrations, 1794–1938* (Leiden, 1939)

Swartz, M., *The Union of Democratic Control in British Politics During the First World War* (Oxford, 1971)

Taylor, A.J.P., *Off the Record: Political Interviews of W.P. Crozier, 1933–43* (London, 1973)

Taylor, Peter J., *Britain and the Cold War: 1945 as Geopolitical Transition* (London, 1990)

Thal, H. van, ed., *The Prime Ministers* (2 vols., London, 1967)

Thorne, Christopher, *The Limits of Foreign Policy: The West, the League and the Far Eastern Crisis, 1931–1933* (London, 1972)

Allies of a Kind: The United States, Britain and the War against Japan, 1941–1945 (London, 1978)

Trevelyan, Humphrey, *Diplomatic Channels* (London, 1979)

Trotter, A., *Britain and East Asia* (Cambridge, 1975)

Tucker, W.R., *The Attitude of the British Labour Party Towards European and Collective Security Problems, 1920–1939* (Geneva, 1950)

Tulloch, Hugh, *James Bryce's American Commonwealth* (Woolbridge, 1988)

Turner, J., *Lloyd George's Secretariat* (Cambridge, 1980)

Tyrkova-Williams, A., *Cheerful Giver: The Life of Harold Williams* (London, 1935)

Vansittart, Lord, *Events and Shadows* (London, n.d.)

The Mist Procession. The Autobiography of Lord Vansittart (London, 1958)

Walpurga, Lady Paget, *Embassies of Other Days* (2 vols., London, 1923)

Waterfield, Gordon, *Professional Diplomat* (London, 1973)

Watt, D. Cameron, *Personalities and Policies: Studies in the Formulation of British Foreign Policy in the Twentieth Century* (London, 1965)

Succeeding John Bull: America in Britain's Place, 1900–1975 (Cambridge, 1984)

How War Came: The Immediate Origins of the Second World War (London, 1989)

Weaver, J.R.H., ed., *Dictionary of National Biography* (London, 1937)

Webster, Charles, *The Foreign Policy of Castlereagh* (London, 1925)

Weinburg, Gerhard, *The Foreign Policy of Hitler's Germany: Diplomatic Revolution in Europe, 1933–1936* (Chicago, 1970)

Wellesley, V.A.H., *Diplomacy in Fetters* (London, 1944)

Wight, M., *Systems of States* (Leicester, 1977)

Williams, Francis, *Ernest Bevin* (London, 1952)

Wilson, Keith M., ed., *British Foreign Secretaries and Foreign Policy: From Crimean War to First World War* (London, 1987)

Wilson, Theodore A., *The First Summit: Roosevelt and Churchill at Placentia Bay, 1941*, 2nd edn (Lawrence, KS, 1991)

Woodward, Sir Llewellyn, *British Foreign Policy in the Second World War* (5 vols., London, 1971–6)

Wrigley, Chris, *Arthur Henderson* (Cardiff, 1990)

Zametica, John, ed., *British Officials and Foreign Policy, 1945–50* (Leicester, 1990)

Articles

Andrew, Christopher, 'The British Secret Service and Anglo-Soviet relations in the 1920s: Part I, From trade negotiations to the Zinoviev Letter', *Historical Journal*, 20 (1977)

Andrew, Christopher, and Neilson, Keith, 'Tsarist codebreakers and British codes', *Intelligence and National Security*, 1:1 (1986)

Baker, Vaughan A., 'Nevile Henderson in Berlin', *Red River Valley Historical Journal*, 2:4 (1977)

Bourette-Knowles, S., 'The global Micawber: Sir Robert Vansittart, the Treasury and the global balance of power, 1933–1935', *Diplomacy and Statecraft*, 6 (1995)

Cairns, John C., 'A nation of shopkeepers in search of a suitable France', *American Historical Review*, 79:3 (June 1974)

Cannadine, David, 'Politics, propaganda and art: the case of two "Worcester Lads" ', *Midlands History* (1977)

Charmley, John, 'The price of victory', *Times Literary Supplement*, 13 May 1994

Crowe, S., 'The Zinoviev Letter', *Journal of Contemporary History*, 10 (1975)

Dell, R., 'Peace, disarmament and the League', *New Statesman*, 23 (2 Aug. 1924)

Dutton, David, 'Simon and Eden at the Foreign Office, 1931–1935', *Review of International Studies*, 20:1 (January 1994)

Feldman, E., 'British diplomats and British diplomacy and the 1905 pogroms in Russia', *Slavonic and East European Review*, 65:4 (1987)

'Reports from British diplomats in Russia on the participation of Jews in revolutionary activity in Northwest Russia and the Kingdom of Poland, 1905–6', *Studies in Contemporary Jewry*, 3 (1987)

Ferris, J.R., 'Worthy of some better enemy: the British estimate of the Imperial Japanese Army, 1919–1941, and the fall of Singapore', *Canadian Journal of History*, 28 (1993)

Ferris, J.R., and Bar-Joseph, U., 'Getting Marlowe to hold his tongue: the Conservative Party, the Intelligence Services and the Zinoviev Letter', *Intelligence and National Security*, 8:4 (1993)

Frazier, Robert, 'Did Britain start the Cold War? Bevin and the Truman Doctrine', *Historical Journal*, 27 (1984)

Gorodestsky, G., 'The Hess Affair and Anglo-Soviet relations on the eve of "Barbarossa" ', *English Historical Review*, 101 (1986)

Hall, H.H. III, 'The foreign policy–making process in Britain, 1934–1935, and the origins of the Anglo-German Naval Agreement', *Historical Journal*, 19 (1976)

Hauner, Milan, 'Did Hitler want a world dominion?' *Journal of Contemporary History*, 13 (1978)

Hendrickson, A., 'The geographical "mental maps" of American foreign policy makers', *International Political Science Review*, 1:4 (1980)

Hoffman, Peter, 'The question of Western allied co-operation with the German anti-Nazi conspiracy', *The Historical Journal*, 34:3 (1991)

Jacobson, J., 'The conduct of Locarno diplomacy', *Review of Politics*, 34 (1972)

Jones, R., 'The social structure of the British Diplomatic Service, 185–1914', *Histoire Sociale–Social History*, 14:27 (1981)

Kaiser, A., 'Lord D'Abernon und die Entstenhung der Locarno-Vertrage', *Vierteljahshefte fur Zeitgeschicht*, 34 (1986)

Keyserlingk, Robert R., 'Die Deutsche Komponente in Churchills Strategie der Nationalen Erhebungen, 1940–1942', *Vierteljharshefte fur Zeitgeschichte*, 31 (1983)

Lammers, Donald S., 'From Whitehall after Munich; the Foreign Office and the future course of British foreign policy', *Historical Journal*, 16 (1974)

Langhorne, R., 'Regulating diplomatic relations: from the beginnings to the Vienna Convention (1961)', *Review of International Studies*, 18 (1992)

Macdonald, C.A., 'Economic appeasement and the German "Moderates", 1937–1939; an introductory essay', *Past and Present*, 56 (1972)

Marx, R., 'Stereotype et decision; le paradoxe du rapprochement franco-britannique de 1903–1904', *Recherches Anglaises et Nord-Americaines*, 25 (1982)

McKercher, B.J.C., 'A British view of American foreign policy: the settlement of blockade claims, 1924–1927', *International History Review*, 3 (1981)

McKercher, B.J.C., 'A sane and sensible diplomacy: Austen Chamberlain, Japan and the naval balance of power in the Pacific Ocean, 1924–29', *Canadian Journal of History*, 21 (1968)

'Austen Chamberlain's control of British foreign policy, 1924–1929', *International History Review*, 6 (1984)

'From enmity to cooperation: the second Baldwin government and the improvement of Anglo–American relations, November 1928–June 1929', *Albion*, 24 (1992)

'The last old diplomat: Sir Robert Vansittart and the verities of British foreign policy, 1903–1930', *Diplomacy and Statecraft*, 6 (1995)

Merrick, R., 'The Russia Committee of the British Foreign Office and the Cold War, 1946–7', *Journal of Contemporary History*, 20 (1985)

Michaelis, Meir, 'World power status or world domination?', *Historical Journal*, 15 (1972)

Morgan, K.O., 'Lloyd George's premiership: a study in "Prime ministerial government"', *Historical Journal*, 13 (1970)

Morrisey, C., and Ramsay, M., ' "Giving a lead in the right direction": Sir Robert Vansittart and the DRC', *Diplomacy and Statecraft*, 6 (1993)

Munch-Peterson, T., ' "Commonsense not bravado": The Butler–Prytz interview of 17 June 1949', *Scandia*, 52:1 (1986)

Neilson, Keith, 'Russian foreign purchasing in the Great War: a test case', *Slavonic and East European Review*, 60 (1982)

' "My Beloved Russians": Sir Arthur Nicolson and Russia, 1906–1916', *International History Review*, 9:4 (1987)

'Tsars and commissars: W. Somerset Maugham, *Ashenden* and images of Russia in British adventure fiction, 1890–1930', *Canadian Journal of History*, 28:3 (1992)

' "Pursued by a Bear": British estimates of Soviet military strength and Anglo–Soviet relations, 1922–1939', *Canadian Journal of History*, 28 (1993)

Pronay, Nicholas, and Taylor, Philip M., ' "An improper use of broadcasting". The British government and clandestine radio propaganda operations against Germany during the Munich crisis and after', *Journal of Contemporary History*, 18 (1983)

Quarteraro, Rosario, 'Appendice a Inghilterra e Italia', *Storia Contemporanea*, 7:4 (1976)

Reynolds, David, '1940: Fulcrum of the twentieth century?', *International History*, 66:1 (Jan. 1990)

Roi, M.L., 'From the Stressa Front to the Triple Entente: Sir Robert Vansittart, the Abyssinian Crisis and the containment of Germany', *Diplomacy and Statecraft*, 6 (1995)

Sharp, A., 'The Foreign Office in eclipse, 1919–1922', *History*, 61 (1976)

Smith, Raymond, 'A climate of opinion: British officials and the development of British Soviet policy, 1945–7', *International Affairs*, 64 (1988)

Smith, Raymond, and Zametica, John, 'The Cold Warrior: Clement Attlee reconsidered, 1945–7', *International Affairs*, 612 (1985)

Stafford, D., 'The detonator concept: British strategy, SOE and European resistance after the Fall of France', *Journal of Contemporary History*, 10 (1975)

Steele, Richard W., 'American public opinion and the war against Germany: the issue of a negotiated peace, 1942', *Journal of American History*, 65 (1978)

Stoler, Mark A., 'The "Pacific First" alternative in American World War II strategy', *International History Review*, 2 (1980)

Strange, Joseph L., 'The British rejection of Operation SLEDGE-HAMMER, an alternative motive', *Military Affairs*, 46:1 (Feb. 1982)

Trotter, A., 'Tentative steps for an Anglo–Japanese rapprochement in 1934', *Modern Asian Studies*, 8 (1974)

Warman, Roberta, 'The erosion of Foreign Office influence in the making of foreign policy, 1916–1918', *Historical Journal*, 15:11 (1972)

Warner, Geoffrey, 'The United States and France and Italy', in The Open University Course A324, *Liberation and Reconstruction: Politics, Culture and Society in France and Italy, 1943–1954* (Milton Keynes, 1990)

Watt, D.C., 'Sir Lewis Namier and contemporary European history', *Cambridge Review* (June 1954)

'The Anglo–German Naval Agreement of 1935: an interim judgment', *Journal of Modern History*, 28 (1956)

'Appeasement. The rise of a revisionist school?', *Political Quarterly*, 36:2 (1965)

'Roosevelt and Chamberlain: two appeasers', *International Journal*, 28:2 (1973)

'Hitler's visit to Rome and the May Weekend Crisis: a study in Hitler's response to external stimuli', *Journal of Contemporary History*, 9:1 (1974)

'British historians, the war-guilt issue and post-war Germanophobia: a documentary note', *Historical Journal*, 36:1 (1993)

Weinberg, Gerhard, 'The secret Benes–Hitler negotiations in 1936–37', *Journal of Central European Affairs*, 19:4 (1960)

'Hitler and England, 1933–1945: pretence and reality', *German Studies Review*, 8 (1985)

Winter, J.M., 'Arthur Henderson, the Russian Revolution and the reconstruction of the Labour Party', *Historical Journal*, 15 (1972)

Theses

Albert, John C., 'Attlee, the Chiefs of Staff and the restructuring of "Commonwealth Defence" between VJ Day and the outbreak of the Korean War' (Oxford D.Phil., 1986)

Aster, S., 'British policy towards the USSR and the onset of the Second World War, March 1938–September 1939' (London Ph.D., 1969)

Baer, G.W., 'The coming of the Italo–Ethiopian War' (Cambridge MA, 1967)

Best, A.M., 'Avoiding war: the diplomacy of Sir Robert Craigie and Shigemitsu Marnoru' (London Ph.D., 1992)

Rotunda, D.J., 'The Rome Embassy of Sir Eric Drummond, 16th Earl of Perth' (London Ph.D., 1972)

Index